CRE▲TIVE
HOMEOWNER®

W9-BEJ-513

The House Plans Bible

CREATIVE HOMEOWNER®, Upper Saddle River, New Jersey

COPYRIGHT © 2006

CREATIVE
HOMEOWNER®

A Division of Federal Marketing Corp.
Upper Saddle River, NJ

All floor plans and elevations copyright by the individual designers and may not be reproduced by any means without permission. All text and other illustrative material ©2006 Creative Homeowner and may not be reproduced, either in part or in its entirety, in any form, by any means, without written permission from the publisher, with the exception of brief excerpts for purposes of radio, television, or published review. All rights, including the right of translation, are reserved. Although all possible measures have been taken to ensure the accuracy of the material presented, the publisher is not liable in case of misinterpretation or typographical error.

Creative Homeowner® is a registered trademark of Federal Marketing Corporation.

VP/Publisher: Brian H. Toolan
VP/Editorial Director: Timothy O. Bakke
Production Manager: Kimberly H. Vivas

Home Plans Editor: Kenneth D. Stuts
Home Plans Designer Liaison: Maureen Mulligan

Design and Layout: Arrowhead Direct (David Kroha, Cindy DiPierdomenico, Judith Kroha)

Cover Design: 3r1 Group

Printed in China

Current Printing (last digit)
10 9 8 7 6 5 4 3 2

The House Plans Bible, First Edition
Library of Congress Control Number: 2005909003
ISBN-10: 1-58011-300-1
ISBN-13: 978-1-58011-300-7

CREATIVE HOMEOWNER®
A Division of Federal Marketing Corp.
24 Park Way
Upper Saddle River, NJ 07458
www.creativehomeowner.com

Note: The homes as shown in the photographs and renderings in this book may differ from the actual blueprints. When studying the house of your choice, please check the floor plans carefully.

PHOTO CREDITS

Front cover: *main* plan 441031, pages 208–209; *inserts top to bottom* plan 181221, pages 238–239; plan 441031, pages 208–209; plan 181228, pages 110–111 **back cover:** *both* plan 291015, pages 386–387 **page 1:** plan 131055, pages 180–181 **page 3:** *top* plan 161101, page 469; *center* plan 441015, pages 220–221; *bottom* plan 181228, pages 110–111 **page 4:** plan 111003, page 411 **page 5:** plan 331005, page 230 **page 6:** *top* plan 141028, page 481; *bottom* plan 161002, page 118 **page 7:** plan 221022, page 10 **page 100:** Henry Cabala/Beateworks.com **page 101:** *all* courtesy of Wilsonart International **page 102:** James Bennett/Beateworks.com **page 103:** Henry Cabala/Beateworks.com **page 104:** Philip Clayton-Thompson, design: Franc Valles/French Tradition **page 105:** davidduncanlivingston.com **pages 106–108:** *all* courtesy of KraftMaid Cabinetry **page 196:** Carolynbates.com **page 197:** *top* courtesy of Ondine Shower Systems; *center* courtesy of DunLeavy Cordun Associates Inc.; *bottom* courtesy of HEWI **page 198:** *top* courtesy of Grohe Plumbing; *bottom* davidduncanlivingston.com **page 199:** Brett Drury Photography, builder: Dakota Builders **page 200:** *left* davidduncanlivingston.com; *right* courtesy of HEWI **page 201:** Mark Samu **page 202:** melabee m miller, cabinetry by Merillat Industries **page 203:** davidduncanlivingston.com **page 204:** courtesy of Johnson Hardware **page 205:** courtesy of DunLeavy Cordun Associates Inc. **page 206:** melabee m miller, builder: Doyle Builders **page 300:** Mark Liscombe/Elizabethwhiting.com, design: Laura Ashley **page 301:** *top* Brian Harrison/Elizabethwhiting.com, design: Allen & Batson; *center* courtesy of Brewster Wallcoverings; *bottom* courtesy of Seabrook Wallcoverings **page 302:** Jessie Walker **page 304:** Brian Harrison/Elizabethwhiting.com **page 305:** Maggie Cole, design: Dianne Lowenthal, ASID **page 306:** Nick Carter/Elizabethwhiting.com **page 307:** Jessie Walker, design: Susan Reese Interiors **page 308:** Tim Street-Porter/Beateworks.com, design: Tom Beeton **page 309:** Mark Samu, design: Carolyn Miller **page 456:** Mark Lohman **page 457:** *top* courtesy of Hunter Douglas; *center* Mark Lohman; *bottom* Mark Samu **pages 458–459:** *both* Mark Lohman **page 460:** *left* davidduncanlivingston.com; *right* Tria Giovan, design: Suzanne Rheinstein **page 461:** davidduncanlivingston.com **pages 462–463:** *all* Mark Lohman **page 549:** plan 371092, pages 18–19 **page 558:** plan 181151, page 135 **page 559:** plan 181151, page 135

Contents

Getting Started

Maybe you can't wait to bang the first nail. Or you may be just as happy leaving town until the windows are cleaned. The extent of your involvement with the construction phase is up to you. Your time, interests, and abilities can help you decide how to get the project from lines on paper to reality. But building a house requires more than putting pieces together. Whoever is in charge of the process must competently manage people as well as supplies, materials, and construction. He or she will have to

- Make a project schedule to plan the orderly progress of the work. This can be a bar chart that shows the time period of activity by each trade.
- Establish a budget for each category of work, such as foundation, framing, and finish carpentry.
- Arrange for a source of construction financing.
- Get a building permit and post it conspicuously at the construction site.
- Line up supply sources and order materials.
- Find subcontractors and negotiate their contracts.
- Coordinate the work so that it progresses smoothly with the fewest conflicts.
- Notify inspectors at the appropriate milestones.
- Make payments to suppliers and subcontractors.

You as the Builder

You'll have to take care of every logistical detail yourself if you decide to act as your own builder or general contractor. But along with the responsibilities of managing the project, you gain the flexibility to do as much of your own work as you want and subcontract out the rest. Before taking this path, however, be sure you have the time and capabilities. Do you also have the time and ability to schedule the work, hire and coordinate subs, order materials, and keep ahead of the accounting required to manage the project successfully? If you do, you stand to save the amount that a general contractor would charge to take on these responsibilities, normally 15 to 30 percent of the construction cost. If you take this responsibility on but mismanage the project, the potential savings will erode and may even cost you more than if you had hired a builder in the first place. A subcontractor might charge extra for hav-

Acting as the builder, above, requires the ability to hire and manage subcontractors.

Building a home, opposite, includes the need to schedule building inspections at the appropriate milestones.

ing to return to the site to complete work that was originally scheduled for an earlier date. Or perhaps because you didn't order the windows at the beginning, you now have to pay for a recent cost increase. (If you had hired a builder in the first place he or she would absorb the increase.)

Hiring a Builder to Handle Construction

A builder or general contractor will manage every aspect of the construction process. Your role after signing the construction contract will be to make regular progress payments and ensure that the work for which you are paying has been completed. You will also consult with the builder and agree to any changes that may have to be made along the way.

Leads for finding builders might come from friends or neighbors who have had contractors build, remodel, or add to their homes. Real-estate agents and bankers may have some names handy but are more likely familiar with the builder's ability to complete projects on time and budget than the quality of the work itself.

The next step is to narrow your list of candidates to three or four who you think can do a quality job and work harmoniously with you. Phone each builder to see whether he or she is interested in being considered for your project. If so, invite the builder to an interview at your home. The meeting will serve two purposes. You'll be able to ask the candidate about his or her experience, and you'll be able to see whether or not your personalities are compatible. Go over the plans with the builder to make certain that he or she understands the scope of the project. Ask if they have constructed similar houses. Get references, and check the builder's standing with the Better Business Bureau. Develop a short list of builders, say three, and ask them to submit bids for the project.

Contracts

Lump-Sum Contracts

A lump-sum, or fixed-fee, contract lets you know from the beginning just what the project will cost, barring any changes made because of your requests or unforeseen conditions. This form works well for projects that promise few surprises and are well defined from the outset by a complete set of contract documents. You can enter into a fixed-price contract by negotiating with a single builder on your short list or by obtaining bids from three or four builders. If you go the latter route, give each bidder a set of documents and allow at least two weeks for them to submit their bids. When you get the bids, decide who you want and call the others to thank them for their efforts. You don't have to accept the lowest bid, but it probably makes sense to do so since you have already honed the list to builders you trust. Inform this builder of your intentions to finalize a contract.

Cost-Plus-Fee Contracts

Under a cost-plus-fee contract, you agree to pay the builder for the costs of labor and materials, as verified by receipts, plus a fee that represents the builder's overhead and profit. This arrangement is sometimes referred to as "time and materials." The fee can range between 15 and 30 percent of the incurred costs. Because you ultimately pick up the tab—whatever the costs—the contractor is never at risk, as he is with a lump-sum contract. You won't know the final total cost of a cost-plus-fee contract until the project is built and paid for. If you can live with that uncertainty, there are offsetting advantages. First, this form allows you to accommodate unknown conditions much more easily than does a lump-sum contract. And rather than being tied down by the project documents, you will be free to make changes at any point along the way. This can be a trap, though. Watching the project take shape will spark the desire to add something or do something differently. Each change costs more, and the accumulation can easily exceed your budget. Because of the uncertainty of the final tab and the built-in advantage to the contractor, you should think twice before entering into this form of contract.

Contract Content

The conditions of your agreement should be spelled out thoroughly in writing and signed by both parties, whatever contractual arrangement you make with your builder. Your contract should include provisions for the following:

- The names and addresses of the owner and builder.
- A description of the work to be included ("As described in the plans and specifications dated . . .").
- The date that the work will be completed if time is of the essence.
- The contract price for lump-sum contracts and the builder's allowed profit and overhead costs for changes.
- The builder's fee for cost-plus-fee contracts and the method of accounting and requesting payment.
- The criteria for progress payments (monthly, by project milestones) and the conditions of final payment.
- A list of each drawing and specification section that is to be included as part of the contract.
- Requirements for guarantees. (One year is the standard period for which contractors guarantee the entire project, but you may require specific guarantees on

When submitting bids, all of the builders should base their estimates on the same specifications. Once the work begins, communicate with your builder to keep the work proceeding smoothly.

Inspect your newly built home, if possible, before the builder closes it up and finishes it.

certain parts of the project, such as a 20-year guarantee on the roofing.)
- Provisions for insurance.
- A description of how changes in the work orders will be handled.

The builder may have a standard contract that you can tailor to the specifics of your project. These contain complete specific conditions with blanks that you can fill in to fit your project and a set of "general conditions" that cover a host of issues from insurance to termination provisions. It's always a good idea to have an attorney review the draft of your completed contract before signing it.

Working with Your Builder

The construction phase officially begins when you have a signed copy of the contract and copies of any insurance required from the builder. It's not unheard of for a builder to request an initial payment of 10 to 20 percent of the total cost to cover mobilization costs, those costs associated with obtaining permits and getting set up to begin the actual construction. If you agree to this, keep a careful eye on the progress of the work to ensure that the total paid out at any one time doesn't get too far out of sync with the actual work completed.

What about changes? From here on, it's up to you and your builder to proceed in good faith and to keep the channels of communication open. Even so, changes of one sort or another beset every project, and they usually add to its cost.

Light at the End of the Tunnel.

The builder's request for a final inspection marks the end of the construction phase— almost. At the final inspection meeting, you and the builder will inspect the work, noting any defects or incomplete items on a "punch list." When the builder tidies up the punch list items, you should reinspect. Sometimes, builders go on to another job and take forever to clean up the last few details, so only after all items on the list have been completed satisfactorily should you release the final payment, which often accounts for the builder's profit.

Some Final Words

Having a positive attitude is important when undertaking a project as large as building a home. A positive attitude can help you ride out the rigors and stress of the construction process.

Stay Flexible. Expect problems, because they certainly will occur. Weather can upset the schedule you have established for subcontractors. A supplier may get behind on deliveries, which also affects the schedule. An unexpected pipe may surprise you during excavation. Just as certain, every problem that comes along has a solution if you are open to it.

Be Patient. The extra days it may take to resolve a construction problem will be forgotten once the project is completed.

Express Yourself. If what you see isn't exactly what you thought you were getting, don't be afraid to look into changing it. Or you may spot an unforeseen opportunity for an improvement. Changes usually cost more money, though, so don't make frivolous decisions.

Finally, watching your home go up is exciting, so stay upbeat. Get away from your project from time to time. Dine out. Take time to relax. A positive attitude will make for smoother relations with your builder. An optimistic outlook will yield better-quality work if you are doing your own construction. And though the project might seem endless while it is under way, keep in mind that all the planning and construction will fade to a faint memory at some time in the future, and you will be getting a lifetime of pleasure from a home that is just right for you.

Plan #181126

Dimensions: 35' W x 30' D
Levels: 2
Square Footage: 1,468
Main Level Sq. Ft.: 958
Upper Level Sq. Ft.: 510
Bedrooms: 3
Bathrooms: 2
Foundation: Basement
Materials List Available: Yes
Price Category: B

Images provided by designer/architect.

This home, as shown in the photograph, may differ from the actual blueprints. For more detailed information, please check the floor plans carefully.

A multiple-gabled roof and a covered entry give this home a charming appearance.

Features:

- Entry: You'll keep heating and cooling costs down with this air-lock entry. There is also a large closet here.

- Kitchen: This efficient L-shaped eat-in kitchen has access to the rear deck.

- Great Room: This two-story space has a cozy fireplace and is open to the kitchen.

- Master Bedroom: Located on the main level, this area has access to the main bathroom, which has an oversized tub and a compart-mentalized lavatory.

- Bedrooms: The two secondary bedrooms are located on the upper level and share a common bathroom.

Great Room

Main Level Floor Plan

30'-0"
9,0 m

12'-0" X 12'-0"
3,60 X 3,60

19'-8" X 14'-0"
5,90 X 4,20

14'-0" X 13'-0"
4,20 X 3,90

13'-0" X 9'-0"
3,90 X 2,70

35'-0"
10,5 m

Upper Level Floor Plan

Copyright by designer/architect.

10'-0" X 11'-0"
3,00 X 3,30

15'-0" X 11'-0"
4,50 X 3,30

Dining Room

Kitchen

Rear View

Stairs

Plan #221022

Dimensions: 79' W x 55' D
Levels: 2
Square Footage: 3,382
Main Level Sq. Ft.: 2,376
Upper Level Sq. Ft.: 1,006
Bedrooms: 4
Bathrooms: 3½
Foundation: Basement
Materials List Available: No
Price Category: G

The traditional-looking facade of stone, brick, and siding opens into a home you'll love for its spaciousness, comfort, and great natural lighting.

Images provided by designer/architect.

Features:

- Ceiling Height: 9 ft.

- Great Room: The two-story ceiling here emphasizes the dimensions of this large room, and the huge windows make it bright and cheery.

- Sunroom: Use this area as a den or an indoor conservatory where you can relax in the midst of health-promoting and beautiful plants.

- Kitchen: This well-planned kitchen features a snacking island and opens into a generous dining nook where everyone will gather.

- Master Suite: Located on the main floor for privacy, this area includes a walk-in closet and a deluxe full bathroom.

- Upper Level: Look into the great room and entryway as you climb the stairs to the three large bedrooms and full bath on this floor.

Rear View

Main Level Floor Plan

Upper Level Floor Plan

Copyright by designer/architect.

Images provided by designer/architect.

Plan #121009

Dimensions: 50' W x 58' D
Levels: 1
Square Footage: 1,422
Bedrooms: 3
Bathrooms: 2
Foundation: Basement
Materials List Available: Yes
Price Category: B

This amenity-filled home is perfect for the growing family or as a retirement retreat.

Features:

- Ceiling Height: 8 ft. unless otherwise noted.
- Great Room: This inviting space is the perfect place for gatherings of all sizes. It shares 12-ft. ceilings with the dining room and kitchen.

- Dining Room: In addition to the 12-ft. ceiling, arched openings, and built-in book cases make this an elegant place to dine.
- Private Porch: After dinner, step through a door in the dining room to enjoy a summer breeze in this inviting porch.
- Master Suite: The boxed ceiling lends drama to this suite and a walk-in closet adds convenience. Luxury comes from the whirlpool bath.
- Garage: You won't be short of parking and storage space in this two-bay garage. As a bonus there is space for a workbench.

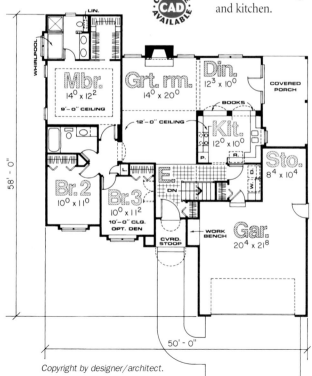

Copyright by designer/architect.

SMARTtip
Window Cornices

You can transform plain rooms by making jogs in cornice molding that will hold shades, blinds, and other window treatments. You can create individual pockets over each window or continue the molding past narrow wall sections between windows to form a more expansive detail. Housings below the cornice can be painted or papered.

Plan #121011

Dimensions: 50' W x 50' D
Levels: 1
Square Footage: 1,724
Bedrooms: 3
Bathrooms: 2
Foundation: Slab, basement
Materials List Available: Yes
Price Category: C

This home, as shown in the photograph, may differ from the actual blueprints. For more detailed information, please check the floor plans carefully.

Images provided by designer/architect.

This one-level home is perfect for retirement or for convenient living for the growing family.

Features:

- Ceiling Height: 8 ft.
- Master Suite: For privacy and quiet, the master suite is segregated from the other bedrooms.
- Family Room: Sit by the fire and read as light streams through the windows flanking the fireplace. Or enjoy the built-in entertainment center.
- Breakfast Area: Located just off the family room, the sunny breakfast area will lure you to linger over impromptu family meals. Here you will find a built-in desk for compiling shopping lists and menus.
- Private Porch: Step out of the breakfast area to enjoy a breeze on this porch.
- Kitchen: Efficient and attractive, this kitchen offers an angled pantry and an island that doubles as a snack bar.

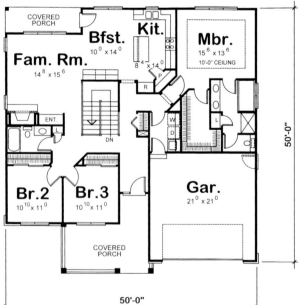

Copyright by designer/architect.

SMARTtip

Measuring for Kitchen Countertops

Custom cabinetmakers will sometimes come to your house to measure for a countertop, but home centers and kitchen stores may require that you come to them with the dimensions already in hand. Be sure to double-check measurements carefully. Being off by only ½ in. can be quite upsetting.

To ensure accuracy, sketch out the countertop on a sheet of graph paper. Include all the essential dimensions. To be on the safe side, have someone else double-check your numbers.

Plan #151001

Dimensions: 70' W x 88' D
Levels: 1
Square Footage: 3,124
Bedrooms: 4
Bathrooms: 3½
Foundation: Crawl space, slab
CompleteCost List Available: Yes
Price Category: G

Images provided by designer/architect.

From the double front doors to sleek arches, columns, and a gallery with arched openings to the bedrooms, you'll love this elegant home.

Features:

- Grand Room: With a 13-ft. pan ceiling and column entry, this room opens to the rear covered porch as well as through French doors to the bay-windowed morning room that, in turn, leads to the gathering room.

- Gathering Room: A majestic fireplace, built-in entertainment center, and book shelves give comfort and ease.

- Kitchen: A double oven, built-in desk, and a work island add up to a design for efficiency.

- Master Suite: Enjoy the practicality of walk-in closets, the comfort of a private sitting area, and the convenience of an adjacent study or nursery. The bath features a step-up whirlpool tub and separate shower.

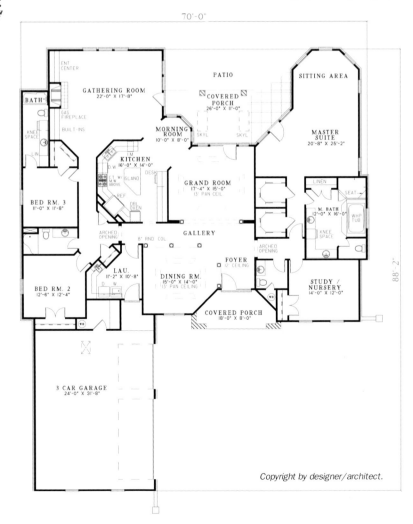

Copyright by designer/architect.

Plan #121029

Dimensions: 58'8" W x 54' D
Levels: 2
Square Footage: 2,576
Main Level Sq. Ft.: 1,735
Upper Level Sq. Ft.: 841
Bedrooms: 4
Bathrooms: 2½
Foundation: Basement
Materials List Available: Yes
Price Category: E

Images provided by designer/architect.

This gracious home is designed with the contemporary lifestyle in mind.

Features:

- Ceiling Height: 8 ft. unless otherwise noted.

- Great Room: This room features a fireplace and entertainment center. It's equally suited for family gatherings and formal entertaining.

- Breakfast Area: The fireplace is two-sided so it shares its warmth with this breakfast area — the perfect spot for informal family meals.

- Master Suite: Halfway up the staircase you'll find double-doors into this truly distinctive suite featuring a barrel-vault ceiling, built-in bookcases, and his and her walk-in closets. Unwind at the end of the day by stretching out in the oval whirlpool tub.

- Computer Loft: This loft overlooks the great room. It is designed as a home office with a built-in desk for your computer.

- Garage: Two bays provide plenty of storage in addition to parking space.

CAD FILE AVAILABLE

Main Level Floor Plan

Upper Level Floor Plan

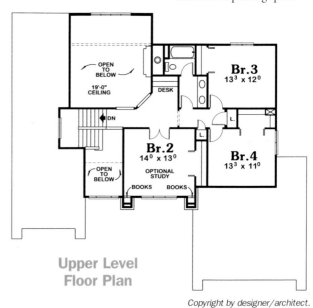

Copyright by designer/architect.

Plan #121015

Dimensions: 52' W x 47'4" D

Levels: 2

Square Footage: 1,999

Main Level Sq. Ft.: 1,421

Upper Level Sq. Ft.: 578

Bedrooms: 4

Bathrooms: 2½

Foundation: Basement

Materials List Available: Yes

Price Category: D

Images provided by designer/architect.

Hipped roofs and a trio of gables bring distinction to this plan.

Features:

- Ceiling Height: 8 ft.

- Open Floor Plan: The rooms flow into each other and are flanked by an abundance of windows. The result is a light and airy space that seems much larger than it really is.

- Formal Dining Room: Here is the perfect room for elegant entertaining.

- Breakfast Nook: This bright, bayed nook is the perfect place to start the day. It's also great for intimate get-togethers.

- Great Room: The family will enjoy gathering in this spacious area.

- Bedrooms: This large master bedroom, along with three secondary bedrooms and an extra room, provides plenty of room for a growing family.

- Attached Garage: The garage provides two bays of parking plus plenty of storage space.

Main Level Floor Plan

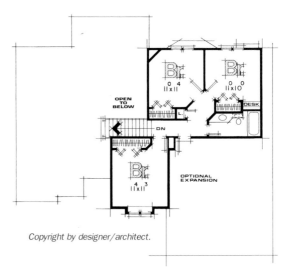

Upper Level Floor Plan

Copyright by designer/architect.

Plan #151593

Dimensions: 59'6" W x 64'2" D
Levels: 1.5
Square Footage: 2,542
Bonus (unfinished): 473
Bedrooms: 3
Bathrooms: 3
Foundation: Crawl space or slab
CompleteCost List Available: Yes
Price Category: E

Images provided by designer/architect.

This classic split-bedroom brick home invites guests in with vaulted ceilings in the front porch and foyer.

Features:

- Dining Room: This roomy formal room has a 12-ft.-high ceiling and a conveniently located butler's pantry.

- Great Room: In this room the fireplace warms guests while they enjoy the media center.

- Kitchen: This work space provides for all with an island and snack bar that opens to the breakfast room. Afternoon barbecues on the rear grilling porch will be a neighborhood favorite.

- Master Suite: Relax in this private suite, which has a bath with a corner whirlpool tub, split vanities, a separate shower, and a walk-in closet.

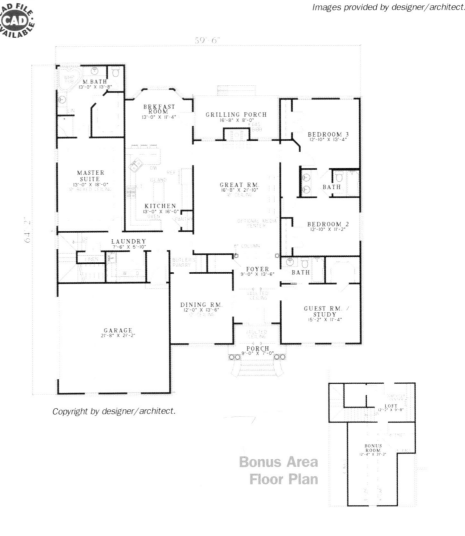

Copyright by designer/architect.

Bonus Area Floor Plan

Plan #101019

Dimensions: 58'4" W x 55'2" D

Levels: 2

Square Footage: 2,954

Main Level Sq. Ft. 2093

Upper Level Sq. Ft. 861

Bedrooms: 4

Bathrooms: 3½

Foundation: Crawl space, slab, or basement

Materials List Available: No

Price Category: F

Images provided by designer/architect.

This luxurious home features a spectacular open floor plan and a brick exterior.

Features:

• Ceiling Height: 9 ft. unless otherwise noted.

• Foyer: This inviting two-story foyer, which vaults to 18 ft., will greet guests with an impressive "welcome."

• Dining Room: To the right of the foyer is this spacious dining room surrounded by decorative columns.

• Family Room: There's plenty of room for all kinds of family activities in this enormous room, with its soaring two-story ceiling.

• Master Suite: This sumptuous retreat boasts a tray ceiling. Optional pocket doors provide direct access to the study. The master bath features his and her vanities and a large walk-in closet.

• Breakfast Area: Perfect for informal family meals, this bayed breakfast area has real flair.

• Secondary Bedrooms: Upstairs are three large bedrooms with 8-ft. ceilings. One has a private bath.

Main Level Floor Plan

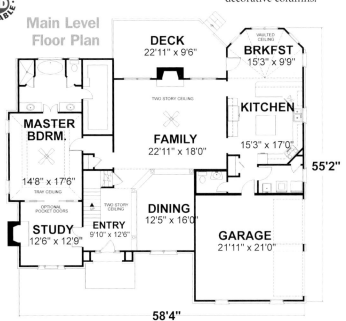

Upper Level Floor Plan

Copyright by designer/architect.

Plan #371092

Dimensions: 71'6" W x 70'8" D
Levels: 2
Square Footage: 3,836
Main Level Sq. Ft.: 2,981
Upper Level Sq. Ft.: 855
Bedrooms: 5
Bathrooms: 4
Foundation: Slab
Materials List Available: No
Price Category: H

Images provided by designer/architect.

This grand home has an arched covered entry and great styling that would make this home a focal point of the neighborhood.

CAD FILE AVAILABLE

Features:

- **Family Room:** This large gathering area boasts a fireplace flanked by a built-in media center. Large windows flood the room with natural light, and there is access to the rear porch.

- **Kitchen:** This large island kitchen has a raised bar and is open to the family room. Its walk-in pantry has plenty of room for supplies.

- **Master Suite:** This retreat features a stepped ceiling and a see-through fireplace to the master bath, which has a large walk-in closet, dual vanities, a glass shower, and a marble tub.

- **Secondary Bedrooms:** Bedrooms 2 and 3 are located on the main level and share a common bathroom. Bedrooms 4 and 5 are located on the upper level and share a Jack-and-Jill bathroom.

Upper Level Floor Plan

Main Level Floor Plan

Foyer

Living Room

Living Room to Backyard

Kitchen

Master Bath

Plan #221034

Dimensions: 63'8" W x 56'4" D
Levels: 2
Square Footage: 2,415
Main Level Sq. Ft.: 1,691
Upper Level Sq. Ft.: 724
Bedrooms: 4
Bathrooms: 2½
Foundation: Basement
Materials List Available: No
Price Category: E

This spacious two-story brick home features tons of amenities that you would normally expect in a much larger home.

Features:

- **Kitchen:** The breakfast bar in this kitchen overlooks both the nook and the great room, creating the illusion of additional space.

- **Great Room:** The two-story ceiling in this room is made comfortable by a wall that features a fireplace and built-ins.

- **Master Suite:** This suite features a spacious bath and large walk-in closet, while the bedroom itself has a stepped ceiling.

- **Upper Level:** Upstairs you'll love the balcony, which overlooks the great room from above, and you'll be pleasantly surprised to find three additional bedrooms and a full bathroom.

Images provided by designer/architect.

Rear Elevation

Copyright by designer/architect.

Plan #121031

Dimensions: 52' W x 51'4" D

Levels: 2

Square Footage: 1,772

Main Level Sq. Ft.: 1,314

Upper Level Sq. Ft.: 458

Bedrooms: 3

Bathrooms: 2½

Foundation: Basement

Materials List Available: Yes

Price Category: C

Images provided by designer/architect.

This home features architectural details reminiscence of earlier fine homes.

Features:

- Ceiling Height: 8 ft. unless otherwise noted.
- Foyer: This grand entry soars two-stories high. The U-shaped staircase with window leads to a second-story balcony.
- Great Room: You'll be drawn to the impressive views through the triple-arch

windows at the front and rear of this room.

- Kitchen: Designed for maximum efficiency, this kitchen is a pleasure to be in. It features a center island, a full pantry, and a desk for added convenience.
- Breakfast Area: This area adjoins the kitchen. Both rooms are flooded with sunlight streaming from a shared bay window.
- Master Suite: The stylish bedroom includes a walk-in closet. Luxuriate in the whirlpool tub at the end of a long day .

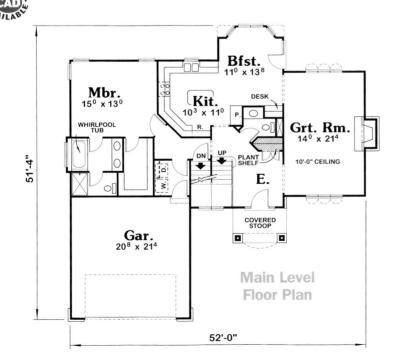

Main Level Floor Plan

Copyright by designer/architect.

Upper Level Floor Plan

Plan #111015

Dimensions: 64' W x 58' D
Levels: 1
Square Footage: 2,208
Bedrooms: 4
Bathrooms: 2
Foundation: Slab
Materials List Available: No
Price Category: E

Images provided by designer/architect.

Copyright by designer/architect.

Plan #451200

Dimensions: 40' W x 45' D
Levels: 2
Square Footage: 2,142
Main Level Sq. Ft.: 1,303
Upper Level Sq. Ft.: 839
Bedrooms: 3
Bathrooms: 3
Foundation: Crawl space
Materials List Available: No
Price Category: D

Images provided by designer/architect.

Main Level Floor Plan

Copyright by designer/architect.

Lower Level Floor Plan

Upper Level Floor Plan

Plan #151469

Dimensions: 50'6" W x 54'8" D
Levels: 2
Square Footage: 2,401
Main Level Sq. Ft.: 1,495
Upper Level Sq. Ft.: 546
Bedrooms: 4
Bathrooms: 2½
Foundation: Crawl space or slab
CompleteCost List Available: Yes
Price Category: D

Images provided by designer/architect.

The interesting roofline makes this home stand out from the rest.

Features:

- Foyer: This beautiful entry space has a 10-ft.-high ceiling that leads into a massive great room.

- Kitchen: Featuring access to the breakfast room and grilling porch, this cooking center has a bar area for extra seating.

- Master Suite: This main-level master suite has a 10-ft.-high ceiling and two large closets, which lead to the amenity-filled private bath.

- Bedrooms: Upstairs you'll find three bedrooms and full bathroom with an optional bonus area.

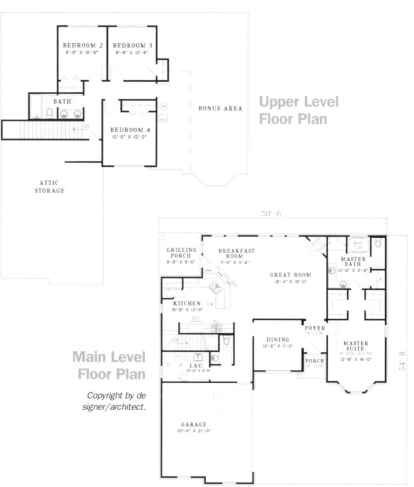

Upper Level Floor Plan

BEDROOM 2
9'-9" X 10'-6"

BEDROOM 3
9'-9" X 10'-6"

BATH

BONUS AREA

BEDROOM 4
10'-8" X 13'-0"

ATTIC STORAGE

Main Level Floor Plan

Copyright by designer/architect.

50'-6"

GRILLING PORCH
9'-8" X 9'-6"

BREAKFAST ROOM
11'-0" X 11'-4"

MASTER BATH
12'-8" X 11'-4"

GREAT ROOM
16'-4" X 18'-0"

PANTRY

KITCHEN
15'-8" X 12'-0"

FOYER

DINING
10'-6" X 11'-0"

MASTER SUITE
12'-8" X 16'-0"

LAU.
10'-4" X 6'-6"

PORCH

54'-8"

GARAGE
20'-0" X 21'-10"

Plan #121025

Dimensions: 60' W x 59'4" D

Levels: 2

Square Footage: 2,562

Main Level Sq. Ft.: 1,875

Upper Level Square Footage: 687

Bedrooms: 4

Bathrooms: 2½

Foundation: Basement

Materials List Available: Yes

Price Category: E

Images provided by designer/architect.

Dramatic arches are the reoccurring architectural theme in this distinctive home.

Features:

• Ceiling Height: 8 ft. unless otherwise noted.

• Foyer: This is a grand two-story entrance. Plants will thrive on the plant shelf thanks to light streaming through the arched window.

• Great Room: The foyer flows into the great room through dramatic 15-ft.-high arched openings.

• Kitchen: An island is the centerpiece of this highly functional kitchen that includes a separate breakfast area.

• Office: French doors open into this versatile office that features a 10-ft. ceiling and transom-topped windows.

• Master Suite: The master suite features a volume ceiling, built-in dresser, and two closets. You'll unwind in the beautiful corner whirlpool bath with its elegant window treatment.

Main Level Floor Plan

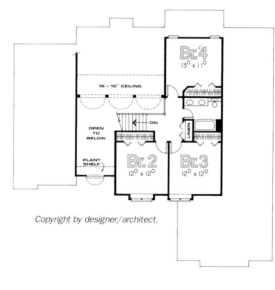

Upper Level Floor Plan

Copyright by designer/architect.

Plan #271018

Dimensions: 67' W x 37' D
Levels: 2
Square Footage: 2,445
Main Level Sq. Ft.: 1,290
Upper Level Sq. Ft.: 1,155
Bedrooms: 4
Bathrooms: 2½
Foundation: Basement
Materials List Available: Yes
Price Category: E

Images provided by designer/architect.

This traditional home re-creates the charm and character of days gone by.

Features:

• Living Room: A dramatic skylighted entry preludes this formal, sunken living room, which includes a stunning corner fireplace, a vaulted ceiling, and an adjoining formal dining room.

• Dining Room: This quiet space offers a built-in hutch beneath a vaulted ceiling.

• Kitchen: A built-in desk and a pantry mark this smartly designed space, which opens to a breakfast room and the family room beyond.

• Family Room: Sunken and filled with intrigue, this gathering room features a fireplace flanked by windows, plus French doors that open to a backyard deck.

• Master Suite: This luxurious upper-floor retreat boasts a vaulted ceiling, an angled walk-in closet, and a private bath.

Main Level Floor Plan

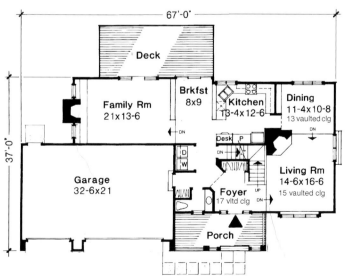

Upper Level Floor Plan

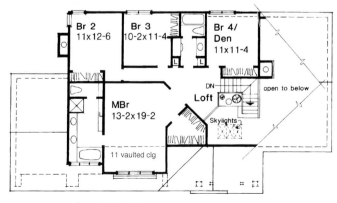

Copyright by designer/architect.

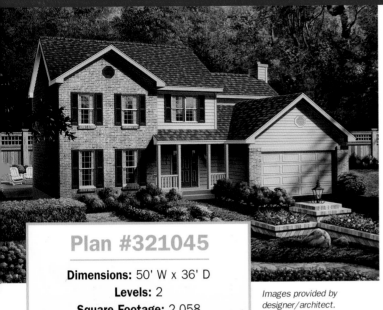

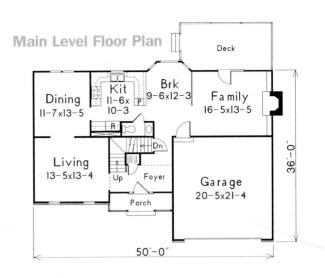

Deck

Dining
11-7x13-5

Kit
11-6x
10-3

Brk
9-6x12-3

Family
16-5x13-5

Living
13-5x13-4

Up   Foyer   Dn

Porch

Garage
20-5x21-4

36'-0"

50'-0"

Images provided by designer/architect.

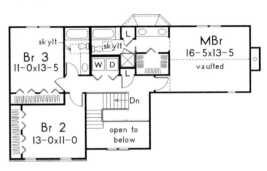

Upper Level Floor Plan

skylt   skylt

Br 3
11-0x13-5

L

W D

L

MBr
16-5x13-5
vaulted

Br 2
13-0x11-0

open to below

Dn

Copyright by designer/architect.

Plan #321045

Dimensions: 50' W x 36' D
Levels: 2
Square Footage: 2,058
Main Level Sq. Ft.: 1,098
Upper Level Sq. Ft.: 960
Bedrooms: 3
Bathrooms: 2½
Foundation: Crawl space, slab, or basement
Materials List Available: Yes
Price Category: D

65' 2"

M. BATH

MASTER SUITE
16'-8" X 13'-10"

BRKFST. RM.
13'-0" X 9'-2"

STORAGE

KITCHEN
13'-0" X 10'-2"

GARAGE
20'-10" X 22'-8"

DINING RM.
11'-0" X 12'-0"

PATIO
32'-6" X 8'-0"

COVERED PORCH
32'-6" X 9'-0"

GREAT RM.
19'-6" X 17'-0"

FOYER

PORCH

BEDROOM 4
14'-4" X 11'-0"

BATH

BEDROOM 2
10'-6" X 12'-0"

BEDROOM 3
10'-0" X 12'-0"

Images provided by designer/architect.

Copyright by designer/architect.

Plan #151447

Dimensions: 65'2" W x 63'8" D
Levels: 1
Square Footage: 2,147
Bedrooms: 4
Bathrooms: 2½
Foundation: Crawl space and slab
CompleteCost List Available: Yes
Price Category: D

Plan #151386

Dimensions: 64'2" W x 49' D

Levels: 1

Square Footage: 1,989

Bedrooms: 4

Bathrooms: 3

Foundation: Crawl space, slab, basement, or walkout

CompleteCost List Available: Yes

Price Category: D

Images provided by designer/architect.

CAD FILE AVAILABLE

Copyright by designer/architect.

Floor plan rooms: BATH, BREAKFAST ROOM 12'-4" X 9'-6", PORCH, MASTER SUITE 13'-4" X 16'-8", GUEST ROOM/BEDROOM 4 12'-8" X 11'-6", GREAT ROOM 15'-0" X 18'-4", KITCHEN 12'-4" X 13'-4", M.BATH 8'-10" X 27'-0", LAU. 12'-4" X 5'-10", BATH, FOYER 7'-4" X 7'-10", DINING ROOM 12'-2" X 13'-4", BEDROOM 3 11'-0" X 10'-4", BEDROOM 2 11'-2" X 11'-6", GARAGE 20'-10" X 25'-0", PORCH 7'-0" X 5'-6"

Plan #151383

Dimensions: 70'4" W x 57'2" D

Levels: 1

Square Footage: 2,534

Bedrooms: 3

Bathrooms: 2

Foundation: Crawl space or slab

CompleteCost List Available: Yes

Price Category: E

Images provided by designer/architect.

CAD FILE AVAILABLE

Front View

Copyright by designer/architect.

Floor plan rooms: BEDROOM 3 11'-10" X 14'-6", COVERED PORCH 36'-4" X 10'-0", MASTER SUITE 21'-2" X 14'-8", BATH, BREAKFAST AREA 13'-2" X 10'-10", M.BATH 17'-4" X 12'-0", GREAT ROOM 22'-6" X 22'-0", KITCHEN 19'-2" X 13'-6", LAU. 8'-10" X 8'-0", BEDROOM 2 11'-10" X 13'-6", STUDY 10'-0" X 12'-4", FOYER 7'-4" X 9'-8", DINING ROOM 12'-8" X 16'-4", GARAGE 24'-2" X 29'-2", PORCH 7'-4" X 6'-0"

Plan #441007

Dimensions: 70' W x 64' D
Levels: 1
Square Footage: 2,197
Bedrooms: 4
Bathrooms: 2½
Foundation: Crawl space
Materials List Available: No
Price Category: D

Images provided by designer/architect.

Welcome to this roomy ranch, embellished with a brick facade, intriguing roof peaks, and decorative quoins on all the front corners.

CAD FILE AVAILABLE

Features:

- **Great Room:** There's a direct sightline from the front door through the trio of windows in this room. The rooms are defined by columns and changes in ceiling height rather than by walls, so light bounces from dining room to breakfast nook to kitchen.

- **Kitchen:** The primary workstation in this kitchen is a peninsula, which faces the fireplace. The peninsula is equipped with a sink, dishwasher, downdraft cooktop, and snack counter.

- **Den/Home Office:** Conveniently located off the foyer, this room would work well as a home office.

- **Master Suite:** The double doors provide an air of seclusion for this suite. The vaulted bedroom features sliding patio doors to the backyard and an arch-top window. The adjoining bath is equipped with a whirlpool tub, shower, double vanity, and walk-in closet.

- **Secondary Bedrooms:** The two additional bedrooms, each with direct access to the shared bathroom, occupy the left wing of the ranch.

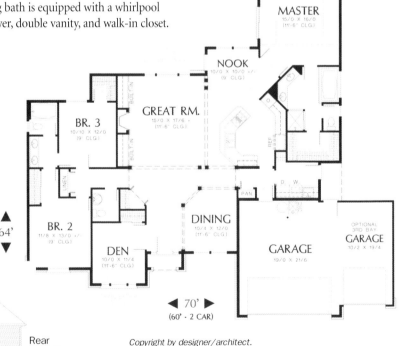

Copyright by designer/architect.

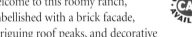
Rear Elevation

Plan #181246

Dimensions: 44' W x 29'8" D

Levels: 2

Square Footage: 1,485

Main Level Sq. Ft.: 750

Upper Level Sq. Ft.: 735

Bedrooms: 3

Bathrooms: 1½

Foundation: Basement

Materials List Available: Yes

Price Category: B

Images provided by designer/architect.

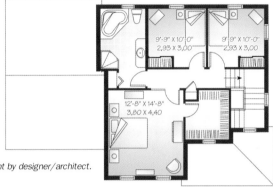

Main Level Floor Plan

Upper Level Floor Plan

Copyright by designer/architect.

Plan #181247

Dimensions: 32' W x 48' D

Levels: 2

Square Footage: 1,767

Main Level Sq. Ft.: 910

Upper Level Sq. Ft.: 857

Bedrooms: 3

Bathrooms: 2½

Foundation: Basement

Materials List Available: Yes

Price Category: C

Images provided by designer/architect.

Main Level Floor Plan

Upper Level Floor Plan

Copyright by designer/architect.

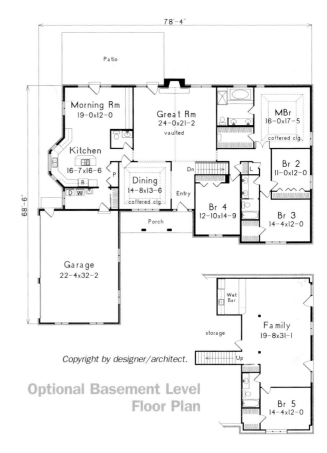

Images provided by designer/architect.

Plan #321036

Dimensions: 78'4" W x 68'6" D

Levels: 1

Square Footage: 2,900

Bedrooms: 4

Bathrooms: 2½

Foundation: Basement

Materials List Available: No

Price Category: F

Copyright by designer/architect.

Optional Basement Level Floor Plan

Images provided by designer/architect.

Plan #261008

Dimensions: 68'W x 64'6" D

Levels: 2

Square Footage: 2,226

Main Level Sq. Ft.: 1,689

Upper Level Sq. Ft.: 537

Bedrooms: 4

Bathrooms: 3

Foundation: Basement

Materials List Available: No

Price Category: E

Main Level Floor Plan

Upper Level Floor Plan

Copyright by designer/architect.

Plan #121017

Dimensions: 54' W x 50' D
Levels: 2
Square Footage: 2,353
Main Level Sq. Ft.: 1,653
Upper Level Sq. Ft.: 700
Bedrooms: 4
Bathrooms: 2½
Foundation: Basement
Materials List Available: Yes
Price Category: E

Images provided by designer/architect.

The dramatic two-story entry with bent staircase is the first sign that this is a gracious home.

Features:

• Ceiling Height: 8 ft. except as noted.

• Great Room: A row of transom-topped windows and a tall, beamed ceiling add a sense of spaciousness to this family gathering area.

• Formal Dining Room: The bayed window helps make this an inviting place to entertain.

• See-through Fireplace: This feature spreads warmth and coziness throughout the informal areas of the home.

• Breakfast Area: This sunny area shares a see-through fireplace with the great room. It's the perfect place to start the day.

• Master Suite: Here are all the features you expect to find in large luxury homes. Wake up to tall, sloped ceilings, and enjoy the corner whirlpool, separate shower, and vanity. A large walk-in closet provides plenty of wardrobe storage.

Main Level Floor Plan

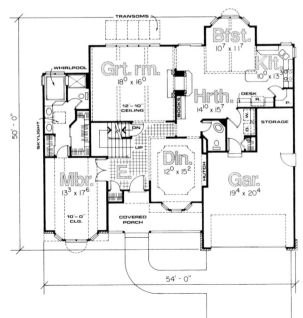

Upper Level Floor Plan

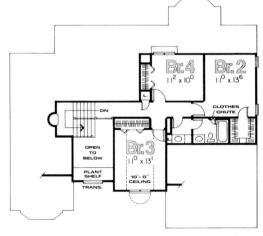

Copyright by designer/architect.

Plan #321051

Dimensions: 69'8" W x 46' D
Levels: 2
Square Footage: 2,624
Main Level Sq. Ft.: 1,774
Upper Level Sq. Ft.: 850
Bedrooms: 4
Bathrooms: 2½
Foundation: Basement
Materials List Available: Yes
Price Category: F

If you're looking for a home that deserves to be called "grand" and "elegant," you will love this spacious beauty.

This home, as shown in the photograph, may differ from the actual blueprints. For more detailed information, please check the floor plans carefully.   *Images provided by designer/architect.*

Features:

- **Entryway:** Two stories high, this area sets the tone for the whole house.

- **Great Room:** The 18-ft. ceiling in this room gives a bright and airy feeling that the three magnificent Palladian windows surely enhance.

- **Dining Room:** A classic colonnade forms the entry to this lovely bayed room.

- **Kitchen:** Designed for gourmet cooks who love efficient work spaces, this kitchen will delight the whole family.

- **Master Suite:** Relax in the comfort of this luxurious suite at the end of the day. You'll find walk-in closets, a large bay window, and plant shelves in the bedroom, as well as a sunken tub in the bathroom.

Master Bath

Main Level Floor Plan

Copyright by designer/architect.

Upper Level Floor Plan

Plan #421009

Dimensions: 64'9" W x 59' D
Levels: 1
Square Footage: 2,649
Bedrooms: 3
Bathrooms: 2
Foundation: Crawl space, slab, or basement
Materials List Available: Yes
Price Category: F

Images provided by designer/architect.

Main Level Floor Plan

Alternate Floor Plan

Copyright by designer/architect.

Plan #181260

Dimensions: 54' W x 43' D
Levels: 2
Square Footage: 3,251
Main Level Sq. Ft.: 1,536
Upper Level Sq. Ft.: 1,715
Bedrooms: 4
Bathrooms: 3½
Foundation: Basement
Materials List Available: Yes
Price Category: G

Images provided by designer/architect.

Main Level Floor Plan

Upper Level Floor Plan

Copyright by designer/architect.

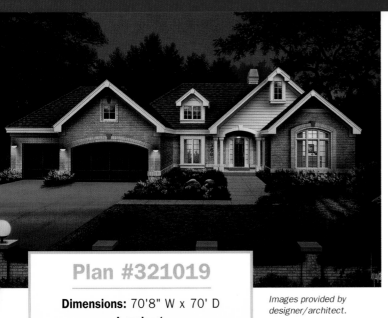

Plan #321019

Dimensions: 70'8" W x 70' D
Levels: 1
Square Footage: 2,452
Bedrooms: 4
Bathrooms: 2½
Foundation: Basement
Materials List Available: Yes
Price Category: E

Images provided by designer/architect.

Copyright by designer/architect.

Main Level Floor Plan

Plan #181264

Images provided by designer/architect.

Dimensions: 51' W x 39' D
Levels: 2
Square Footage: 2,090
Main Level Sq. Ft.: 1,075
Upper Level Sq. Ft.: 1,015
Bedrooms: 3
Bathrooms: 2½
Foundation: Basement
Materials List Available: Yes
Price Category: D

Upper Level Floor Plan

Copyright by designer/architect.

Plan #121020

Dimensions: 64' W x 46' D

Levels: 2

Square Footage: 2,480

Main Level Sq. Ft.: 1,369

Upper Level Sq. Ft.: 1,111

Bedrooms: 4

Bathrooms: 3

Foundation: Basement

Materials List Available: Yes

Price Category: E

Images provided by designer/architect.

Tapered columns and an angled stairway give this home a classical style.

Features:

• Ceiling Height: 8 ft.

• Living Room: Just off the dramatic two-story entry is this distinctive living room, with its tapered columns, transom-topped windows, and boxed ceiling.

• Formal Dining Room: The tapered columns, transom-topped windows, and boxed ceiling found in the living room continue into this gracious dining space.

• Family Room: Located on the opposite side of the house from the living room and dining room, the family room features a beamed ceiling and fireplace framed by windows.

• Kitchen: An island is the centerpiece of this convenient kitchen.

• Master Suite: Upstairs, a tiered ceiling and corner windows enhance the master bedroom, which is served by a pampering bath.

Main Level Floor Plan

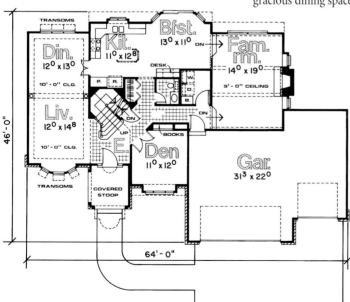

Upper Level Floor Plan

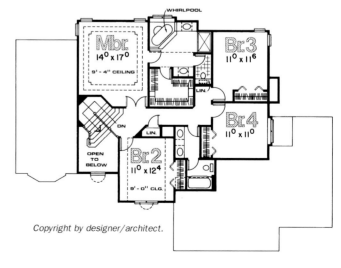

Copyright by designer/architect.

Plan #151548

Dimensions: 55'10" W x 52' D
Levels: 1
Square Footage: 1,763
Bedrooms: 3
Bathrooms: 2
Foundation: Crawl space or slab
CompleteCost List Available: Yes
Price Category: C

Images provided by designer/architect.

Round-top windows and a sleek roofline provide a sense of elegance in this plan.

Features:

- Entertaining: A spacious great room with a fireplace and a backyard view blends with the kitchen and breakfast room, which has access to the grilling porch, creating the perfect area for entertaining.

- Master Suite: Indulge yourself in this private suite. The bath has a relaxing whirlpool tub, with a privacy glass-block window above, as well as a walk-in closet and split vanities.

- Garage: This front-loading two-car garage has extra storage space.

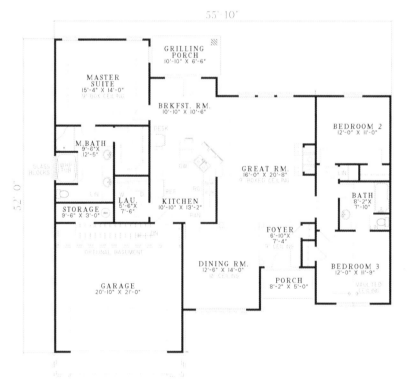

Copyright by designer/architect.

Plan #181266

Dimensions: 58' W x 54' D
Levels: 2
Square Footage: 2,991
Main Level Sq. Ft.: 1,927
Upper Level Sq. Ft.: 1,064
Bedrooms: 4
Bathrooms: 3½
Foundation: Basement
Materials List Available: Yes
Price Category: F

Images provided by designer/architect.

CAD FILE AVAILABLE

Main Level Floor Plan

Upper Level Floor Plan

Copyright by designer/architect.

Plan #181309

Dimensions: 34' W x 39' D
Levels: 1
Square Footage: 1,114
Bedrooms: 2
Bathrooms: 1
Foundation: Basement
Materials List Available: Yes
Price Category: B

Images provided by designer/architect.

CAD FILE AVAILABLE

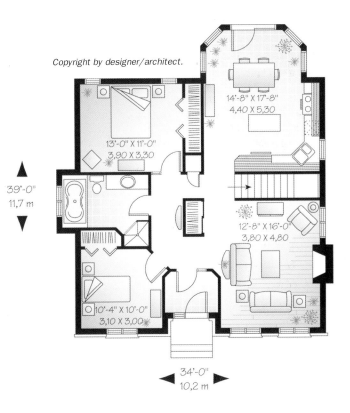

Copyright by designer/architect.

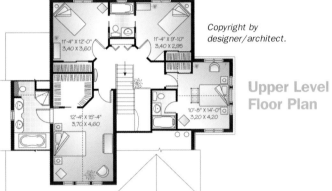

Main Level Floor Plan

Images provided by designer/architect.

Copyright by designer/architect.

Upper Level Floor Plan

Plan #181295

Dimensions: 46' W x 40' D
Levels: 2
Square Footage: 2,265
Main Level Sq. Ft.: 1,090
Upper Level Sq. Ft.: 1,175
Bedrooms: 4
Bathrooms: 3½
Foundation: Basement
Materials List Available: Yes
Price Category: E

CAD FILE AVAILABLE · CAD ·

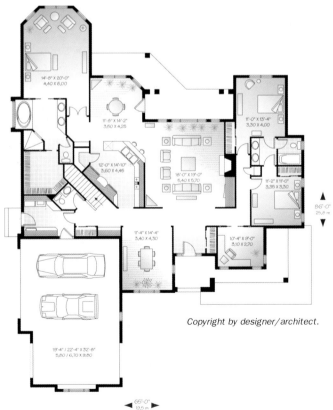

Images provided by designer/architect.

CAD FILE AVAILABLE · CAD ·

Copyright by designer/architect.

Plan #181281

Dimensions: 65' W x 86' D
Levels: 1
Square Footage: 2,620
Bedrooms: 3
Bathrooms: 2½
Foundation: Basement
Materials List Available: Yes
Price Category: F

Plan #121024

Dimensions: 60' W x 58' D

Levels: 2

Square Footage: 3,057

Main Level Sq. Ft.: 1,631

Second Level Sq. Ft.: 1,426

Bedrooms: 4

Bathrooms: 2½

Foundation: Basement

Materials List Available: Yes

Price Category: G

Images provided by designer/architect.

This distinctive home offers plenty of space and is designed for gracious and convenient living.

Features:

- Ceiling Height: 8 ft. unless otherwise noted.

- Foyer: A curved staircase in this elegant entry will greet your guests.

- Living Room: This room invites you with a volume ceiling flanked by transom-topped windows that flood the room with sunlight.

- Screened Veranda: On warm summer nights, throw open the French doors in the living room and enjoy a breeze on the huge screened veranda.

- Dining Room: This distinctive room is overlooked by the veranda.

- Family Room: At the back of the home is this comfortable family retreat with its soaring cathedral ceiling and handsome fireplace flanked by bookcases.

- Master Bedroom: This bayed bedroom features a 10-ft. vaulted ceiling.

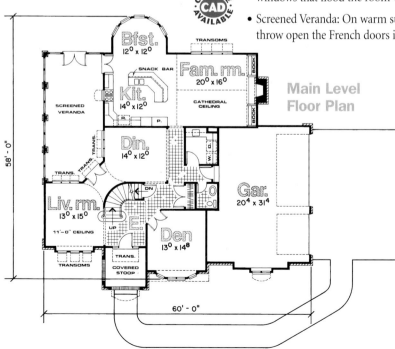

Main Level Floor Plan

Upper Level Floor Plan

Copyright by designer/architect.

Plan #151281

Dimensions: 48'6" W x 48'4" D
Levels: 1
Square Footage: 1,461
Bedrooms: 3
Bathrooms: 2
Foundation: Walkout basement
CompleteCost List Available: Yes
Price Category: B

Images provided by designer/architect.

This brick ranch is the perfect home in which to raise your family.

Features:

- **Great Room:** Just off the entry is this large room, with its cozy fireplace and access to the rear porch.

- **Kitchen:** This fully equipped kitchen has a raised bar and is open to the great room and dining area.

- **Master Suite:** Located in the rear of the home, this suite has a large walk-in closet and a private bath with his and her vanities.

- **Bedrooms:** The two secondary bedrooms have large closets and share a hall bathroom.

- **Garage:** This front-loading two-car garage has plenty of room for cars and storage.

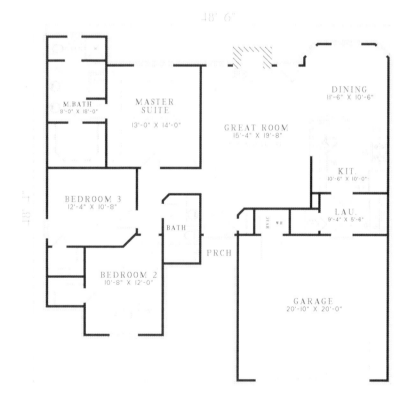

Copyright by designer/architect.

Plan #131033

Dimensions: 84'10" W x 48' D
Levels: 2
Square Footage: 2,813
Main Level Sq. Ft.: 1,890
Upper Level Sq. Ft.: 923
Bedrooms: 5
Bathrooms: 3½
Foundation: Crawl space, slab, or basement
Materials List Available: Yes
Price Category: G

Contemporary styling, luxurious amenities, and the classics that make a house a home are all available here.

Features:

- **Family Room:** A sloped ceiling with skylight and a railed overlook to make this large space totally up to date.

- **Living Room:** Sunken for comfort and with a cathedral ceiling for style, this room features a fireplace flanked by windows and sliding glass doors.

- **Master Suite:** Unwind in this room, with its cathedral ceiling, with a skylight, walk-in closet, and private access to the den.

- **Upper Level:** A bridge overlooks the living room and foyer and leads through the family room to three bedrooms and a bath.

- **Optional Guest Suite:** 500 sq. ft. above the master suite and den provides total comfort.

Images provided by designer/architect.

Main Level Floor Plan

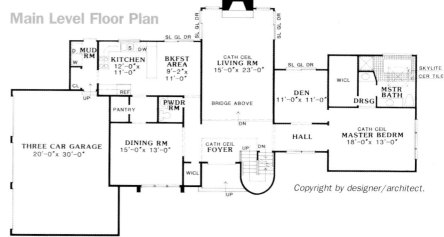

Copyright by designer/architect.

Upper Level Floor Plan

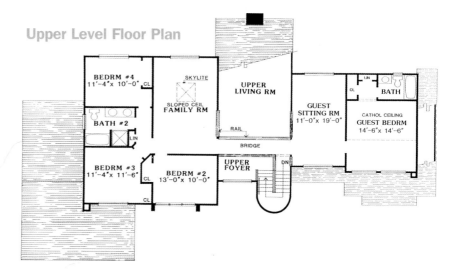

Plan #161031

Dimensions: 99'8" W x 68'8" D

Levels: 2

Square Footage: 5,381

Main Level Sq. Ft.: 3,793

Upper Level Sq. Ft.: 1,588

Bedrooms: 4

Bathrooms: 3½

Foundation: Basement

Materials List Available: Yes

Price Category: I

Images provided by designer/architect.

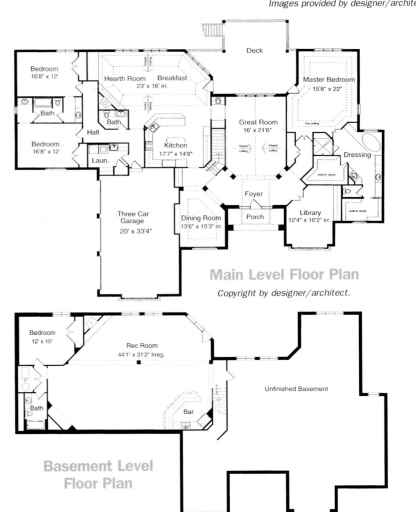

Main Level Floor Plan

Copyright by designer/architect.

Basement Level Floor Plan

If you're looking for a compatible mixture of formal and informal areas in a home, look no further!

Features:

- **Great Room:** Columns at the entry to this room and the formal dining room set a gracious tone that is easy around which to decorate.

- **Library:** Set up an office or just a cozy reading area in this quiet room.

- **Hearth Room:** Spacious and inviting, this hearth room is positioned so that friends and family can flow from here to the breakfast area and kitchen.

- **Master Suite:** The luxury of this area is capped by the access it gives to the rear yard.

- **Lower Level:** Enjoy the 9-ft.-tall ceilings as you walk out to the rear yard from this area.

Main Level Floor Plan

Copyright by designer/architect.

Plan #451149

Dimensions: 35'2" W x 42' D
Levels: 2
Square Footage: 2,130
Main Level Sq. Ft.: 1,085
Upper Level Sq. Ft.: 455
Bedrooms: 3
Bathrooms: 2
Foundation: Walk-out basement
Materials List Available: No
Price Category: D

Images provided by designer/architect.

Garage Level Floor Plan

Upper Level Floor Plan

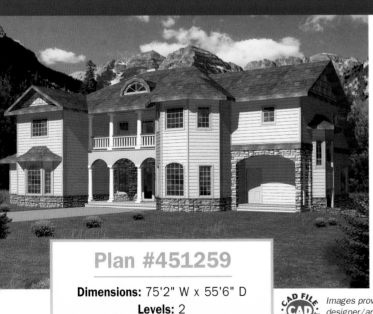

Main Level Floor Plan

Copyright by designer/architect.

Upper Level Floor Plan

Images provided by designer/architect.

Plan #451259

Dimensions: 75'2" W x 55'6" D
Levels: 2
Square Footage: 3,798
Main Level Sq. Ft.: 2,485
Upper Level Sq. Ft.: 1,313
Bedrooms: 6
Bathrooms: 6½
Foundation: Walk-out basement
Materials List Available: No
Price Category: H

Basement Level Floor Plan

Plan #111031

Dimensions: 56' W x 53' D
Levels: 2
Square Footage: 2,869
Main Level Sq. Ft.: 2,152
Upper Level Sq. Ft.: 717
Bedrooms: 4
Bathrooms: 3
Foundation: Slab, crawl space
Materials List Available: No
Price Category: F

This home is ideal for any family, thanks to its spaciousness, beauty, and versatility.

Images provided by designer/architect.

Features:

- Ceiling Height: 9 ft.

- Front Porch: The middle of the three French doors with circle tops here opens to the foyer.

- Living Room: Archways from the foyer open to both this room and the equally large dining room.

- Family Room: Also open to the foyer, this room features a two-story sloped ceiling and a balcony from the upper level. You'll love the fireplace, with its raised brick hearth and the

two French doors with circle tops, which open to the rear porch.

- Kitchen: A center island, range with microwave, built-in desk, and dining bar that's open to the breakfast room add up to comfort and efficiency.

- Master Suite: A Palladian window and linen closet grace this suite's bedroom, and the bath has an oversized garden tub, standing shower, two walk-in closets, and double vanity.

Copyright by designer/architect.

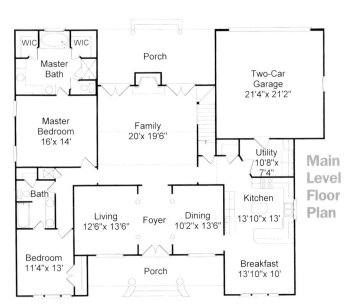

Main Level Floor Plan

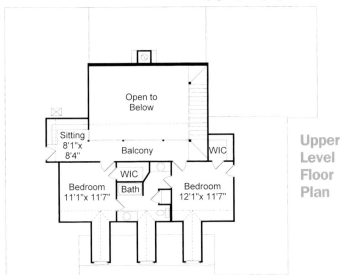

Upper Level Floor Plan

Entry

Kitchen

Living Room

Living Room

SMARTtip

Preparing to Use a Clay Chiminea

Before getting started, there are a couple of general rules about using a clay chiminea. Make sure the chiminea is completely dry before lighting a fire, or else it will crack. Also, line the bottom of the pot with about 4 inches of sand. Finally, always build the fire slowly, and never use kerosene or charcoal lighter fluid.

To cure a new clay chiminea, follow these simple steps:

- Build a small paper fire inside the pot. For kindling, use strips of newspaper rolled into a few balls. Place one newspaper ball on the sand inside the chiminea. Ignite it with a match. Then add another ball, and another, one at a time, until the outside walls of the chiminea are slightly warm. Allow the fire to burn out; then let the pot cool completely before the next step.

- Once the chiminea feels cool, light another small fire, this time using wood. Again, let the fire burn out naturally, and then allow the unit to completely cool.

- Repeat the process of lighting a wood fire three more times, adding more kindling and building a larger fire with each consecutive attempt. Remember to let the chiminea cool completely between fires.

After the fifth fire, the chiminea should be cured and ready to use anytime you want a cozy fire.

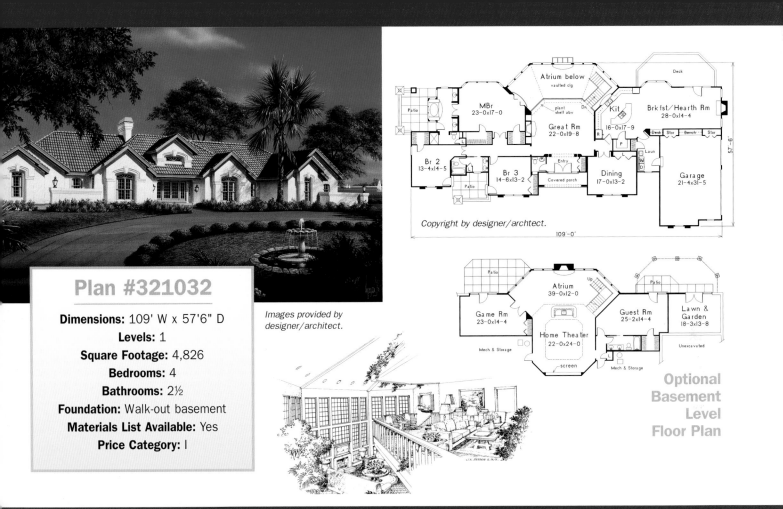

Copyright by designer/archtect.

109'-0"

57'-6"

Optional
Basement
Level
Floor Plan

Plan #321032

Dimensions: 109' W x 57'6" D
Levels: 1
Square Footage: 4,826
Bedrooms: 4
Bathrooms: 2½
Foundation: Walk-out basement
Materials List Available: Yes
Price Category: I

Images provided by
designer/architect.

Plan #221036

Dimensions: 70' W x 62'4" D
Levels: 1
Square Footage: 2,504
Bedrooms: 3
Bathrooms: 3
Foundation: Basement
Materials List Available: No
Price Category: E

Images provided by
designer/architect.

Copyright by designer/architect.

Rear Elevation

Plan #121062

Dimensions: 70' W x 62' D
Levels: 2
Square Footage: 3,448
Main Level Sq. Ft.: 2,375
Upper Level Sq. Ft.: 1,073
Bedrooms: 4
Bathrooms: 3½
Foundation: Basement
Materials List Available: Yes
Price Category: G

Images provided by designer/architect.

You'll love this design if you're looking for a comfortable home with dimensions and details that create a sense of grandeur.

Features:

• Entry: A soaring ceiling, curved staircase, and balcony that overlooks a tall plant shelf combine to create your first impression of grandeur in this home.

• Great Room: A transom-topped bowed window highlights this room, with its 11-ft., beamed ceiling, built-in wet bar, and see-through fireplace.

• Kitchen: Designed for the gourmet cook, this kitchen has every amenity you could desire.

• Breakfast Room: Adjacent to the great room and the kitchen, this gazebo-shaped breakfast area lights both the kitchen and hearth room.

Main Level Floor Plan

Upper Level Floor Plan

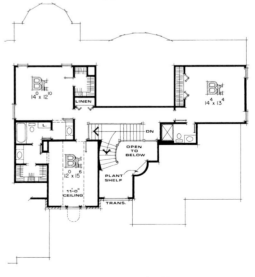

Copyright by designer/architect.

Plan #151004

Dimensions: 64'8" W x 62'1" D

Levels: 1

Square Footage: 2,107

Bedrooms: 4

Bathrooms: 2½

Foundation: Crawl space, slab, or basement

CompleteCost List Available: Yes

Price Category: D

Images provided by designer/architect.

You'll love the spacious feeling in this comfortable home designed for a family.

Features:

- Foyer: A 10-ft. ceiling greets you in this home.

- Great Room: A 10-ft. ceiling complements this large room, with its fireplace, built-in cabinets, and easy access to the rear covered porch.

- Dining Room: The 9-ft. boxed ceiling in this large room helps to create a beautiful formal feeling.

- Kitchen: The island in this kitchen is open to the breakfast room for true convenience.

- Breakfast Room: Morning light will stream through the bay window here.

- Master Suite: A 9-ft. pan ceiling adds a distinctive note to this room with access to the rear porch. In the bath, you'll find a whirlpool tub, separate shower, double vanities, and two walk-in closets.

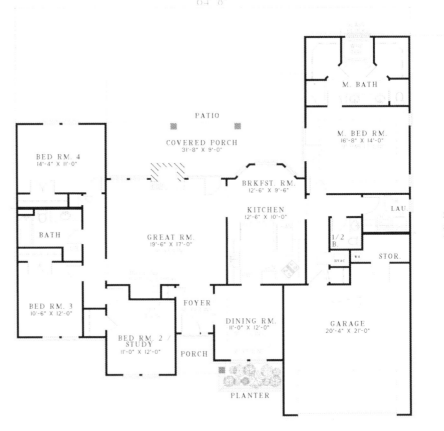

Copyright by designer/architect.

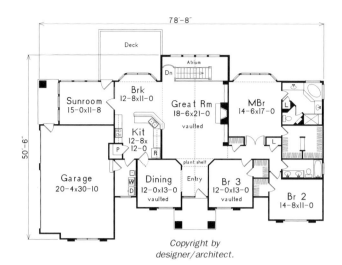

Copyright by
designer/architect.

Images provided by
designer/architect.

Plan #321037

Dimensions: 78'8" W x 50'6" D
Levels: 1
Square Footage: 2,397
Bedrooms: 3
Bathrooms: 2
Foundation: Basement or walkout
Materials List Available: Yes
Price Category: E

**Optional
Basement Level
Floor Plan**

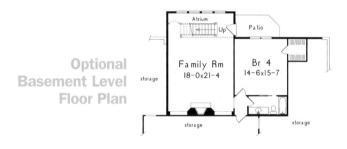

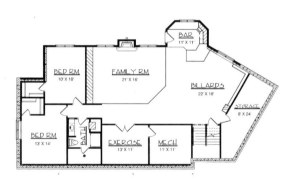

Optional Basement Level Floor Plan

Plan #271079

Dimensions: 104' W x 55' D
Levels: 1
Square Footage: 2,228
Bedrooms: 1-3
Bathrooms: 1½
Foundation: Daylight basement
Materials List Available: No
Price Category: E

Images provided by
designer/architect.

CAD FILE AVAILABLE

Copyright by
designer/architect.

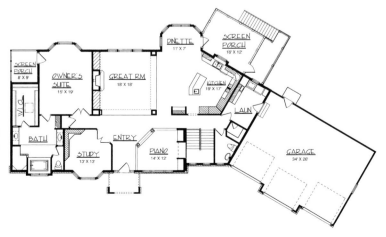

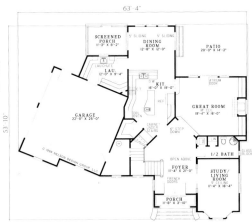

Main Level Floor Plan

Images provided by designer/architect.

CAD FILE AVAILABLE

Plan #151019

Dimensions: 63'4" W x 53'10" D
Levels: 2
Square Footage: 2,947
Main Level Sq. Ft.: 1,407
Upper Level Sq. Ft.: 1,540
Bedrooms: 3
Bathrooms: 2½
Foundation: Crawl space, slab; optional full basement plan available for extra fee
CompleteCost List Available: Yes
Price Category: F

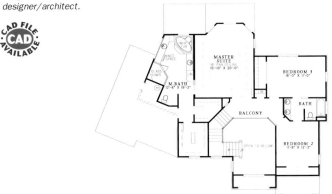

Upper Level Floor Plan

Copyright by designer/architect.

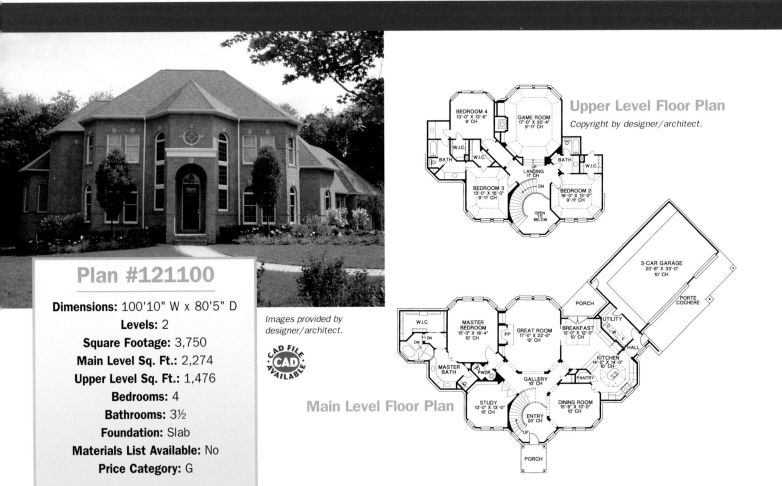

Upper Level Floor Plan

Copyright by designer/architect.

Plan #121100

Dimensions: 100'10" W x 80'5" D
Levels: 2
Square Footage: 3,750
Main Level Sq. Ft.: 2,274
Upper Level Sq. Ft.: 1,476
Bedrooms: 4
Bathrooms: 3½
Foundation: Slab
Materials List Available: No
Price Category: G

Images provided by designer/architect.

CAD FILE AVAILABLE

Main Level Floor Plan

Plan #151002

Dimensions: 67' W x 66' D

Levels: 1

Square Footage: 2,444

Bedrooms: 3

Bathrooms: 2½

Foundation: Crawl space, slab, or basement

CompleteCost List Available: Yes

Price Category: E

Images provided by designer/architect.

This gracious, traditional home is designed for practicality and convenience.

Features:

• **Ceiling Height:** 9 ft. except as noted below.

• **Great Room:** This room is ideal for entertaining, thanks to its lovely fireplace and French doors that open to the covered rear porch. Built-in cabinets give convenient storage space.

• **Family Room:** With access to the kitchen as well as the rear porch, this room will become your family's "headquarters."

• **Study:** Enjoy the quiet in this room with its 12-ft. ceiling and doorway to a private patio on the side of the house.

• **Dining Room:** Take advantage of the 8-in. wood columns and 12-ft. ceilings to create a formal dining area.

• **Kitchen:** An eat-in bar is a great place to snack, and the handy computer nook allows the kids to do their homework while you cook.

• **Breakfast Room:** Opening from the kitchen, this area gives added space for the family to gather any time.

• **Master Suite:** Featuring a 10-ft. boxed ceiling, the master bedroom also has a door way that opens onto the covered rear porch. The master bathroom has a step-up whirlpool tub, separate shower, and twin vanities with a makeup area.

Copyright by designer/architect.

Plan #161016

Dimensions: 59'4" W x 58'8" D
Levels: 2
Square Footage: 2,101
Main Level Sq. Ft.: 1,626
Upper Level Sq. Ft.: 475
Bedrooms: 3
Bathrooms: 2½
Foundation: Basement, optional crawl space available for extra fee
Materials List Available: Yes
Price Category: D

Note: Home in photo reflects a modified garage entrance.

Images provided by designer/architect.

Features:

- **Great Room:** Made for relaxing and entertaining, the great room is sunken to set it off from the rest of the house. A balcony from the second floor looks down into this spacious area, making it easy to keep track of the kids while they are playing.

- **Kitchen:** Convenience marks this well laid-out kitchen where you'll love to cook for guests and for family.

- **Master Bedroom:** A vaulted ceiling complements the unusual octagonal shape

of the master bedroom. Located on the first floor, this room allows some privacy from the second floor bedrooms. It is also ideal for anyone who no longer wishes to climb stairs to reach a bedroom.

Rear Elevation

You'll love the exciting roofline that sets this elegant home apart from its neighbors as well as the embellished, solid look that declares how well-designed it is—from the inside to the exterior.

CAD FILE AVAILABLE

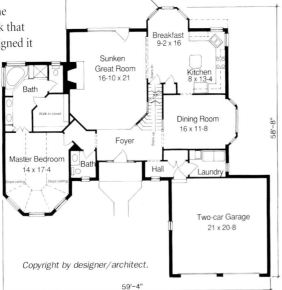

Main Level Floor Plan

Deck

Bath

Walk-in closet

Sunken Great Room 16-10 x 21

Breakfast 9-2 x 16

Kitchen 8 x 13-4

Dining Room 16 x 11-8

Foyer

Master Bedroom 14 x 17-4

Bath

Hall

Laundry

Two-car Garage 21 x 20-8

58'-8"

59'-4"

Copyright by designer/architect.

Upper Level Floor Plan

Bedroom 15x 10-8

Great Room Below

Bath

Bedroom 14x 10-6

Foyer Below

Plan #221037

Dimensions: 83'8" W x 64'4" D
Levels: 1
Square Footage: 3,002
Bedrooms: 3
Bathrooms: 2 full, 2 half
Foundation: Basement
Materials List Available: No
Price Category: G

Images provided by designer/architect.

This spacious ranch features most of the amenities you would expect in a home of this size.

Features:

• Kitchen: The breakfast bar in this efficient work space overlooks the nook and flows into the great room, providing a spacious area for entertaining even the largest of groups.

• Master Suite: This suite features his and her walk-in closets and a centered Jacuzzi tub and two lavatories in the bath.

• Bedrooms: You'll find two additional bedrooms, each with its own bathroom, on the opposite side of the home, allowing for privacy for mom and dad.

• Garage: This three-bay garage has extra storage for the kids' bikes as well as your cars.

Copyright by designer/architect.

Rear Elevation

Plan #211002

Dimensions: 68' W x 62' D
Levels: 1
Square Footage: 1,792
Bedrooms: 3
Bathrooms: 2
Foundation: Crawl space
Materials List Available: Yes
Price Category: C

Images provided by designer/architect.

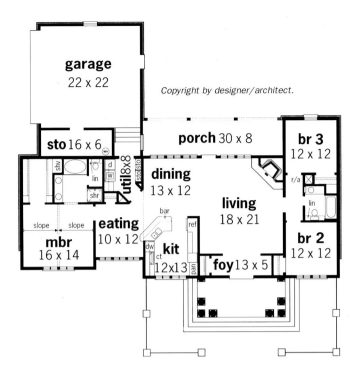

Copyright by designer/architect.

Plan #151108

Dimensions: 84'6" W x 58'6" D
Levels: 1
Square Footage: 2,742
Bedrooms: 4
Bathrooms: 2½
Foundation: Crawl space, slab, or basement
CompleteCost List Available: Yes
Price Category: F

Images provided by designer/architect.

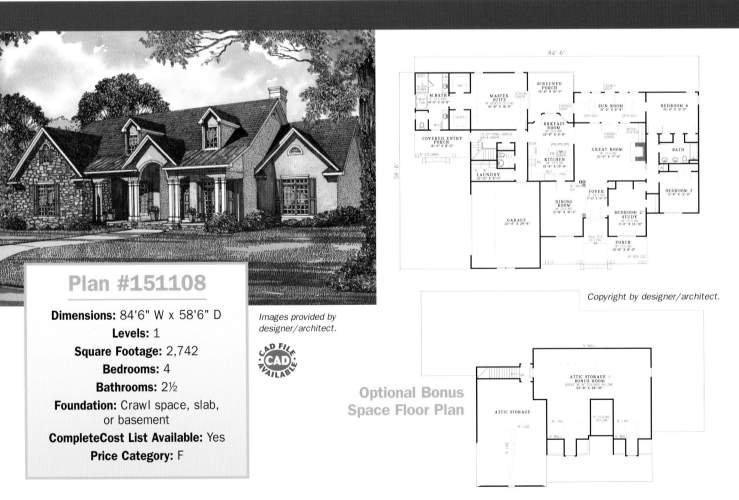

Copyright by designer/architect.

Optional Bonus Space Floor Plan

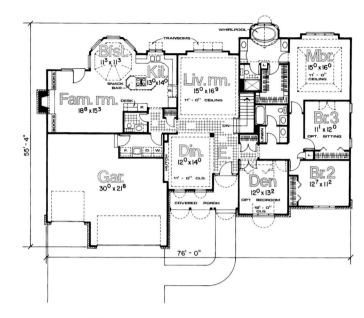

Plan #121003

Dimensions: 76' W x 55'4" D

Levels: 1

Square Footage: 2,498

Bedrooms: 4

Bathrooms: 2½

Foundation: Basement

Materials List Available: Yes

Price Category: E

Images provided by designer/architect.

Copyright by designer/architect.

Plan #221035

Dimensions: 69' W x 64' D

Levels: 2

Square Footage: 3,101

Main Level Sq. Ft.: 2,205

Upper Level Sq. Ft.: 896

Bedrooms: 4

Bathrooms: 3½

Foundation: Basement

Materials List Available: No

Price Category: G

Images provided by designer/architect.

Main Level Floor Plan

Copyright by designer/architect.

Upper Level Floor Plan

Rear Elevation

Plan #121023

Dimensions: 85'5" W x 74'8" D
Levels: 2
Square Footage: 3,904
Main Level Sq. Ft.: 2,813
Upper Level Sq. Ft.: 1,091
Bedrooms: 4
Bathrooms: 3½
Foundation: Basement
Materials List Available: Yes
Price Category: H

Images provided by designer/architect.

Spacious and gracious, here are all the amenities you expect in a fine home.

Features:

• Ceiling Height: 8 ft. except as noted.

• Foyer: This magnificent entry features a graceful curved staircase with balcony above.

• Sunken Living Room: This sunken room is filled with light from a row of bowed windows. It's the perfect place for social gatherings both large and small.

• Den: French doors open into this truly distinctive den with its 11-ft. ceiling and built-in bookcases.

• Formal Dining Room: Entertain guests with style and grace in this dining room with corner column.

• Master Suite: Another set of French doors leads to this suite that features two walk-in closets, a whirlpool flanked by vanities, and a private sitting room with built-in bookcases.

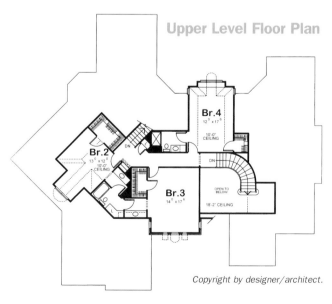

Copyright by designer/architect.

Plan #151010

Dimensions: 38'4" W x 68'6" D
Levels: 1
Square Footage: 1,379
Bedrooms: 3
Bathrooms: 2
Foundation: Crawl space, slab
CompleteCost List Available: Yes
Price Category: B

Images provided by designer/architect.

This French Country home has a spacious great room for friends and family to gather, but you can sneak away to the covered rear porch or patio off the master suite for cozy tête-à-têtes.

Features:

• Entry: Take advantage of the marvelous 10-ft. ceilings to hang groups of potted flowering plants.

• Great Room: This spacious room, with an optional 10-ft. boxed ceiling, is the place to curl up by the gas fireplace on a cold winter night.

• Kitchen: The kitchen includes a bar for casual meals, and is open to the breakfast room.

• Rear Porch: Enjoy leisurely meals on the covered rear porch that you can access from both the master suite and the breakfast room.

• Master Suite: The 10-ft. boxed ceiling in the bedroom and the master bath with a whirlpool tub and separate shower make this suite a luxurious place to end a long day.

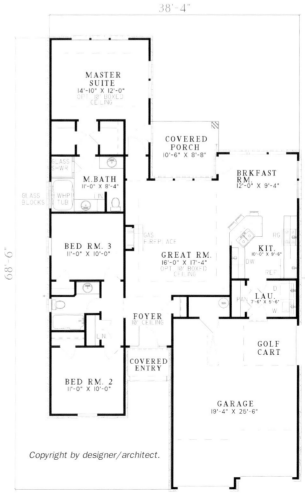

Copyright by designer/architect.

Plan #211011

Dimensions: 84' W x 54' D
Levels: 1
Square Footage: 2,791
Bedrooms: 3 or 4
Bathrooms: 2
Foundation: Slab or crawl space
Materials List Available: Yes
Price Category: F

Images provided by designer/architect.

Plenty of room plus an open, flexible floor plan make this a home that will adapt to your needs.

Features:

- Ceiling Height: 8 ft. unless otherwise noted.

- Living Room: This distinctive room features a 12-ft. ceiling and is designed so that it can also serve as a master suite with a sitting room.

- Family Room: The whole family will want to gather in this large, inviting family room.

- Morning Room: The family room blends

into this sunny spot, which is perfect for informal family meals.

- Kitchen: This spacious kitchen offers a smart layout. It is also contiguous to the family room.

- Master Suite: You'll look forward to the end of the day when you can enjoy this master suite. It includes a huge, luxurious master bath with two large walk-in closets and two vanity sinks.

- Optional Bedroom: This optional fourth bedroom is located so that it can easily serve as a library, den, office, or music room.

SMARTtip

Types of Decks

Ground-level decks resemble a low platform and are best for flat locations. They can be the most economical type to build because they don't require stairs.

Raised decks can rise just a few steps up or meet the second story of a house. Lifted high on post supports, they adapt well to uneven or sloped locations.

Multilevel decks feature two or more stories and are connected by stairways or ramps. They can follow the contours of a sloped lot, unifying the deck with the outdoors.

Copyright by designer/architect.

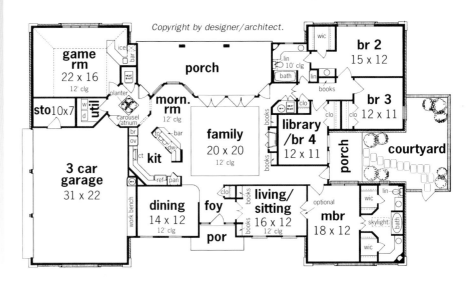

Plan #121046

Dimensions: 65'3" W x 57'2" D

Levels: 2

Square Footage: 2,655

Main Level Sq. Ft.: 1,906

Upper Level Sq. Ft.: 749

Bedrooms: 4

Bathrooms: 2

Foundation: Slab

Materials List Available: Yes

Price Category: F

CAD FILE AVAILABLE

Images provided by designer/architect.

This home beautifully blends traditional architectural detail with modern amenities.

Features:

• Ceiling Height: 8 ft. unless otherwise noted.

• Foyer: This two-story entry enjoys views of the uniquely shaped study, a second-floor balcony, and the formal dining room.

• Formal Dining Room: With its elegant corner column, this dining room sets the stage for formal entertaining as well as family gatherings.

• Kitchen: This well-appointed kitchen features a center island for efficient food preparation. It has a butler's pantry near the dining room and another pantry in the service entry.

• Breakfast Area: Here's the spot for informal family meals or lingering over coffee.

• Rear Porch: Step out through French doors in the master bedroom and the breakfast area.

Main Level Floor Plan

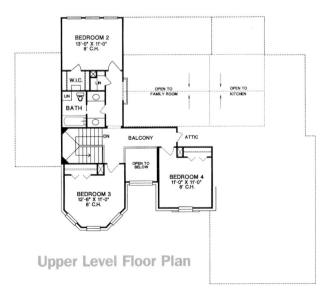

Upper Level Floor Plan

Copyright by designer/architect.

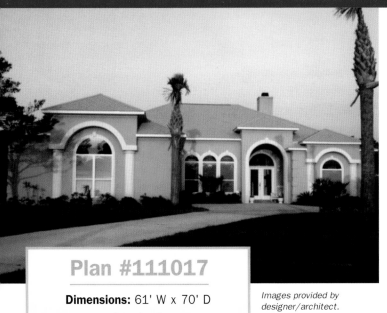

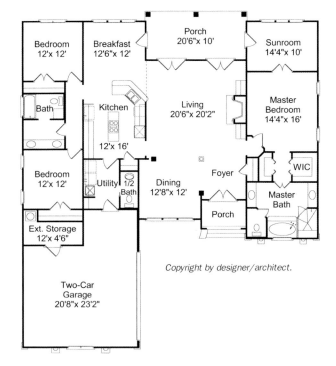

Porch
20'6"x 10'

Bedroom
12'x 12'

Breakfast
12'6"x 12'

Sunroom
14'4"x 10'

Bath

Kitchen

Living
20'6"x 20'2"

Master
Bedroom
14'4"x 16'

12'x 16'

Bedroom
12'x 12'

Utility

1/2
Bath

Dining
12'8"x 12'

Foyer

WIC

Master
Bath

Ext. Storage
12'x 4'6"

Porch

Two-Car
Garage
20'8"x 23'2"

Images provided by designer/architect.

Copyright by designer/architect.

Plan #111017

Dimensions: 61' W x 70' D
Levels: 1
Square Footage: 2,323
Bedrooms: 3
Bathrooms: 2½
Foundation: Monolithic slab
Materials List Available: No
Price Category: E

Plan #121082

Dimensions: 68'8" W x 60' D
Levels: 2
Square Footage: 2,932
Main Level Sq. Ft.: 2,084
Upper Level Sq. Ft.: 848
Bedrooms: 4
Bathrooms: 3½
Foundation: Basement
Materials List Available: Yes
Price Category: F

Images provided by designer/architect.

Main Level Floor Plan

Copyright by designer/architect.

Upper Level Floor Plan

Images provided by designer/architect.

Copyright by designer/architect.

Rear Elevation

Plan #221039

Dimensions: 89'8" W x 64' D

Levels: 1

Square Footage: 2,839

Bedrooms: 3

Bathrooms: 2½

Foundation: Basement

Materials List Available: No

Price Category: F

Copyright by designer/architect.

Images provided by designer/architect.

Plan #321034

Dimensions: 75'8" W x 52'6" D

Levels: 1

Square Footage: 3,508

Bedrooms: 4

Bathrooms: 3

Foundation: Basement, walkout

Materials List Available: Yes

Price Category: H

Optional Basement Level Floor Plan

Plan #121073

Dimensions: 70' W x 52' D
Levels: 2
Square Footage: 2,579
Main Level Sq. Ft.: 1,933
Upper Level Sq. Ft.: 646
Bedrooms: 4
Bathrooms: 2½
Foundation: Basement
Materials List Available: Yes
Price Category: E

Images provided by designer/architect.

Luxury will surround you in this home with contemporary styling and up-to-date amenities at every turn.

Features:

• Great Room: This large room shares both a see-through fireplace and a wet bar with the adjacent hearth room. Transom-topped windows add both light and architectural interest to this room.

• Den: Transom-topped windows add visual interest to this private area.

• Kitchen: A center island and corner pantry add convenience to this well-planned kitchen, and a lovely ceiling treatment adds beauty to the bayed breakfast area.

• Master Suite: A built-in bookcase adds to the ambiance of this luxury-filled area, where you're sure to find a retreat at the end of the day.

Main Level Floor Plan

Upper Level Floor Plan

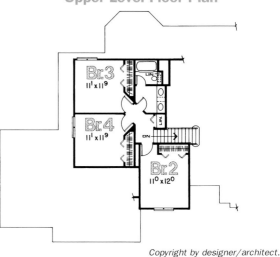

Copyright by designer/architect.

Images provided by designer/architect.

Plan #151011

Dimensions: 59'6" W x 74'4" D
Levels: 2
Square Footage: 3,437
Main Level Sq. Ft.: 2,184
Upper Level Sq. Ft.: 1,253
Bedrooms: 5
Bathrooms: 4
Foundation: Crawl space or slab; basement or daylight basement for fee
CompleteCost List Available: Yes
Price Category: G

Beauty, comfort, and convenience are yours in this luxurious, split-level home.

Features:

- Ceiling Height: 10 ft. unless otherwise noted.
- Master Suite: The 11-ft. pan ceiling sets the tone for this secluded area, with a lovely bay window that opens onto a rear porch, a pass-through fireplace to the great room, and a sitting room.
- Great Room: The pass-through fireplace makes this spacious room a cozy spot,

while the French doors leading to a rear porch make it a perfect spot for entertaining.

- Dining Room: Gracious 8-in. columns set off the entrance to this room.
- Kitchen: An island bar provides an efficient work area that's fitted with a sink.
- Breakfast Room: Open to the kitchen, this room is defined by a bay window and a spiral staircase to the second floor.
- Laundry Room: Large enough to accommodate a folding table, this room can also be fitted with a swinging pet door.
- Play Room: French doors in the children's playroom open onto a balcony where they can continue their games.
- Bedrooms: The 9-ft. ceilings on the second story make the rooms feel bright and airy.

Copyright by designer/architect.

Main Level Floor Plan

Upper Level Floor Plan

Plan #161001

Dimensions: 67'2" W x 47' D

Levels: 1

Square Footage: 1,782

Bedrooms: 3

Bathrooms: 2

Foundation: Basement

Materials List Available: Yes

Price Category: C

An all-brick exterior displays the solid strength that characterizes this gracious home.

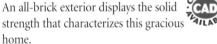

Features:

- **Gathering Area:** A feeling of spaciousness permeates this gathering area, created by the foyer, great room, and dining room. Multiple windows provide natural light that dances along a sloped ceiling, spilling onto decorative columns and a fireplace.

- **Breakfast Area:** A continuation of the sloped ceiling leads to this breakfast area, where French doors open to a screened porch.

- **Kitchen:** An abundance of cabinets and counter space are the hallmarks of this large kitchen, with its easy access to a spacious laundry room and storage area.

- **Master Suite:** A tray ceiling and spacious walk-in closet in the master bedroom, along with a whirlpool tub and double-bowl vanity in the bathroom, enable you to pamper yourself.

Images provided by designer/architect.

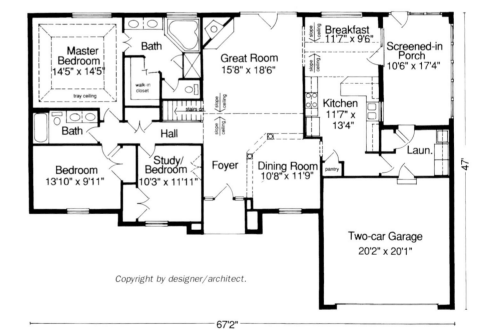

Copyright by designer/architect.

Great Room/Foyer

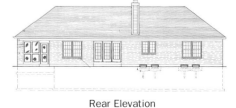

Rear Elevation

Plan #121019

Dimensions: 70' W x 60' D
Levels: 2
Square Footage: 3,775
Main Level Sq. Ft.: 1,923
Upper Level Sq. Ft.: 1,852
Bedrooms: 4
Bathrooms: 3
Foundation: Basement
Materials List Available: Yes
Price Category: H

CAD FILE AVAILABLE

Images provided by designer/architect.

The grand exterior presence is carried inside, beginning with the dramatic curved staircase.

Features:

- Ceiling Height: 8 ft.
- Den: French doors lead to this sophisticated den, with its bayed windows and wall of bookcases.
- Living Room: A curved wall and a series of arched windows highlight this large space.
- Formal Dining Room: This room shares the curved wall and arched windows found in the living room.
- Screened Porch: This huge space features skylights and is accessible by another French door from the dining room.
- Family Room: Family and guests alike will be drawn to this room, with its trio of arched windows and fireplace flanked by bookcases.
- Kitchen: An island adds convenience and distinction to this large, functional kitchen.
- Garage: This spacious three-bay garage provides plenty of space for cars and storage.

Main Level Floor Plan

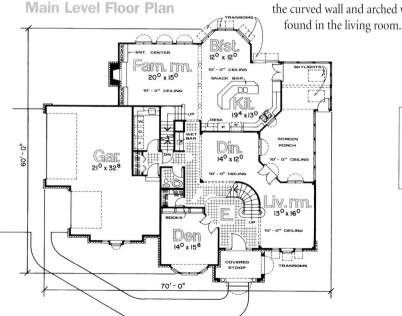

Upper Level Floor Plan

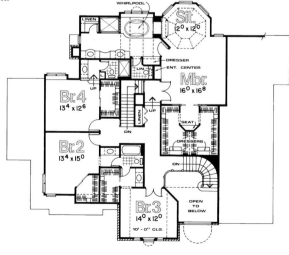

Copyright by designer/architect.

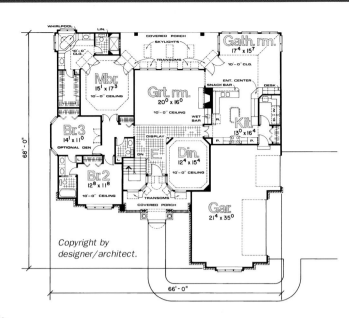

Plan #121053

Dimensions: 66' W x 68' D
Levels: 1
Square Footage: 2,456
Bedrooms: 3
Bathrooms: 2½
Foundation: Basement
Materials List Available: Yes
Price Category: E

Images provided by designer/architect.

This home, as shown in the photograph, may differ from the actual blueprints. For more detailed information, please check the floor plans carefully.

SMARTtip

Installing Plastic Molding

Foam trim is best cut with a backsaw. Power miter saws with fine-toothed blades also work. Larger-toothed blades tend to tear the foam unevenly.

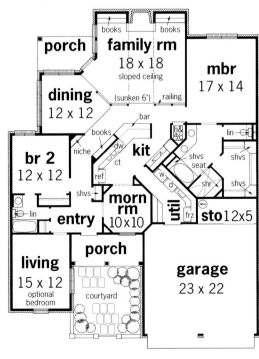

Plan #211041

Dimensions: 49' W x 64' D
Levels: 1
Square Footage: 1,891
Bedrooms: 3
Bathrooms: 2
Foundation: Slab
Materials List Available: Yes
Price Category: D

Images provided by designer/architect.

Copyright by designer/architect.

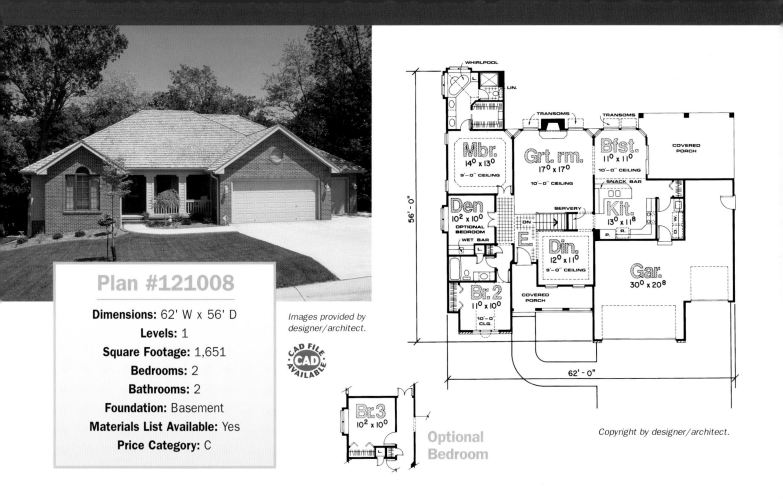

Plan #121008

Dimensions: 62' W x 56' D
Levels: 1
Square Footage: 1,651
Bedrooms: 2
Bathrooms: 2
Foundation: Basement
Materials List Available: Yes
Price Category: C

Images provided by designer/architect.

CAD FILE AVAILABLE

Optional Bedroom

Copyright by designer/architect.

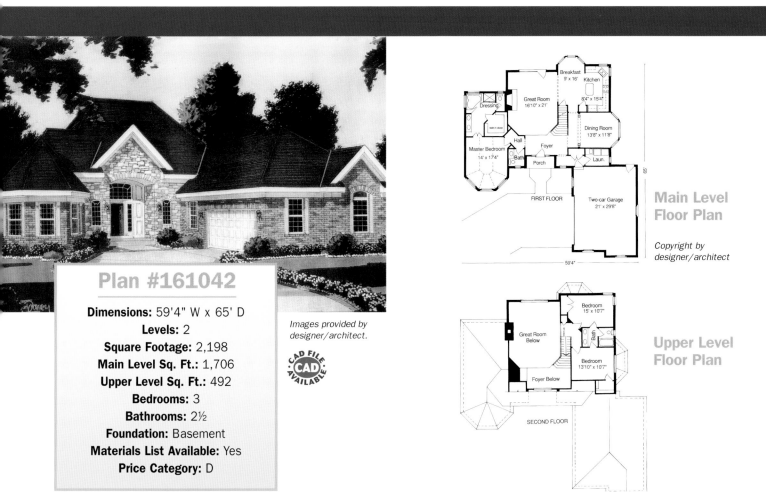

Plan #161042

Dimensions: 59'4" W x 65' D
Levels: 2
Square Footage: 2,198
Main Level Sq. Ft.: 1,706
Upper Level Sq. Ft.: 492
Bedrooms: 3
Bathrooms: 2½
Foundation: Basement
Materials List Available: Yes
Price Category: D

Images provided by designer/architect.

CAD FILE AVAILABLE

Main Level Floor Plan

Copyright by designer/architect

Upper Level Floor Plan

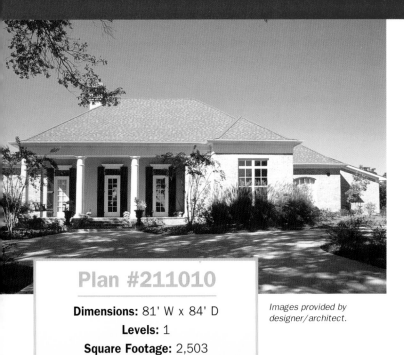

Plan #211010

Dimensions: 81' W x 84' D

Levels: 1

Square Footage: 2,503

Bedrooms: 3

Bathrooms: 2½

Foundation: Slab

Materials List Available: Yes

Price Category: E

Images provided by designer/architect.

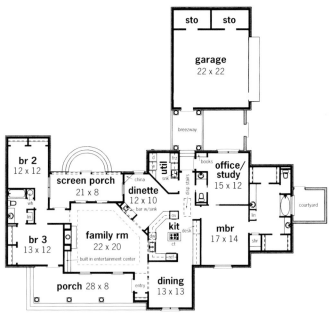

Copyright by designer/architect.

Plan #321018

Dimensions: 88'4" W x 48'4" D

Levels: 1

Square Footage: 2,523

Bedrooms: 3

Bathrooms: 2

Foundation: Basement

Materials List Available: Yes

Price Category: E

Images provided by designer/architect.

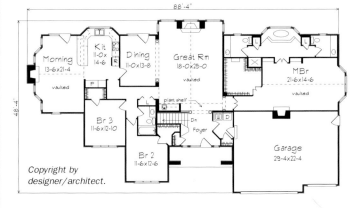

Copyright by designer/architect.

SMARTtip

Tiebacks

You don't have to limit yourself to tiebacks made from matching or contrasting fabric. Achieve creative custom looks by making tiebacks from unexpected items. Some materials to consider are old cotton bandannas or silk scarves, strings of beads, lengths of leather, or old belts and chains.

Plan #351001

Dimensions: 72'8" W x 51' D

Levels: 1

Square Footage: 1,855

Bedrooms: 3

Bathrooms: 2½

Foundation: Crawl space, slab, or basement

Materials List Available: Yes

Price Category: D

From the lovely arched windows on the front to the front and back covered porches, this home is as comfortable as it is beautiful.

Features:

- **Great Room:** Come into this room with 12-ft. ceilings, and you're sure to admire the corner gas fireplace and three windows overlooking the porch.

- **Dining Room:** Set off from the open design, this room is designed to be used formally or not.

- **Kitchen:** You'll love the practical walk-in pantry, broom closet, and angled snack bar here.

- **Breakfast Room:** Brightly lit and leading to the covered porch, this room will be a favorite spot.

- **Bonus Room:** Develop a playroom or study in this area.

- **Master Suite:** The large bedroom is complemented by the private bath with garden tub, separate shower, double vanity, and spacious walk-in closet.

Images provided by designer/architect.

Copyright by designer/architect.

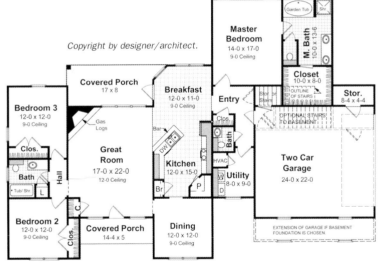

Kitchen/Great Room

Bonus Area Floor Plan

Plan #151007

Dimensions: 54'2" W x 56'2" D
Levels: 1
Square Footage: 1,787
Bedrooms: 3
Bathrooms: 2
Foundation: Crawl space, slab, basement, or walkout
CompleteCost List Available: Yes
Price Category: C

Images provided by designer/architect.

This compact, well-designed home is graced with amenities usually reserved for larger houses.

Features:

- Foyer: A 10-ft. ceiling creates unity between the foyer and the dining room just beyond it.

- Dining Room: 8-in. boxed columns welcome you to this dining room, with its 10-ft. ceilings.

- Great Room: The 9-ft. boxed ceiling suits the spacious design. Enjoy the fireplace in the winter and the rear-grilling porch in the summer.

- Breakfast Room: This bright room is a lovely spot for any time of day.

- Master Suite: Double vanities and a large walk-in closet add practicality to this quiet room with a 9-ft. pan ceiling. The master bath includes whirlpool tub with glass block and a separate shower.

- Bedrooms: Bedroom 2 features a bay window, and both rooms are convenient to the bathroom.

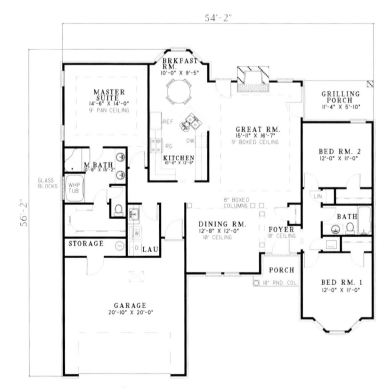

Copyright by designer/architect.

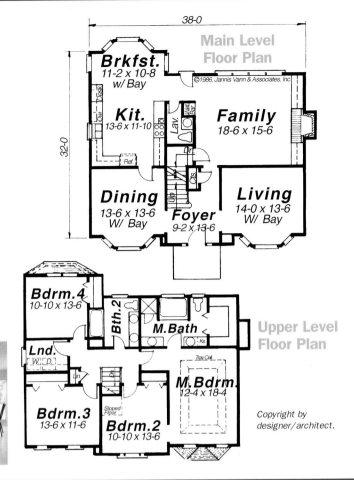

Main Level Floor Plan

Brkfst.
11-2 x 10-8
w/ Bay

©1986, Jannis Vann & Associates, Inc.

Kit.
13-6 x 11-10

Family
18-6 x 15-6

Lav

Dining
13-6 x 13-6
W/ Bay

Foyer
9-2 x 13-6

Living
14-0 x 13-6
W/ Bay

38-0

32-0

Ref.

Up

Dn

Plan #141030

Dimensions: 38' W x 32' D

Levels: 2

Square Footage: 2,323

Main Level Sq. Ft.: 1,179

Upper Level Sq. Ft.: 1,144

Bedrooms: 4

Bathrooms: 2½

Foundation: Basement

Materials List Available: Yes

Price Category: E

Images provided by designer/architect.

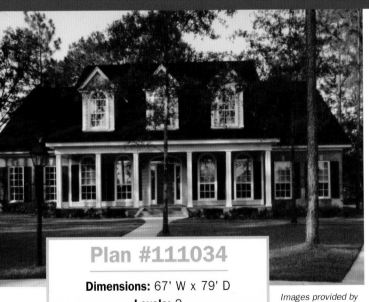

Bdrm.4
10-10 x 13-6

Bth.2

M.Bath

Upper Level Floor Plan

Lnd.
W.D.

Lin

Tray Ceil

M.Bdrm.
12-4 x 18-4

Bdrm.3
13-6 x 11-6

Sloped Ceil

Bdrm.2
10-10 x 13-6

Copyright by designer/architect.

Main Level Floor Plan

Two-Car Garage
22'6"x 24'9"

Patio
19'x 10'

Porch
19'x 9'5"

Storage
12'4"x 7'7"

Master Bath

Master Bedroom
14'x 20'

Family Room
20'x 20'

Utility

Kitchen
13'2"x 16'8"

Walk-In Closet

Walk-In Closet

Bath

Bedroom
13'2"x 12'

Living
12'1"x 14'

Foyer

Dining
12'1"x 14'

Breakfast
13'2"x 11'

Porch
32'10"x 6'

Unfinished Gameroom

Upper Level Floor Plan

Storage

Open to Below

Balcony

Bedroom
12'x 13'

Bedroom
13'x 13'

Bath

Copyright by designer/architect.

Plan #111034

Dimensions: 67' W x 79' D

Levels: 2

Square Footage: 3,085

Main Level Sq. Ft.: 2,439

Upper Level Sq. Ft.: 646

Bedrooms: 4

Bathrooms: 3

Foundation: Basement

Materials List Available: No

Price Category: G

Images provided by designer/architect.

Images provided by designer/architect.

Plan #441014

Dimensions: 119'6" W x 87'6" D
Levels: 1
Square Footage: 3,940
Bedrooms: 3
Bathrooms: 3 full, 2 half
Foundation: Crawl space; slab or basement available for fee
Materials List Available: No
Price Category: H

CAD FILE AVAILABLE

Though this is but a single-story home, it satisfies and delights on many levels. The exterior has visual appeal, with varied rooflines, a mixture of materials, and graceful traditional lines.

Features:

- **Great Room:** This huge room boasts a sloped, vaulted ceiling, a fireplace, and built-ins. There is also a media room with double-door access.

- **Kitchen:** This kitchen has an island, two sink prep areas, a butler's pantry connecting it to the formal dining room, and a walk-in pantry.

- **Bedrooms:** Family bedrooms sit at the front of the plan and are joined by a Jack-and-Jill bathroom.

- **Master Suite:** This master suite is on the far right side. Its grand salon has an 11-ft.-high ceiling, a fireplace, built-ins, a walk-in closet, and a superb bathroom.

- **Garage:** If you need extra space, there's a bonus room on an upper level above the three-car garage.

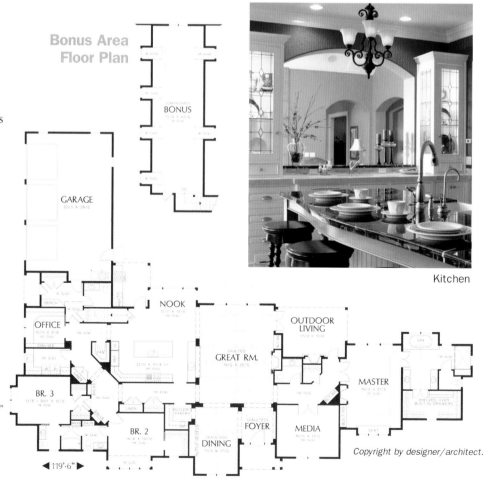

Kitchen

Copyright by designer/architect.

Rear Elevation

Dining Room

Kitchen

Master Bath

Great Room

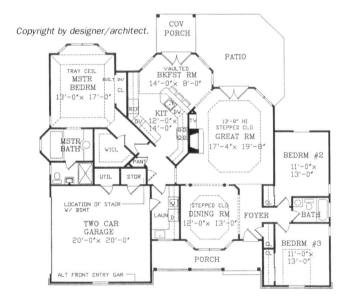

Copyright by designer/architect. ◀70▶

Plan #101010

Dimensions: 70' W x 47' D

Levels: 1

Square Footage: 2,187

Bedrooms: 4

Bathrooms: 2½

Foundation: Crawl space, slab, or basement

Materials List Available: Yes

Price Category: D

Images provided by designer/architect.

SMARTtip

Using Slipcovers in Your Dining Area

Change the look of your dining room by slipcovering chairs. Short-skirted slipcovers give a more informal appearance; fabrics in graphic patterns, such as checks or floral prints, complement this style of slipcover best. Long-skirted covers are elegant additions to a formal dining room, particularly in solid color or tone-on-tone fabrics. Ties, buttons, or trim can add personality.

Copyright by designer/architect.

Plan #131015

Dimensions: 57'4" W x 56'10" D

Levels: 1

Square Footage: 1,860

Bedrooms: 3

Bathrooms: 2

Foundation: Crawl space, slab, or basement

Materials List Available: Yes

Price Category: E

Images provided by designer/architect.

Rear Elevation

Great Room

Plan #321016

Dimensions: 88' W x 70'8" D
Levels: 1
Square Footage: 3,814
Main Level Sq. Ft.: 3,566
Lower Level Sq. Ft.: 248
Bedrooms: 3
Bathrooms: 2½
Foundation: Daylight basement
Materials List Available: Yes
Price Category: H

Images provided by designer/architect.

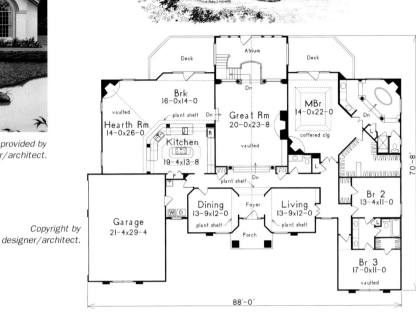

Rear View

Copyright by designer/architect.

Plan #321026

Dimensions: 67' W x 42'4" D
Levels: 1
Square Footage: 1,712
Bedrooms: 3
Bathrooms: 2½
Foundation: Crawl space
Materials List Available: Yes
Price Category: C

Images provided by designer/architect.

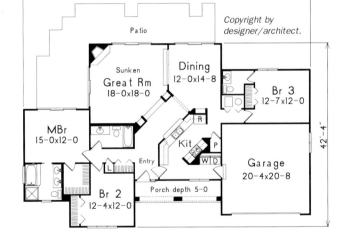

Copyright by designer/architect.

SMARTtip

Deck Design with Computers

Consider using a computer-aided design (CAD) program to plan your deck. Some programs let you see three-dimensional views of your design complete with railings, stairs, planters, hot tubs, and the surrounding landscaping.

Plan #121007

Dimensions: 74' W x 67'8" D

Levels: 1

Square Footage: 2,512

Bedrooms: 3

Bathrooms: 2½

Foundation: Basement

Materials List Available: Yes

Price Category: E

Images provided by designer/architect.

A series of arches brings grace to this home's interior and exterior.

Features:

- Ceiling Height: 8 ft.

- Formal Dining Room: Tapered columns give this dining room a classical look that lends elegance to any dinner party.

- Great Room: Just beyond the dining room is this light-filled room, with its wall of arched windows and see-through fireplace.

- Hearth Room: On the other side of the fire place you will find this cozy area, with its corner entertainment center.

- Dinette: A gazebo-shaped dinette is the architectural surprise of the house layout.

- Kitchen: This well-conceived working kitchen features a generous center island.

- Garage: With three garage bays you'll never be short of parking space or storage.

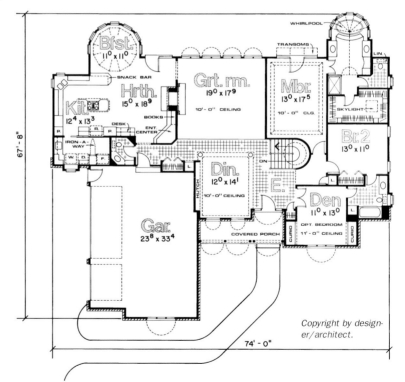

Copyright by designer/architect.

Optional Bedroom

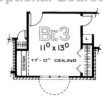

Plan #121069

Dimensions: 58' W x 59'4" D
Levels: 2
Square Footage: 2,914
Main Level Sq. Ft.: 1,583
Upper Level Sq. Ft.: 1,331
Bedrooms: 4
Bathrooms: 3½
Foundation: Basement
Materials List Available: Yes
Price Category: F

Images provided by designer/architect.

You'll love this design if you're looking for a home to complement a site with a lovely rear view.

Features:

- **Great Room:** A trio of lovely windows looks out to the front entry of this home. The French doors in this room open to the breakfast area for everyone's convenience.

- **Kitchen:** Designed to suit a gourmet cook, this kitchen includes a roomy pantry and an island with a snack bar.

- **Breakfast Area:** The boxed window here is perfect for houseplants or a collection of culinary herbs. A door leads to the rear porch, where you'll love to dine in good weather.

- **Master Suite:** On the upper level, the bedroom features a cathedral ceiling, two walk-in closets, and a window seat. The bath also has a cathedral ceiling and includes dual lavatories, a large dressing area, and a sunlit whirlpool tub.

Main Level Floor Plan

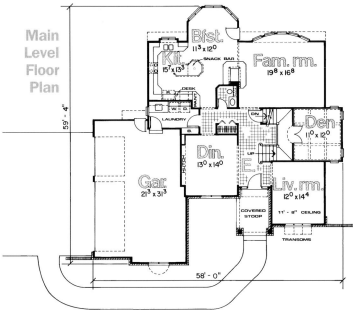

Upper Level Floor Plan

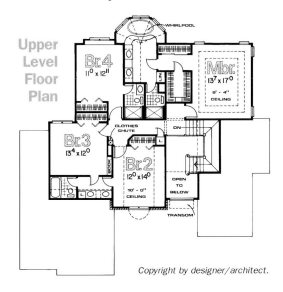

Copyright by designer/architect.

Plan #151003

Dimensions: 51'6" W x 52'4" D
Levels: 1
Square Footage: 1,680
Bedrooms: 3
Bathrooms: 2
Foundation: Crawl space, slab, or basement
CompleteCost List Available: Yes
Price Category: C

A lovely front porch, bay windows, and dormers add sparkle to this country-style home.

Features:

- Great Room: Perfect for entertaining, this room features a tray ceiling, wet bar, and a quiet screened porch nearby.

- Dining Room: This bayed dining room facing the front porch is cozy yet roomy enough for family parties during the holidays.

- Kitchen: This eat-in kitchen also faces the front and is ideal for preparing meals for any occasion.

- Master Suite: The tray ceiling here gives an added feeling of space, while the distance from the other bedrooms allows for all the privacy you'll need.

Images provided by designer/architect.

This home, as shown in the photograph, may differ from the actual blueprints. For more detailed information, please check the floor plans carefully.

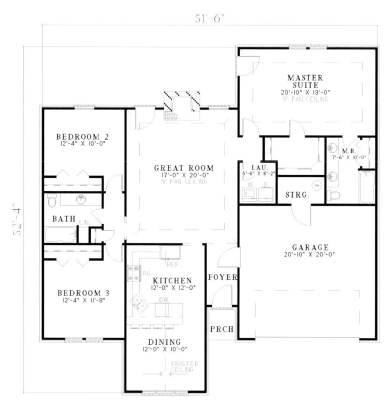

Copyright by designer/architect.

Plan #121074

Dimensions: 68'8" W x 47'8" D
Levels: 2
Square Footage: 2,486
Main Level Sq. Ft.: 1,829
Upper Level Sq. Ft.: 657
Bedrooms: 4
Bathrooms: 2½
Foundation: Basement
Materials List Available: Yes
Price Category: E

Images provided by designer/architect.

Enjoy the natural light that streams through the many lovely windows in this well-designed home.

Features:

- **Living Room:** This room is sure to be your family's headquarters, thanks to the lovely 15-ft. ceiling, stacked windows, central location, and cozy fireplace.
- **Dining Room:** A boxed ceiling adds formality to this well-positioned room.
- **Kitchen:** The island cooktop in this kitchen is so large that it includes a snack bar area. A pantry gives ample storage space, and a built-in desk—where you can set up a computer station or a record-keeping area—adds efficiency.
- **Master Suite:** For the sake of privacy, this master suite is located on the opposite side of the home from the other living areas. You'll love the roomy bedroom and luxuriate in the private bath with its many amenities.

Main Level Floor Plan

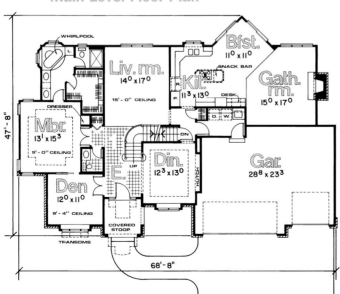

Upper Level Floor Plan

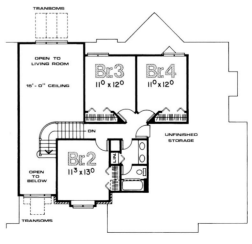

Copyright by designer/architect.

Plan #151057

Dimensions: 73'6" W x 80'6" D
Levels: 1
Square Footage: 2,951
Bedrooms: 4
Bathrooms: 3
Foundation: Crawl space, slab, or basement
CompleteCost List Available: Yes
Price Category: F

Images provided by designer/architect.

The stucco exterior and large windows give this ranch an elegant look.

Features:

• **Foyer:** Enter the covered porch, and walk through the beautiful front door to this large foyer with entry closet.

• **Entertaining:** The large great room has a cozy fireplace and built-ins for casual get-togethers. The formal living room, also with a fireplace, is for special entertaining.

• **Kitchen:** This large U-shaped island kitchen has a raised bar and is open to the breakfast area and the great room. A short step though the door brings you onto the rear lanai.

• **Master Suite:** This private retreat has a fireplace and a sitting area with access to the rear lanai. The master bath features dual vanities, a whirlpool tub, a glass shower, and a compartmentalized toilet area.

• **Bedrooms:** Three large bedrooms are located on the opposite side of the home to give the master suite privacy. Two bedrooms share a Jack-and-Jill bathroom. The third bedroom has access to a common bathroom.

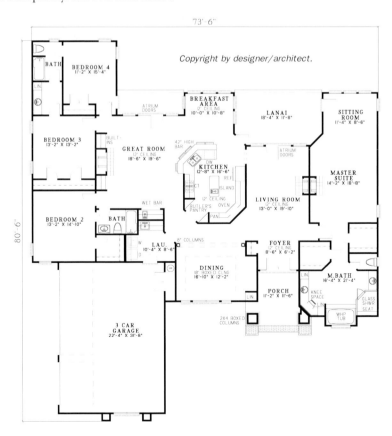

Copyright by designer/architect.

Plan #121065

Dimensions: 62' W x 55'4" D
Levels: 2
Square Footage: 3,407
Main Level Sq. Ft.: 1,719
Upper Level Sq. Ft.: 1,688
Bedrooms: 4
Bathrooms: 2½
Foundation: Basement
Materials List Available: Yes
Price Category: G

CAD FILE CAD AVAILABLE

Images provided by designer/architect.

If you love contemporary design, the unusual shapes of the rooms in this home will delight you.

Features:

• Entry: You'll see a balcony from the upper level that overlooks this entryway, as well as the lovely curved staircase to this floor.

• Great Room: This room is sunken to set it apart. A fireplace, wet bar, spider-beamed ceiling, and row of arched windows give it character.

• Dining Room: Columns define this lovely octagon room, where you'll love to entertain guests or create lavish family dinners.

• Master Suite: A multi-tiered ceiling adds a note of grace, while the fireplace and private library create a real retreat. The gracious bath features a gazebo ceiling and a skylight.

Main Level Floor Plan

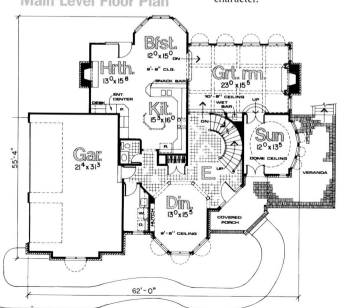

Upper Level Floor Plan

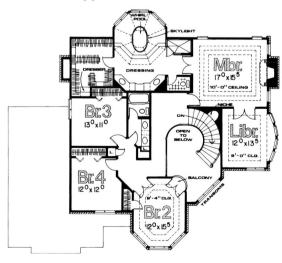

Copyright by designer/architect.

Plan #211039

Dimensions: 62' W x 64' D

Levels: 1

Square Footage: 1,868

Bedrooms: 3

Bathrooms: 2

Foundation: Slab

Materials List Available: Yes

Price Category: D

Images provided by designer/architect.

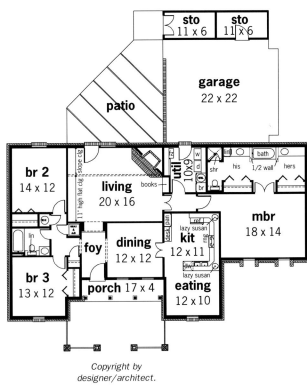

Copyright by designer/architect.

Plan #151054

Dimensions: 71'2" W x 54'10" D

Levels: 1

Square Footage: 1,746

Bedrooms: 3

Bathrooms: 2

Foundation: Crawl space or slab (basement option for fee)

CompleteCost List Available: Yes

Price Category: C

Images provided by designer/architect.

Copyright by designer/architect.

SMARTtip

Mixing and Matching Windows

Windows, both fixed and operable, are made in various styles and shapes. While mixing styles should be carefully avoided, a variety of interesting window sizes and shapes may nevertheless be combined to achieve symmetry, harmony, and rhythm on the exterior of a home.

Plan #121067

Dimensions: 56' W x 59'4" D
Levels: 2
Square Footage: 2,708
Main Level Sq. Ft.: 1,860
Upper Level Sq. Ft.: 848
Bedrooms: 4
Bathrooms: 3½
Foundation: Basement
Materials List Available: Yes
Price Category: F

Images provided by designer/architect.

CAD FILE AVAILABLE

Upper Level Floor Plan

Main Level Floor Plan

Copyright by designer/architect.

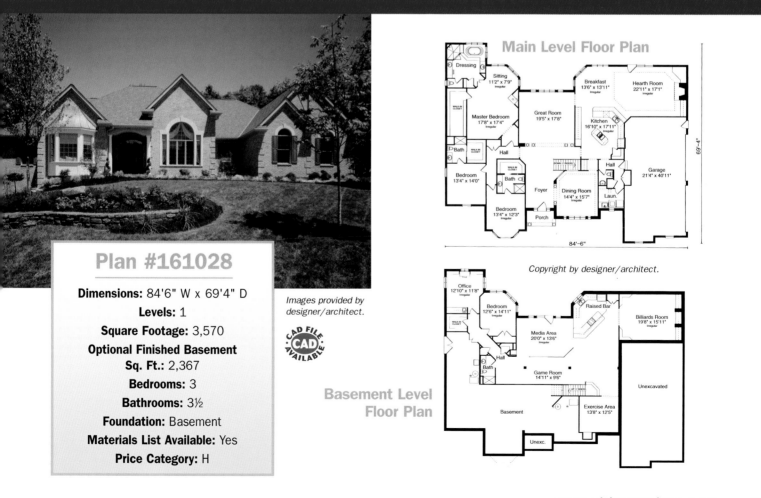

Plan #161028

Dimensions: 84'6" W x 69'4" D
Levels: 1
Square Footage: 3,570
Optional Finished Basement Sq. Ft.: 2,367
Bedrooms: 3
Bathrooms: 3½
Foundation: Basement
Materials List Available: Yes
Price Category: H

Images provided by designer/architect.

CAD FILE AVAILABLE

Main Level Floor Plan

Copyright by designer/architect.

Basement Level Floor Plan

Plan #121050

Dimensions: 64' W x 50' D
Levels: 1
Square Footage: 1,996
Bedrooms: 2
Bathrooms: 2
Foundation: Basement
Materials List Available: Yes
Price Category: D

Images provided by designer/architect.

This compact design includes features usually reserved for larger homes and has styling that is typical of more-exclusive home designs.

Features:

- Entry: As you enter this home, you'll see the formal living and dining rooms—both with special ceiling detailing—on either side.

- Great Room: Located in the rear of the home for convenience, this great room is likely to be your favorite spot. The fireplace is framed by transom-topped windows, so you'll love curling up here, no matter what the weather or time of day.

- Kitchen: Ample counter and cabinet space make this kitchen a dream in which to work.

- Master Suite: A tray ceiling and lovely corner windows create an elegant feeling in the bedroom, and two walk-in closets make it easy to keep this space tidy and organized. The private bath has a skylight, corner whirlpool tub, and two separate vanities.

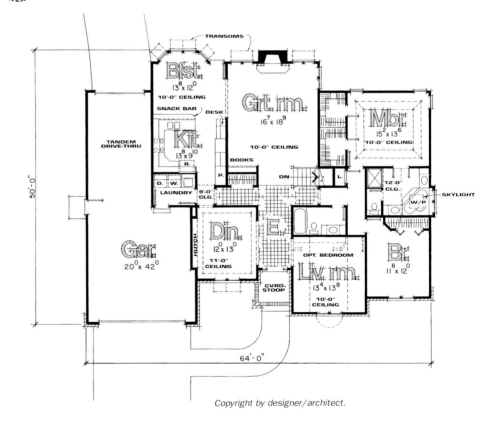

Copyright by designer/architect.

Plan #271093

Dimensions: 74' W x 52' D
Levels: 2
Square Footage: 2,813
Main Level Sq. Ft.: 1,828
Upper Level Sq. Ft.: 985
Bedrooms: 3
Bathrooms: 3
Foundation: Basement
Materials List Available: No
Price Category: F

This Craftsman-style home will be the envy of your neighbors.

CAD FILE AVAILABLE

Images provided by designer/architect.

Features:

- Entry: Enter the home through the covered porch and into this entry with a view into the great room.

- Great Room: This large gathering area, with two-sided fireplace, has window looking out to the backyard.

- Kitchen: This peninsula kitchen has plenty of cabinets and counter space. The garage is just a few steps away though the laundry room.

- Hearth Room: Just off the kitchen this hearth room shares the fireplace with the great room and is open into the dining room.

- Master Suite: Located upstairs, with a secondary bedroom, this suite has a sitting area, large closet, and master bath.

Great Room

Kitchen

Main Level Floor Plan

Copyright by designer/architect.

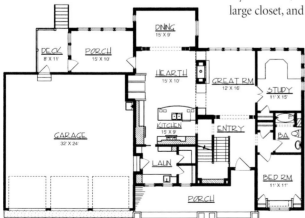

Upper Level Floor Plan

Plan #171004

Dimensions: 72' W x 52' D
Levels: 1
Square Footage: 2,256
Bedrooms: 3
Bathrooms: 2
Foundation: Crawl space, slab
Materials List Available: Yes
Price Category: E

This home greets you with a front porch featuring a high roofline and stucco columns.

Copyright by designer/architect.

Images provided by designer/architect.

Features:

- Ceiling Height: 9 ft. unless otherwise noted.
- Foyer: Step through the front porch into this impressive foyer, which opens to the formal dining room and the study.
- Dining Room: This dining room's 12-ft. ceiling enhances its sense of spaciousness, with plenty of room for large dinner parties.
- Family Room: With plenty of room for all kinds of family activities, this room also has a 12-ft. ceiling, a fireplace, and two paddle fans.

- Kitchen: This kitchen has all the counter space you'll need to prepare your favorite recipes. There's a pantry, desk, and angled snack bar.
- Master Bedroom: This master retreat is separate from the other bedrooms for added privacy. It has an elegant, high step-up ceiling and a paddle fan.
- Master Bath: This master bath features a large walk-in closet, deluxe corner bath, walk-in shower, and his and her vanities.

SMARTtip

Windows – Privacy

You can easily stencil a work of art onto a windowpane, perhaps only as a border around the edge. Choose or create a design that gives you as little or as much privacy and light control as you need. Use a ready-made stencil or a piece of openwork fabric such as lace, or mask a design onto the glass using tape and a razor knife. Then apply glass paint or frosted glass spray, referring to the instructions and guidelines that come with the product.

Plan #121063

Dimensions: 84' W x 52' D

Levels: 2

Square Footage: 3,473

Main Level Sq. Ft.: 2,500

Upper Level Sq. Ft.: 973

Bedrooms: 4

Bathrooms: 3½

Foundation: Basement

Materials List Available: Yes

Price Category: G

Images provided by designer/architect.

Enjoy the many amenities in this well-designed and gracious home.

Features:

• **Entry:** A large sparkling window and a tapering split staircase distinguish this lovely entryway.

• **Great Room:** This spacious great room will be the heart of your new home. It has a 14-ft. spider-beamed window that serves to highlight its built-in bookcase, built-in entertainment center, raised hearth fireplace,

wet bar, and lovely arched windows topped with transoms.

• **Kitchen:** Anyone who walks into this kitchen will realize that it's designed for both convenience and efficiency.

• **Master Suite:** The tiered ceiling in the bedroom gives an elegant touch, and the bay window adds to it. The two large walk-in closets and the spacious bath, with columns setting off the whirlpool tub and two vanities, complete this dream of a suite.

Main Level Floor Plan

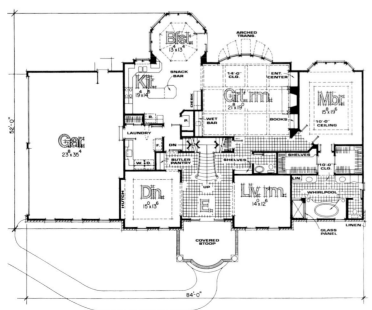

Upper Level Floor Plan

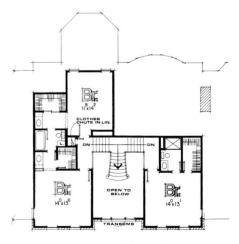

Copyright by designer/architect.

Plan #121018

Dimensions: 95'9" W x 70'2" D

Levels: 2

Square Footage: 3,950

Main Level Sq. Ft.: 2,839

Upper Level Square Footage: 1,111

Bedrooms: 4

Bathrooms: 2 full, 2 half

Foundation: Basement

Materials List Available: Yes

Price Category: H

Images provided by designer/architect.

A spectacular two-story entry with a floating curved staircase welcomes you home.

Features:

- Ceiling Height: 8 ft. except as noted.

- Den: To the left of the entry, French doors lead to a spacious and stylish den featuring a spider-beamed ceiling.

- Living Room: The volume ceiling, transom windows, and large fireplace evoke a gracious traditional style.

- Gathering Rooms: There is plenty of space for large-group entertaining in the gathering rooms that also feature fireplaces and transom windows.

- Master Suite: Here is the height of luxurious living. The suite features an oversized walk-in closet, tiered ceilings, and a sitting room with fireplace. The pampering bath has a corner whirlpool and shower.

- Garage: An angle minimizes the appearance of the four-car garage.

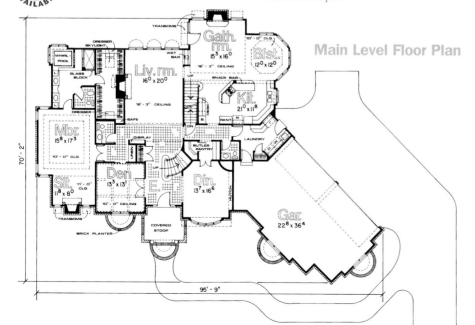

Main Level Floor Plan

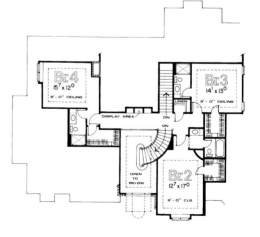

Upper Level Floor Plan

Copyright by designer/architect.

Plan #401029

Dimensions: 37'6" W x 48'4" D

Levels: 2

Square Footage: 2,163

Main Level Sq. Ft.: 832

Upper Level Sq. Ft.: 1,331

Bedrooms: 3

Bathrooms: 2½

Foundation: Basement

Materials List Available: Yes

Price Category: D

Images provided by designer/architect.

This two-level plan has a bonus—a roof deck with hot tub! A variety of additional outdoor spaces makes this one wonderful plan.

Features:

- **First Level:** Family bedrooms, a full bath room, and a cozy den are on the first level, along with a two-car garage.

- **Living Area:** The living spaces are on the second floor and include a living/dining room combination with a deck and fireplace. The dining room has buffet space.

- **Family Room:** Featuring a fireplace and a built-in entertainment center, the gathering area is open to the breakfast room and sky lighted kitchen.

- **Master Bedroom:** This room features a private bath with a whirlpool tub and two-person shower, a walk-in closet, and access to still another deck.

Upper Level Floor Plan

CAD FILE AVAILABLE

Copyright by designer/architect.

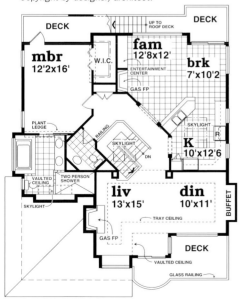

Rear Elevation

Dining Room/Kitchen

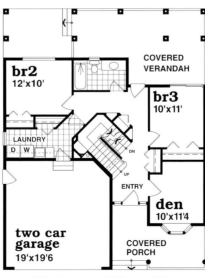

Main Level Floor Plan

Plan #121051

Dimensions: 64' W x 44' D
Levels: 1
Square Footage: 1,808
Bedrooms: 3
Bathrooms: 2½
Foundation: Basement
Materials List Available: Yes
Price Category: D

Images provided by designer/architect.

You'll love the way that natural light pours into this home from the gorgeous windows you'll find in room after room.

Features:

- Great Room: You'll notice the bayed, transom-topped window in this lovely great room as soon as you step into the home. A wet-bar makes the room a natural place for entertaining, and the see-through fireplace makes it cozy on chilly days and winter evenings.

- Kitchen: This well-designed kitchen will be a delight for everyone who cooks here, not only because of the ample counter and cabinet space but also because of its location in the home.

- Master Suite: Angled ceilings in both the bedroom and the bathroom of this suite make it feel luxurious, and the picturesque window in the bedroom gives it character. The bath includes a corner whirlpool tub where you'll love to relax at the end of the day.

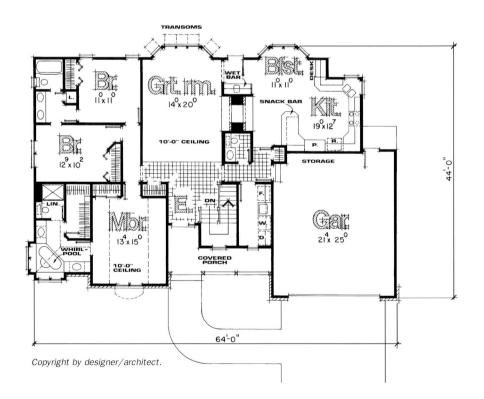

Copyright by designer/architect.

Images provided by designer/architect.

Plan #121092

Dimensions: 65'4" W x 52'8" D
Levels: 1
Square Footage: 1,887
Bedrooms: 3
Bathrooms: 2½
Foundation: Basement
Materials List Available: Yes
Price Category: D

This is the design if you want a home that will be easy to expand as your family grows.

Features:

- Entry: Both the dining room and great room are immediately accessible from this lovely entry.

- Great Room: The transom-topped bowed windows highlight the spacious feeling here.

- Gathering Room: Also with an angled ceiling, this room has a fireplace as well as built-in entertainment center and bookcases.

- Dining Room: This elegant room features a 13-ft. boxed ceiling and majestic window around which you'll love to decorate.

- Kitchen: Designed for convenience, this kitchen includes a lovely angled ceiling and gazebo-shaped breakfast area.

- Basement: Use the plans for finishing a family room and two bedrooms when the time is right.

Main Level Floor Plan

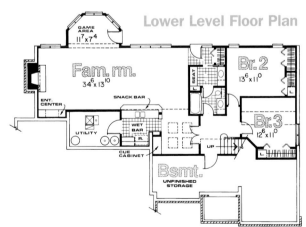

Lower Level Floor Plan

Copyright by designer/architect.

Plan #211058

Dimensions: 74'6" W x 68' D
Levels: 1
Square Footage: 2,564
Bedrooms: 4
Bathrooms: 4
Foundation: Slab
Materials List Available: No
Price Category: E

Images provided by designer/architect.

The style of this spacious home is traditional but the amenities are attuned to modern life.

SMARTtip
Outdoor Furniture

Too much of the same is too much! Avoid matched sets of outdoor furniture. Instead, pair a cast-iron table with wooden chairs, for example. Another trick is to choose all the same chairs from one collection, but buy them in several different finishes. Finally, when it comes time for chair cushions, select fabrics that feel and look good together but don't necessarily match each other or that of the umbrella.

Features:

• Ceiling Height: 8 ft.

• Family Room: This is a great room for family gatherings and relaxation. Everyone will want to gather around the handsome fireplace. A built-in television niche makes maximum use of floor space.

• Home Office: Whether you work full-time at home or just need a spot for the home computer and bill-paying, you'll appreciate this generous office. It even has its own full bath, so all you need is a sofa bed for double-duty as a guest room.

• Porch: Step through sliding glass doors in the family room onto this generous porch, which is also accessible to the bedroom hallway and the garage.

• Courtyard: This private courtyard off the porch adds offers another spot for relaxation.

• Garage: The garage offers parking for three cars, along with plenty of extra storage.

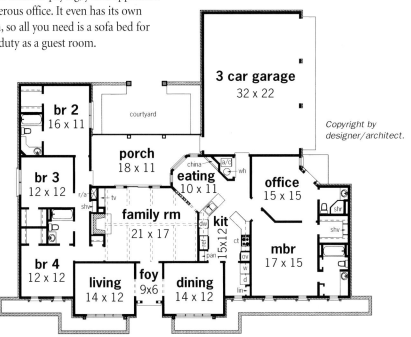

Copyright by designer/architect.

Plan #211006

Dimensions: 61' W x 77' D
Levels: 1
Square Footage: 2,177
Bedrooms: 3
Bathrooms: 2
Foundation: Crawl space or slab
Materials List Available: Yes
Price Category: D

Images provided by designer/architect.

This traditional home with a stucco exterior is distinguished by its 9-ft. ceilings throughout and its sleek, contemporary interior.

Features:

- Living Room: A series of arched openings that surround this room adds strong visual interest. Settle down by the fireplace on cold winter nights.

- Dining Room: Step up to enter this room with a raised floor that sets it apart from other areas.

- Kitchen: Ideal for cooking as well as casual socializing, this kitchen has a stovetop island and a breakfast bar.

- Master Suite: The sitting area in this suite is so big that you might want to watch TV here or make it a study. In the bath, you'll find a skylight above the angled tub with a mirror surround and well-placed plant ledge.

- Rear Porch: This 200-sq.-ft. covered porch gives you plenty of space for entertaining.

SMARTtip

DECK Furniture Style

Mix-and-match tabletops, frames, and legs are stylish. Combine materials such as glass, metal, wood, and mosaic tiles.

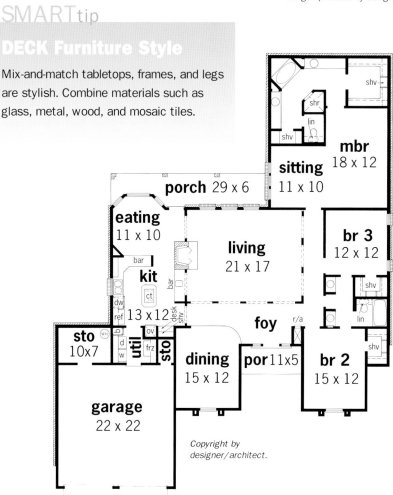

Copyright by designer/architect.

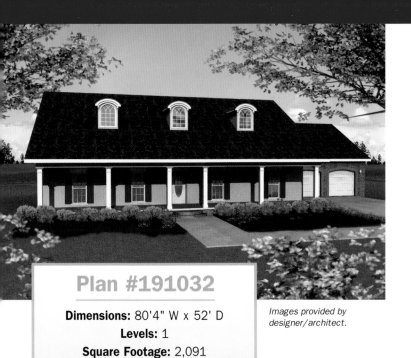

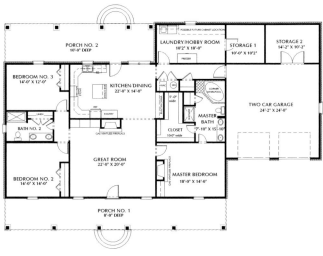

Images provided by designer/architect.

Plan #191032

Dimensions: 80'4" W x 52' D

Levels: 1

Square Footage: 2,091

Bedrooms: 3

Bathrooms: 2

Foundation: Slab

Materials List Available: No

Price Category: D

Copyright by designer/architect.

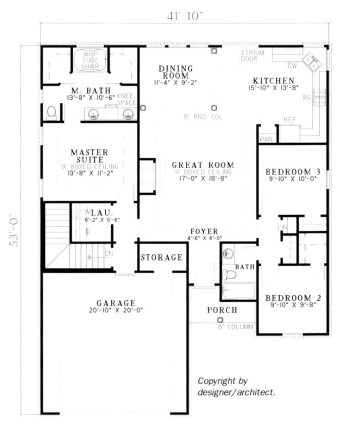

Images provided by designer/architect.

CAD FILE AVAILABLE

Plan #151059

Dimensions: 41'10" W x 53' D

Levels: 1

Square Footage: 1,382

Bedrooms: 3

Bathrooms: 2

Foundation: Crawl space, slab, with basement option for fee

CompleteCost List Available: Yes

Price Category: B

Copyright by designer/architect.

Plan #211062

Dimensions: 96'6" W x 43' D

Levels: 1

Square Footage: 2,719

Bedrooms: 4

Bathrooms: 2½

Foundation: Slab

Materials List Available: Yes

Price Category: F

Images provided by designer/architect.

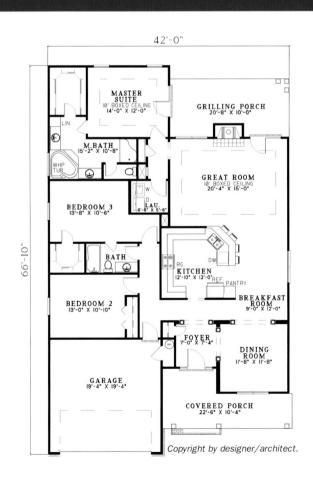

Copyright by designer/architect.

- 3 car garage 22 x 32
- br 2 16 x 11
- wic
- bath
- courtyard
- screen porch 25 x 11
- eating 11 x 10
- china
- bath
- office 15 x 11
- wic
- br 3 12 x 12
- wic
- bath
- t.v.
- family rm 21 x 17
- 11' clg
- kit 15x12
- ct
- shr
- mbr 17 x 13
- lin
- br 4 12 x 12
- wic
- living 19 x 14
- 11' clg
- dining 13 x 12
- 2 story clg
- util 12x6
- porch 26 x 5

Plan #151008

Dimensions: 42' W x 66'10" D

Levels: 1

Square Footage: 1,892

Bedrooms: 3

Bathrooms: 2

Foundation: Crawl space, slab, basement, or daylight basement

CompleteCost List Available: Yes

Price Category: D

Images provided by designer/architect.

CAD FILE AVAILABLE

This home, as shown in the photograph, may differ from the actual blueprints. For more detailed information, please check the floor plans carefully.

42'-0"

- MASTER SUITE 10' BOXED CEILING 14'-0" X 12'-0"
- GRILLING PORCH 20'-8" X 10'-0"
- LIN.
- M.BATH 15'-2" X 10'-8"
- WHP TUB
- GREAT ROOM 10' BOXED CEILING 20'-4" X 15'-0"
- BEDROOM 3 13'-8" X 10'-6"
- W. D. LAU. 6'-6" X 5'-6"
- KITCHEN 12'-10" X 12'-0"
- DW
- BATH
- 66'-10"
- RG.
- REF.
- PANTRY
- BEDROOM 2 13'-0" X 10'-10"
- BREAKFAST ROOM 9'-0" X 12'-0"
- FOYER 7'-0" X 7'-4"
- DINING ROOM 11'-8" X 11'-8"
- GARAGE 19'-4" X 19'-4"
- COVERED PORCH 22'-6" X 10'-4"

Copyright by designer/architect.

Upper Level
Floor Plan

Copyright by
designer/architect.

*Images provided by
designer/architect.*

**Main Level
Floor Plan**

Plan #121089

Dimensions: 54' W x 51'8" D
Levels: 2
Square Footage: 1,976
Main Level Sq. Ft.: 1,413
Upper Level Sq. Ft.: 563
Bedrooms: 4
Bathrooms: 2½
Foundation: Basement
Materials List Available: Yes
Price Category: D

CAD FILE
CAD
AVAILABLE

Plan #171003

Dimensions: 69' W x 64' D
Levels: 1
Square Footage: 2,098
Bedrooms: 3
Bathrooms: 3
Foundation: Crawl space, slab
Materials List Available: Yes
Price Category: D

*Images provided by
designer/architect.*

*Copyright by
designer/architect.*

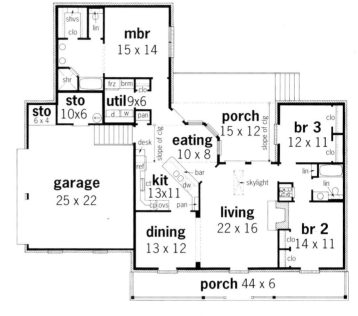

Plan #211040

Dimensions: 66' W x 60' D

Levels: 1

Square Footage: 1,800

Bedrooms: 3

Bathrooms: 2

Foundation: Slab

Materials List Available: Yes

Price Category: D

Images provided by designer/architect.

Copyright by designer/architect.

Plan #151046

Dimensions: 63'4" W x 59'10" D

Levels: 1

Square Footage: 2,525

Bedrooms: 3

Bathrooms: 2

Foundation: Crawl space, slab, or basement

CompleteCost List Available: Yes

Price Category: E

Images provided by designer/architect.

Copyright by designer/architect.

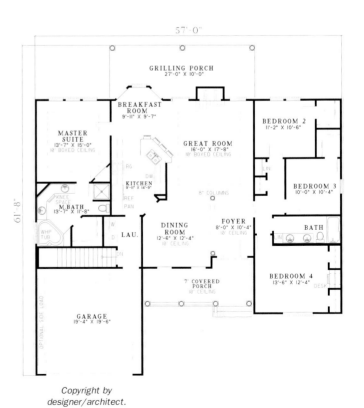

Copyright by designer/architect.

Plan #171010

Dimensions: 76' W x 61' D
Levels: 1
Square Footage: 1,972
Bedrooms: 3
Bathrooms: 2
Foundation: Slab, crawl space
Materials List Available: Yes
Price Category: D

Images provided by designer/architect.

SMARTtip

Testing Grill Hoses for Leaks

Hoses on gas grills can develop leaks. To check the hose on your gas grill, brush soapy water over it. If you see any bubbles, turn off the gas valve and disconnect the tank. Then replace the hose.

Plan #151068

Dimensions: 57' W x 61'8" D
Levels: 1
Square Footage: 1,880
Bedrooms: 4
Bathrooms: 2
Foundation: Crawl space, slab, or basement
CompleteCost List Available: Yes
Price Category: D

Images provided by designer/architect.

CAD FILE AVAILABLE

Copyright by designer/architect.

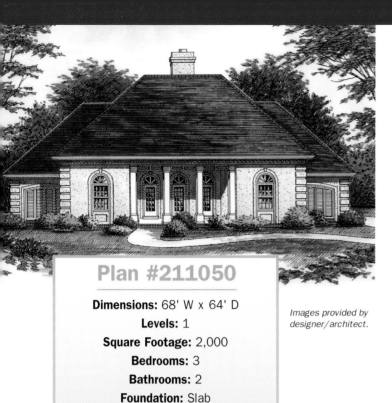

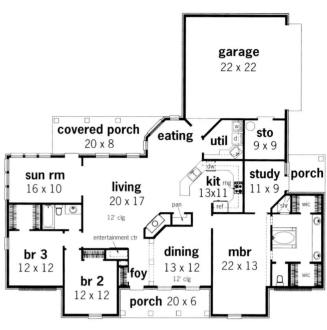

Plan #211050

Dimensions: 68' W x 64' D

Levels: 1

Square Footage: 2,000

Bedrooms: 3

Bathrooms: 2

Foundation: Slab

Materials List Available: Yes

Price Category: D

Images provided by designer/architect.

Copyright by designer/architect.

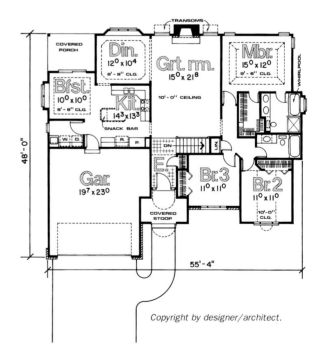

Plan #121004

Dimensions: 55'4" W x 48' D

Levels: 1

Square Footage: 1,666

Bedrooms: 3

Bathrooms: 2

Foundation: Basement

Materials List Available: Yes

Price Category: C

Images provided by designer/architect.

Copyright by designer/architect.

the new Smart Approach to

kitchen design

CREATIVE HOMEOWNER

SUSAN MANEY

This article was reprinted from *The New Smart Approach to Kitchen Design* (Creative Homeowner 2003)

Safety & Comfort in Your Kitchen

By the year 2020 more than 20 percent of the American population will be over the age of 65, according to the United States Census Bureau. Some of these people will suffer disabilities that limit their sight, hearing, or mobility. Universal design addresses their needs, as well as those of multigenerational households: as Baby Boomers bring home their aging parents while raising families of their own, it is not uncommon to have young children and grandparents living under one roof. Indeed, as our population ages it benefits everyone to think about ways to make the kitchen functional—and safe—for every member of the family.

In fact, more building codes govern the kitchen than any other room in the house. That's because so many accidents occur there. Think about it: sharp knives; intense heat; electrical appliances in close proximity to water; hard, unforgiving surfaces; breakable glassware and china. These are some of the ingredients in a perfect recipe for kitchen accidents. They also represent safety concerns that should be considered during the design stage of your kitchen. Although this is true under any circumstances, it is particularly important when those who will be using the kitchen are the most vulnerable: children and the elderly. With that in mind, safety should reign as a primary factor in any kitchen design. The goal should be to lessen the chance of injury while increasing the performance of the room.

Take the following steps when designing for safety. And remember: you don't have to be very young or very old to suffer an injury in the kitchen. One of the most common Sunday morning hospital emergency room visits is by someone who has sliced open a hand while cutting a bagel.

Step One: Use proper lighting.

Never work in a dim space. Good general lighting, supplemented with proper task lighting clearly focused on a work surface, without glare or shadows, can vastly decrease your chance of injury while preparing a meal. In most cases, that means ceiling fixtures to provide general illumination and undercabinet lights for task lighting. Be sure island work areas receive sufficient task lighting. good lighting should be adaptable to meet the needs of younger, as well as older, eyes.

Step Two: Use slip-resistant flooring. Falling with a hot casserole or sharp knife in your hand can have serious consequences. Choose a slip-resistant material for your floor, such as matte-finished wood or laminate, textured vinyl, or a soft-glazed ceramic tile indicated specifically for flooring. If you select tile, it helps to use a throw rug with a non-skid backing—especially around areas that get wet. Remember to inquire about the slip-resistance rating of any flooring material you may be considering for your new kitchen.

Opposite: Slip-resistant floor tile is usually safe, but the cool, hard surface may be uncomfortable to stand on for long periods of time.

Above: Let there be plenty of light. Aging can affect eyesight, so provide adequate lighting in and around the work area. If you install dimmer switches, you'll be able to adjust the level of light as you desire for various tasks or for dining.

Step Three: Keep a fire extinguisher handy. A grease fire in the kitchen can spread rapidly. That's why it's so important to have a fire extinguisher within arm's reach of the ovens and cooktop. For maximum protection, there should be at least two extinguishers in any kitchen—one located in the cooking area and one stored in another part of the room. You want them to be handy; however, you don't want fire extinguishers to fall into the hands of children. Install them high enough so that they are out of reach of curious youngsters.

Step Four: Keep electrical switches, plugs, and lighting fixtures away from water sources and wet hands. In addition, make sure every electrical receptacle is grounded and protected with ground-fault circuit interrupters. These devices cut electrical current if there is a power surge or if moisture is present. Most building codes require them in any room where there is plumbing to protect homeowners against electrical shock.

Step Five: Consider lock-out options. New smart-home technology allows you to lock your range and ovens so that no one can use them while you are out of the house. The simple lock-out device can prevent burns, fires, or worse.

You can choose between lock-out covers or a programmed lock-out system. Or you can install timers on all appliances you don't want in use when you can't supervise the cooking. Installing guard rails around burners is another good idea.

You might also consider designating one wall cabinet for storing cleansers and other toxic substances—the fire extinguisher, for example. Include a lock on the cabinet, and keep the key in a safe place.

Step Six: Regulate water temperature—and devices. Install faucets with antiscald devices that prevent water temperature from rising to dangerously high levels, or buy pressure-balanced valves that equalize hot and cold water. Although pressure-balanced faucets were available only in single-lever styles in the past, now some models with separate hot- and cold-water valves offer this safety feature, too. Another option is a faucet that can be pre-programmed to your desired temperature setting. All of these controls should be childproofed with lock-out features.

Step Seven: Design a safe cooktop. How many times have you been scalded reaching over a boiling pot or a hot element? Avoid this dangerous situation by selecting staggered burners for your cooktop or one straight row of burners. If you can't find single burners, turn two-burner units sideways, placing them parallel to the front of the countertop. Never choose a unit with controls at the rear of the cooktop; controls should be along the side or in front.

Step Eight: Use space efficiently and safely. You can have all the space in the world and still put family members in compromising situations. Avoid swinging doors. When placing appliances, think

Left: Wicker baskets are a smart choice if you're sensitive to the petroleum chemicals in plastics or vinyl-coated wire.

Opposite: A single-lever faucet is the easiest to use. Avoid scalds by regulating water temperature.

104

about how the traffic area will be affected when a door is open. Locate ovens and the microwave at a comfortable height that doesn't necessitate reaching in order to retrieve hot food. Install carousel shelves, Lazy Susans, and slide-out trays and bins in base cabinets to make storage more accessible without doing a lot of bending.

Avoid sharp corners, especially at the end of a run of cabinetry or on the island or peninsula. If space is tight and you can't rearrange most elements, install a rounded-end cabinet and choose a countertop material that will allow a bull-nose edge treatment. Solid-surfacing material is an excellent choice for such an application.

Universal Design

As people age, their capabilities change; some become more challenged than others and need more assistance with day-to-day chores. Universal design is an approach that adapts the home to people of all skills. It evolved as a response to our increasingly aging society.

Incorporating universal concepts into your design is always smart, particularly if you plan to stay in your house as you grow older. Analyze your lifestyle and your family's needs now—and what you anticipate them to be in the future. Do you have young children? Do you expect to have an elderly parent living with you? Will you remain in the house after you retire? Planning to include some

Opposite: The 32½-inch height of these base cabinets meets the recommendations of the American Disabilities Act (ADA). Notice the extra high and deep toekick that allows wheelchair access.

Below: A pullout cutting board provides a sufficient work surface for a seated person.

Right: The sink base conceals plumbing but allows access. The raised dishwasher permits easier loading.

universal-design features in your new kitchen now will save you money later on, because it's more expensive to make changes to an existing plan.

According to the National Kitchen & Bath Association (NKBA), one of the easiest and most practical universal-design elements you can include is the installation of counters at varying heights, which allows you to perform some tasks while seated and others while standing, not bending. Another idea that makes sense for any kitchen is a pullout counter near both the cooktop and another at the oven. They provide handy landing places for hot pots, pans, and dishes. Or design a compact work triangle that eliminates the need for extra steps. For most people, an L-shaped layout accomplishes this most efficiently, but islands can also create compact work areas. Other ideas include digital displays, which are easier to read and fairly stan-

dard on today's appliances; wall-mounted switches and outlets at the universal reach range of 15 to 48 inches from the floor; reserving a base cabinet for storing dishes, making dinnerware easier to reach; wrist-blade-style faucets that don't require grabbing or twisting; and a side-by-side style refrigerator, which places most often-used foods at easily accessible heights. It might also be worthwhile to investigate some of the smart-home technology available. This includes devices

that allow you to call home from any phone to turn on the lights, heat the oven, raise the thermostat, or program dinner to start cooking. Of course, this sophisticated technology is expensive. If any of these features will destroy your budget, don't use them.

SMARTtip
Electrical Outlets and Switches

Sometimes the special needs of the disabled may seem to conflict with those of the very young. A case point is accessible switch and outlet placement, which is lower on a wall. As an alternative, the NKBA recommends locating them inside the front of a tilt-down drawer to conceal them from children. Alternatively, an outlet strip can be kept out of a child's reach and at a convenient adult location while lessening the reach to plugs and switches installed in the backsplash.

You may have heard the terms accessible and adaptable design used interchangeably and with universal design. However, all of these are different. You've just learned about universal design; here's an explanation of the other two.

Accessible design

Accessible design normally means that a home—or in this case a kitchen—is barrier-free. It also indicates that the room complies with design guidelines for disabled people found in government regulations such as the American National Standards Institute's A117.1 (ANSI A117.1-1986). There are a number of guidelines governing accessible design, the goal of which is to provide criteria for designing for the wheelchair-bound. Most accessible homes incorporate a number of fixed features that give a disabled person easy access.

If a disabled person in your family will use the new kitchen, plan the space accordingly, making sure there is adequate room for that person to move around. Design appropriate clearances. A standard wheelchair occupies 10 square feet and has a turning diameter of 5 feet. Therefore, doorways must be at least 32 inches wide, and aisles must be a minimum of 42 inches wide, according to the NKBA.

A lowered cooktop with an angled non-fogging mirror installed above the surface lets someone seated see what's cooking. If you don't like the look of an open space below the cooktop, install retractable doors that open to accommodate the wheelchair and close for a finished look. An induction cooktop is probably the most practical choice for this situation. It features an automatic shutoff, has a cool-to-the-touch cooking surface, and is easy to keep clean. Low, shallow base cabinets outfitted with pullout and slide-out bins and trays, carousel shelves, and Lazy Susans maximize accessibility, as do lower counter heights—31 inches as opposed to the standard 36 inches. Light-colored countertops with a contrasting edge

Right: An oven that can be operated from a seated position is recommended for anyone in a wheelchair. Locating the oven this way is also practical for people who have trouble bending. Plus, it's a safe position for lifting hot casseroles and roasts from the oven.

treatment are recommended for people with impaired vision.

More than one cabinet manufacturer has introduced a line of cabinets and accessories that accommodate everyone in the family, including those with special needs. Features include a lowered base cabinet; an oven cabinet accessible from a seated position; a raised dishwasher enclosure for easy loading and unloading; a sink base that allows seated use but conceals plumbing; a 9-inch-deep toekick to permit wheelchair access; a tambour-door base cabinet unit; base microwave cabinets; and knife hinges for barrier-free door opening. Each one of these features reflects an idea that should be designed into any all-accessible kitchen.

You might also want to consider having a second microwave near the kitchen table. The cabinet in which you choose to house it should have a drop-down door to provide a shelf for resting hot dishes straight from the oven.

And if you have the space, keep one or two rolling carts in the kitchen that allow someone to easily transport several items around the room—especially foods on large serving platters—at the same time.

Adaptable design

Adaptable design refers to features that can be easily modified for use by a disabled person. Such design features are normally found in multifamily rental housing so that a landlord is able to rent to anyone. The adaptable-design kitchen incorporates some concealed traditional accessible features—for example, doors under the sink that can be removed to allow accessibility for someone in a wheelchair.

Plan #181228

Dimensions: 68' W x 36' D

Levels: 2

Square Footage: 2,393

Main Level Sq. Ft.: 1,279

Upper Level Sq. Ft.: 1,114

Bedrooms: 4

Bathrooms: 2

Foundation: Slab

Materials List Available: Yes

Price Category: E

Come home to this fine home, and relax on the front or rear porch.

Features:

- Living Room: This large, open entertaining area has a cozy fireplace and is flooded with natural light.

- Kitchen: This fully equipped kitchen has an abundance of cabinets and counter space. Access the rear porch is through a glass door.

- Laundry Room: Located on the main level, this laundry area also has space for storage.

- Upper Level: Climb the U-shaped staircase, and you'll find four large bedrooms that share a common bathroom.

Images provided by designer/architect.

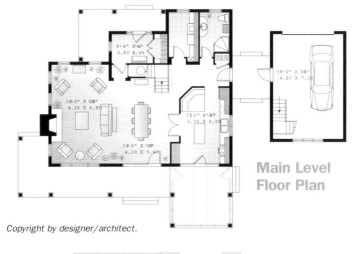

Main Level Floor Plan

Copyright by designer/architect.

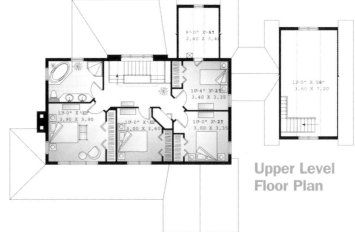

Upper Level Floor Plan

Rear View

Dining Room

Living Room

Living Room

Kitchen

Master Bath

Plan #151712

Dimensions: 66'4" W x 58'7" D
Levels: 2
Square Footage: 2,783
Main Level Sq. Ft.: 2,029
Upper Level Sq. Ft.: 754
Bedrooms: 3
Bathrooms: 2
Foundation: Crawl space or basement
CompleteCost List Available: Yes
Price Category: D

Images provided by designer/architect.

You'll enjoy entertaining family and friends during those frigid winter months as holiday visitors gather around the inviting fireplaces in this stunning two-story home.

Features:

- **Hearth Room:** Located just off the kitchen, this casual area has a cozy fireplace.
- **Kitchen:** The open floor plan allows everyone plenty of room to roam, and this expansive work space allows for effortless service to all living areas.
- **Master Suite:** This luxurious suite features a private bath with a corner whirlpool tub, ample natural lighting, and a 10-ft.-high boxed ceiling.
- **Guest Room:** Located upstairs, this room will allow your overnight guests to enjoy the view from their window seat snuggled within an entire wall of built-in bookshelves.

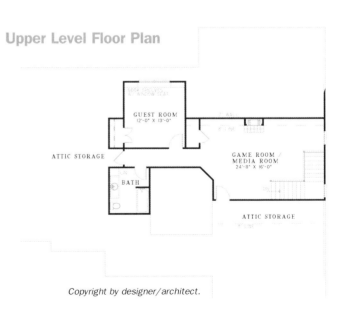

Copyright by designer/architect.

Plan #321027

Dimensions: 72' W x 68' D

Levels: 1

Square Footage: 2,758

Bedrooms: 4

Bathrooms: 2½

Foundation: Basement

Materials List Available: Yes

Price Category: F

Images provided by designer/architect.

This stone-and-wood-sided four-bedroom home has country charm.

Features:

• Dining Room: You'll find this high-ceilinged room just off the entry.

• Great Room: This large gathering area has a vaulted ceiling with skylights and a corner fireplace.

• Kitchen: This large kitchen has an abundance of cabinets and opens into the breakfast area with a vaulted ceiling.

• Master Suite: This private area features a vaulted ceiling and a walk-in closet. The master bath has a double vanity and soaking tub.

• Bedrooms: Three additional bedrooms share a common bath.

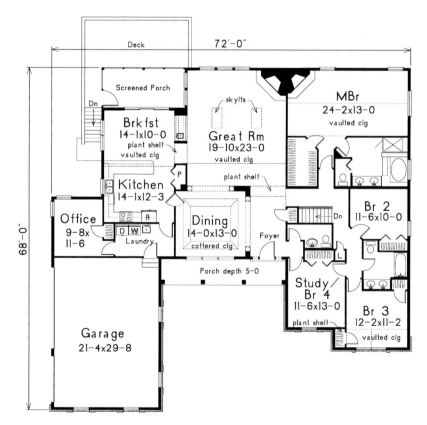

Copyright by designer/architect.

Plan #441002

Dimensions: 70' W x 51' D
Levels: 1
Square Footage: 1,873
Bedrooms: 3
Bathrooms: 2
Foundation: Crawl space
Materials List Available: No
Price Category: D

Images provided by designer/architect.

Shutters flank tall windows to adorn the front of this charming home. A high roofline gives presence to the façade and allows vaulted ceilings in all the right places inside.

CAD FILE AVAILABLE

Features:

• Great Room: The entry hall overlooks this room, where a fireplace warms gatherings on chilly evenings and built-in shelves, to the right of the fireplace, add space that might be used as an entertainment center. A large three-panel window wall allows for a rear-yard view.

• Dining Room: This area is connected directly to the great room and features double doors to a covered porch.

• Kitchen: This open work area contains ample counter space with an island cooktop and large pantry.

• Bedrooms: The bedrooms are split, with the master suite in the back and additional bedrooms at the front.

• Master Suite: This suite boasts a 9-ft.-high ceiling and is graced by a luxurious bathroom and a walk-in closet.

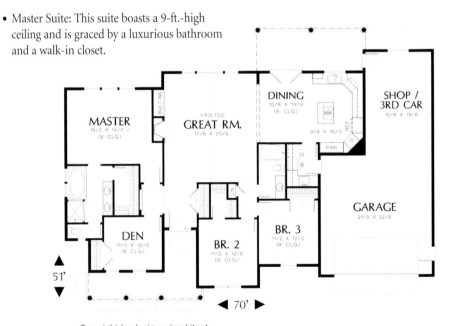

Copyright by designer/architect.

Rear Elevation

Plan #131002

Dimensions: 70'1" W x 60'7" D
Levels: 1
Square Footage: 1,709
Bedrooms: 3
Bathrooms: 2½
Foundation: Crawl space, slab, or basement
Materials List Available: Yes
Price Category: D

Images provided by designer/architect.

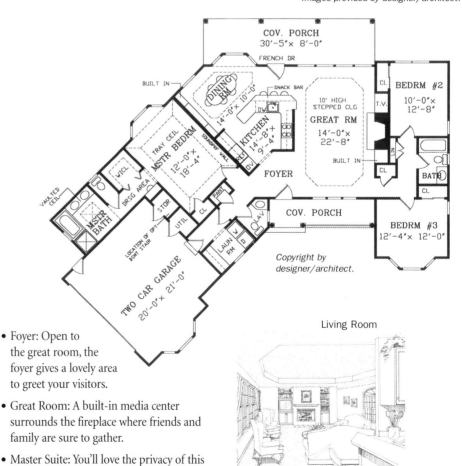

Copyright by designer/architect.

Rear View

You'll love the way this angled ranch brings out the best in a corner lot or on a slope.

Features:

- Ceiling Height: 8 ft.

- Front Porch: Hang baskets of plants from the roof of this porch, which is just the right size for a couple of rockers and a side table.

- Dining Room: Well-placed windows flood this room with sunlight during the day and a built-in cabinet gives ample storage space for all your china, linens, and collectables.

- Foyer: Open to the great room, the foyer gives a lovely area to greet your visitors.

- Great Room: A built-in media center surrounds the fireplace where friends and family are sure to gather.

- Master Suite: You'll love the privacy of this somewhat isolated but easily accessed room. Decorate to show off the large bay window and tray ceiling, and enjoy the luxury of a compartmented bathroom.

Living Room

Plan #421017

Dimensions: 63' W x 61' D
Levels: 2
Square Footage: 2,433
Main Level Sq. Ft.: 1,590
Upper Level Sq. Ft.: 843
Bedrooms: 4
Bathrooms: 2½
Foundation: Crawl space, slab, or basement
Materials List Available: Yes
Price Category: E

Images provided by designer/architect.

Main Level Floor Plan

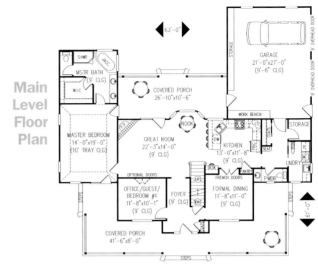

Optional Great Room Floor Plan

Upper Level Floor Plan

Copyright by designer/architect.

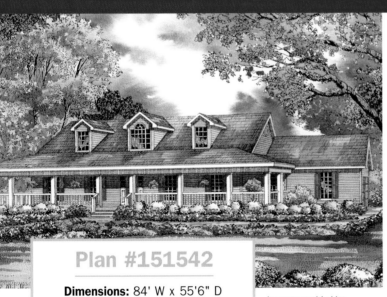

Plan #151542

Dimensions: 84' W x 55'6" D
Levels: 1.5
Square Footage: 1,921
Bedrooms: 3
Bathrooms: 3
Foundation: Crawl space, slab, basement, or walk-out
CompleteCost List Available: Yes
Price Category: D

Images provided by designer/architect.

Main Level Floor Plan

Copyright by designer/architect.

Upper Level Floor Plan

Images provided by designer/architect.

Plan #211048

Dimensions: 66' W x 60' D

Levels: 1

Square Footage: 2,002

Bedrooms: 3

Bathrooms: 2

Foundation: Crawl space, slab

Materials List Available: Yes

Price Category: D

Copyright by designer/architect.

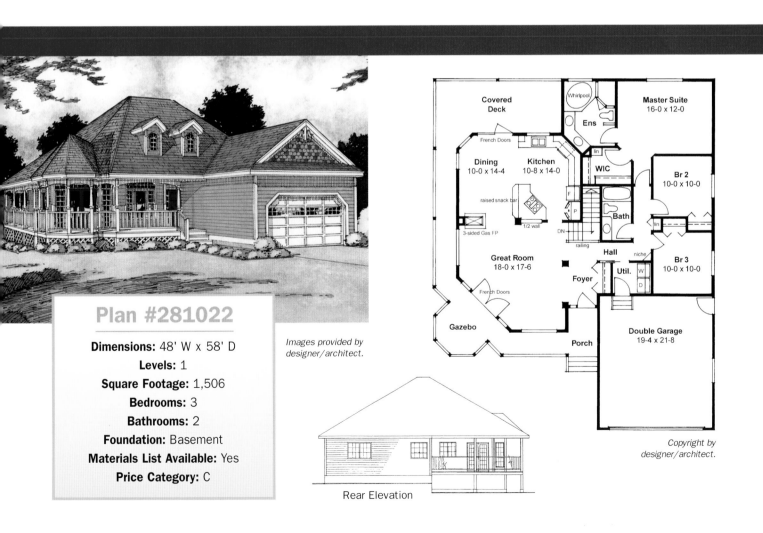

Images provided by designer/architect.

Plan #281022

Dimensions: 48' W x 58' D

Levels: 1

Square Footage: 1,506

Bedrooms: 3

Bathrooms: 2

Foundation: Basement

Materials List Available: Yes

Price Category: C

Rear Elevation

Copyright by designer/architect.

Great Room/Foyer

Plan #161002

Dimensions: 64'2" W x 44'2" D

Levels: 1

Square Footage: 1,860

Bedrooms: 3

Bathrooms: 2

Foundation: Basement

Materials List Available: Yes

Price Category: D

CAD FILE AVAILABLE

Images provided by designer/architect.

Copyright by designer/architect.

Rear Elevation

Plan #441013

Dimensions: 69' W x 59' D

Levels: 2

Square Footage: 3,317

Main Level Sq. Ft.: 2,657

Lower Level Sq. Ft.: 600

Bedrooms: 4

Bathrooms: 3½

Foundation: Slab

Materials List Available: No

Price Category: G

Images provided by designer/architect.

CAD FILE AVAILABLE

Main Level Floor Plan

Lower Level Floor Plan

Copyright by designer/architect.

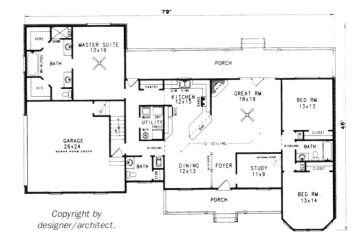

Images provided by designer/architect.

Copyright by designer/architect.

Plan #171015

Dimensions: 79' W x 52' D
Levels: 1
Square Footage: 2,089
Bedrooms: 3
Bathrooms: 2½
Foundation: Slab, crawl space
Materials List Available: Yes
Price Category: D

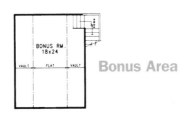

Bonus Area

Plan #441012

Dimensions: 65' W x 55' D
Levels: 1
Square Footage: 3,682
Main Level Sq. Ft.: 2,192
Basement Level Sq. Ft.: 1,490
Bedrooms: 4
Bathrooms: 4
Foundation: Slab
Materials List Available: No
Price Category: H

Images provided by designer/architect.

CAD FILE AVAILABLE

Main Level Floor Plan

Basement Level Floor Plan

Copyright by designer/architect.

Rear Elevation

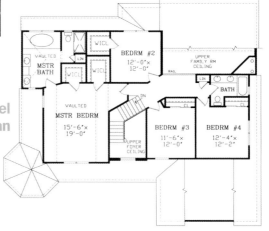

Main Level Floor Plan

Images provided by designer/architect.

Plan #131021

Dimensions: 60' W x 52'4" D
Levels: 2
Square Footage: 3,110
Main Level Sq. Ft.: 1,818
Upper Level Sq. Ft.: 1,292
Bedrooms: 5
Bathrooms: 2½
Foundation: Crawl space, slab, or basement
Materials List Available: Yes
Price Category: H

Upper Level Floor Plan

Copyright by designer/architect.

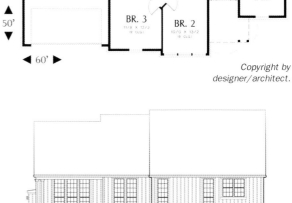

Plan #441008

Dimensions: 60' W x 50' D
Levels: 1
Square Footage: 2,001
Bedrooms: 3
Bathrooms: 2
Foundation: Crawl space; slab or basement available for fee
Materials List Available: No
Price Category: D

Images provided by designer/architect.

Copyright by designer/architect.

Rear Elevation

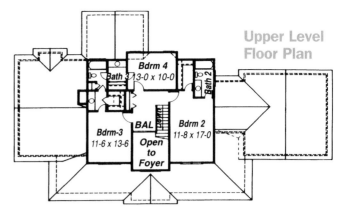

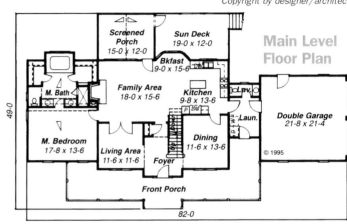

Copyright by designer/architect.

Upper Level Floor Plan

Main Level Floor Plan

Plan #141017

Dimensions: 82' W x 49' D

Levels: 2

Square Footage: 2,480

Main Level Sq. Ft.: 1,581

Upper Level Sq. Ft.: 899

Bedrooms: 4

Bathrooms: 3½

Foundation: Basement, crawl space, or slab

Materials List Available: No

Price Category: E

Images provided by designer/architect.

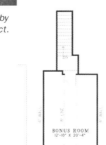

Plan #151490

Dimensions: 52' W x 69'6" D

Levels: 1

Square Footage: 1,869

Bedrooms: 3

Bathrooms: 2

Foundation: Crawl space or slab

CompleteCost List Available: Yes

Price Category: D

Images provided by designer/architect.

CAD FILE AVAILABLE

Bonus Area Floor Plan

Copyright by designer/architect.

Plan #241017

Dimensions: 74'4" W x 55'4" D

Levels: 1

Square Footage: 2,431

Bedrooms: 4

Bathrooms: 2½

Foundation: Slab

Materials List Available: No

Price Category: E

Images provided by designer/architect.

The turret, arched window details, and wraparound porch hint at the interesting interior design of this lovely home.

Features:

- **Great Room:** This room features a 12-ft. ceiling, angled walls, a corner fireplace, and sliding doors leading to the rear porch.

- **Dining Room:** Located in the turret, the highlights of this room are the deep bay and 10-ft. ceiling.

- **Morning Room:** The angled walls and windows over the rear porch echo those in the great room.

- **Kitchen:** With an angled snack bar accessible from the great room and morning room, this well-designed kitchen is ideal for the family cooks.

- **Master Suite:** Situated for privacy, the master suite has an angled wall in the bedroom and a door onto the rear porch. The bath has two walk-in closets, two vanities, a garden tub, and a separate shower stall.

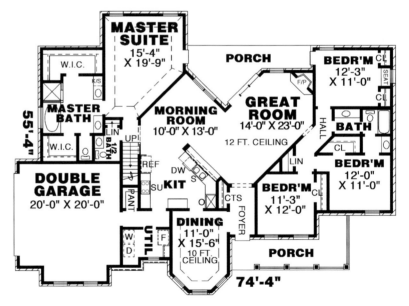

Copyright by designer/architect.

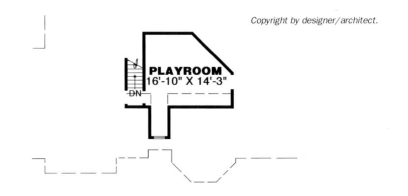

Plan #181094

Dimensions: 50' W x 39' D
Levels: 2
Square Footage: 2,099
Main Level Sq. Ft.: 1,060
Upper Level Sq. Ft.: 1,039
Bedrooms: 4
Bathrooms: 2½
Foundation: Basement
Materials List Available: Yes
Price Category: D

Images provided by designer/architect.

The curved covered porch makes this is a great place to come home to.

Features:

• Entry: This air-lock entry area with closet will help keep energy costs down.

• Family Room: This gathering area features a fireplace and is open to the kitchen and the dining area.

• Kitchen: U-shaped and boasting an island and a walk-in pantry, this kitchen is open to the dining area.

• Master Suite: This large retreat features a fireplace and a walk-in closet. The master bath has dual vanities, a separate shower, and a large tub.

• Bedrooms: Located upstairs with the master suite are three additional bedrooms. They share a common bathroom, and each has a large closet.

Rear View

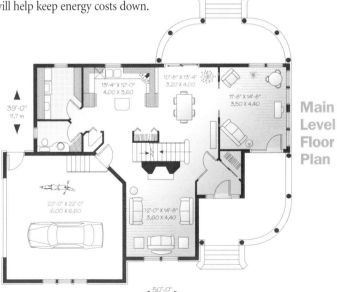

Main Level Floor Plan

Upper Level Floor Plan

Copyright by designer/architect.

Plan #181085

Dimensions: 56'4" W x 44' D
Levels: 2
Square Footage: 2,183
Main Level Sq. Ft.: 1,232
Second Level Sq. Ft.: 951
Bedrooms: 3
Bathrooms: 2½
Foundation: Basement
Materials List Available: Yes
Price Category: D

This country home features an inviting front porch and a layout designed for modern living.

Images provided by designer/architect.

CAD FILE AVAILABLE

Features:

- Ceiling Height: 8 ft.
- Solarium: Sunlight streams through the windows of this solarium at the front of the house.
- Living Room: Walk through French doors, and you will enter this inviting living room. Family and friends will be drawn to the corner fireplace.
- Formal Dining Room: Usher your guests directly from the living room into this formal dining room. The kitchen is located on the

other side of the dining room for convenient service.

- Kitchen: This generously sized kitchen is a delight, it offers a center island, separate eat-in area, and access to the back deck.
- Bonus Room: This room just off the entry hall can become a family room, a bedroom, or an office.
- Master Suite: Curl up by the corner fireplace in this master retreat, with its walk-in closet and lavish bath with separate shower and tub.

Main Level Floor Plan

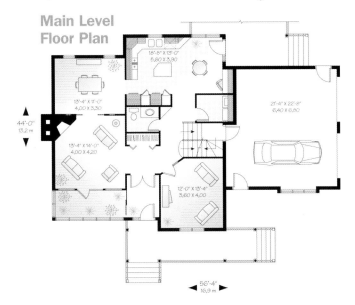

Upper Level Floor Plan

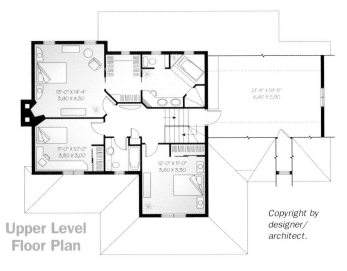

Copyright by designer/architect.

Plan #151307

Dimensions: 34'6" W x 32'6" D

Levels: 1

Square Footage: 1,029

Bedrooms: 3

Bathrooms: 1½

Foundation: Crawl space or slab

CompleteCost List Available: Yes

Price Category: B

Images provided by designer/architect.

This charming country house is the perfect starter home.

Features:

• Front Porch: Visit with neighbors on this front porch as the children ride their bikes.

• Great Room: Entering the home, you'll feel all the comforts of home in this spacious room, which provides a relaxed atmosphere with an open view to the kitchen.

• Kitchen: This eat-in kitchen has a bar and plenty of cabinet space.

• Master Suite: This suite features a walk-in closet with private access to the bath. Listening for that newborn baby is made easier with the nursery close by.

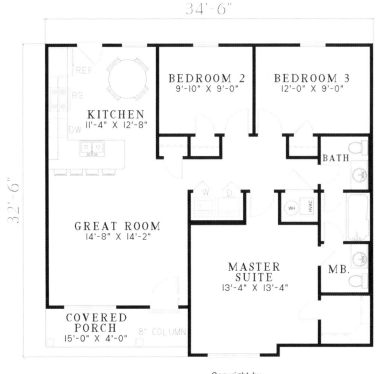

Copyright by designer/architect.

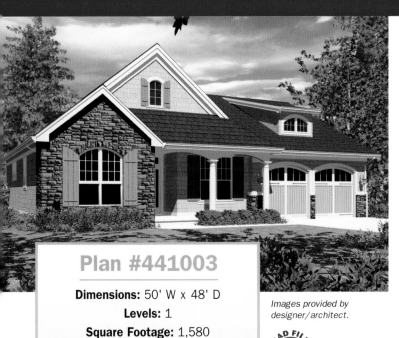

Plan #441003

Dimensions: 50' W x 48' D

Levels: 1

Square Footage: 1,580

Bedrooms: 3

Bathrooms: 2½

Foundation: Crawl space; slab or basement available for fee

Materials List Available: No

Price Category: C

Images provided by designer/architect.

Copyright by designer/architect.

Rear Elevation

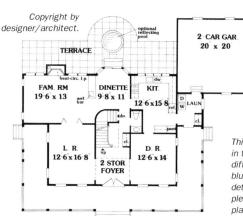

Plan #131051

Dimensions: 64'4" W x 53'4" D

Levels: 2

Square Footage: 2,431

Main Level Sq. Ft.: 1,293

Upper Level Sq. Ft.: 1,138

Bedrooms: 4

Bathrooms: 2½

Foundation: Crawl space, slab, or basement

Materials List Available: Yes

Price Category: F

Images provided by designer/architect.

Copyright by designer/architect.

Main Level Floor Plan

This home, as shown in the photograph, may differ from the actual blueprints. For more detailed information, please check the floor plans carefully.

Optional 3rd Level Floor Plan

Upper Level Floor Plan

Plan #421013

Dimensions: 68'10" W x 51'2" D
Levels: 2
Square Footage: 2,327
Main Level Sq. Ft.: 1,484
Upper Level Sq. Ft.: 843
Bedrooms: 4
Bathrooms: 2½
Foundation: Crawl space, slab, or basement
Materials List Available: Yes
Price Category: E

Images provided by designer/architect.

Main Level Floor Plan

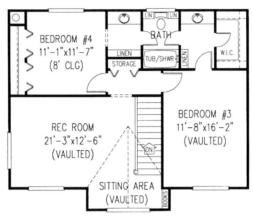

Upper Level Floor Plan

Copyright by designer/architect.

Plan #441010

Dimensions: 108' W x 59' D
Levels: 1
Square Footage: 2,973
Bedrooms: 4
Bathrooms: 4½
Foundation: Crawl space; slab or basement available for fee
Materials List Available: No
Price Category: F

Images provided by designer/architect.

Copyright by designer/architect.

Bonus Area Floor Plan

Rear Elevation

Images provided by designer/architect.

Plan #131030

Dimensions: 51' W x 41'10" D

Levels: 2

Square Footage: 2,470

Main Level Sq. Ft.: 1,290

Upper Level Sq. Ft.: 1,180

Bedrooms: 4

Bathrooms: 2½

Foundation: Crawl space, slab, basement, or walk-out basement

Materials List Available: Yes

Price Category: F

If high ceilings and spacious rooms make you happy, you'll love this gorgeous home.

Features:

• **Family Room:** An 18-ft. vaulted ceiling that's open to the balcony above, a corner fireplace, and a wall of windows make this room feel special.

• **Dining Room:** This formal room, which flows into the living room, also opens to the front porch and optional backyard deck.

• **Kitchen:** A bright breakfast room joins with this kitchen and opens to the backyard deck.

• **Master Suite:** You'll smile when you see the 11-ft. vaulted ceiling, stunning arched window, and two walk-in closets in the bedroom. A skylight lets natural light into the private bath, with its spa tub, separate shower, and dual-sink vanity.

• **Bedrooms:** To reach these three charming bedrooms, you'll admire the view into the family room below as you walk along the balcony hall.

Main Level Floor Plan

Copyright by designer/architect.

Upper Level Floor Plan

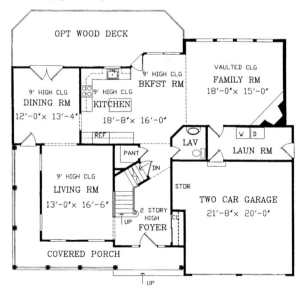

Plan #121083

Dimensions: 72' W x 45'4" D
Levels: 2
Square Footage: 2,695
Main Level Sq. Ft.: 1,881
Upper Level Sq. Ft.: 814
Bedrooms: 4
Bathrooms: 3½
Foundation: Basement
Materials List Available: Yes
Price Category: F

Images provided by designer/architect.

You'll love this home for its soaring entryway ceiling and well-designed layout.

Features:

- Entry: A balcony from the upper level looks down into this two-story entry, which features a decorative plant shelf.

- Great Room: Comfort is guaranteed in this large room, with its built-in bookcases framing a lovely fireplace and trio of transom-topped windows along one wall.

- Living Room: Save both this formal room and the formal dining room, both of which flank the entry, for guests and special occasions.

- Kitchen: This convenient work space includes a gazebo-shaped breakfast area where friends and family will gather at any time of day.

Main Level Floor Plan

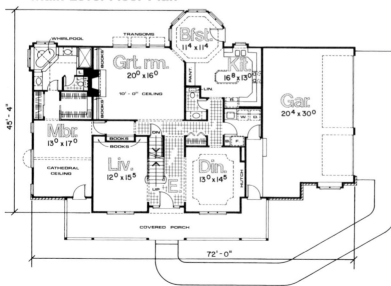

Upper Level Floor Plan

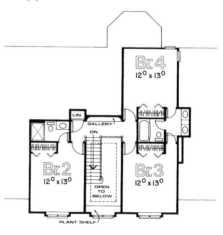

Copyright by designer/architect.

Plan #131047

Dimensions: 69'10" W x 51'8" D
Levels: 1
Square Footage: 1,793
Bedrooms: 3
Bathrooms: 2
Foundation: Crawl space, slab, or basement
Materials List Available: Yes
Price Category: C

Images provided by designer/architect.

The country charm of this well-designed home is mixed with the convenience and luxury normally reserved for more contemporary plans.

Features:

• Great Room: The spaciousness of this great room is enhanced by the 11-ft. stepped ceiling. A fireplace makes it cozy on cool evenings or on chilly winter days, and two sets of French sliding glass doors open to the back porch.

• Kitchen: In addition to the convenient layout of this design, you'll also love its bright, airy position. It includes an old-fashioned pantry,

a sink under a window, and a sunny breakfast area that opens to the wraparound porch.

• Master Suite: You'll find 11-ft. ceilings in both the master bedroom and the bayed sitting area that the suite includes. In the bath, the circular spa tub is surrounded by a glass-block wall.

• Bonus Space: A permanent staircase leads to an unfinished bonus space on the upper level.

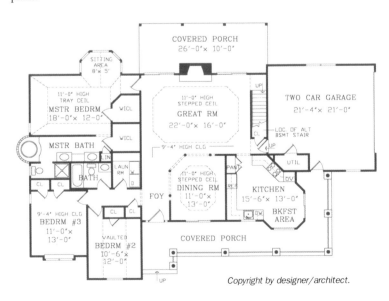

Copyright by designer/architect.

Rear Elevation

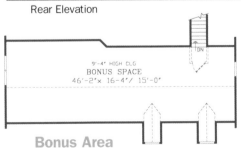

Bonus Area

Plan #441011

Dimensions: 67' W x 46' D
Levels: 1
Square Footage: 2,898
Main Level Sq. Ft.: 1,744
Basement Level Sq. Ft.: 1,154
Bedrooms: 3
Bathrooms: 2½
Foundation: Walk-out basement
Materials List Available: No
Price Category: F

Images provided by designer/architect.

CAD FILE AVAILABLE

Main Level Floor Plan

Basement Level Floor Plan

Copyright by designer/architect.

Rear Elevation

Plan #421011

Dimensions: 64'6" W x 47'7" D
Levels: 2
Square Footage: 2,266
Main Level Sq. Ft.: 1,216
Upper Level Sq. Ft.: 1,050
Bedrooms: 4
Bathrooms: 2½
Foundation: Crawl space, slab, or basement
Materials List Available: Yes
Price Category: E

Images provided by designer/architect.

CAD FILE AVAILABLE

Main Level Floor Plan
Copyright by designer/architect.

Alternate Upper Level Bath/Laundry

Upper Level Floor Plan

Plan #131027

Dimensions: 62'4" W x 53'6" D
Levels: 2
Square Footage: 2,567
Main Level Sq. Ft.: 2,017
Upper Level Sq. Ft.: 550
Bedrooms: 4
Bathrooms: 3
Foundation: Crawl space, slab, or basement
Materials List Available: Yes
Price Category: F

Images provided by designer/architect.

The features of this home are so good that you may have trouble imagining all of them at once.

Features:

- Great Room: Imagine a stepped ceiling, corner fireplace, built-media center, and wall of windows with a glass door to the backyard—in one room.

- Dining Room: A stepped ceiling and server with a sink add to the elegance of this formal room.

- Breakfast Room: Eat at the bar this room shares with the island kitchen, and admire the 12-ft. cathedral ceiling and bayed group of

8- and 9-ft. windows. Or go through the sliding glass door to the covered side porch.

- Master Suite: The bedroom has a tray ceiling and cozy sitting area, and a whirlpool tub, shower, and walk-in closet are in the skylighted bath.

- Optional Study: The private bath in bedroom 2 makes it ideal for a study or home office.

- Bonus Room: Enjoy the extra 300 sq. ft.

Breakfast Nook

Rear View

Great Room

Main Level Floor Plan

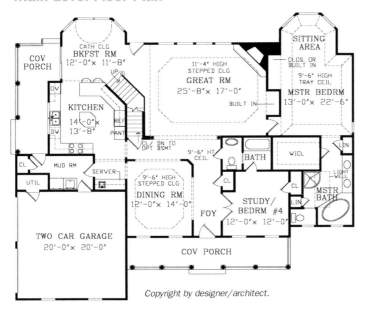

Copyright by designer/architect.

Upper Level Floor Plan

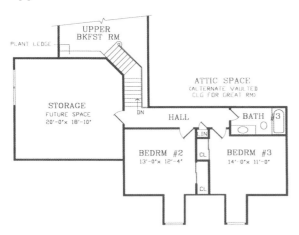

As with any skill, there is a right and a wrong way to paint. There is a right way to hold a brush, a right way to maneuver a roller, a right way to spray a wall, etc. Follow these basic professional tips:

Brushing vs. Rolling. Some painters insist that only a brush-painted job looks right. However, most painters will "cut in" the edges with a brush, and then finish the main body of a wall or ceiling using a roller. Brushing alone can be time-consuming, and it is typically reserved for architectural woodwork.

Using the Right Brush. Use the largest brush with which you are comfortable. Professional painters seldom pick up anything smaller than a 4-inch brush. Most homeowners will achieve good results using a 4-inch brush for "cutting in" and for large surfaces, and an angled 2½- to 3-inch sash brush for trim around windows and doors. Be sure, also, to use brushes that are appropriate for the type of paint being applied. Oil-based paints require a natural bristle (also called "China bristles"), while water-based paints are applied with a synthetic bristle brush.

Handling a Brush. Many people grip a paintbrush as if they were shaking someone's hand. It is better to grip a brush more like a pencil, with the fingers and thumb wrapped around the metal ferrule. This grip provides the hand and wrist with a wider range of motion and therefore greater speed and precision. If your hand cramps, switch hands or switch temporarily to the handshake grip.

Wiping Rags. Before you begin painting, put a dust rag in your pocket. This is helpful for clearing away cobwebs and dust before painting. It is also handy for wiping off paint drips before they have a chance to dry.

Paint Hooks. When working on a ladder, use a good-quality paint hook to secure the paint bucket to your ladder. Avoid makeshift hooks made with wire or coat hangers. Paint hooks are inexpensive and available at virtually all paint and hardware stores.

Main Level Floor Plan

Great Rm 19-4x15-0
Breakfast 11-8x13-0
Kit 12-0x14-6
Entry
Up
Porch Depth 7-8
Dining 15-0x12-0
Garage 21-4x21-10

48'-8"
57'-0"

Images provided by designer/architect.

Upper Level Floor Plan

MBr 19-4x13-0 Vaulted
Br 2 14-0x11-0
Dn
Br 3 12-9x12-0 Vaulted

Copyright by designer/architect.

Plan #321052

Dimensions: 57' W x 48'8" D
Levels: 2
Square Footage: 2,182
Main Level Sq. Ft.: 1,112
Upper Level Sq. Ft.: 1,070
Bedrooms: 3
Bathrooms: 3½
Foundation: Basement
Materials List Available: Yes
Price Category: D

Main Level Floor Plan

66'-6"

COVERED PORCH
NOOK
GREAT ROOM 24'-5"x15'-1" (9' CLG)
KITCHEN 12'-3"x13'-1" (9' CLG)
LNDRY
SHOP/STORAGE 11'-10"x16'-10"
SHELVES
WORK BENCH
48'-0"
OFFICE/ GUEST/ HOME SCHOOL 12'-0"x11'-0" (9' CLG)
FOYER (9' CLG)
PANTRY
French Doors
PWDR
SHELVES
FORMAL DINING 12'-0"x12'-0" (9' CLG)
GARAGE 21'-0"x22'-0"
COVERED PORCH
STEPS

Images provided by designer/architect.

CAD FILE AVAILABLE

FOYER (9' CLG)

Alternate Foyer Area Floor Plan

MASTER BATH
W.I.C.
BEDROOM #2 11'-0"x10'-9"
BEDROOM #3 11'-0"x10'-9"
BONUS ROOM 20'-5"x18'-0"
MASTER BEDROOM 12'-0"x16'-0" (VAULTED)
SITTING ROOM 14'-11"x14'-11" (VAULTED)
HALL BATH
LINEN
STORAGE

Upper Level Floor Plan
Copyright by designer/architect.

Plan #421015

Dimensions: 66'6" W x 48' D
Levels: 2
Square Footage: 2,198
Main Level Sq. Ft.: 1,201
Upper Level Sq. Ft.: 997
Bedrooms: 4
Bathrooms: 2½
Foundation: Crawl space, slab, or basement
Materials List Available: Yes
Price Category: D

Images provided by designer/architect.

Plan #181151

Dimensions: 50' W x 46' D
Levels: 2
Square Footage: 2,283
Main Level Sq. Ft.: 1,274
Second Level Sq. Ft.: 1,009
Bedrooms: 3
Bathrooms: 2½
Foundation: Basement
Materials List Available: Yes
Price Category: E

Multiple porches, stately columns, and arched multi-paned windows adorn this country home.

CAD FILE AVAILABLE

Features:

- Ceiling Height: 8 ft. unless otherwise noted.
- Great Room: The second-floor mezzanine overlooks this great room. With its soaring ceiling, this dramatic room is the centerpiece of a spacious and flowing design that is just as suited to entertaining as it is to family life.
- Dining Area: Guests will naturally flow into this dining area when it is time to eat. After dinner they can step directly out onto the porch to enjoy coffee and dessert when the weather is fair.
- Kitchen: This efficient and well-designed kitchen has double sinks and offers a separate eating area for those impromptu family meals.
- Master Bedroom: This master retreat has a walk-in closet and its own sumptuous bath.
- Home Office: Whether you work at home or just need a place for the family computer and keeping track of family finances, this home office fills the bill.

Main Level Floor Plan

Upper Level Floor Plan

Copyright by designer/architect.

Plan #221028

Dimensions: 50' W x 67' D

Levels: 1

Square Footage: 1,773

Bedrooms: 2

Bathrooms: 2

Foundation: Basement

Materials List Available: No

Price Category: C

Images provided by designer/architect.

This chateau-style ranch home feels as if it belongs on a French countryside somewhere.

Features:

• Entry: This octagonal shaped space has a tray ceiling, giving a grand, open feeling to the area.

• Master Suite: This suite has a tray ceiling in the bedroom, a Jacuzzi tub in the bath, and a spacious walk-in closet with ample storage space.

• Bedroom: This second bedroom can be found at the front of the house just off the entry, along with a full bathroom for guests.

• Garage: This large front-loading three-car garage has room for cars plus storage.

Rear Elevation

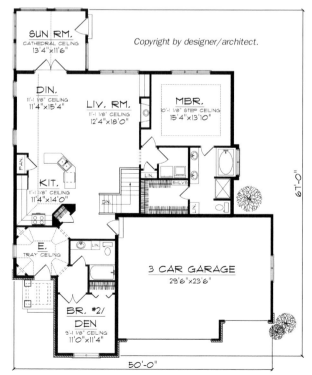

Copyright by designer/architect.

Plan #161087

Dimensions: 48'10" W x 53'4" D

Levels: 1

Square Footage: 1,664

Bedrooms: 3

Bathrooms: 2

Foundation: Walkout basement

Materials List Available: Yes

Price Category: C

A brick-and-stone facade with cedar shakes, a large front porch, arches, and a double gable decorate the exterior of this charming cottage-style home.

Features:

- Great Room: This area has plenty of space for entertaining or just relaxing. It features a gas fireplace and access to the rear deck.

- Kitchen: This well equipped cooking center has everything the chef in the family could want. It is open to the dining room and great room.

- Master Suite: This private space boasts a large sleeping area with a bath that has two vanities.

- Expansion: The lower level can be finished to add an additional bedroom, bathroom, and recreation room.

Images provided by designer/architect.

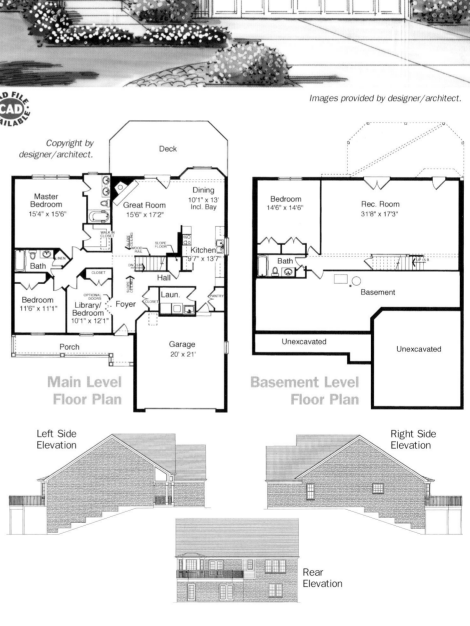

Plan #351070

Dimensions: 63'4" W x 53' D
Levels: 1
Square Footage: 1,818
Bedrooms: 3
Bathrooms: 3
Foundation: Basement
Materials List Available: No
Price Category: D

Images provided by designer/architect.

This charming farmhouse has everything, including three bedrooms, three bathrooms and a two-car garage.

Features:

- **Great Room:** Enjoy the vaulted ceiling, gas log fireplace, and built-ins in this expansive room.

- **Flex Space:** This space is provided for uses such as an office/media center, half bathroom, hobby room, or winter-wear closet.

- **Master Suite:** This suite has a tray ceiling, a large closet for him and her, a jetted tub, an oversized shower, and a large vanity next to her closet.

- **Bedrooms:** All bedrooms feature walk-in closets with their own private bathroom. Bedroom 2 could be used as an in-law suite.

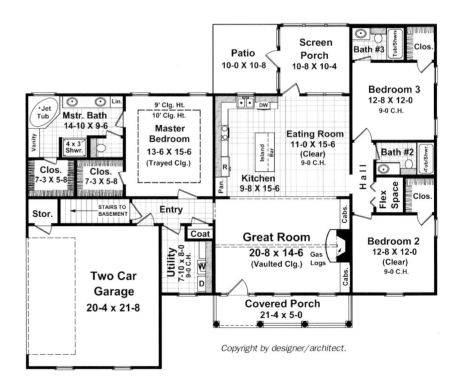

Copyright by designer/architect.

Images provided by designer/architect.

Plan #121006

Dimensions: 46' W x 58' D

Levels: 1

Square Footage: 1,762

Bedrooms: 3

Bathrooms: 2

Foundation: Slab

Materials List Available: Yes

Price Category: C

The entry has a trio of arched openings that leads you to other areas of this amenity-packed home.

Features:

- Ceiling Height: 8 ft. except as noted.

- Eating Bar: Conveniently located between the kitchen and family room, this is sure to be a favorite spot for informal entertaining and family gatherings.

- Family room: A wall of windows, a fireplace, and a vaulted ceiling stretching to 11 ft. work together to make this a bright and warm room.

- Kitchen: There's no shortage of counter space in this well-planned kitchen that features a center island in addition to the eating bar.

- Master Suite: Luxuriate at the end of the day in this large bedroom with its decorative tray ceiling and walk-in closet. Enjoy the pampering bath with its sunlit corner whirlpool flanked by vanities.

- Garage: Two bays provide room for cars and plenty of storage as well.

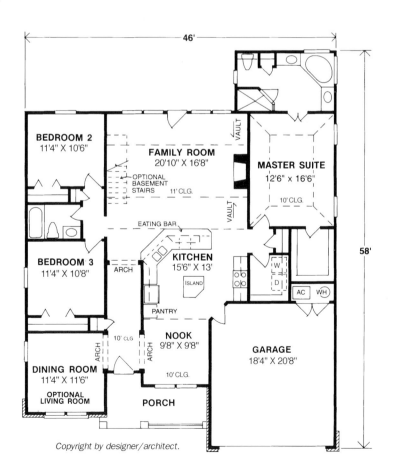

Copyright by designer/architect.

11'-8" X 16'-4"
3,50 X 4,90

26'-0" X 15'-0"
7,80 X 4,50

20'-4" X 21'-4"
6,10 X 6,40

12'-4" X 14'-0"
3,70 X 4,20

18'-4" X 20'-0"
5,50 X 6,00

◄ 60'-0" ►
18,3 m

Plan #181034

Dimensions: 60' W x 44' D

Levels: 2

Square Footage: 2,687

Main Level Sq. Ft.: 1,297

Upper Level Sq. Ft.: 1,390

Bedrooms: 3

Bathrooms: 2½

Foundation: Full basement

Materials List Available: Yes

Price Category: F

Images provided by designer/architect.

CAD FILE CAD AVAILABLE

11'-0" X 11'-0"
3,30 X 3,30

11'-8" X 16'-4"
3,50 X 4,90

18'-0" X 15'-0"
5,40 X 4,50

Upper Level Floor Plan

12'-4" X 13'-0"
3,70 X 4,00

12'-4" X 14'-0"
3,70 X 4,20

12'-0" X 21'-0"
3,60 X 6,40

11'-8" X 9'-8"
3,50 X 2,90

Copyright by designer/architect.

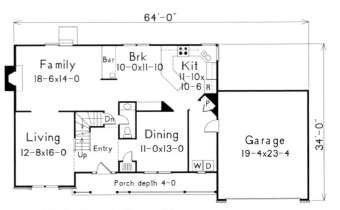

64'-0"

Family
18-6x14-0

Bar

Brk
10-0x11-10

Kit
11-10x
10-6

R

34'-0"

Living
12-8x16-0

Up | Dn | Entry

Dining
11-0x13-0

Garage
19-4x23-4

W D

P

Porch depth 4-0

Main Level Floor Plan

Plan #321041

Dimensions: 64' W x 34' D

Levels: 2

Square Footage: 2,286

Main Level Sq. Ft.: 1,283

Upper Level Sq. Ft.: 1,003

Bedrooms: 4

Bathrooms: 2½

Foundation: Crawl space, slab, or basement

Materials List Available: No

Price Category: E

Images provided by designer/architect.

Br 4
10-2x
10-8

Br 3
11-7x10-8

MBr
12-8x15-11
vaulted

Dn

open to below

Br 2
12-4x10-8

Upper Level Floor Plan

Copyright by designer/architect.

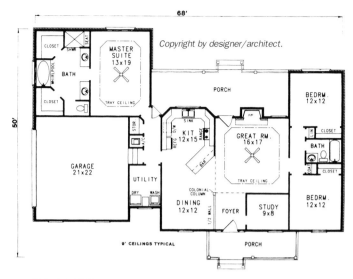

Copyright by designer/architect.

Images provided by designer/architect.

Plan #171009

Dimensions: 68' W x 50' D
Levels: 1
Square Footage: 1,771
Bedrooms: 3
Bathrooms: 2
Foundation: Crawl space, slab
Materials List Available: Yes
Price Category: C

SMARTtip

Deck Awnings

Awnings come in bright colors. As light filters through, it will cast a hue to anything under the deck. Warm colors, such as red or pink, will create a rosy glow; cool colors, such blues or greens, will enhance the shade.

Plan #421003

Dimensions: 59' W x 61' D
Levels: 1
Square Footage: 1,698
Bedrooms: 3
Bathrooms: 2½
Foundation: Crawl space, slab, or basement
Materials List Available: Yes
Price Category: C

Images provided by designer/architect.

CAD FILE AVAILABLE

Copyright by designer/architect.

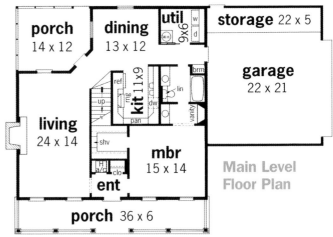

Main Level Floor Plan

porch 14 x 12

dining 13 x 12

util 9 x 6

storage 22 x 5

garage 22 x 21

living 24 x 14

kit 11 x 9

mbr 15 x 14

ent

porch 36 x 6

Plan #211069

Dimensions: 58' W x 42' D
Levels: 1½
Square Footage: 1,600
Main Level Sq. Ft.: 1,136
Upper Level Sq. Ft.: 464
Bedrooms: 3
Bathrooms: 2
Foundation: Crawl space
Materials List Available: Yes
Price Category: C

Images provided by designer/architect.

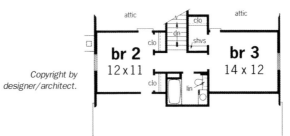

Copyright by designer/architect.

attic

br 2 12 x 11

br 3 14 x 12

attic

Upper Level Floor Plan

Plan #421012

Dimensions: 64'4" W x 56'4" D
Levels: 2
Square Footage: 2,795
Main Level Sq. Ft.: 1,787
Upper Level Sq. Ft.: 1,008
Bedrooms: 4
Bathrooms: 3½
Foundation: Crawl space, slab, or basement
Materials List Available: Yes
Price Category: F

Images provided by designer/architect.

Main Level Floor Plan

MASTER BEDROOM 14'-0"x17'-0" (11' TRAY)

COVERED PORCH 29'-0"x8'-0"

NOOK 11'-3"x10'-0" (9' CLG)

GREAT ROOM 28'-5"x19'-5" (9' CLG)

MASTER BATH

LAUNDRY/ 1/2 BATH

KITCHEN 11'-3"x 11'-4" (9' CLG)

GARAGE 24'-0"x22'-0" (9'-6" CLG)

DINING ROOM 11'-0"x15'-8" (9' CLG)

FOYER 9' CLG

PWDR

WRAP AROUND PORCH 25'-0"x8'-0"

Upper Level Floor Plan

FUTURE (UNFINISHED) 18'-5"x18'-7" (8' CLG)

BEDROOM #4 10'-10"x11'-0" (8' CLG)

BEDROOM #3 10'-10"x11'-0" (8' CLG)

BEDROOM #2 11'-0"x13'-0" (8' CLG)

FAMILY ROOM 16'-1"x19'-1" (VAULTED)

Copyright by designer/architect.

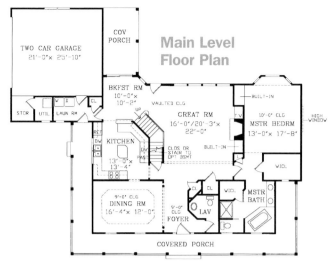

Main Level Floor Plan

Images provided by designer/architect.

Upper Level Floor Plan

Copyright by designer/architect.

Plan #131046

Dimensions: 68' W x 57'6" D
Levels: 2
Square Footage: 2,245
Main Level Sq. Ft.: 1,720
Upper Level Sq. Ft.: 525
Bedrooms: 3
Bathrooms: 2½
Foundation: Crawl space, slab, or basement
Materials List Available: Yes
Price Category: F

Main Level Floor Plan

Images provided by designer/architect.

Alternate Main Level Floor Plan

Alternate Main Level Floor Plan

Copyright by designer/architect.

Upper Level Floor Plan

Alternate Upper Level Floor Plan

Alternate Upper Level Floor Plan

Plan #421019

Dimensions: 71'10" W x 44'7" D
Levels: 2
Square Footage: 2,750
Main Level Sq. Ft.: 1,700
Upper Level Sq. Ft.: 1,050
Bedrooms: 5
Bathrooms: 3½
Foundation: Crawl space, slab, or basement
Materials List Available: Yes
Price Category: F

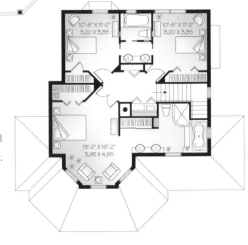

Main Level Floor Plan

Images provided by designer/architect.

Plan #181291

Dimensions: 32' W x 34' D
Levels: 2
Square Footage: 1,898
Main Level Sq. Ft.: 949
Upper Level Sq. Ft.: 949
Bedrooms: 3
Bathrooms: 2½
Foundation: Basement
Materials List Available: Yes
Price Category: D

Upper Level Floor Plan

Copyright by designer/architect.

Main Level Floor Plan

Images provided by designer/architect.

Copyright by designer/architect.

Plan #421025

Dimensions: 71'8" W x 57' D
Levels: 2
Square Footage: 2,599
Main Level Sq. Ft.: 1,602
Upper Level Sq. Ft.: 997
Bedrooms: 5
Bathrooms: 2½
Foundation: Crawl space, slab, or basement
Materials List Available: Yes
Price Category: E

Alternate Foyer Area Floor Plan

Upper Level Floor Plan

Plan #121014

Dimensions: 52' W x 47'4" D
Levels: 2
Square Footage: 1,869
Main Level Sq. Ft.: 1,421
Upper Level Sq. Ft.: 448
Bedrooms: 3
Bathrooms: 2½
Foundation: Basement
Materials List Available: Yes
Price Category: D

Images provided by designer/architect.

This compact home is packed with all the amenities you'll need for a gracious lifestyle.

Features:

• Ceiling Height: 8 ft. except as noted.

• Great Room: A soaring ceiling and six tall transom-topped windows make this a light and airy spot for entertaining.

• Formal Dining Room: This elegant room is ideal for entertaining dinner guests.

• Breakfast Area: This sunny area shares a see-through fireplace with the great room. It's the perfect place to start the day.

• Master Suite: Here are all the features you expect to find in large luxury homes. Wake up to tall, sloped ceilings, and enjoy the corner whirlpool, separate shower, and vanity. A large walk-in closet provides plenty of wardrobe storage.

• Attached Garage: The garage provides two bays of parking plus plenty of storage space.

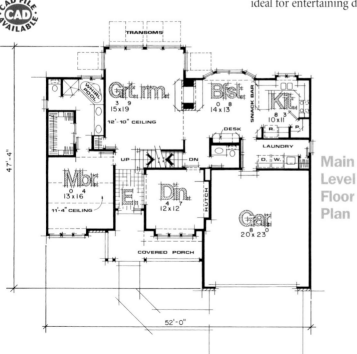

Main Level Floor Plan

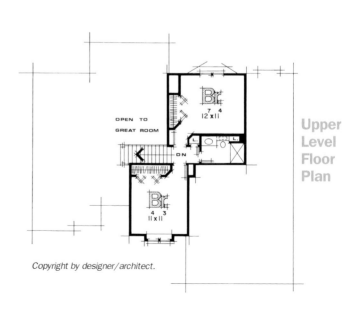

Upper Level Floor Plan

Copyright by designer/architect.

Plan #151537

Dimensions: 70'2" W x 53'4" D
Levels: 2
Square Footage: 2,603
Main Level Sq. Ft.: 1,813
Upper Level Sq. Ft.: 790
Bedrooms: 4
Bathrooms: 2½
Foundation: Crawl space or slab
CompleteCost List Available: Yes
Price Category: F

Images provided by designer/architect.

Eye-catching covered porches and columns are used on both the front and rear of this traditional home.

Features:

- **Great Room:** A vaulted ceiling, balcony, and built-in media center enhance this great room, which is open to the kitchen and breakfast room.

- **Kitchen:** This large kitchen, with a raised bar, has an abundance of cabinets and a walk-in pantry.

- **Master Suite:** This suite and an additional bedroom or study are located on the main level for privacy and convenience.

- **Upper Level:** The upstairs has a balcony overlooking the great room. In addition, it has two bedrooms, a full bathroom, a built-in computer nook, and a large bonus room.

Main Level Floor Plan

Upper Level Floor Plan

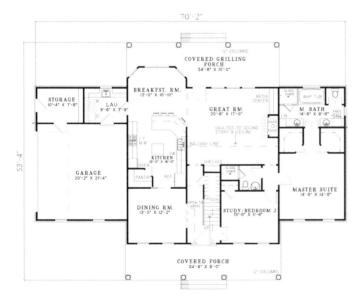

Copyright by designer/architect.

Plan #101014

Dimensions: 52' W x 28' D
Levels: 2
Square Footage: 1,598
Main Level Sq. Ft.: 812
Upper Level Sq. Ft.: 786
Bedrooms: 3
Bathrooms: 2½
Foundation: Slab, crawl space
Materials List Available: No
Price Category: C

Images provided by designer/architect.

This lovely Victorian home has a perfect balance of ornamental features and modern amenities.

Features:

- Ceiling Height: 8 ft. unless otherwise noted.

- Foyer: An impressive beveled glass-front door invites you into this roomy foyer.

- Kitchen: This bright and open kitchen offers an abundance of counter space to make cooking a pleasure.

- Breakfast Room: You'll enjoy plenty of informal family meals in this sunny and open spot next to the kitchen.

- Family Room: The whole family will be attracted to this handsome room. A full-width bay window adds to the Victorian charm.

- Master Suite: This dramatic suite features a multi-faceted vaulted ceiling and his and her closets and vanities. A separate shower and 6-ft. garden tub complete the lavish appointments.

CAD FILE AVAILABLE

Main Level Floor Plan

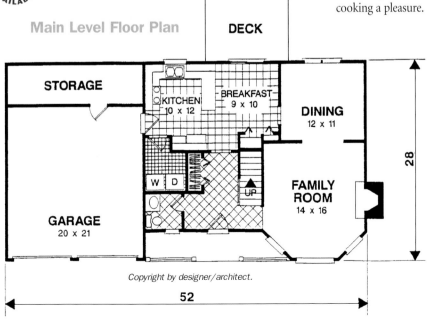

Copyright by designer/architect.

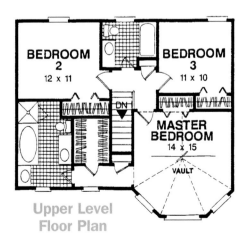

Upper Level Floor Plan

Main Level Floor Plan

Images provided by designer/architect.

Copyright by designer/architect.

Plan #181243

Dimensions: 67' W x 40' D
Levels: 2
Square Footage: 2,219
Main Level Sq. Ft.: 1,232
Upper Level Sq. Ft.: 987
Bedrooms: 3
Bathrooms: 3½
Foundation: Basement
Materials List Available: Yes
Price Category: E

Upper Level Floor Plan

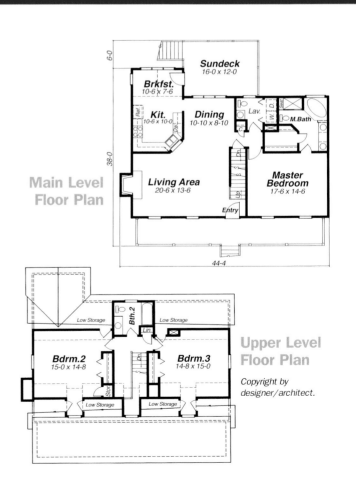

Main Level Floor Plan

Upper Level Floor Plan

Copyright by designer/architect.

Images provided by designer/architect.

Plan #141012

Dimensions: 44'4" W x 38' D
Levels: 2
Square Footage: 1,870
Main Level Sq. Ft.: 1,159
Upper Level Sq. Ft.: 711
Bedrooms: 3
Bathrooms: 2½
Foundation: Basement
Materials List Available: Yes
Price Category: D

Plan #151016

Dimensions: 60'2" W x 39'10" D
Levels: 2
Square Footage: 1,783;
2,107 with bonus
Main Level Sq. Ft.: 1,124
Upper Level Sq. Ft.: 659
Bonus Room Sq. Ft.: 324
Bedrooms: 3
Bathrooms: 2½
Foundation: Crawl space, slab,
or basement
CompleteCost List Available: Yes
Price Category: C

Images provided by designer/architect.

Features:

- Great Room: Enjoy the fireplace in this spacious, versatile room.
- Dining Room: Entertaining is easy, thanks to the open design with the kitchen.
- Master Suite: Luxury surrounds you in this suite, with its large walk-in closet, double vanities, and a bathroom with a whirlpool tub and separate shower.

- Upper Bedrooms: Window seats make wonderful spots for reading or relaxing, and a nook between the windows of these rooms is a ready-made play area.
- Bonus Area: Located over the garage, this space could be converted to a home office, a studio, or a game room for the kids.
- Attic: There's plenty of storage space here.

An open design characterizes this spacious home built for family life and entertaining.

Bonus Room Above Garage

Copyright by designer/architect.

Main Level Floor Plan

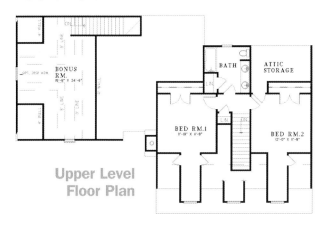

Upper Level Floor Plan

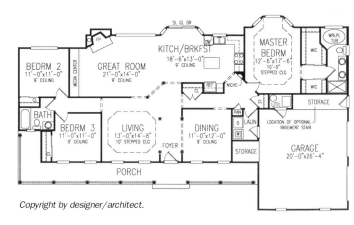

Copyright by designer/architect.

Images provided by
designer/architect.

Plan #131016

Dimensions: 75' W x 45' D

Levels: 1

Square Footage: 1,902

Bedrooms: 3

Bathrooms: 2

Foundation: Basement, crawl space,
or slab

Materials List Available: Yes

Price Category: E

Great Room

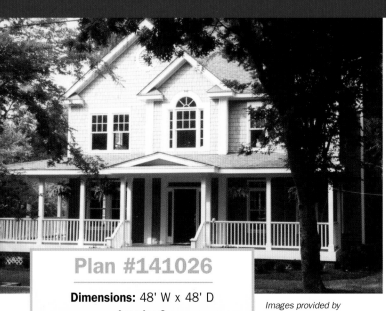

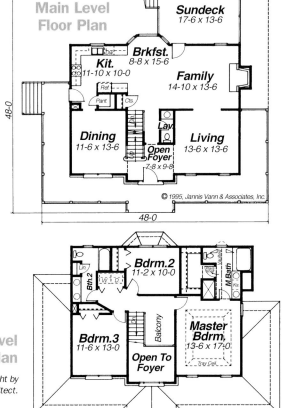

Images provided by
designer/architect.

Plan #141026

Dimensions: 48' W x 48' D

Levels: 2

Square Footage: 1,993

Main Level Sq. Ft.: 1,038

Upper Level Sq. Ft.: 955

Bedrooms: 3

Bathrooms: 2½

Foundation: Basement

Materials List Available: Yes

Price Category: D

Copyright by
designer/architect.

Plan #181310

Dimensions: 32'8" W x 42' D

Levels: 1

Square Footage: 1,094

Bedrooms: 2

Bathrooms: 1

Foundation: Basement

Materials List Available: Yes

Price Category: B

Images provided by designer/architect.

CAD FILE AVAILABLE

Copyright by designer/architect.

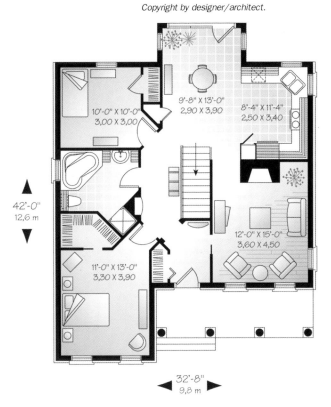

42'-0"
12,6 m

10'-0" X 10'-0"
3,00 X 3,00

9'-8" X 13'-0"
2,90 X 3,90

8'-4" X 11'-4"
2,50 X 3,40

11'-0" X 13'-0"
3,30 X 3,90

12'-0" X 15'-0"
3,60 X 4,50

32'-8"
9,8 m

Plan #281002

Dimensions: 54' W x 33' D

Levels: 2

Square Footage: 1,859

Main Level Sq. Ft.: 959

Second Level Sq. Ft.: 900

Bedrooms: 3

Bathrooms: 2½

Foundation: Basement

Materials List Available: Yes

Price Category: D

Images provided by designer/architect.

Front View

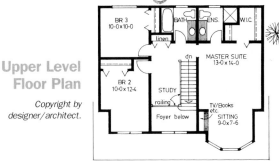

Upper Level Floor Plan

Copyright by designer/architect.

BR 3
10-0 x 10-0

BATH

ENS.

W.I.C.

linen

MASTER SUITE
13-0 x 14-0

dn

BR 2
10-0 x 12-4

STUDY

railing

Foyer below

TV/Books
etc.

SITTING
9-0 x 7-6

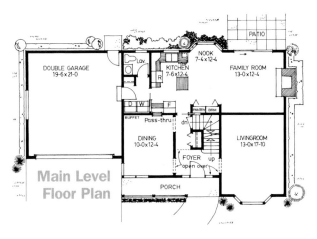

PATIO

DOUBLE GARAGE
19-6 x 21-0

Lav.

NOOK
7-4 x 12-4

KITCHEN
7-6 x 12-4

FAMILY ROOM
13-0 x 12-4

D W F

PANTRY BRM

BUFFET

Pass-thru

dn

DINING
10-0 x 12-4

FOYER
open over

up

LIVINGROOM
13-0 x 17-10

Main Level Floor Plan

PORCH

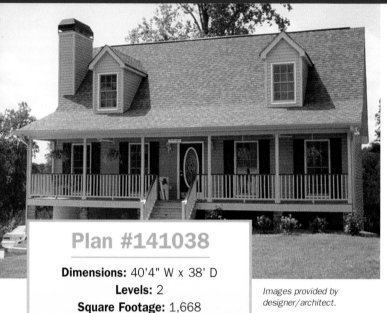

Copyright by designer/architect.

Upper Level Floor Plan

Plan #141038

Dimensions: 40'4" W x 38' D
Levels: 2
Square Footage: 1,668
Main Level Sq. Ft.: 1,057
Upper Level Sq. Ft.: 611
Bedrooms: 3
Bathrooms: 2½
Foundation: Basement with drive-under garage
Materials List Available: Yes
Price Category: C

Images provided by designer/architect.

Main Level Floor Plan

Main Level Floor Plan

Plan #181307

Dimensions: 46' W x 40' D
Levels: 2
Square Footage: 2,028
Main Level Sq. Ft.: 971
Upper Level Sq. Ft.: 1,057
Bedrooms: 3
Bathrooms: 2½
Foundation: Basement
Materials List Available: Yes
Price Category: D

Images provided by designer/architect.

Upper Level Floor Plan

Copyright by designer/architect.

Plan #221040

Dimensions: 50' W x 66' D
Levels: 1
Square Footage: 1,822
Bedrooms: 2
Bathrooms: 2
Foundation: Basement
Materials List Available: No
Price Category: D

Images provided by designer/architect.

This narrow ranch home has timeless curb appeal with its perfect combination of stone and shingle siding.

Features:

- **Kitchen:** This kitchen features a breakfast bar that overlooks both the dining room and great room, all with 11-ft.-high ceilings.

- **Master Suite:** This suite is sure to please, with its stepped ceiling, large walk-in closet, and spacious bath with Jacuzzi tub.

- **Bedroom:** The second bedroom and another full bathroom can be found at the front of the home, away from the master, for maximum privacy.

- **Garage:** This three-bay garage provides ample storage and makes the narrow home attractive for today's economically minded buyer.

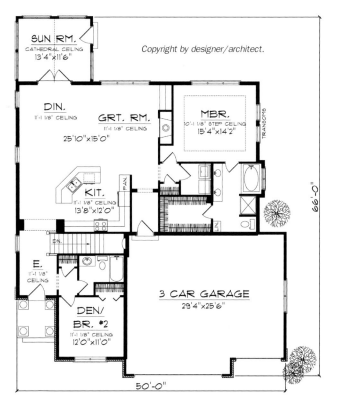

Copyright by designer/architect.

Rear Elevation

Plan #131029

Dimensions: 56'4" W x 46'6" D
Levels: 2
Square Footage: 2,936
Main Level Sq. Ft.: 1,680
Upper Level Sq. Ft.: 1,256
Bedrooms: 4
Bathrooms: 2½
Foundation: Crawl space, slab, or basement
Materials List Available: Yes
Price Category: G

Images provided by designer/architect.

This home is ideal if you love the look of a country-style farmhouse.

Features:

• **Foyer:** Walk across the large wraparound porch that defines this home to enter this two-story foyer.

• **Living Room:** French doors from the foyer lead into this living room.

• **Family Room:** The whole family will love this room, with its vaulted ceiling, fireplace, and sliding glass doors that open to the wooden rear deck.

• **Kitchen:** A beautiful sit-down center island opens to the family room. There's also a breakfast nook with a lovely bay window.

• **Master Suite:** Luxury abounds with vaulted ceilings, walk-in closets, private bath with whirlpool tub, separate shower, and dual sinks.

• **Loft:** A special place with vaulted ceiling and view into the family room below.

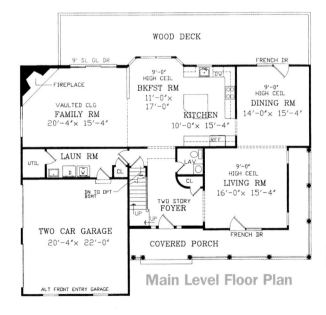

Main Level Floor Plan

Upper Level Floor Plan

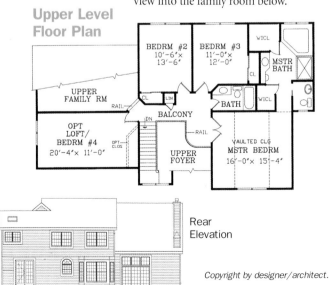

Rear Elevation

Copyright by designer/architect.

Dining Room

Breakfast Area

Kitchen Island

Kitchen

Master Bathroom

Plan #151408

Dimensions: 34'4" W x 48'4" D
Levels: 1.5
Square Footage: 1,544
Main Level Sq. Ft.: 1,031
Upper Level Sq. Ft.: 513
Bedrooms: 3
Bathrooms: 2
Foundation: Crawl space
CompleteCost List Available: Yes
Price Category: C

Images provided by designer/architect.

This cozy cottage will make the perfect year-round or weekend getaway home.

Features:

- Great Room: Enter this large room from the entry porch. Feel the warmth from the stone fireplace rising up through the vaulted ceiling.

- Kitchen: The L-shaped design and large island make this kitchen ideal for daily meals or entertaining.

- Dining Room: This dining room has a door to the rear grilling porch and is open to the kitchen, giving it a large, open feeling.

- Loft: This area has an ample amount of storage, plus a third bedroom and full bathroom.

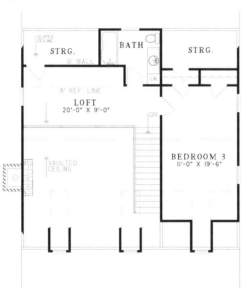

Upper Level Floor Plan

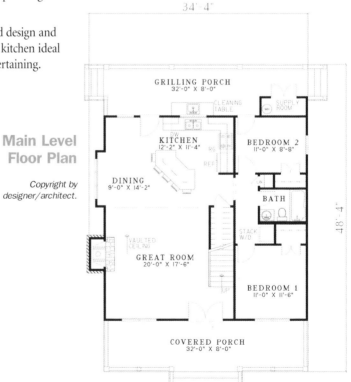

Main Level Floor Plan

Copyright by designer/architect.

Plan #441032

Dimensions: 45' W x 55' D
Levels: 2
Square Footage: 1,944
Main Level Sq. Ft.: 1,514
Upper Level Sq. Ft.: 430
Bedrooms: 3
Bathrooms: 2½
Foundation: Crawl space; slab or basement available for fee
Materials List Available: No
Price Category: D

It's the little things—decorative eave vents, wooden shutters, a porch column, and multiple-pane windows—that create the initial impression of this home.

Features:

• Great Design: The master suite is on the main level, while family bedrooms are upstairs, creating convenient separation and allowing full livability of the main level for empty nesters.

• Kitchen: This kitchen features an island work area and has the use of a walk-in pantry just around the corner.

• Master Suite: Don't overlook amenities in this suite: a large walk-in closet, a fully appointed bath, and a lovely wide window with views of the backyard.

• Garage: This garage holds extra space that can become a workshop, if you choose, or a place for those coveted big-boy toys.

Images provided by designer/architect.

Main Level Floor Plan

Upper Level Floor Plan

Copyright by designer/architect.

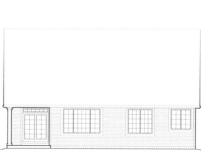

Rear Elevation

Plan #181308

Dimensions: 50'4" W x 48' D

Levels: 1

Square Footage: 2,161

Bedrooms: 3

Bathrooms: 2

Foundation: Basement

Materials List Available: Yes

Price Category: D

Images provided by designer/architect.

Copyright by designer/architect.

Plan #421005

Dimensions: 51' W x 50'9" D

Levels: 2

Square Footage: 1,784

Main Level Sq. Ft.: 1,112

Upper Level Sq. Ft.: 672

Bedrooms: 3

Bathrooms: 2½

Foundation: Crawl space, slab, or basement

Materials List Available: Yes

Price Category: C

Images provided by designer/architect.

Main Level Floor Plan

Upper Level Floor Plan

Copyright by designer/architect.

Plan #181306

Dimensions: 54' W x 42' D
Levels: 2
Square Footage: 2,768
Main Level Sq. Ft.: 1,296
Upper Level Sq. Ft.: 1,472
Bedrooms: 4
Bathrooms: 3½
Foundation: Basement
Materials List Available: Yes
Price Category: F

Images provided by designer/architect.

Main Level Floor Plan

Upper Level Floor Plan

Copyright by designer/architect.

Plan #121021

Dimensions: 46' W x 48' D
Levels: 2
Square Footage: 2,270
Main Level Sq. Ft.: 1,150
Upper Level Sq. Ft.: 1,120
Bedrooms: 4
Bathrooms: 2½
Foundation: Basement
Materials List Available: Yes
Price Category: E

Images provided by designer/architect.

This home, as shown in the photograph, may differ from the actual blueprints. For more detailed information, please check the floor plans carefully.

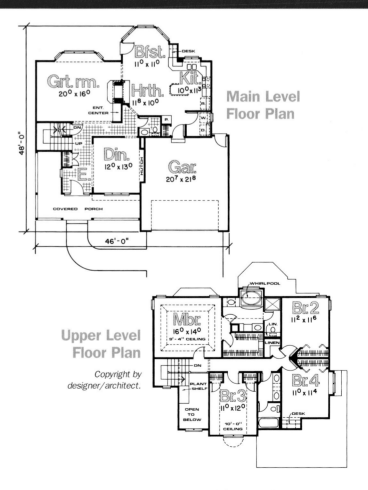

Main Level Floor Plan

Upper Level Floor Plan

Copyright by designer/architect.

Copyright by designer/architect.

Main Level Floor Plan

Images provided by designer/architect.

CAD FILE AVAILABLE · CAD

Plan #181305

Dimensions: 56'4" W x 65'4" D

Levels: 2

Square Footage: 3,085

Main Level Sq. Ft.: 2,018

Upper Level Sq. Ft.: 1,067

Bedrooms: 4

Bathrooms: 2½

Foundation: Basement

Materials List Available: Yes

Price Category: G

Upper Level Floor Plan

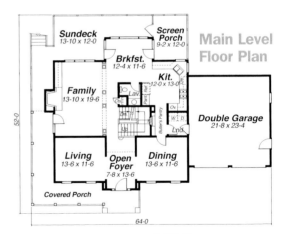

Plan #141016

Dimensions: 64' W x 52' D

Levels: 2

Square Footage: 2,416

Main Level Sq. Ft.: 1,250

Upper Level Sq. Ft.: 1,166

Bedrooms: 4

Bathrooms: 2½

Foundation: Basement

Materials List Available: Yes

Price Category: E

Images provided by designer/architect.

Main Level Floor Plan

Sundeck 13-10 x 12-0

Screen Porch 9-2 x 12-0

Brkfst. 12-4 x 11-6

Kit. 12-0 x 13-0

Family 13-10 x 19-6

Double Garage 21-8 x 23-4

Living 13-6 x 11-6

Open Foyer 7-8 x 13-6

Dining 13-6 x 11-6

Covered Porch

52-0

64-0

Upper Level Floor Plan

Sundeck 9-2 x 12-0

Bdrm. 4 13-6 x 11-6

Master Bdrm. 12-4 x 17-6

M.Bath

Bath 2

Storage

Bdrm. 3 13-6 x 11-6

Open Foyer

Bdrm. 2 13-6 x 11-6

Copyright by designer/architect.

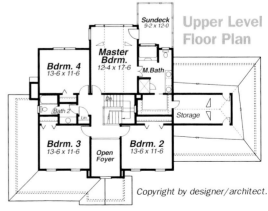

Plan #131043

Dimensions: 65'8" W x 43'10" D
Levels: 2
Square Footage: 1,945
Main Level Sq. Ft.: 1,375
Upper Level Sq. Ft.: 570
Bedrooms: 3
Bathrooms: 2½
Foundation: Crawl space, slab, or basement
Materials List Available: Yes
Price Category: D

Images provided by designer/architect.

This home will delight you with its three dormers and half-round transom windows, which give a nostalgic appearance, and its amenities and conveniences that are certainly contemporary.

Features:

• Porch: This covered porch forms the entryway.

• Great Room: Enjoy the fireplace in this large, comfortable room, which is open to the dining area. A French door here leads to the

covered porch at the rear of the house.

• Kitchen: This large, country-style kitchen has a bayed nook, and oversized breakfast bar, and pass-through to the rear porch to simplify serving and make entertaining a pleasure.

• Master Suite: A tray ceiling sets an elegant tone for this room, and the bay window adds to it. The large walk-in closet is convenient, and the bath is sumptuous.

• Bedrooms: These comfortable rooms have convenient access to a bath.

Main Level Floor Plan

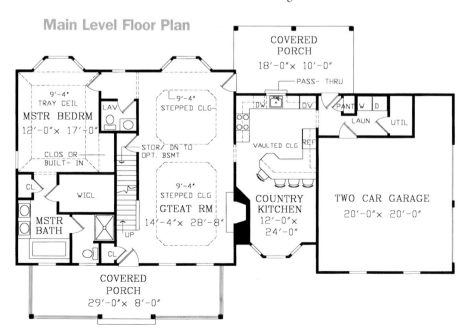

Upper Level Floor Plan

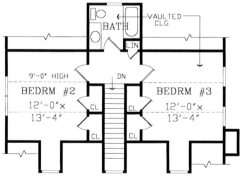

Copyright by designer/architect.

Plan #101020

Dimensions: 55'8" W x 49'2" D
Levels: 2
Square Footage: 2,972
Main Level Sq. Ft.: 1,986
Upper Level Sq. Ft.: 986
Bedrooms: 4
Bathrooms: 3½
Foundation: Basement
Materials List Available: No
Price Category: F

Images provided by designer/architect.

This luxurious country home has an open-design main level that maximizes the use of space.

Features:

- Ceiling Height: 9 ft. unless otherwise noted.

- Foyer: Guests will be greeted by this grand two-story entry, with its graceful angled staircase.

- Dining Room: At nearly 12 ft. x 15 ft., this elegant dining room has plenty of room for large parties.

- Family Room: Everyone will be drawn to this 17-ft. x 19-ft. room, with its dramatic two-story ceiling and its handsome fireplace.

- Kitchen: This spacious kitchen is open to the family room and features a breakfast bar and built-in table in the cooktop island.

- Master Suite: This elegant retreat includes a bayed 18-ft.-5-in. x 14-ft.-9-in. bedroom and a beautiful corner his and her bath/closet arrangement.

- Secondary Bedrooms: Upstairs you'll find three spacious bathrooms, one with a private bath and two with access to a shared bath.

Main Level Floor Plan

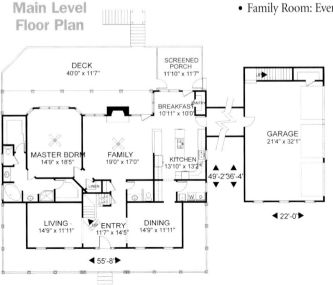

Upper Level Floor Plan

Copyright by designer/architect.

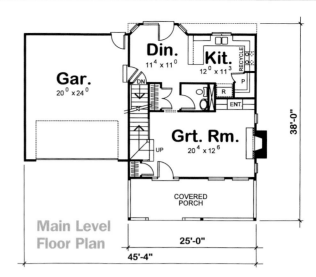

Main Level Floor Plan

Gar. 20⁰ x 24⁰
Din. 11⁴ x 11⁰
Kit. 12⁰ x 11³
Grt. Rm. 20⁴ x 12⁶
COVERED PORCH

38'-0"
25'-0"
45'-4"

Plan #121035

Dimensions: 45'4" W x 38' D
Levels: 2
Square Footage: 1,471
Main Level Sq. Ft.: 716
Upper Level Sq. Ft.: 755
Bedrooms: 3
Bathrooms: 2½
Foundation: Basement
Materials List Available: Yes
Price Category: B

Images provided by designer/architect.

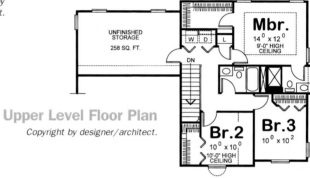

Upper Level Floor Plan
Copyright by designer/architect.

UNFINISHED STORAGE 258 SQ. FT.
Mbr. 14⁰ x 12⁰ 9'-0" HIGH CEILING
Br.2 10⁰ x 10⁰ 10'-0" HIGH CEILING
Br.3 10⁰ x 10²

Plan #441009

Dimensions: 94' W x 53' D
Levels: 1
Square Footage: 2,650
Bedrooms: 4
Bathrooms: 2½
Foundation: Crawl space;
slab or basement available for fee
Materials List Available: No
Price Category: F

Images provided by designer/architect.

Copyright by designer/architect.

Rear Elevation

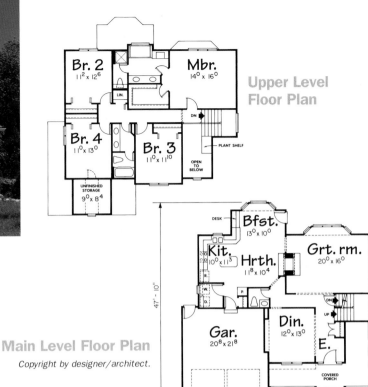

Images provided by designer/architect.

Upper Level Floor Plan

Main Level Floor Plan

Copyright by designer/architect.

Plan #121037

Dimensions: 46' W x 47'10" D
Levels: 2
Square Footage: 2,292
Main Level Sq. Ft.: 1,158
Upper Level Sq. Ft.: 1,134
Bedrooms: 4
Bathrooms: 2½
Foundation: Basement
Materials List Available: Yes
Price Category: E

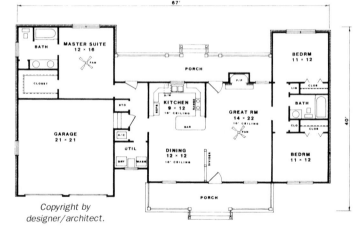

Copyright by designer/architect.

Images provided by designer/architect.

Plan #171002

Dimensions: 67' W x 40' D
Levels: 1
Square Footage: 1,458
Bedrooms: 3
Bathrooms: 2
Foundation: Crawl space, slab
Materials List Available: Yes
Price Category: B

SMARTtip

Accent Landscape Lighting

Accent highlights elements in your landscape. It creates ambiance and helps integrate the garden with the deck. Conventional low-voltage floodlights are excellent for creating effects such as wall grazing, silhouetting, and uplighting.

**Main Level
Floor Plan**

*Images provided by
designer/architect.*

CAD FILE AVAILABLE

Plan #181300

Dimensions: 58' W x 43' D
Levels: 2
Square Footage: 2,149
Main Level Sq. Ft.: 1,337
Upper Level Sq. Ft.: 812
Bedrooms: 4
Bathrooms: 3½
Foundation: Basement
Materials List Available: Yes
Price Category: D

**Upper Level
Floor Plan**

*Copyright by
designer/architect.*

**Main
Level
Floor
Plan**

Copyright by designer/architect.

*Images provided by
designer/architect.*

CAD FILE AVAILABLE

Plan #181302

Dimensions: 48' W x 62' D
Levels: 2
Square Footage: 3,719
Main Level Sq. Ft.: 2,452
Upper Level Sq. Ft.: 1,267
Bedrooms: 3
Bathrooms: 3½
Foundation: Basement
Materials List Available: No
Price Category: H

**Upper Level
Floor Plan**

Plan #131013

Dimensions: 50' W x 41'8" D
Levels: 1
Square Footage: 1,489
Bedrooms: 3
Bathrooms: 2
Foundation: Crawl space, slab or basement
Materials List Available: Yes
Price Category: C

You'll love the Victorian details on the exterior of this charming ranch-style home.

Features:

• Front Porch: This porch is large enough so that you can sit out on warm summer nights to catch a breeze or create a garden of potted ornamentals.

• Great Room: Running from the front of the house to the rear, this great room is bathed in natural light from both directions. The volume ceiling adds a luxurious feeling to it, and the fireplace creates a cozy place on chilly afternoons.

• Kitchen: Cooking will be a pleasure in this kitchen, thanks to the thoughtful layout and well-designed work areas.

• Master Suite: Enjoy the quiet in this room, where it will be easy to relax and unwind, no matter what the time of day. The walk-in closet gives you plenty of storage space, and you're sure to appreciate both the privacy and large size of the master bath.

Images provided by designer/architect.

Copyright by designer/architect.

Rear Elevation

Plan #151413

Dimensions: 32' W x 42' D

Levels: 1.5

Square Footage: 1,400

Main Level Sq. Ft.: 948

Upper Level Sq. Ft.: 452

Bedrooms: 2

Bathrooms: 2

Foundation: Crawl space or slab

CompleteCost List Available: Yes

Price Category: B

Images provided by designer/architect.

Relax on the front porch of this lovely little cottage. It's a great starter home or a weekend getaway.

Features:

• Great Room: Enter from the front porch into this large room, with its vaulted ceiling and stone fireplace.

• Kitchen: This large kitchen has plenty of cabinets and counter space; there is even a raised bar.

• Grilling Porch: Just off the kitchen is this porch. Bedroom 1 has access to this area as well.

• Upper Level: Located on this level are a loft area, a full bathroom, and a bedroom.

32'-0"

GRILLING PORCH
15'-8" X 8'-0"

BEDROOM 1
12'-4" X 11'-4"

KITCHEN
15'-4" X 11'-10"

BATH

STACKED W/D

42'-0"

Main Level Floor Plan

BALCONY LINE

GREAT RM.
17'-0" X 16'-2"

DINING
10'-6" X 13'-6"

VAULTED CEILING OPEN TO ABOVE

UP

COVERED PORCH
32'-0" X 8'-0"

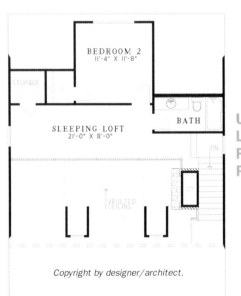

BEDROOM 2
11'-4" X 11'-8"

STORAGE

BATH

SLEEPING LOFT
21'-0" X 8'-0"

Upper Level Floor Plan

DN

VAULTED CEILING

Copyright by designer/architect.

Plan #121045

Dimensions: 40' W x 48' D

Levels: 2

Square Footage: 1,575

Main Level Sq. Ft.: 787

Upper Level Sq. Ft.: 788

Bedrooms: 3

Bathrooms: 2½

Foundation: Basement

Materials List Available: Yes

Price Category: C

This home, as shown in the photograph, may differ from the actual blue-prints. For more detailed information, please check the floor plans carefully.

Images provided by designer/architect.

This home is carefully laid out to provide the convenience demanded by busy family life.

Features:

• Ceiling Height: 8 ft.

• Family Room: This charming family room, with its fireplace and built-in cabinetry, will become the central gathering place for family and friends.

• Kitchen: This kitchen offers a central island that makes food preparation more convenient and doubles

as a snack bar for a quick bite on the run. The breakfast area features a pantry and planning desk.

• Computer Loft: The second-floor landing includes this loft designed to accommodate the family computer.

• Room to Grow: Also on the second-floor landing you will find a large unfinished area waiting to accommodate the growing family.

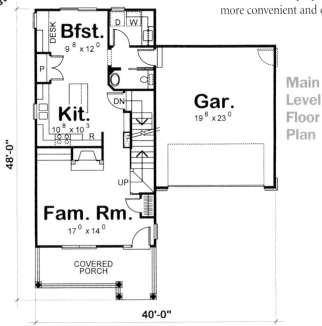

Main
Level
Floor
Plan

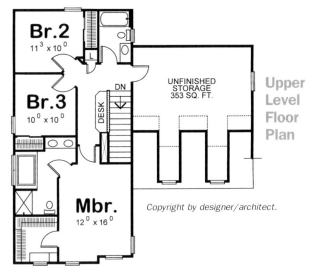

Upper
Level
Floor
Plan

Copyright by designer/architect.

Main Level Floor Plan

NOOK 8/8 X 8/10

DINING 9/10 X 10/4

VAULTED MASTER 16/0 X 11/10

TWO STORY GREAT RM. 15/10 X 19/8

GARAGE 19/4 X 21/8

◄ 40' ► ▲ 53' ▼

Images provided by designer/architect.

Plan #441017

Dimensions: 40' W x 53' D
Levels: 2
Square Footage: 1,707
Main Level Sq. Ft.: 1,230
Upper Level Sq. Ft.: 477
Bedrooms: 3
Bathrooms: 2½
Foundation: Crawl space; slab or basement available for fee
Materials List Available: No
Price Category: C

BR. 3 12/6 X 12/2 +/-

BR. 2 10/9 X 12/2 +/-

OPEN TO GREAT RM. BELOW

BONUS RM. 13/6 X 12/6

ATTIC STORAGE

Upper Level Floor Plan

Copyright by designer/architect.

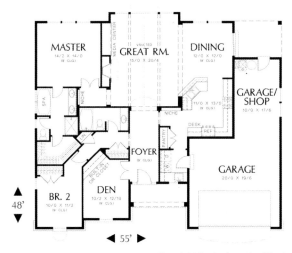

MASTER 14/2 X 14/0 (9' CLG.)

VAULTED GREAT RM. 15/0 X 20/4

DINING 12/0 X 12/0 (9' CLG.)

GARAGE/ SHOP 10/0 X 17/6

FOYER (9' CLG.)

GARAGE 20/0 X 19/6

BR. 2 10/0 X 11/2 (9' CLG.)

DEN 10/2 X 12/10 (9' CLG.)

▲ 48' ▼

◄ 55' ►

Images provided by designer/architect.

Copyright by designer/architect.

Plan #441004

Dimensions: 55' W x 48' D
Levels: 1
Square Footage: 1,728
Bedrooms: 2
Bathrooms: 2
Foundation: Crawl space; slab or basement available for fee
Materials List Available: No
Price Category: C

Rear Elevation

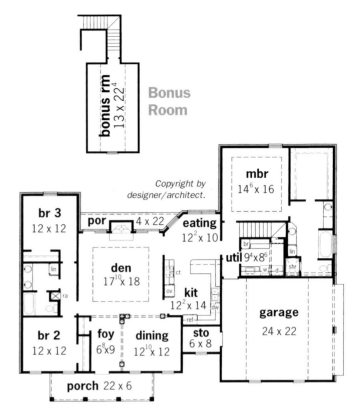

Bonus Room

bonus rm 13 x 22⁴

Copyright by designer/architect.

mbr 14⁶ x 16

br 3 12 x 12

por 4 x 22

eating 12² x 10

den 17¹⁰ x 18

util 9⁴ x 8⁶

kit 12² x 14

garage 24 x 22

br 2 12 x 12

foy 6⁸ x 9

dining 12¹⁰ x 12

sto 6 x 8

porch 22 x 6

Plan #201084

Dimensions: 66'10" W x 54'5" D

Levels: 1

Square Footage: 2,056

Bedrooms: 3

Bathrooms: 2

Foundation: Crawl space, slab

Materials List Available: Yes

Price Category: D

Images provided by designer/architect.

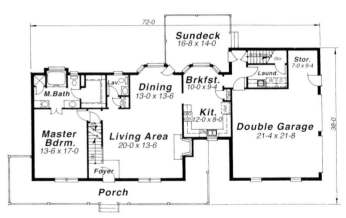

Main Level Floor Plan

72-0

Sundeck 16-8 x 14-0

M.Bath

Dining 13-0 x 13-6

Brkfst. 10-0 x 9-4

Laund.

Stor. 7-0 x 9-4

Master Bdrm. 13-6 x 17-0

Living Area 20-0 x 13-6

Kit. 12-0 x 8-0

Double Garage 21-4 x 21-8

38-0

Foyer

Porch

Plan #141014

Dimensions: 72' W x 38' D

Levels: 2

Square Footage: 2,091

Main Level Sq. Ft.: 1,362

Upper Level Sq. Ft.: 729

Bedrooms: 3

Bathrooms: 2½

Foundation: Basement

Materials List Available: Yes

Price Category: D

Images provided by designer/architect.

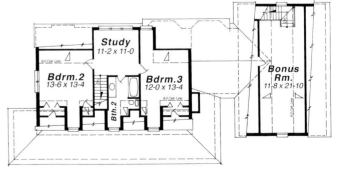

Study 11-2 x 11-0

Bdrm.2 13-6 x 13-4

Bdrm.3 12-0 x 13-4

Bth.2

Bonus Rm. 11-8 x 21-10

Copyright by designer/architect.

Upper Level Floor Plan

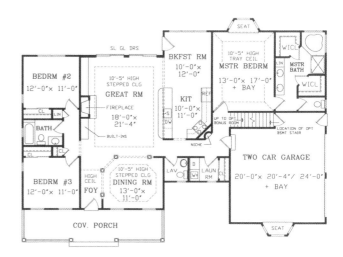

Plan #131035

Dimensions: 65'4" W x 45'10" D
Levels: 1
Square Footage: 1,892
Bedrooms: 3
Bathrooms: 2½
Foundation: Crawl space, slab, or basement
Materials List Available: Yes
Price Category: D

Images provided by designer/architect.

Rear Elevation

Bonus Area

Copyright by designer/architect.

Plan #131041

Dimensions: 42' W x 45' D
Levels: 2
Square Footage: 1,679
Main Level Sq. Ft.: 1,134
Upper Level Sq. Ft.: 545
Bedrooms: 3
Bathrooms: 2½
Foundation: Crawl space, slab, or basement
Materials List Available: Yes
Price Category: D

Images provided by designer/architect.

Great Room

Main Level Floor Plan

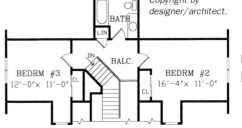

Copyright by designer/architect.

Upper Level Floor Plan

Plan #351069

Dimensions: 78' W x 49'6" D
Levels: 1
Square Footage: 2,008
Bedrooms: 3
Bathrooms: 2½
Foundation: Crawl space or slab
Materials List Available: No
Price Category: F

This is a great house with a functional split-floor-plan layout.

Features:

- **Entertaining Areas:** A large dining area for those family get-togethers and an expansive great room with a gas log fireplace and vaulted ceiling will make entertaining easy.

- **Master Suite:** This expansive suite has a large sitting area, his and her walk-in closets, a jetted tub, and a walk-in shower.

- **Storage Areas:** The home features plenty of storage space; a large utility room will help stow away your odds and ends.

- **Expansion:** Flex space can be used as a home office/study, playroom, and/or entertainment center. There is even a bonus room above the garage.

Images provided by designer/architect.

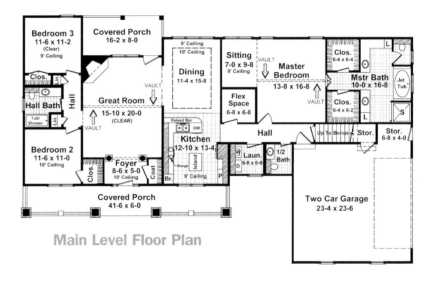

Main Level Floor Plan

Upper Level Floor Plan

Copyright by designer/architect.

Plan #131001

Dimensions: 72'4" W x 32'4" D
Levels: 1
Square Footage: 1,615
Bedrooms: 3
Bathrooms: 2
Foundation: Crawl space, slab, basement, or walkout
Materials List Available: Yes
Price Category: D

Cathedral ceilings and illuminating skylights add drama and beauty to this practical ranch house.

Features:

• Ceiling Height: 8 ft.

• Front Porch: Watch the rain in comfort from the covered front porch.

• Foyer: The stone-tiled foyer flows into the living areas.

• Living Room: Oriented towards the front of the house, the living room opens to the dining room and shares a lovely three-sided fireplace with the family room.

• Family Room: Conveniently located to share the fireplace with the living room, this room is bright and cheery thanks to its skylights as well as the sliding glass doors that open onto the rear patio.

• Kitchen: An island makes this sunny room both efficient and attractive.

Images provided by designer/architect.

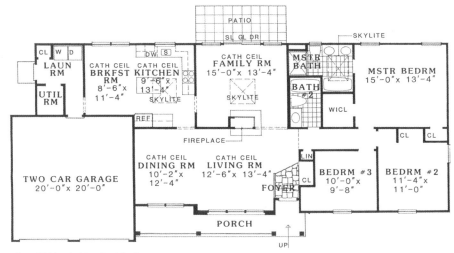

Copyright by designer/architect.

• Breakfast Nook: Located just off the kitchen, this area can serve double-duty as a spot for kitchen visitors to sit.

• Dining Room: The open design between the dining and living rooms adds to the spacious feeling that the cathedral ceiling creates in this area.

• Laundry Room: This area opens from the kitchen for convenience.

• Master Suite: A walk-in closet makes this room practical, but the master bathroom with a skylight, dual-sink vanity, soaking tub, and separate shower makes it luxurious.

• Bedrooms: The two additional bedrooms share a bathroom.

Plan #151411

Dimensions: 44'2" W x 39' D
Levels: 1.5
Square Footage: 1,472
Main Level Sq. Ft.: 1,140
Upper Level Sq. Ft.: 332
Bedrooms: 4
Bathrooms: 2
Foundation: Crawl space or slab
CompleteCost List Available: Yes
Price Category: B

Images provided by designer/architect.

The front porch and roof dormers add a genuine country look to this home.

Features:

• **Great Room:** This large gathering area features a fireplace and windows looking onto the front yard.

• **Kitchen:** This large U-shaped kitchen has a raised bar and is open to the dining room.

• **Bedrooms:** Two bedrooms are located on the main level and share a common bathroom. The remaining two bedrooms are located on the upper level and share a full bathroom.

• **Loft:** This large area overlooks the great room and is ideal for extra sleeping areas for overnight guests.

Main Level Floor Plan

44'-2"

BATH

BEDROOM 1
11'-0" X 13'-0"

BEDROOM 2
10'-8" X 9'-2"

GRILLING PORCH
13'-4" X 9'-6"

CLEANING TABLE

SUPPLY ROOM

STACKED W/D

PAN

REF   RG

39'-0"

GREAT RM.
17'-0" X 16'-0"

KITCHEN
13'-4" X 12'-6"

DW

8' COVERED PORCH

DINING
13'-4" X 12'-6"

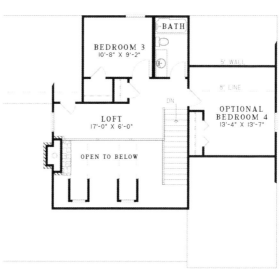

Upper Level Floor Plan
Copyright by designer/architect.

BATH

BEDROOM 3
10'-8" X 9'-2"

5' WALL

8' LINE

DN

LOFT
17'-0" X 6'-0"

OPTIONAL BEDROOM 4
13'-4" X 13'-7"

OPEN TO BELOW

Plan #121047

Dimensions: 67'8" W x 57' D

Levels: 2

Square Footage: 3,072

Main Level Sq. Ft.: 2,116

Upper Level Sq. Ft.: 956

Bedrooms: 4

Bathrooms: 3½

Foundation: Slab

Materials List Available: Yes

Price Category: G

Images provided by designer/architect.

A long porch and a trio of roof dormers give this gracious home a sophisticated country look.

Features:

- Ceiling Height: 8 ft. unless otherwise noted.

- Balcony: This balcony overlooks the entry and the staircase hall.

- Dining Room: Columns and a cased opening lend elegance, making this the perfect venue for stylish dinner parties.

- Family Room: A cathedral ceiling gives this room a light and airy feel. The handsome fireplace framed by windows is sure to become a favorite family gathering place.

- Master Bedroom: This architecturally distinctive bedroom features a bayed sitting area and a tray ceiling.

- Bedrooms: One of the bedrooms enjoys a private bath, making it a perfect guest room. Other bedrooms feature walk-in closets.

Main Level Floor Plan

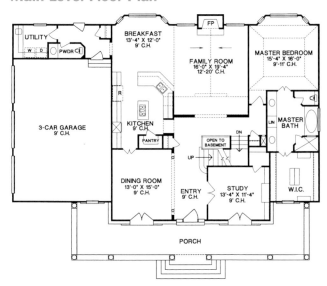

Upper Level Floor Plan

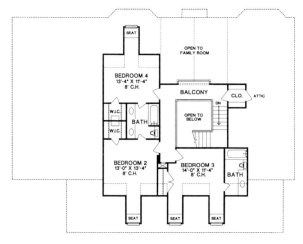

Copyright by designer/architect.

Plan #221044

Dimensions: 60'4" W x 55' D

Levels: 1

Square Footage: 1,781

Bedrooms: 3

Bathrooms: 2

Foundation: Basement

Materials List Available: No

Price Category: C

CAD FILE AVAILABLE · CAD

This adorable ranch home, with its blend of stone, shutters, and shingle siding is sure to capture your attention.

Features:

- Great Room: This spacious room shares a see-through fireplace with the den and features an 11-ft.-high ceiling.

- Kitchen: This island kitchen boasts a walk-in pantry and is open to the dining area. Just off the kitchen is a mudroom and then the garage.

- Master Suite: This suite features a large walk-in closet, spacious bath with Jacuzzi tub, and stepped ceiling in the bedroom.

- Bedrooms: On the other side of the home you'll find two additional bedrooms, one of which has a cathedral ceiling.

Images provided by designer/architect.

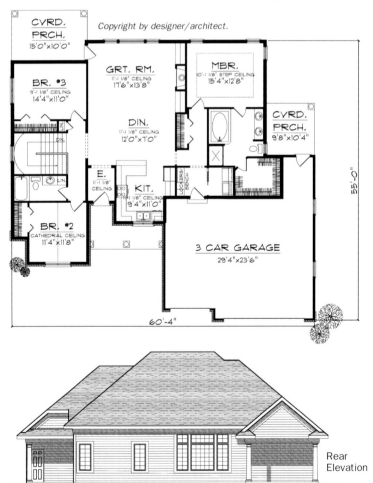

Rear Elevation

Plan #281015

Dimensions: 32' W x 48' D

Levels: 2

Square Footage: 1,660

Main Level Sq. Ft.: 964

Upper Level Sq. Ft.: 696

Bedrooms: 4

Bathrooms: 2½

Foundation: Basement

Materials List Available: Yes

Price Category: C

You'll love the gracious features and amenities in this charming home, which is meant for a narrow lot.

Features:

• Foyer: This two-story foyer opens into the spacious living room.

• Living Room: The large bay window in this room makes a perfect setting for quiet times alone or entertaining guests.

• Dining Room: The open flow between this room and the living room adds to the airy feeling.

• Family Room: With a handsome fireplace and a door to the rear patio, this room will be the heart of your home.

• Kitchen: The U-shaped layout, pantry, and greenhouse window make this room a joy.

• Master Suite: The bay window, large walk-in closet, and private bath make this second-floor room a true retreat.

Images provided by designer/architect.

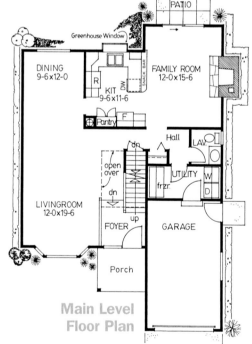

Main Level Floor Plan

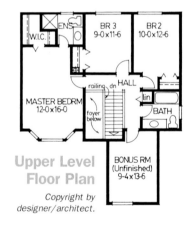

Upper Level Floor Plan

Copyright by designer/architect.

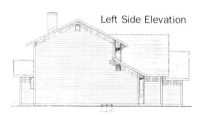

Left Side Elevation

Rear Elevation

Right Side Elevation

Images provided by designer/architect.

Plan #221041

Dimensions: 50' W x 60'4" D

Levels: 1

Square Footage: 1,627

Bedrooms: 3

Bathrooms: 2

Foundation: Basement

Materials List Available: No

Price Category: C

This narrow ranch home packs many amenities into a limited amount of square feet, making it attractive yet affordable.

Features:

• Great Design: Inside you'll find tall ceilings throughout, which only add to the overall feeling that the home is larger than it really is.

The open floor plan was carefully crafted to make use of every square inch of living space.

• Kitchen: From this kitchen you can look into both the dining room and the great room, and you'll love the breakfast bar, which provides additional eating space for family and friends.

• Master Suite: This restful retreat includes a large walk-in closet, spacious bath with

Jacuzzi tub, and stepped ceiling in the bedroom.

• Bedrooms: On the opposite side of the home you'll find two additional bedrooms, allowing for maximum privacy for mom and dad.

Rear Elevation

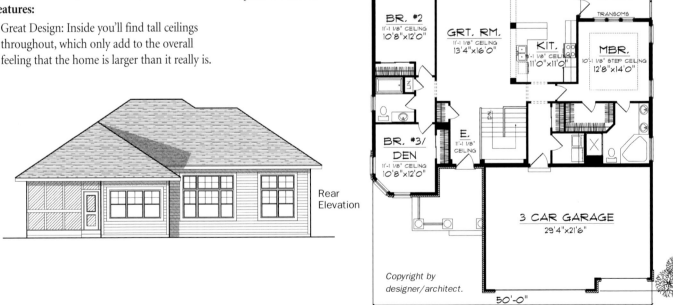

Copyright by designer/architect.

Plan #321039

Dimensions: 31'8" W x 45' D

Levels: 1

Square Footage: 1,231

Bedrooms: 2

Bathrooms: 2

Foundation: Basement

Materials List Available: Yes

Price Category: B

Images provided by designer/architect.

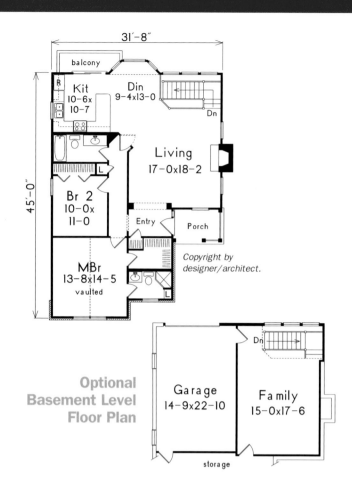

Copyright by designer/architect.

Optional Basement Level Floor Plan

Plan #221047

Dimensions: 60' W x 82' D

Levels: 1

Square Footage: 2,067

Bedrooms: 3

Bathrooms: 2

Foundation: Basement

Materials List Available: No

Price Category: D

Images provided by designer/architect.

CAD FILE AVAILABLE

Rear Elevation

Copyright by designer/architect.

Plan #131055

Dimensions: 62'4" W x 53'6" D
Levels: 1.5
Square Footage: 2,575
Main Level Sq. Ft.: 2,007
Upper Level Sq. Ft.: 568
Bedrooms: 4
Bathrooms: 3
Foundation: Crawl space, slab, or basement
Materials List Available: Yes
Price Category: E

This is a classic-looking farmhouse on the outside, but inside you will find everything today's family wants in a home.

Features:

- **Great Room:** This room has a large corner fireplace and high ceilings, and it leads directly into a grand master-bedroom suite.

- **Dining Room:** This open room looks into the great room and across the foyer into an optional fourth bedroom or study.

- **Kitchen:** With a center island workspace and a snack bar, this large, spacious kitchen opens into the bay window breakfast room.

- **Master Suite:** This private space is located on the main level away from the secondary bedrooms. It features a large bedroom and sitting area, plus a private bath.

Images provided by designer/architect.

Main Level Floor Plan

Copyright by designer/architect.

Stairs

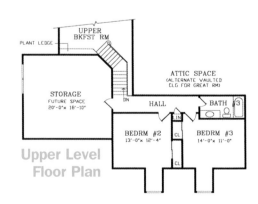

Upper Level Floor Plan

Rear View

Great Room

Kitchen

Dining Room

Master Bedroom

Master Bath

Plan #221032

Dimensions: 60' W x 55' D

Levels: 1

Square Footage: 1,844

Bedrooms: 3

Bathrooms: 2

Foundation: Basement

Materials List Available: No

Price Category: D

Three columns frame the front porch on this charming ranch home.

Features:

- **Great Room:** You'll love the view out the back of the home from the wall of windows in this room, which is sure to catch your eye as you enter.

- **Open Plan:** The kitchen, dining room, and great room all work together in this open floor plan to create volume. The three-sided fireplace, which is shared by the great room and dining room, is sure to be a crowd pleaser.

- **Master Suite:** This retreat is located on the right side of the home and features a stepped ceiling, a spacious bath with Jacuzzi tub, a walk-in closet, and an additional closet for more storage space.

- **Bedrooms:** On the opposite side of the home you'll find two additional bedrooms and a full bathroom.

Images provided by designer/architect.

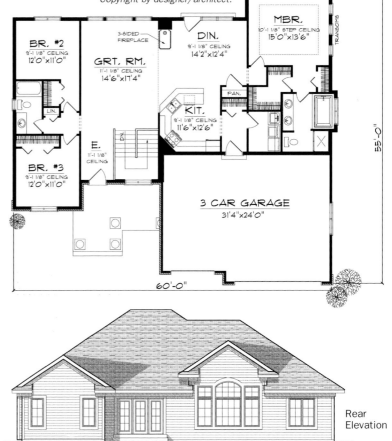

Rear Elevation

Plan #221054

Dimensions: 63'8" W x 75'4" D
Levels: 2
Square Footage: 3,206
Main Level Sq. Ft.: 2,064
Upper Level Sq. Ft.: 1,142
Bedrooms: 4
Bathrooms: 2 full, 2 half
Foundation: Basement
Materials List Available: No
Price Category: G

The large turret of this European beauty is sure to capture your attention as you enter the two-story home.

Features:

- **Great Room:** This room features a two-story ceiling, a wall of windows, and a see-through fireplace to the master suite.

- **Kitchen:** This kitchen, with its eat-in island overlooking the dining room and hearth room, works together with those two rooms to create a comfortable living area.

- **Master Suite:** You'll be impressed by the large walk-in closet of this suite, which opens directly to a main floor laundry room, as well as the spacious master bath.

- **Bedrooms:** Upstairs you can look over the railing into the great room below as you proceed to one of the three additional bedrooms. Bedroom 4 has its own full bathroom, while the remaining two share a Jack and Jill bathroom.

Images provided by designer/architect.

Upper Level Floor Plan
Copyright by designer/architect.

Rear Elevation

Main Level Floor Plan

Plan #181081

Dimensions: 58' W x 33' D
Levels: 2
Square Footage: 2,350
Main Level Sq. Ft.: 1,107
Second Level Sq. Ft.: 1,243
Bedrooms: 3
Bathrooms: 2½
Foundation: Basement
Materials List Available: Yes
Price Category: E

Images provided by designer/architect.

This traditional country home features a wrap-around porch and a second-floor balcony.

Features:

- Ceiling Height: 8 ft. unless otherwise noted.

- Family Room: Double French doors and a fireplace in this inviting front room enhance the beauty and warmth of the home's open floor plan.

- Kitchen: You'll love working in this bright and convenient kitchen. The breakfast bar is the perfect place to gather for informal meals.

- Master Suite: You'll look forward to retiring to this elegant upstairs suite at the end of a busy day. The suite features a private bath with separate shower and tub, as well as dual vanities.

- Secondary Bedrooms: Two family bedrooms share a full bath with a third room that opens onto the balcony.

- Basement: An unfinished full basement provides plenty of storage and the potential to add additional finished living space.

Main Level Floor Plan

Copyright by designer/architect.

Upper Level Floor Plan

Plan #441019

Dimensions: 38' W x 35' D
Levels: 3
Square Footage: 2,044
Main Level Sq. Ft.: 1,106
Upper Level Sq. Ft.: 872
Lower Level Sq. Ft.: 66
Bedrooms: 3
Bathrooms: 2½
Foundation: Slab
Materials List Available: No
Price Category: D

Designed for a sloping lot, this tri-level home intrigues the eye and lifts the spirits.

Features:

• Open Plan: Sunlight filters into the grand two-story foyer and living room from tall windows.

• Living Room: From the loft overlooking this room you can view flames dancing in the fireplace, which is shared by the family room.

• Dining Room: From the windows or optional French doors in this space you can behold the outdoor vista.

• Kitchen: This spacious kitchen houses an island with a downdraft cooktop. Serve food informally in front of the breakfast-nook windows or at the island.

• Master Suite: This master bedroom is embellished with a vaulted ceiling and elegant front-facing windows; the attached master bath has a separate tub and shower and a private toilet enclosure.

Images provided by designer/architect.

Main Level Floor Plan

Garage Level Floor Plan

Copyright by designer/architect.

Upper Level Floor Plan

Rear Elevation

Plan #441025

Dimensions: 70' W x 101'6" D
Levels: 2
Square Footage: 3,457
Main Level Sq. Ft.: 2,222
Upper Level Sq. Ft.: 1,235
Bedrooms: 4
Bathrooms: 3 full, 2 half
Foundation: Crawl space;
slab or basement available for fee
Materials List Available: No
Price Category: G

Images provided by designer/architect.

Classic Craftsman tradition shines through in this spectacular two-story home.

Features:

- Great Room: This open room features two sets of double doors to the rear yard, a fireplace, and a built-in media center.

- Kitchen: Casual dining takes place in the breakfast nook, which is open to this island kitchen and leads to a vaulted porch.

- Master Suites: One master suite is found on the first floor. It glows with appointments, from double-door access to the rear yard to a fine bath with spa tub, separate shower, and double sinks. The second master suite, on the second floor, holds a window seat and a private bath with spa tub.

- Bedrooms: Two additional bedrooms (or a bedroom and a study) share a full compart-mented bathroom with private vanities for each room.

- Garage: This four-car garage connects to the main house at a laundry/mud room with a half-bath, coat closet, built-in bench, and washer/dryer space. Extra room in the garage can be used as a workshop or for storage space.

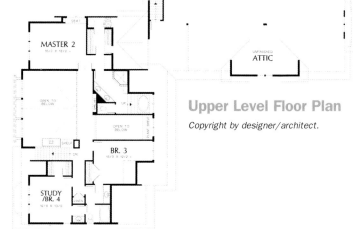

Main Level Floor Plan

Upper Level Floor Plan

Copyright by designer/architect.

Plan #121027

Dimensions: 46' W x 48' D
Levels: 2
Square Footage: 1,660
Main Level Sq. Ft.: 1,265
Upper Level Sq. Ft.: 395
Bedrooms: 3
Bathrooms: 2½
Foundation: Basement
Materials List Available: Yes
Price Category: C

Images provided by designer/architect.

This elegant home is designed for architectural interest and gracious living.

Features:

- Ceiling Height: 8 ft. unless otherwise noted.
- Great Room: Family and guests will be drawn to this inviting, sun-filled room with its 13-ft. ceiling and raised-hearth fireplace.
- Formal Dining Room: An angled ceiling lends architectural interest to this elegant room. Alternately, this room can be used as a parlor.

- Master Bedroom: Corner windows are designed to ease window placement.
- Master Bath: The master bedroom is served by a private bath. The sunlit whirlpool bath invites you to take time to luxuriate and rejuvenate. There's a double vanity, separate shower, and a walk-in closet.
- Garage: This two bay garage offers plenty of space for storage in addition to parking.

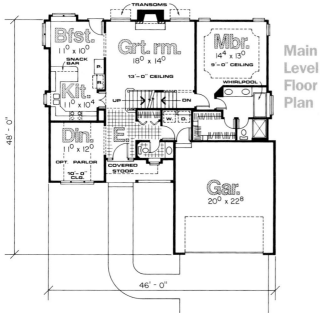

Main Level Floor Plan

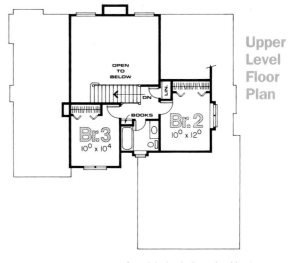

Upper Level Floor Plan

Copyright by designer/architect.

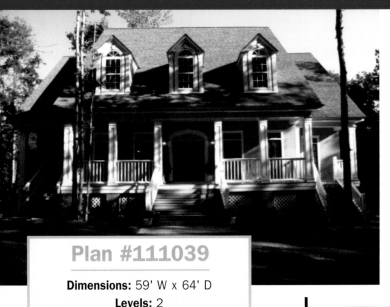

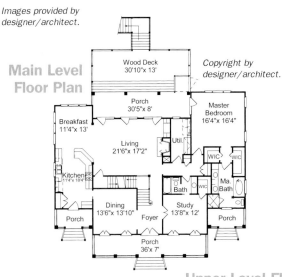

Images provided by designer/architect.

Main Level Floor Plan

Wood Deck 30'10"x 13'

Porch 30'5"x 8'

Breakfast 11'4"x 13'

Master Bedroom 16'4"x 16'4"

Living 21'6"x 17'2'

Util

WIC   WIC

Kitchen 11'4 18'4'

Bath   WIC   Ma. Bath

Dining 13'6"x 13'10"   Study 13'8"x 12'

Porch   Foyer   Porch

Porch 36'x 7'

Copyright by designer/architect.

Plan #111039

Dimensions: 59' W x 64' D
Levels: 2
Square Footage: 3,335
Main Level Sq. Ft.: 2,129
Upper Level Sq. Ft.: 1,206
Bedrooms: 4
Bathrooms: 4
Foundation: Basement
Materials List Available: No
Price Category: G

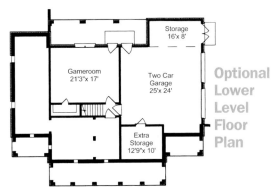

Optional Lower Level Floor Plan

Storage 16'x 8'

Gameroom 21'3"x 17'

Two Car Garage 25'x 24'

Extra Storage 12'9"x 10'

Upper Level Floor Plan

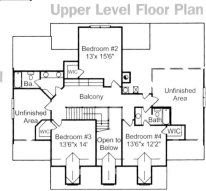

Bedroom #2 13'x 15'6"

WIC

Ba.

Balcony

Unfinished Area

Unfinished Area

Bedroom #3 13'6"x 14'   Open to Below   Bedroom #4 13'6"x 12'2"

WIC   Bath   WIC

Plan #441046

Dimensions: 50' W x 42' D
Levels: 2
Square Footage: 2,606
Main Level Sq. Ft.: 1,216
Upper Level Sq. Ft.: 1,390
Bedrooms: 4
Bathrooms: 2½
Foundation: Crawl space; slab or basement for fee
Materials List Available: No
Price Category: F

CAD FILE AVAILABLE

Images provided by designer/architect.

Rear Elevation

SHOP

NOOK

GREAT RM.

GARAGE

DINING

DEN

42'

50'

Main Level Floor Plan

BR. 4

MASTER

BR. 3

BR. 2

Upper Level Floor Plan

Copyright by designer/architect.

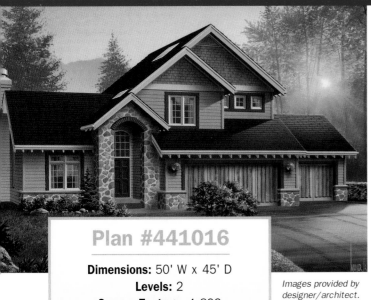

**Upper Level
Floor Plan**

Plan #441016

Dimensions: 50' W x 45' D
Levels: 2
Square Footage: 1,893
Main Level Sq. Ft.: 1,087
Upper Level Sq. Ft.: 806
Bedrooms: 3
Bathrooms: 2½
Foundation: Crawl space; slab or basement for fee
Materials List Available: No
Price Category: D

Images provided by designer/architect.

**Main Level
Floor Plan**

Copyright by designer/architect.

45'

◄ 50' ►
40' - 2 CAR GARAGE

Plan #451194

Dimensions: 87'8" W x 58' D
Levels: 1
Square Footage: 2,618
Bedrooms: 3
Bathrooms: 2½
Foundation: Crawl space
Materials List Available: No
Price Category: F

Images provided by designer/architect.

Copyright by designer/architect.

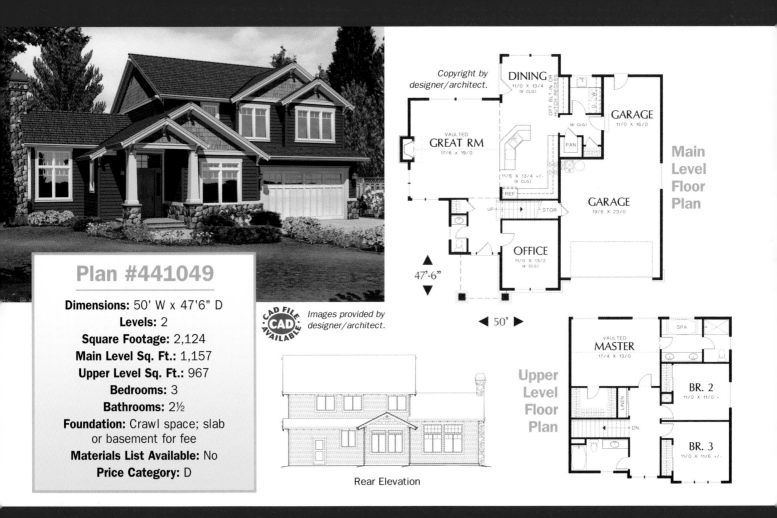

Plan #441049

Dimensions: 50' W x 47'6" D
Levels: 2
Square Footage: 2,124
Main Level Sq. Ft.: 1,157
Upper Level Sq. Ft.: 967
Bedrooms: 3
Bathrooms: 2½
Foundation: Crawl space; slab or basement for fee
Materials List Available: No
Price Category: D

Images provided by designer/architect.

Rear Elevation

Main Level Floor Plan

Copyright by designer/architect.

Upper Level Floor Plan

Plan #441050

Dimensions: 50' W x 52'6" D
Levels: 2
Square Footage: 2,296
Main Level Sq. Ft.: 1,464
Upper Level Sq. Ft.: 832
Bedrooms: 3
Bathrooms: 2½
Foundation: Crawl space; slab or basement for fee
Materials List Available: No
Price Category: E

Images provided by designer/architect.

Rear Elevation

Main Level Floor Plan

Copyright by designer/architect.

Upper Level Floor Plan

Plan #441026

Dimensions: 60' W x 52' D
Levels: 2
Square Footage: 3,623
Main Level Sq. Ft.: 1,835
Upper Level Sq. Ft.: 1,788
Bedrooms: 4
Bathrooms: 2½
Foundation: Crawl space
Materials List Available: No
Price Category: H

Images provided by designer/architect.

Crazy about Craftsman styling? This exquisite plan has it in abundance and doesn't skimp on the floor plan, either. Massive stone bases support the Arts and Crafts columns at the entry porch.

Features:

- Living Room: This large gathering area features a cozy fireplace.

- Dining Room: This formal room is connected to the island kitchen via a butler's pantry.

- Master Suite: Located upstairs, this suite features a walk-in closet and luxury bath.

- Bedrooms: The three family bedrooms share a centrally located compartmented bathroom.

Rear
Elevation

Main Level Floor Plan

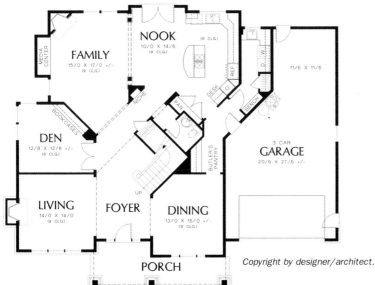

Copyright by designer/architect.

Upper Level Floor Plan

Plan #101011

Dimensions: 71'2" W x 58'1" D
Levels: 1
Square Footage: 2,184
Bedrooms: 3
Bathrooms: 3
Foundation: Crawl space, slab, basement, walkout
Materials List Available: Yes
Price Category: D

A classic design and spacious interior add up to a flexible design suitable to any modern lifestyle.

Features:

- Ceiling Height: 9 ft. unless otherwise noted.

- Formal Dining Room: A decorative square column and a tray ceiling adorn this elegant dining room.

- Screened Porch: Enjoy summer breezes in style by stepping out of the French doors into this vaulted screened porch.

- Kitchen: Does everyone want to hang out in the kitchen while you are cooking? No problem. True to the home's country style, this huge 14-ft.-3-in. x 22-ft.-6-in. has plenty of room for helpers.

- The kitchen is open to the vaulted family room.

Images provided by designer/architect.

- Patio or Deck: This pleasant outdoor area is accessible from both the screened porch and the master bedroom.

- Master Suite: This luxurious suite includes a double tray ceiling, a sitting area, two walk-in closets, and an exquisite bath.

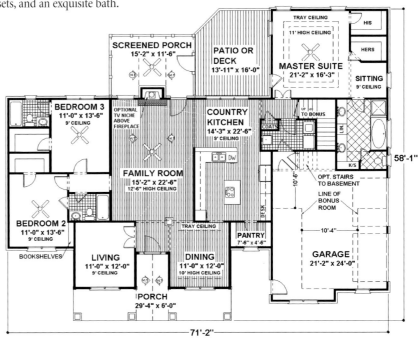

Copyright by designer/architect.

Kitchen

Dining Room

Family Room

Living Room

Master Bath

Master Bedroom

Plan #221056

Dimensions: 54' W x 58' D

Levels: 1

Square Footage: 1,917

Bedrooms: 2

Bathrooms: 2

Foundation: Basement

Materials List Available: No

Price Category: D

You'll think this home was built many years ago because of its perfect blend of shingle siding and stone. With an open floor plan, this ranch home packs a lot of amenities in a small footprint.

Features:

- Open Plan: From the breakfast bar that overlooks the nook and great room, to the 10-ft.-high ceilings throughout, this home feels spacious and roomy enough for any size family.

- Great Room: This gathering area has a cozy fireplace, a built-in cabinet, and views of the backyard.

- Master Suite: This master suite features a stepped ceiling, a Jacuzzi tub in the bath, and a spacious walk-in closet.

- Bedrooms: Two additional bedrooms are located on the opposite side of the home, allowing for plenty of privacy for mom and dad.

Images provided by designer/architect.

NOOK
10'-1 1/8" CEILING
13'4"x10'0"

GRT. RM.
10'-1 1/8" CEILING
14'8"x18'0"

MBR.
10'-1 1/8" STEP CEILING
15'8"x14'0"

KIT.
10'-1 1/8" CEILING
13'4"x11'4"

DIN./DEN/BR. #3
10'-1 1/8" CEILING
13'4"x11'4"

E.
10'-1 1/8" CEILING

BR. #2
10'-1 1/8" CEILING
12'0"x12'0"

3 CAR GARAGE
30'8"x24'0"

54'-0"

58'-0"

BR. #3/DEN
10'-1 1/8" CEILING
11'8"x11'4"

**Dining Room
Den
Bedroom 3
Optional
Floor Plan**

Copyright by designer/architect.

Rear Elevation

Plan #341053

Dimensions: 44'10" W x 50'6" D
Levels: 1.5
Square Footage: 1,903
Main Level Sq. Ft.: 1,185
Upper Level Sq. Ft.: 718
Bedrooms: 3
Bathrooms: 2½
Foundation: Crawl space
Materials List Available: Yes
Price Category: D

Images provided by designer/architect.

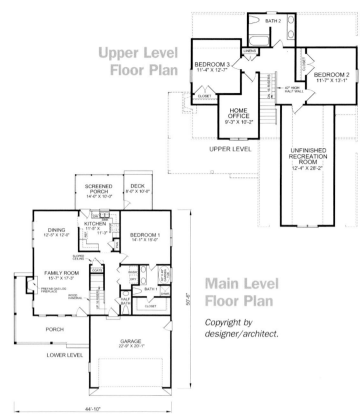

Upper Level Floor Plan

Main Level Floor Plan

Copyright by designer/architect.

Plan #341054

Dimensions: 47' W x 53'8" D
Levels: 1.5
Square Footage: 1,370
Main Level Sq. Ft.: 1,370
Bonus Room Sq. Ft.: 261
Bedrooms: 3
Bathrooms: 2
Foundation: Crawl space
Materials List Available: Yes
Price Category: B

Images provided by designer/architect.

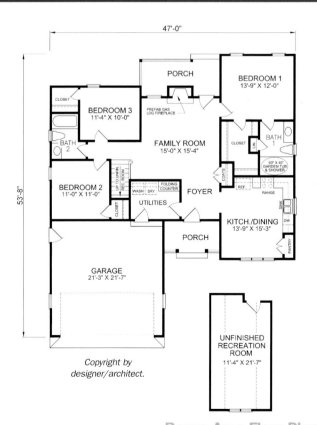

Copyright by designer/architect.

Bonus Area Floor Plan

This article was reprinted from *The New Smart Approach to Bath Design* (Creative Homeowner 2003).

Safety & Comfort in Your Bathroom

Wet floors. Bare feet. Various stages of dress. Contact lenses in, contact lenses out. Sleepy nights, groggy mornings. Electrical appliances in close proximity to water. These are some of the reasons why more accidents occur in the bathroom than in any other room in the house. They are also safety concerns to be considered when designing a new bath. This is especially true when those using it are the most vulnerable: children and the elderly. Slips, falls, and hot-water scalds top the injury list.

By the year 2020, more than half of the population of the United States will be over 55 years old. Universal design addresses the needs of that generation, as well as every other one. It is design aimed at multigenerational households. As Baby Boomers bring their aging parents home to live while still raising families of their own, it is not uncommon to have small children and grandparents living under the same roof at the same time. Indeed, as our population ages in general, it behooves everyone to think about design that is usable by each member of the family, today and in the future. Besides, if you have ever broken a bone or have had to use crutches, you already know the problems or obstacles that occur trying to maneuver in a typical home when you are disabled, even temporarily. As with safety, some thoughtful design can help.

Above: Adjustable handheld sprayers in the shower are convenient for people of all heights.

Below: Grab bars, securely mounted into wall studs, are important in showers as well as in tubs.

Opposite: Tile is fine flooring material as long as it is matte finished and slip-resistant. Check the slip-resistance rating of any tile you intend to install on the floor.

Safety First

While form and function are two critical parts of any design, safety should reign as a primary factor in any bathroom plan. Minimizing the risk of bodily injury only makes good sense. Take the following steps when designing for safety. And remember, you don't have to be very young or very old to be at risk of accidents, particularly in the bath.

Step One: Use slip-resistant flooring material. Slips and falls are two of the top three on the injury hit list, so a good flooring choice is critical. Choose a slip-resistant surface such as textured tile or vinyl, or a matte-finish laminate flooring. If you decide on ceramic tile, be sure to purchase the type designed for flooring.

Step Two: Install grab bars. With the aging of society, grab bars are becoming standard accessories in bathrooms. If you don't need them now, you may in the future—even if it is only while you are recuperating from a sports injury or during the last few months of a pregnancy. Consider installing grab bars inside each tub and shower. You may even think about locating grab bars in the toilet area, particularly if there are people in your household who may have difficulty getting up and down.

Many manufacturers offer grab bars in a variety of decorative styles and finishes. The good news is that they can also double as towel racks for added storage. But make sure walls are reinforced to receive the added stress of a person's weight before installing grab bars. Never use towel racks as substitutes for grab bars.

Step Three: Regulate water temperature—and devices. Regulating scalding temperatures in a tub or sink faucet is essential in any home, but especially when there are children or elderly persons using the bath. Install faucets with antiscald devices that prevent water temperatures from rising over 111 degrees Fahrenheit, or opt for pressure-balanced valves that equalize hot and cold water.

Left: Pressure-balanced controls equalize hot and cold water to prevent scalds. Today, even nostalgic styles come with this safety future.

Above: This master bathroom is an example of how principles of universal design can be incorporated into a home with attractive, as well as comfortable, results.

Opposite: A shower should be large enough to accommodate a seat. The glass door must be shatterproof, and it should be installed to open into the room.

Consider a faucet that can be preprogrammed by you to a specific temperature. These controls should be childproof. Besides opting for a faucet with a temperature regulator, you can prevent other related mishaps by installing tub and shower controls so that they are accessible from inside and outside the fixtures. The National Kitchen and Bath Association (NKBA) recommends locating shower controls between 38 and 48 inches above the floor and offset toward the room. Place tub controls between the tub rim and 33 inches above the floor, below the grab bar. Like shower controls, they should be installed offset toward the

room. That way someone outside the tub or shower—or in a wheelchair—can regulate them.

Step Four: Choose shatter-resistant materials. Select tempered or laminated glass, plastic, or other shatterproof materials. Try to avoid any material or product that may break and present another hazard on top of a fall. This is particularly true in children's baths. Children tend to get rambunctious and exert more wear and tear on materials than a manufacturer may have anticipated. (Always choose durable, impact-resistant materials and fixtures in any child's

room.) If you can, opt for a child-safe product over a luxury item if you can't afford both.

Step Five: Design a safe shower environment. Besides shatterproof doors that open into the room, (not into the shower), and temperature-control devices, there are other measures you can take to make showering pleasant and safe. For example, every shower unit should have a seat or bench that is 17 inches to 19 inches high and 15 inches deep, according to the NKBA. That way you won't put yourself at risk by standing on a soapy, slippery surface. Your back will thank you, too, when you don't strain it with deep bending at the waist to reach your feet.

Of course, you'll want a shower that is equipped with the latest in jetted sprayers and showerheads to look as glamorous as it functions, but keep the design simple. Avoid steps; install safety rails; and make the entrance wide enough to get in and out comfortably. Specify a 60-inch-wide entrance for a shower that measures 36 inches deep. For a compact 32-inch-deep shower, plan an entrance that is 42 inches wide.

Step Six: Plan a safe tub. It's not hard to feel like Cleopatra soaking in a luxurious sunk-in tub. And certainly a tub set into a sumptuous platform makes a big fashion statement. But the reality is that a tub that requires you to step up or down stairs can be hazardous. Steps can get wet and slippery, and you may lose your balance. When children will be bathing, supervision is a must. You may want to reconsider this design, especially if you will remain in the house as you age. What appears glamorous now could be impractical and dangerous when you're older.

Step Seven: Keep electrical switches, plugs, and lighting fixtures away from water sources and wet hands. Not only that, but make sure that every electrical receptacle is grounded and protected with ground-fault circuit interrupters. These devices can cut the electrical current if there is a power surge or if moisture is present. Most building codes require installing them in kitchens, bathrooms, and any other rooms with plumbing.

Planning to include a light fixture above the tub or in the shower? For safety's sake, install it so that it is not within the reach of anyone—in either a sitting or standing position. Check local codes regarding this option.

Step Eight: Don't clutter the traffic area. Be realistic, no matter how clever you are about using every square inch of space. If your bathroom is a compact 40 square feet, it can't accommodate an oversize tub or a bidet. Don't crowd in extra amenities and risk tripping over yourself or clogging walkways in the bathroom. There are minimum clearances you should adhere to for your own safety. That is one reason to create a scale drawing of your project. An adjacent toilet/bidet installation, for example, requires a 16-inch minimum clearance to all obstructions. A water closet (toilet compartment) should be at least 3 feet wide by 15½ feet long with a swing-out door.

Step Nine: Make storage accessible. If you can't reach a storage area without standing on the toilet, it's not useful. Ideally, storage for toiletries, linens, and the like should be no higher than 4 feet from the floor. Don't make it too low, either. You can avoid ill-advised bending by keeping storage at least 15 inches from the floor, says the NKBA. Locate storage for personal hygiene products within the reach of a person who is seated on a bidet or a toilet.

Step Ten: Install a safety lock on the door. For some reason the words "Do not lock the door" trigger an irresistible urge in children to do just the opposite. The best solution is to install a safety lock. This device, which is inexpensive, looks just like a standard door knob with a little push-button lock on the inside of the bathroom and a pin hole in the knob on the outside. To release the lock from outside the door, insert an ice pick or other thin tool into the hole and push out the button.

Lastly, use common sense. Some things should be obvious but are often overlooked. For example, people come in all sizes. Take an inventory of family members' heights to avoid placing sharp corners or racks at eye level. Children tend to grow, however, so this presents a challenge. The best approach is to place sharp-cornered items in spots that are away from any traffic patterns. For example, don't put a counter next to the tub where you will bump your hip every day as you step out of the bath.

Designing for safety is not difficult. All you need is a little thought and foresight. Run through the list of your family's functional needs for the bath, and then consider your physical safety. Is there a better way to arrange fixtures that will make it easier to maneuver? Does the design you have sketched out contain enough space for two people to use the bathroom at the same time? Answer these questions now, not after the fixtures have been installed.

Universal Design

By the year 2006, fully one-third of America will be either disabled, chronically ill, or over the age of 65. Our society is aging, and our current housing stock is not designed to meet the changing capabilities of the aged. That is why the smartest trend these days is universal design—an approach that opens the bath, indeed the entire home, to people of all different capabilities.

Universal-designed bathrooms are not the same as "accessible" ones. They are

Left: In a bathroom that incorporates universal design features, the countertop height is determined by the height of the homeowners.

Opposite: A pocket door is an excellent way to provide separation and privacy in different areas in a bath without blocking accessibility.

simply more accommodating to people of all ages, sizes, skills, and capabilities. Begin by analyzing your lifestyle and your family's unique needs. Do you have someone in your house who must sit down while putting on makeup or shaving? Plan kneespace under a sink or vanity. Does anyone have balance problems stepping into a tub? Install safety rails that meet established requirements on the tub-surround walls. Do you have small children who want to get ready for bed all by themselves without help from Mom? Perhaps a lower countertop and sink would encourage independence. Are you planning on having children in the future? What features would make your home more comfortable during pregnancy and your baby's infancy? Will you really be able to step into a sunk-in tub for a handheld shower during your ninth month? Maybe a separate tub and shower

are more practical for the times you will be pregnant.

Before incorporating every universal-design idea you can think of into your bath, decide how long you want to remain in the house. Statistics show that more often than not, today's homeowners stay put longer. If you plan on keeping your house into your golden years, include some accessible features. Good ideas include digital displays, which are easier to read; wider doorways to accommodate walkers, crutches, and wheelchairs; and minimum thresholds on interior and exterior doorways for easy maneuvering. The items specified in a universal design are usable by most people regardless of their level of ability or disability. For example, everyone can use lever door handles more easily than round ones, from people who

have no hands to those whose hands are full. Universal design refers to products or to a more convenient placement of fixtures. Changing the counter heights in a bath may be more ergonomic for a couple whose heights are drastically different. The same would be true about placing a showerhead. Universal design addresses the scope of accessibility and attempts to make all elements and spaces usable by all people.

It may be worthwhile to look into some of the smart home technology—products that allow you to call your home from your cellular phone to turn on the lights, raise the thermostat, start running a bath, preprogram water level and temperature, and turn on the oven for dinner so that you have time for that long, hot soak. There are thousands of ways to make a home more usable. The key is

Opposite: A lever handle on the door that separates the vanity from the bathing area is easiest for all family members to use.

Left: Lowering the sink and storage to an accessible height provides independence for a disabled person.

Accessible Design

Accessible design normally means that a home—or in this case a bathroom—is barrier-free. It also indicates that the room complies with the design guidelines for disabled people found in government regulations, such as the American National Standards Institute's A117.1 (ANSI A117.1-1986). There are a number of guidelines governing accessible design. Their goal is to provide criteria for designing for people who must use wheelchairs. Most accessible homes incorporate a number of fixed features that enable a disabled person to have easy access to areas such as the bathroom.

If there are disabled people in your family who will be using the new bathroom, you'll have to plan space accordingly, making sure there is adequate room for them to move around. You'll also need fixtures and fittings that allow people to care for themselves independently.

In addition to the safety features recommended earlier, there are specific accessible-design guidelines, recommended by the NKBA, that you should follow. Begin by including enough space in your floor plan for a wheelchair-bound person to enter and maneuver around. Start with the entry. Doorways must be a minimum of 32 inches wide but 36 inches is better. Once inside, the person will need a passage that is at least 24 inches deep, moving into the room, and 36 inches wide. When you are sketching out the plan, include enough space for someone in a wheelchair to open or close the door with ease. Because the amount of space depends on the type of door and the approach into the bathroom, you'll have to work it out with the disabled

to look at universal-designed products and match them to your house, your capabilities, and your anticipated future needs. Whatever you do, remember that universal design is supposed to make life easier. If adding these features will destroy your budget, don't add them. But remember safety—and keep the grab

bars for days when you aren't so steady on your feet.

You may have heard the terms "accessible" and "adaptable" bandied about as though they are interchangeable with each other and with "universal design." In fact, they are different.

person in your home. Perhaps there is a similar entry into another room in the house where he or she can practice entering, closing, and opening the door while you take the measurements of the door swing.

With regard to fixture placement, the recommendations for clear floor space offered by the NKBA are listed in the box at right. Just remember two things: First, it's okay to overlap clearances for different fixtures. Second, although you should always try to adhere to these professional guidelines, the available space may limit you. If you have to deviate a few inches here or there, the bathroom will still be the most accessible that you can make it. When you are ready to shop for fixtures and fittings, keep in mind you get what you pay for. As with products for standard bathrooms, there is an array (though more limited) that range from the purely practical to technological marvels.

In general, shop for a tub that allows a disabled person to transfer from a wheelchair to the bath with ease. There are tubs constructed with built-in seats that lift and rotate, allowing a person to slide on, rotate into the unit, and hydraulically lower himself flush with the bottom of the tub. This position is the most comfortable for bathing. A handheld sprayer will be handy, too, for warming up the water or rinsing hair.

Transfer showers permit a wheelchair-bound person to roll next to the unit, adjust the controls from the outside, and then back up and make a parallel transfer onto the shower seat using grab bars—or the wheelchair—as support. Standing individuals can use the shower by flipping down the seat.

In the toilet area, you'll have choices, too. Instead of the standard 15-inch-high

toilet, choose an 18-inch-high model, which makes getting up and down easier—even for people who are not disabled. Add a flush-handle extension and install a toilet-paper holder with a controlled-flow feature. For accessibility, locate the holder 26 inches high on a wall in front of the toilet. A wall-mounted sink or one dropped into a countertop should be replaced at the universal-access height—32 inches. To accommodate someone in a wheelchair, plan a minimum 27-inch-deep-by-30-inch-wide minimum knee space under the vanity or sink. Insulate any exposed undersink pipes to prevent burning. Lever faucets or touch-pad controls are recommended. If your budget permits, install touchless electronic faucets that sense motion. It's

also practical to include a sprayer so that hair can be washed at the lav.

Adaptable Design

Adaptable designs are those that can be easily modified for use by a disabled person. They are normally used in multi-family rental housing so that the landlord can rent to a nondisabled person as well as a disabled one. The adaptable house incorporates some concealment of traditional accessible features. For example, an adaptable bath would have a door on the vanity underneath the sink that could be removed to make room for a wheelchair. There may be no steps at the tub and shower area—a good idea in every situation—or doorways may be extra wide.

SMARTtip

The table below shows the minimum floor clearances, in inches, recommended by the National Kitchen and Bath Association (NKBA) for placing fixtures in an accessible bathroom. Use them as guidelines, but tailor them to your personal situation, available space, and needs as necessary.

Fixture	NKBA Minimum
Lavatory	30 x 48*
Toilet	48 x 48**
Bidet	48 x 48***
Bathtub	60 x 30****

In the case of a shower that is less than 60 inches wide, the minimum clearance should be 36 inches deep by the width of the shower plus 12 inches. A shower that is more than 60 inches wide requires 36 inches of clear floor space by the width of the shower.

* Up to 19 inches can extend under the lavatory.

** At least 16 inches must extend to each centerline of the toilet.

*** You may reduce it to 30 x 48 if space is tight, but that may compromise full use.

**** For a parallel approach. For a perpendicular approach, clearance should be 60 x 48.

Plan #441031

Dimensions: 78'2" W x 68' D
Levels: 2
Square Footage: 4,150
Main Level Sq. Ft.: 2,572
Upper Level Sq. Ft.: 1,578
Bedrooms: 4
Bathrooms: 4½
Foundation: Crawl space;
slab or basement available for fee
Materials List Available: No
Price Category: I

Images provided by designer/architect.

Features:

- **Great Room:** The main level offers this commodious room, with its beamed ceiling, alcove, fireplace, and built-ins.
- **Kitchen:** Go up a few steps to the dining nook and this kitchen, and you'll find a baking center, walk-in pantry, and access to a covered side porch.

- **Formal Dining Room:** This formal room lies a few steps up from the foyer and sports a bay window and hutch space.
- **Guest Suite:** This suite, which is located at the end of the hall, features a private bathroom and walk-in closet.
- **Master Suite:** A fireplace flanked by built-ins warms this suite. Its bath contains a spa tub, compartmented toilet, and huge shower.

Graceful and gracious, this superb shingle design delights with handsome exterior elements. A whimsical turret, covered entry, upper-level balcony, and bay window all bring their charm to the facade.

CAD FILE AVAILABLE

Main Level Floor Plan

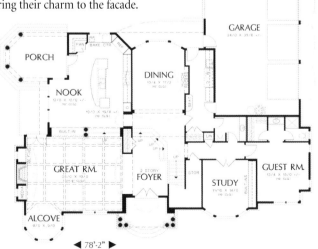

Upper Level Floor Plan

Copyright by designer/architect.

Kitchen

Dining Room

Master Bath

Foyer

Master Bedroom

Great Room

Rear View

Plan #221042

Dimensions: 50' W x 63' D
Levels: 2
Square Footage: 2,704
Main Level Sq. Ft.: 1,797
Upper Level Sq. Ft.: 907
Bedrooms: 4
Bathrooms: 2 full, 2 half
Foundation: Basement
Materials List Available: No
Price Category: F

Stone and shingle siding and graceful columns adorn the front of this European style two-story home.

Features:

• **Great Room:** Upon entering, you'll be pleased with the sight of a wall of windows in this room, providing a tremendous view of the backyard.

• **Kitchen:** This kitchen features a breakfast bar overlooking the dining room and providing additional seating for family and friends.

• **Master Suite:** With its large walk-in closet and spacious bathroom, complete with a Jacuzzi tub, this suite is sure to please.

• Upper Level: Upstairs you'll find a loft with balcony that overlooks the great room below and three additional bedrooms, making this four-bedroom home perfect for just about any size family.

Images provided by designer/architect.

Rear Elevation

Main Level Floor Plan

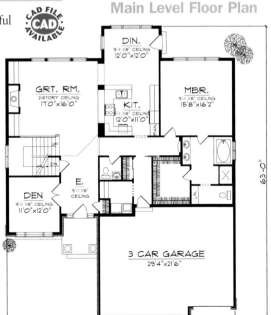

Upper Level Floor Plan

Copyright by designer/architect.

Plan #441001

Dimensions: 44' W x 68' D
Levels: 1
Square Footage: 1,850
Bedrooms: 3
Bathrooms: 2
Foundation: Crawl space
Materials List Available: No
Price Category: D

Images provided by designer/architect.

With all the tantalizing elements of a cottage and the comfortable space of a family-sized home, this Arts and Crafts-style one-story design is the best of both worlds. Exterior accents such as stone wainscot, cedar shingles under the gable ends, and mission-style windows just add to the effect.

CAD FILE AVAILABLE

Features:

- Great Room: A warm hearth lights this room—right next to a built-in media center.

- Dining Room: This area features a sliding glass door to the rear patio for a breath of fresh air.

- Den: This quiet area has a window seat and a vaulted ceiling, giving the feeling of openness and letting your mind wander.

- Kitchen: This open corner kitchen features a 42-in. snack bar and a giant walk-in pantry.

- Master Suite: This suite boasts a tray ceiling and a large walk-in closet.

Rear Elevation

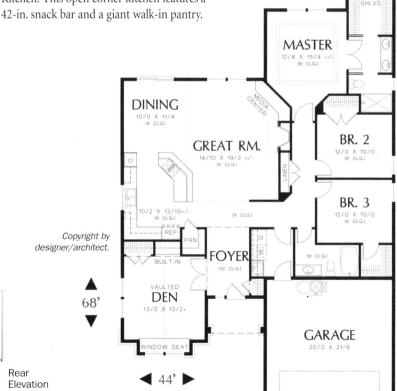

Copyright by designer/architect.

Plan #441005

Dimensions: 50' W x 59' D
Levels: 1
Square Footage: 1,800
Bedrooms: 3
Bathrooms: 2
Foundation: Crawl space
Materials List Available: No
Price Category: D

Images provided by designer/architect.

This home looks as if it's a quaint little abode—with its board-and-batten siding, cedar shingle detailing, and column-covered porch—but even a quick peek inside will prove that there is much more to this plan than meets the eye.

CAD FILE AVAILABLE

Features:

- Foyer: This entry area rises to a 9-ft.-high ceiling. On one side is a washer-dryer alcove with a closet across the way; on the other is another large storage area. Just down the hallway is a third closet.

- Kitchen: This kitchen features a center island, built-in desk/work center, and pantry. This area and the dining area also boast 9-ft.-high ceilings and are open to a vaulted great room with corner fireplace.

- Dining Room: Sliding doors in this area lead to a covered side porch, so you can enjoy outside dining.

- Master Suite: This suite has a vaulted ceiling. The master bath is wonderfully appointed with a separate shower, spa tub, and dual sinks.

- Bedrooms: Three bedrooms (or two plus an office) are found on the right side of the plan.

Rear Elevation

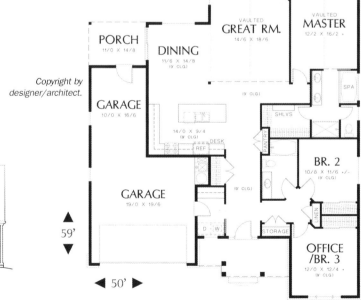

Copyright by designer/architect.

Plan #121032

Dimensions: 54'8" W x 45'4" D
Levels: 2
Square Footage: 2,339
Main Level Sq. Ft.: 1,665
Upper Level Sq. Ft.: 674
Bedrooms: 4
Bathrooms: 2½
Foundation: Basement
Materials List Available: Yes
Price Category: E

Images provided by designer/architect.

This home is designed for gracious living and is distinguished by many architectural details.

Features:

- Ceiling Height: 8 ft. unless otherwise noted.

- Foyer: This is truly a grand foyer with a dramatic ceiling that soars to 18 ft.

- Great Room: The foyer's 18-ft. ceiling extends into the great room where an open staircase adds architectural windows. Warm yourself by the fireplace that is framed by windows.

- Kitchen: An island is the centerpiece of this handsome and efficient kitchen that features a breakfast area for informal family meals. The room also includes a handy desk.

- Private Wing: The master suite and study are in a private wing of the house.

- Room to Expand: In addition to the three bedrooms, the second level has an unfinished storage space that can become another bedroom or office.

Main Level Floor Plan

Upper Level Floor Plan

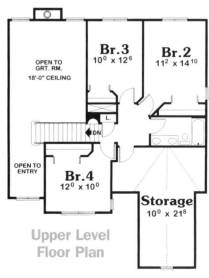

Copyright by designer/architect.

Plan #441006

Dimensions: 48' W x 64' D
Levels: 1
Square Footage: 1,891
Bedrooms: 3
Bathrooms: 2
Foundation: Crawl space
Materials List Available: No
Price Category: D

Images provided by designer/architect.

If you prefer the look of Craftsman homes, you'll love the details this plan includes. Wide-based columns across the front porch, Mission-style windows, and a balanced mixture of exterior materials add up to true good looks.

Features:

- Great Room: A built-in media center and a fireplace in this room make it distinctive.

- Kitchen: A huge skylight over an island eating counter brightens this kitchen. A private office space opens through double doors nearby.

- Dining Room: This room has sliding glass doors opening to the rear patio.

- Bedrooms: Two bedrooms with two bathrooms are located on the right side of the plan. One of the bedrooms is a master suite with a vaulted salon and a bath with a spa tub.

- Garage: You'll be able to reach this two-car garage via a service hallway that contains a laundry room, a walk-in pantry, and a closet.

Copyright by designer/architect.

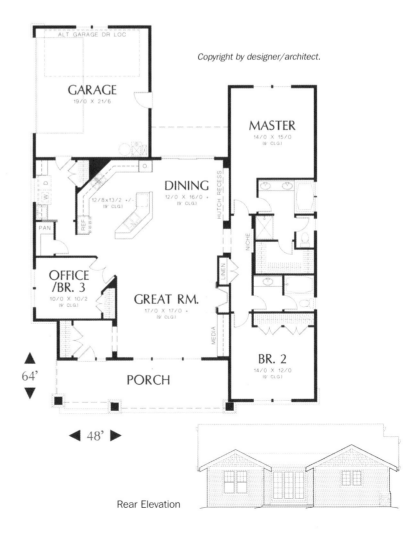

Rear Elevation

Plan #101004

Dimensions: 55'8" W x 56'6" D
Levels: 1
Square Footage: 1,787
Bedrooms: 3
Bathrooms: 2
Foundation: Crawl space, slab, or basement
Materials List Available: Yes
Price Category: C

CAD FILE AVAILABLE

Images provided by designer/architect.

This carefully designed ranch provides the feel and features of a much larger home.

Features:

- Ceiling Height: 9 ft. unless otherwise noted.

- Foyer: Guests will step up onto the inviting front porch and into this foyer, with its impressive 11-ft. ceiling.

- Dining Room: Open to the entry and to its left is this elegant dining room, perfect for entertaining or informal family gatherings.

- Family Room: This family gathering place features an 11-ft. ceiling to enhance its sense of spaciousness.

- Kitchen: This intelligently designed kitchen has an open plan. A breakfast bar and a serving bar are features that add to its convenience.

- Master Suite: This suite is loaded with amenities, including a double-step tray ceiling, direct access to the screened porch, a sitting room, deluxe bath, and his and her walk-in closets.

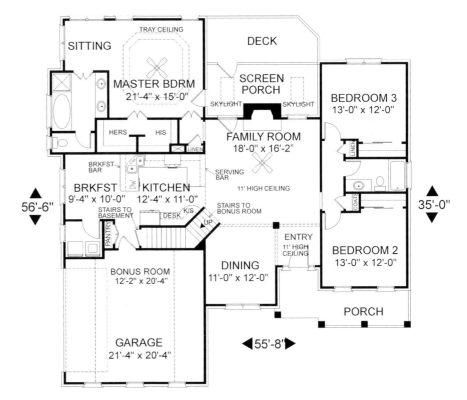

Copyright by designer/architect.

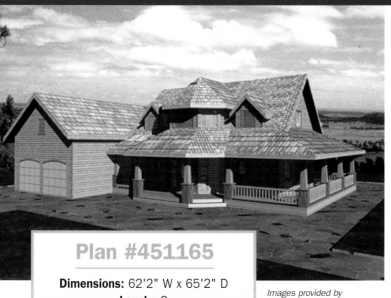

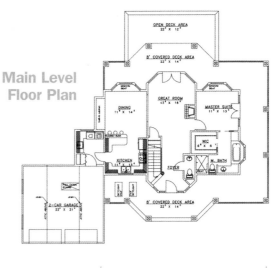

**Main Level
Floor Plan**

*Images provided by
designer/architect.*

Plan #451165

Dimensions: 62'2" W x 65'2" D
Levels: 2
Square Footage: 1,933
Main Level Sq. Ft.: 1,171
Upper Level Sq. Ft.: 762
Bedrooms: 3
Bathrooms: 2½
Foundation: Crawl space
Materials List Available: No
Price Category: D

Upper Level Floor Plan

Copyright by designer/architect.

Plan #341055

Dimensions: 58'9" W x 54'3" D
Levels: 1.5
Square Footage: 1,647
Main Level Sq. Ft.: 1,647
Bonus Room Sq. Ft.: 398
Bedrooms: 3
Bathrooms: 2
Foundation: Crawl space
Materials List Available: Yes
Price Category: C

*Images provided by
designer/architect.*

Main Level Floor Plan

Upper Level Floor Plan

Copyright by designer/architect.

Plan #451182

Dimensions: 102'9" W x 84'6" D
Levels: 2
Square Footage: 3,241
Main Level Sq. Ft.: 2,203
Upper Level Sq. Ft.: 1,038
Bedrooms: 3
Bathrooms: 2½
Foundation: Basement
Materials List Available: No
Price Category: G

Images provided by designer/architect.

CAD FILE AVAILABLE

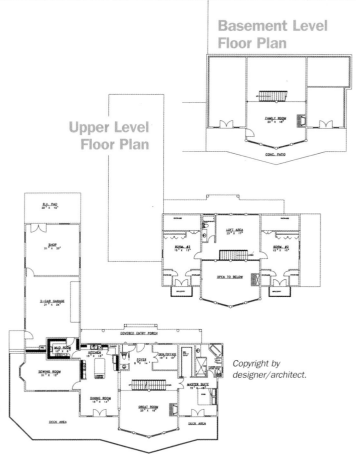

Basement Level Floor Plan

Upper Level Floor Plan

Main Level Floor Plan

Copyright by designer/architect.

Plan #151138

Dimensions: 53' W x 49'4" D
Levels: 1
Square Footage: 2,010
Main Level Sq. Ft.: 1,935
Basement Level Sq. Ft.: 75
Bedrooms: 3
Bathrooms: 2
Foundation: Basement or walk-out
CompleteCost List Available: Yes
Price Category: C

Images provided by designer/architect.

CAD FILE AVAILABLE

Lower Level Floor Plan

Main Level Floor Plan

Copyright by designer/architect.

Main Level Floor Plan

SCREENED PORCH
14'-0" X 10'-0"

KITCHEN
12'-9" X 14'-1"

DINING ROOM
13'-7" X 12'-0"

COVERED PATIO

HALF BATH

FAMILY ROOM
13'-7" X 16'-9"

GARAGE
20'-3" X 21'-0"

PORCH

PREFAB GAS LOG FIREPLACE

BUILT-IN BOOKCASE

44'-4"

35'-0"

Plan #341057

Dimensions: 35' W x 44'4" D
Levels: 2
Square Footage: 1,642
Main Level Sq. Ft.: 762
Upper Level Sq. Ft.: 880
Bedrooms: 3
Bathrooms: 2½
Foundation: Crawl space
Materials List Available: Yes
Price Category: C

Images provided by designer/architect.

CAD FILE AVAILABLE

BEDROOM 3
10'-3" X 10'-1"

BEDROOM 2
10'-9" X 10'-1"

CLOSET

BATH 1

BATH 2

LINENS

WASH DRY

BEDROOM 1
13'-7" X 13'-7"

UNFINISHED REC. ROOM
11'-10" X 12'-0"

Upper Level Floor Plan

Copyright by designer/architect.

Plan #361004

Dimensions: 77' W x 81' D
Levels: 1
Square Footage: 2,191
Bedrooms: 3
Bathrooms: 2
Foundation: Crawl space
Materials List Available: No
Price Category: D

Images provided by designer/architect.

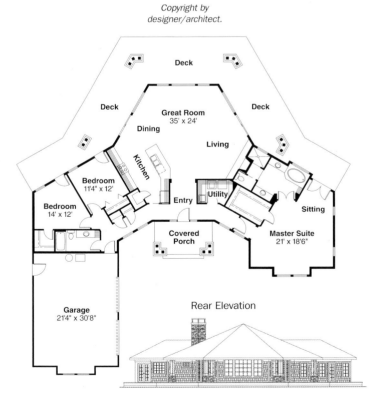

Copyright by designer/architect.

Deck

Deck

Deck

Great Room
35' x 24'

Dining

Living

Kitchen

Bedroom
11'4" x 12'

Bedroom
14' x 12'

Entry

Utility

Sitting

Master Suite
21' x 18'6"

Covered Porch

Garage
21'4" x 30'8"

Rear Elevation

Plan #161089

Dimensions: 64'2" W x 60'10" D
Levels: 2
Square Footage: 2,507
Main Level Sq. Ft.: 1,785
Upper Level Sq. Ft.: 722
Bedrooms: 4
Bathrooms: 2½
Foundation: Basement; crawl-space, slab, walkout for fee
Materials List Available: Yes
Price Category: E

This home will stand out in the neighborhood due to the stone siding, cedar shakes, and covered porch.

Images provided by designer/architect.

Features:

- **Great Room:** This large gathering area features a 14-ft.-high ceiling and a gas fireplace.

- **Kitchen:** This large peninsula kitchen is open to the breakfast area with access to the rear porch.

- **Master Suite:** Located on the main floor away from the secondary bedrooms, this suite has a sloped ceiling. The master bath has a compartmentalized lavatory, large shower, soaking tub, and walk-in closet.

- **Bedrooms:** The three secondary bedrooms are located on the upper level and share a common bathroom.

- **Garage:** This oversized garage has room for two cars plus room for storage.

Rear Elevation

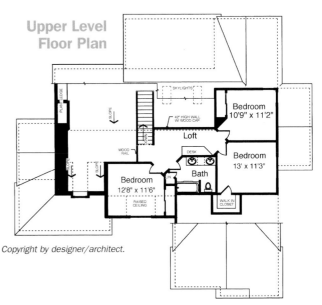

Plan #441015

Dimensions: 130'3" W x 79'3" D
Levels: 1
Square Footage: 4,732
Bedrooms: 4
Bathrooms: 3 full, 2 half
Foundation: Walkout basement
Materials List Available: No
Price Category: I

An artful use of stone was employed on the exterior of this rustic hillside home to complement other architectural elements, such as the angled, oversize four-car garage and the substantial roofline.

Features:

• Great Room: This massive vaulted room features a large stone fireplace at one end and a formal dining area at the other. A built-in media center and double doors separate the great room from a home office with its own hearth and built-ins.

• Kitchen: This kitchen features a walk-in pantry and snack counter and opens to a skylighted outdoor kitchen. Its appointments include a cooktop and a corner fireplace.

• Home Theatre: This space has a built-in viewing screen, a fireplace, and double terrace access.

• Master Suite: This private space is found at the other side of the home. Look closely for expansive his and her walk-in closets, a spa tub, a skylighted double vanity area, and a corner fireplace in the salon.

Images provided by designer/architect.

• Bedrooms: Three family bedrooms are on the lower level; bedroom 4 has a private bathroom and walk-in closet.

• Garage: This large garage has room for four cars; don't miss the dog shower and grooming station just off the garage.

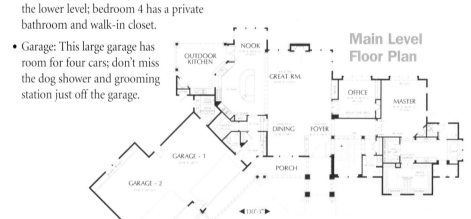

Copyright by designer/architect.

Entry

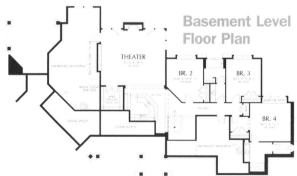

Master Bath

Rear View

Foyer

Dining Room

Great Room

Plan #161090

Dimensions: 69'4" W x 42'4" D
Levels: 1
Square Footage: 1,563
Bedrooms: 3
Bathrooms: 2
Foundation: Basement
Materials List Available: Yes
Price Category: C

This charming ranch with stone accents is a great starter home.

Features:

- Great Room: This large entertaining area has a sloped ceiling, a gas fireplace, and a view of the backyard.

- Kitchen: This peninsula kitchen is open to the dining area and is just a few steps away from the laundry area and the garage.

- Master Suite: This suite has a raised ceiling and a large walk-in closet. The master bath has an oversized tub.

- Bedrooms: The two secondary bedrooms have large closets and share a hall bathroom.

- Garage: This front-loading two-car garage has room for cars or any needed extra storage place.

Images provided by designer/architect.

Copyright by designer/architect.

Rear Elevation

Left Side Elevation

Right Side Elevation

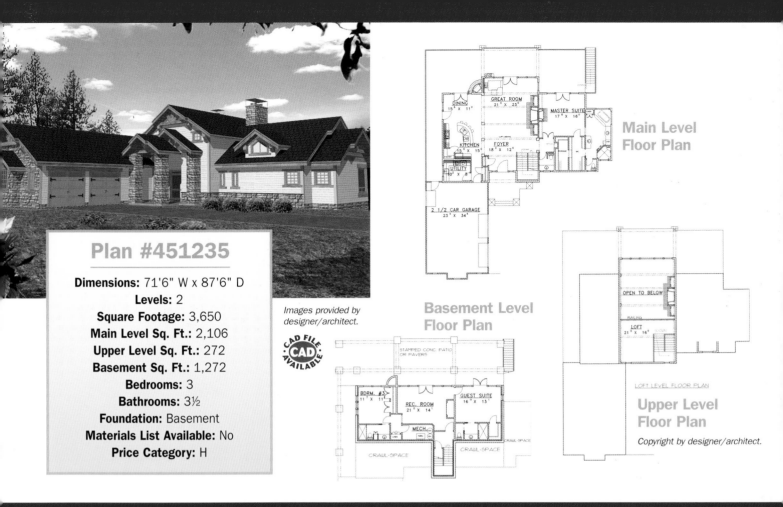

Plan #451235

Dimensions: 71'6" W x 87'6" D
Levels: 2
Square Footage: 3,650
Main Level Sq. Ft.: 2,106
Upper Level Sq. Ft.: 272
Basement Sq. Ft.: 1,272
Bedrooms: 3
Bathrooms: 3½
Foundation: Basement
Materials List Available: No
Price Category: H

Main Level Floor Plan

Basement Level Floor Plan

Upper Level Floor Plan

Images provided by designer/architect.

Copyright by designer/architect.

Plan #341059

Dimensions: 53' W x 51'6" D
Levels: 1.5
Square Footage: 1,554
Main Level Sq. Ft.: 1,554
Bonus Room Sq. Ft.: 622
Bedrooms: 3
Bathrooms: 2
Foundation: Crawl space
Materials List Available: Yes
Price Category: C

Images provided by designer/architect.

Main Level Floor Plan

Upper Level Floor Plan
Copyright by designer/architect.

Plan #441018

Dimensions: 36' W x 44' D
Levels: 2
Square Footage: 1,500
Main Level Sq. Ft.: 716
Upper Level Sq. Ft.: 784
Bedrooms: 3
Bathrooms: 2½
Foundation: Crawl space
Materials List Available: No
Price Category: C

Images provided by designer/architect.

A trio of gables and a porch entry create a charming exterior for this home. With a compact footprint especially suited for smaller lots, it offers all the amenities important to today's sophisticated homebuyer.

Features:

• Great Room: From the entry, view this spacious two-story room, which features a fireplace and a wall of windows overlooking the porch.

• Dining Room: A French door to the porch is located in this room, along with a planning desk and a large pantry.

• Kitchen: Family will gravitate to this corner kitchen. It offers plenty of cabinet space and countertops including a center island, complete with a breakfast bar to add more space and convenience.

• Master Suite: Located upstairs, this vaulted suite features a walk-in closet and private bathroom.

Main Level Floor Plan

Copyright by designer/architect.

Upper Level Floor Plan

Main Level Floor Plan

Images provided by designer/architect.

Plan #451217

Dimensions: 103'6" W x 53'11" D
Levels: 1
Square Footage: 4,711
Main Level Sq. Ft.: 2,470
Lower Level Sq. Ft.: 2,241
Bedrooms: 4
Bathrooms: 3
Foundation: Walk-out basement
Materials List Available: No
Price Category: I

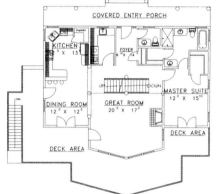

Basement Level Floor Plan

Copyright by designer/architect.

Images provided by designer/architect.

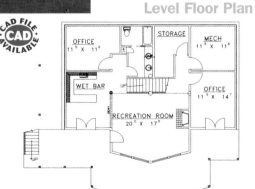

Main Level Floor Plan

Copyright by designer/architect.

Upper Level Floor Plan

Plan #451249

Dimensions: 52' W x 54'8" D
Levels: 2
Square Footage: 2,281
Main Level Sq. Ft.: 1,436
Upper Level Sq. Ft.: 845
Bedrooms: 3
Bathrooms: 3
Foundation: Walk-out basement
Materials List Available: No
Price Category: E

Basement Level Floor Plan

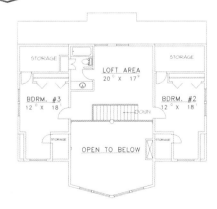

Main Level Floor Plan

Copyright by designer/architect.

Dining 13' x 15'

Breakfast 15'2" x 9'

Great Room 16' x 23'10"

Kitchen 16'6" x 9'

Laun.

Hall

Dressing

walk-in closet

Two-car Garage 22' x 22'

Raised Foyer

Porch

Master Bedroom 13'2" x 16'

Upper Level Floor Plan

Images provided by designer/architect.

Rear View

Bedroom 12'10" x 11'6"

Bedroom 11' x 11'6"

Bath

Balcony

Great Room Below

walk-in closet

Bonus Room 11' x 11'11"

Plan #161034

Dimensions: 56' W x 53' D
Levels: 2
Square Footage: 2,156
Main Level Sq. Ft.: 1,605
Upper Level Sq. Ft.: 551
Bedrooms: 3
Bathrooms: 2½
Foundation: Basement
Materials List Available: No
Price Category: D

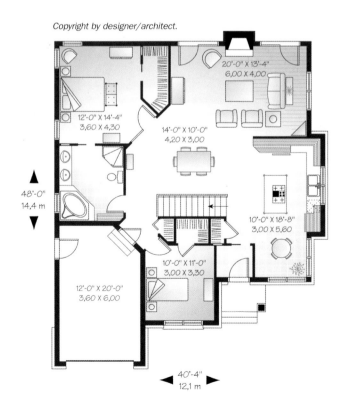

Copyright by designer/architect.

20'-0" X 13'-4"
6,00 X 4,00

12'-0" X 14'-4"
3,60 X 4,30

14'-0" X 10'-0"
4,20 X 3,00

48'-0"
14,4 m

10'-0" X 18'-8"
3,00 X 5,60

10'-0" X 11'-0"
3,00 X 3,30

12'-0" X 20'-0"
3,60 X 6,00

40'-4"
12,1 m

Plan #181274

Images provided by designer/architect.

Dimensions: 40'4" W x 48' D
Levels: 1
Square Footage: 1,355
Bedrooms: 2
Bathrooms: 1
Foundation: Basement
Materials List Available: Yes
Price Category: B

Main Level Floor Plan

Plan #181301

Dimensions: 68' W x 64' D

Levels: 2

Square Footage: 3,943

Main Level Sq. Ft.: 2,486

Upper Level Sq. Ft.: 1,457

Bedrooms: 4

Bathrooms: 3½

Foundation: Basement

Materials List Available: Yes

Price Category: H

Images provided by designer/architect.

Upper Level Floor Plan

Copyright by designer/architect.

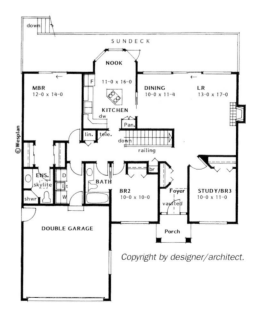

Plan #281009

Dimensions: 46' W x 52' D

Levels: 1

Square Footage: 1,423

Bedrooms: 3

Bathrooms: 2

Foundation: Walk-out basement

Materials List Available: Yes

Price Category: B

Images provided by designer/architect.

Copyright by designer/architect.

Rear Elevation

Plan #281016

Dimensions: 46' W x 44' D
Levels: 2
Square Footage: 1,945
Main Level Sq. Ft.: 1,211
Upper Level Sq. Ft.: 734
Bedrooms: 3
Bathrooms: 3
Foundation: Combination basement/slab
Materials List Available: Yes
Price Category: D

Images provided by designer/architect.

Main Level Floor Plan

Upper Level Floor Plan

Copyright by designer/architect.

Rear Elevation

Plan #441028

Dimensions: 53'6" W x 73' D
Levels: 2
Square Footage: 3,165
Main Level Sq. Ft.: 1,268
Upper Level Sq. Ft.: 932
Lower Level Sq. Ft.: 966
Bedrooms: 4
Bathrooms: 3½
Foundation: Slab
Materials List Available: No
Price Category: G

Images provided by designer/architect.

Main Level Floor Plan

Upper Level Floor Plan

Lower Level Floor Plan

Copyright by designer/architect.

Plan #441035

Dimensions: 50' W x 56' D
Levels: 2
Square Footage: 2,196
Main Level Sq. Ft.: 1,658
Upper Level Sq. Ft.: 538
Bedrooms: 4
Bathrooms: 2½
Foundation: Crawl space;
slab or basement available for fee
Materials List Available: No
Price Category: D

Images provided by designer/architect.

- **Bonus Space:** This huge space, located on the second level, provides for a future bedroom, game room, or home office. Two dormer windows grace it.

- **Garage:** A service hall, with laundry alcove, opens to this garage. There is space enough here for three cars or two and a workshop.

This home's stone-and-cedar-shingle facade is delightfully complemented by French Country detailing, dormer windows, and shutters at the large arched window and its second-story sister.

CAD FILE AVAILABLE

Features:

- **Great Room:** Containing a fireplace and double doors to the rear yard, this large room is further enhanced by a vaulted ceiling.

- **Kitchen:** This cooking center has an attached nook with corner windows overlooking the backyard.

- **Master Suite:** This suite is well designed with a vaulted ceiling and Palladian window. Its bath sports a spa tub.

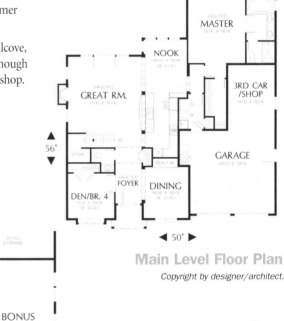

Upper Level Floor Plan

Main Level Floor Plan

Copyright by designer/architect.

Rear Elevation

Plan #331005

Dimensions: 85'11" W x 55'7" D
Levels: 2
Square Footage: 3,585
Main Level Sq. Ft.: 2,691
Upper Level Sq. Ft.: 894
Bedrooms: 4
Bathrooms: 3½
Foundation: Crawl space, slab, or basement
Materials List Available: No
Price Category: H

Images provided by designer/architect.

You'll love the stately, traditional exterior design and the contemporary, casual interior layout as they are combined in this elegant home.

Features:

- Foyer: The highlight of this spacious area is the curved stairway to the balcony over head.

- Family Room: The two-story ceiling and second-floor balcony overlooking this room add to its spacious feeling, but you can decorate around the fireplace to create a cozy, intimate area.

- Study: Use this versatile room as a guest room, home office or media room.

- Kitchen: Designed for the modern cook, this kitchen features a step-saving design, an island for added work space, and ample storage space.

- Master Suite: Step out to the rear deck from the bedroom to admire the moonlit scenery or bask in the morning sun. The luxurious bath makes an ideal place to relax in privacy.

Main Level Floor Plan

Rear View

Copyright by designer/architect.

Upper Level Floor Plan

Images provided by designer/architect.

Plan #441038

Dimensions: 59' W x 51'6" D
Levels: 2
Square Footage: 2,518
Main Level Sq. Ft.: 1,464
Upper Level Sq. Ft.: 1,054
Bedrooms: 4
Bathrooms: 3
Foundation: Crawl space; slab or basement available for fee
Materials List Available: No
Price Category: E

Features:

- Kitchen: This kitchen contains gourmet appointments with an island countertop, a large pantry, and a work desk built in.
- Dining Room: This formal room connects directly to the kitchen for convenience.
- Master Suite: This suite features a fine bath with a spa tub and separate shower.
- Bedrooms: A bedroom (or make it a home office) is tucked away behind the two-car garage and has the use of a full bathroom across the hall. Three additional bedrooms are found on the upper level, along with a large bonus space that could be developed later into bedroom 5.

Victorians are such a cherished style; it's impossible not to admire them. This one begins with all the classic details and adds a most up-to-date floor plan.

CAD FILE AVAILABLE

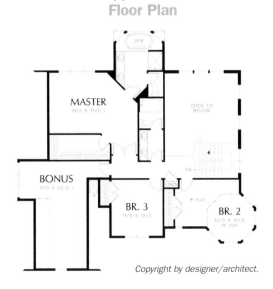

Copyright by designer/architect.

Plan #441044

Dimensions: 54' W x 47' D
Levels: 2
Square Footage: 2,277
Main Level Sq. Ft.: 1,563
Upper Level Sq. Ft.: 714
Bedrooms: 5
Bathrooms: 2½
Foundation: Crawl space;
slab or basement available for fee
Materials List Available: No
Price Category: E

Images provided by designer/architect.

This handsome design takes its initial cues from the American farmhouse style, but it blends in a wonderful mixture of exterior materials to enliven the look. Cedar battens, lap siding, and stone accents work together for an out-of-the-ordinary facade.

Features:

• **Open Living:** The floor plan is thoughtfully created and holds just the right amount of space for exceptional livability. An open living area, comprising a vaulted great room, dining room, and large kitchen, lies to the rear of the main level and can take advantage of back-yard views and a patio.

• **Den:** This room, which is located at the front of the main level, may also become an additional bedroom if you need the space.

• **Master Suite:** This suite is located on the main level. It features a salon with a vaulted ceiling and a bath with a spa tub, separate shower, and compartmented toilet.

• **Bonus Space:** This space on the upper level complements two family bedrooms and a shared full bathroom.

Main Level Floor Plan

Upper Level Floor Plan

Copyright by designer/architect.

Rear Elevation

Plan #441048

Dimensions: 48' W x 40' D
Levels: 2
Square Footage: 2,453
Main Level Sq. Ft.: 1,118
Upper Level Sq. Ft.: 1,335
Bedrooms: 4
Bathrooms: 2½
Foundation: Crawl space
Materials List Available: No
Price Category: E

The perfect-size plan and a pretty facade add up to a great home for your family. The combination of wood siding and stone complements a carriage-style garage door and cedar-shingle detailing on the outside of this home.

Images provided by designer/architect.

Features:

- **Entry:** The interior opens though this angled front entry, with the den on the left and a half-bathroom on the right. The den has a comfortable window seat for dreaming and gazing.

- **Kitchen:** The dining area adjoins this island kitchen, which has a roomy pantry and built-in desk.

- **Master Suite:** This vaulted suite features a spa bath, walk-in closet with window seat, and separate tub and shower.

- **Upper Level:** All bedrooms are located on this level. Bedroom 3 has a walk-in closet. The laundry area is also located here to make wash day trouble free.

Rear Elevation

Copyright by designer/architect.

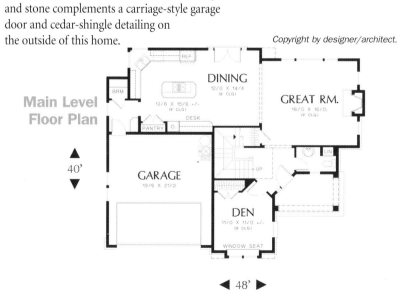

Main Level Floor Plan

Upper Level Floor Plan

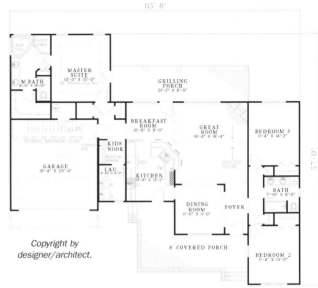

Plan #151510

Dimensions: 65'8" W x 57' D

Levels: 1

Square Footage: 1,813

Bedrooms: 3

Bathrooms: 2

Foundation: Crawl space or slab

CompleteCost List Available: Yes

Price Category: D

Images provided by designer/architect.

Copyright by designer/architect.

CAD FILE AVAILABLE

Plan #181063

Dimensions: 55' W x 41' D

Levels: 2

Square Footage: 2,037

Main Level Sq. Ft.: 1,347

Upper Level Sq. Ft.: 690

Bedrooms: 4

Bathrooms: 2

Foundation: Full basement

Materials List Available: Yes

Price Category: D

CAD FILE AVAILABLE

Images provided by designer/architect.

This home, as shown in the photograph, may differ from the actual blueprints. For more detailed information, please check the floor plans carefully.

Main Level Floor Plan

Upper Level Floor Plan

Copyright by designer/architect.

Plan #181120

Dimensions: 32' W x 40' D
Levels: 2
Square Footage: 1,480
Main Level Sq. Ft.: 1,024
Second Level Sq. Ft.: 456
Bedrooms: 2
Bathrooms: 2
Foundation: Basement
Materials List Available: Yes
Price Category: B

Images provided by designer/architect.

Escape to this charming all-season vacation home with lots of view-capturing windows.

Features:

- Ceiling Height: 8 ft. unless otherwise noted.

- Living/Dining Area: The covered back porch opens into this large, inviting combined area. Its high ceiling adds to the sense of spaciousness.

- Family Room: After relaxing in front of the fireplace that warms this family room, family and guests can move outside onto the porch to watch the sun set.

- Kitchen: Light streams through a triple window in this well-designed kitchen. It's conveniently located next to the dining area and features a center island with a breakfast bar and double sinks.

- Master Suite: This first floor suite is located in the front of the house and is enhanced by its large walk-through closet and the adjoining private bath.

Main Level Floor Plan

Upper Level Floor Plan

Plan #131056

Dimensions: 40' W x 54' D
Levels: 1.5
Square Footage: 1,396
Main Level Sq. Ft.: 964
Upper Level Sq. Ft.: 432
Bedrooms: 3
Bathrooms: 2
Foundation: Slab or basement
Materials List Available: Yes
Price Category: B

This ruggedly handsome home is a true A-frame. The elegance of the roof virtually meeting the ground and the use of rugged stone veneer and log-cabin siding make it stand out.

Features:

- Living Room: This area is the interior high-light of the home. The large, exciting space features a soaring ceiling, a massive fireplace, and a magnificent window wall to capture a view.

- Side Porch: The secondary entry from this side porch leads to a center hall that provides direct access to the first floor's two bedrooms, bathroom, kitchen, and living room.

- Kitchen: This kitchen is extremely efficient and includes a snack bar and access to the screened porch.

- Loft Area: A spiral stairway leads from the living room to this second-floor loft, which overlooks the living room. The area can also double as an extra sleeping room.

Images provided by designer/architect.

Main Level Floor Plan

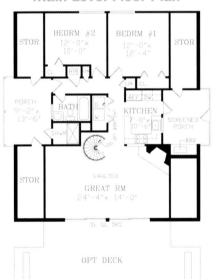

Upper Level Floor Plan

Copyright by designer/architect

Rear View

Great Room

Main Level Floor Plan

10'-0" X 13'-8"
3,00 X 4,10

28'-0"
8,4 m

26'-8" X 13'-0"
8,00 X 3,90

28'-0"
8,4 m

Plan #181244

Dimensions: 28' W x 28' D
Levels: 2
Square Footage: 1,381
Main Level Sq. Ft.: 784
Upper Level Sq. Ft.: 597
Bedrooms: 3
Bathrooms: 1½
Foundation: Basement
Materials List Available: Yes
Price Category: B

Images provided by designer/architect.

CAD FILE AVAILABLE

9'-0" X 10'-0"
2,70 X 3,00

9'-0" X 10'-0"
2,70 X 3,00

15'-0" X 11'-0"
4,50 X 3,30

Upper Level Floor Plan

Copyright by designer/architect.

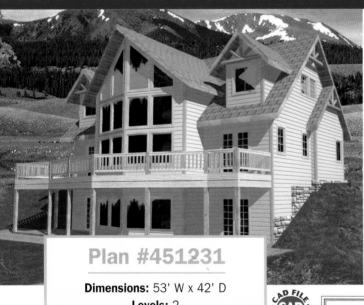

Plan #451231

Dimensions: 53' W x 42' D
Levels: 2
Square Footage: 2,281
Main Level Sq. Ft.: 1,436
Upper Level Sq. Ft.: 845
Bedrooms: 3
Bathrooms: 2½
Foundation: Walk-out basement
Materials List Available: No
Price Category: E

Images provided by designer/architect.

Main Level Floor Plan

Copyright by designer/architect.

COVERED ENTRY PORCH

KITCHEN
13' X 13'

FOYER
6'10" X 14'

DINING ROOM
12' X 12'

MASTER SUITE
12' X 15'10

GREAT ROOM
20' X 17'

DECK AREA

DECK AREA

CAD FILE AVAILABLE

Basement Level Floor Plan

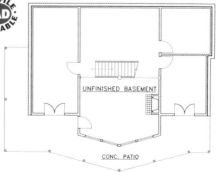

UNFINISHED BASEMENT

CONC. PATIO

Upper Level Floor Plan

STORAGE

STORAGE

LOFT AREA
20' X 17'

BDRM. #3
12' X 18'

BDRM. #2
12' X 18'

OPEN TO BELOW

STORAGE

STORAGE

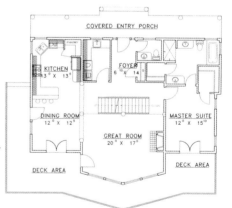

Plan #181221

Dimensions: 60' W x 44' D
Levels: 2
Square Footage: 3,411
Main Level Sq. Ft.: 1,488
Upper Level Sq. Ft.: 603
Basement Level Sq. Ft.: 1,321
Bedrooms: 3
Bathrooms: 2½
Foundation: Basement
Materials List Available: Yes
Price Category: G

Images provided by designer/architect.

This stone- and wood-sided home will be a joy to come home to.

Features:

- Living Room: This large entertaining area features a fireplace and large windows.

- Kitchen: Any cook would feel at home in this island kitchen, which has an abundance of cabinets and counter space.

- Master Bedroom: Located on the main level for privacy, this room features a walk-in closet and access to the main-level full bathroom.

- Bedrooms: One bedroom is located on the upper level and the other is located on the main level. Each has a large closet.

Study

Living Room

Main Level Floor Plan

44'-0"
13,2 m

60'-0"
18.0 m

17'-0" X 14'-1"
5,10 X 4,30

13'-4" X 14'-0"
4,00 X 4,25

16'-4" X 22'-1"
4,90 X 6,80

15'-0" X 15'-1"
4,50 X 4,60

12'-0" X 10'-1"
3,60 X 3,00

Upper Level Floor Plan

Copyright by designer/architect.

12'-6" X 13'-1"
3,75 X 4,20

14'-1" X 11'-1"
4,22 X 3,40

Basement Level Floor Plan

19'-8" X 28'-1"
4,70 X 8,50

13'-0" X 13'-1"
3,90 X 4,20

11'-8" X 27'-1"
3,50 X 8,00

Dining Room/ Kitchen

Foyer

Plan #321040

Dimensions: 35' W x 40'8" D

Levels: 1

Square Footage: 1,084

Bedrooms: 2

Bathrooms: 2

Foundation: Basement

Materials List Available: Yes

Price Category: B

This cute cottage, with its front porch, would make a great starter home or a weekend getaway home.

Features:

- Living Room: This room features an entry closet and a cozy fireplace.

- Kitchen: This well-designed kitchen opens into the breakfast area.

- Master Suite: This retreat has a walk-in closet and a private bath.

- Bedroom: This second bedroom features a walk-in closet and has access to the hall bathroom.

Images provided by designer/architect.

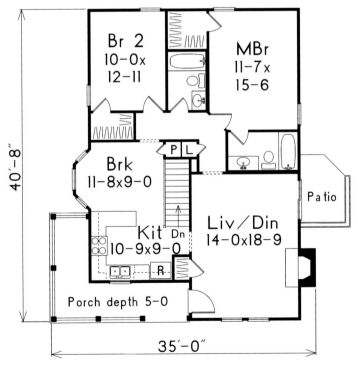

Copyright by designer/architect.

Plan #181133

Dimensions: 38' W x 40' D
Levels: 2
Square Footage: 1,832
Main Level Sq. Ft.: 1,212
Second Level Sq. Ft. 620
Bedrooms: 3
Bathrooms: 2
Foundation: Basement
Materials List Available: Yes
Price Category: D

You'll enjoy sunshine indoors and out with a wraparound deck and windows all around.

CAD FILE AVAILABLE

Images provided by designer/architect.

Features:

- Ceiling Height: 8 ft.

- Family Room: Family and friends will be drawn to this large sunny room. Curl up with a good book before the beautiful see-through fireplace.

- Screened Porch: This porch shares the see-through fireplace with the family room so you can enjoy an outside fire on cool summer nights.

- Master Suite: This romantic first-floor master suite offers a large walk-in closet and a luxurious private bathroom enhanced by dual vanities.

- Secondary Bedrooms: Upstairs you'll find two generous bedrooms with ample closet space. These bedrooms share a full bathroom.

- Basement: This large walkout basement with large glass door is perfectly suited for future expansion.

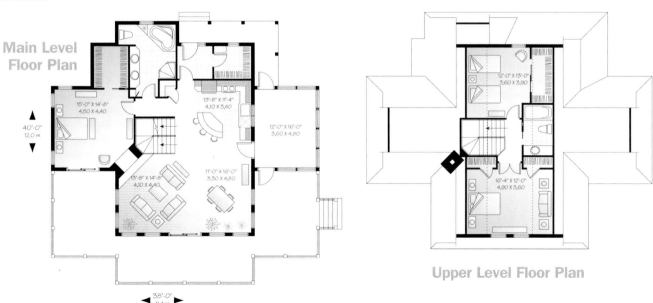

Main Level Floor Plan

Upper Level Floor Plan

Plan #181128

Dimensions: 36' W x 36' D
Levels: 2
Square Footage: 1,634
Main Level Sq. Ft.: 1,087
Second Level Sq. Ft.: 547
Bedrooms: 3
Bathrooms: 2
Foundation: Basement
Materials List Available: Yes
Price Category: C

Images provided by designer/architect.

This stone-accented rustic vacation home offers the perfect antidote to busy daily life.

Features:

- Ceiling Height: 8 ft. unless otherwise noted.
- Family Room: Family and friends will be unable to resist relaxing in this airy two-story family room, with its own handsome fireplace. French doors lead to the front deck.
- Kitchen: This eat-in kitchen features double sinks, ample counter space, and a pantry. It offers plenty of space for the family to gather for informal vacation meals.

- Master Suite: This first-floor master retreat occupies almost the entire length of the home. It includes a walk-in closet and a lavish bath.
- Secondary Bedrooms: On the second floor, two family bedrooms share a full bath.
- Mezzanine: This lovely balcony overlooks the family room.
- Basement: This full unfinished basement offers plenty of space for expansion.

Main Level Floor Plan

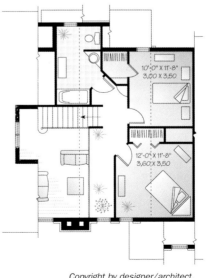

Upper Level Floor Plan

Copyright by designer/architect.

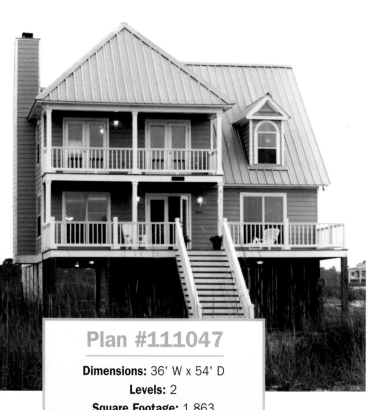

Images provided by designer/architect.

Plan #111047

Dimensions: 36' W x 54' D

Levels: 2

Square Footage: 1,863

Main Level Sq. Ft.: 1,056

Upper Level Sq. Ft.: 807

Bedrooms: 4

Bathrooms: 3

Foundation: Pier

Materials List Available: No

Price Category: D

Designed for a coastline, this home is equally appropriate as a year-round residence or a vacation retreat.

Features:

- **Orientation:** The rear-facing design gives you an ocean view and places the most attractive side of the house where beach-goers can see it.

- **Entryway:** On the waterside, a large deck with a covered portion leads to the main entrance.

- **Carport:** This house is raised on piers that let you park underneath it and that protect it from water damage during storms.

- **Living Room:** A fireplace, French doors, and large windows grace this room, which is open to both the kitchen and the dining area.

- **Master Suite:** Two sets of French doors open to a balcony on the ocean side, and the suite includes two walk-in closets and a fully equipped bath.

Main Level Floor Plan

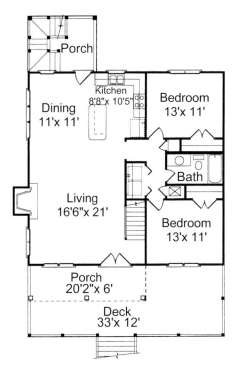

Upper Level Floor Plan

Copyright by designer/architect.

Plan #181001

Dimensions: 38' W x 28' D
Levels: 1
Square Footage: 920
Bedrooms: 2
Bathrooms: 1
Foundation: Basement
Materials List Available: Yes
Price Category: A

Images provided by designer/architect.

This cozy and charming one-story cottage offers many amenities in its well-designed layout.

Features:

- Ceiling Height: 8 ft.

- Porch: Enjoy summer evenings relaxing on the front porch.

- Kitchen: This kitchen has ample work and storage space as well as a breakfast bar and enough room for the family to dine together.

- Family Room: Natural light streaming through the windows makes this an appealing place for family activities.

- Bedrooms: There's a generous master bedroom and one secondary bedroom. Each has its own closet.

- Laundry Room: A fully equipped laundry room is conveniently located adjacent to the kitchen.

- Full Basement: Here is plenty of storage room as well as the opportunity for expanded living space.

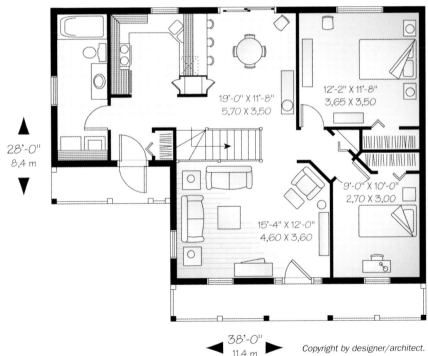

28'-0"
8,4 m

38'-0"
11,4 m

Copyright by designer/architect.

Plan #391001

Dimensions: 32' W x 40' D
Levels: 2
Square Footage: 2,015
Main Level Sq. Ft.: 1,280
Upper Level Sq. Ft.: 735
Bedrooms: 3
Bathrooms: 2½
Foundation: Crawl space
Materials List Available: Yes
Price Category: D

Images provided by designer/architect.

- **Kitchen:** This L-shaped kitchen features an expansive cooktop/lunch counter.

- **Utility Areas:** A utility room handles the laundry and storage, and a half bath with linen closet takes care of other necessities.

- **Master Suite:** This main-floor master suite is just that—sweet! The spa-style bath features

a corner tub nestled against a greenhouse window. Plus, there are double sinks and a separate shower.

- **Upstairs:** The sun-washed loft overlooks the activity below while embracing two dreamy bedrooms and a sizable bath with double sinks.

Follow your dream to this home surrounded with decking. The A-frame front showcases bold windowing (on two levels), and natural lighting fills the house.

Features:

- **Dining Room:** This dining room and the family room are completely open to each other, perfect for hanging out in the warmth of the hearth.

Main Level Floor Plan

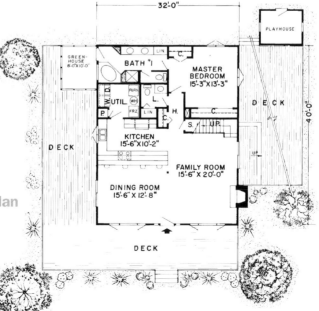

Upper Level Floor Plan

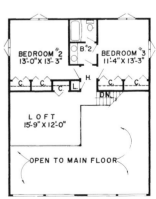

Copyright by designer/architect.

Images provided by designer/architect.

Plan #181122

Dimensions: 62' W x 36'4" D
Levels: 2
Square Footage: 3,105
Main Level Sq. Ft.: 1,470
Upper Level Sq. Ft.: 1,635
Bedrooms: 4
Bathrooms: 3
Foundation: Walkout basement
Materials List Available: Yes
Price Category: G

Upper Level Floor Plan

Copyright by designer/architect.

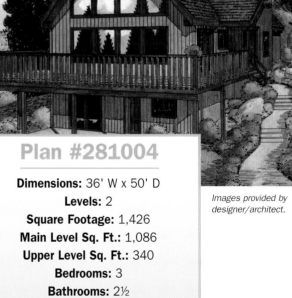

Plan #281004

Dimensions: 36' W x 50' D
Levels: 2
Square Footage: 1,426
Main Level Sq. Ft.: 1,086
Upper Level Sq. Ft.: 340
Bedrooms: 3
Bathrooms: 2½
Foundation: Walk-out basement
Materials List Available: Yes
Price Category: B

Images provided by designer/architect.

Main Level Floor Plan

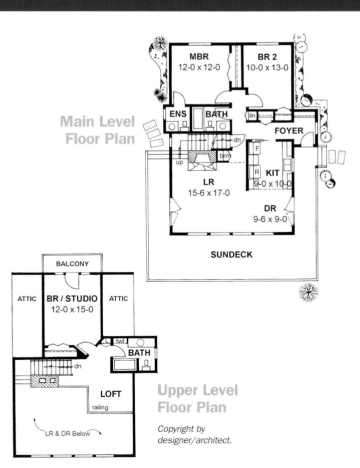

Upper Level Floor Plan

Copyright by designer/architect.

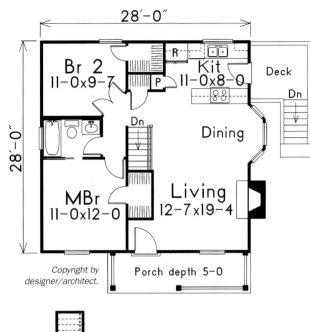

28'-0"

Br 2
11-0x9-7

Kit
11-0x8-0

Deck

Dn

MBr
11-0x12-0

Dn

Dining

Living
12-7x19-4

28'-0"

Copyright by designer/architect.

Porch depth 5-0

Images provided by designer/architect.

Plan #321025

Dimensions: 28' W x 28' D

Levels: 1

Square Footage: 914

Bedrooms: 2

Bathrooms: 1

Foundation: Basement, walk-out

Materials List Available: Yes

Price Category: A

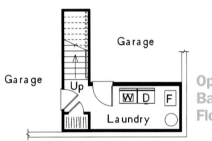

Garage

Garage

Up

W D F

Laundry

Optional Basement Level Floor Plan

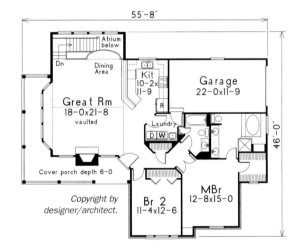

55'-8"

Atrium below

Dn

Dining Area

Kit
10-2x11-9

Garage
22-0x11-9

Great Rm
18-0x21-8
vaulted

Laundry

D W

46'-0"

Cover porch depth 6-0

Br 2
11-4x12-6

MBr
12-8x15-0

Copyright by designer/architect.

Plan #321035

Dimensions: 55'8" W x 46' D

Levels: 1

Square Footage: 1,384

Bedrooms: 2

Bathrooms: 2

Foundation: Walkout

Materials List Available: Yes

Price Category: B

Images provided by designer/architect.

Rear View

Up

Patio

Optional Basement Level Floor Plan

Family Rm
25-0x21-4

Unexcavated

Unfinished Basement

Plan #391046

Dimensions: 67'6" W x 39'6" D
Levels: 2
Square Footage: 1,978
Main Level Sq. Ft.: 1,034
Upper Level Sq. Ft.: 944
Bedrooms: 4
Bathrooms: 2½
Foundation: Crawl space, slab, or basement
Materials List Available: Yes
Price Category: D

This could be your coastal cottage or the pretty place you come home to every day.

Features:

• **Porch:** This wraparound porch leads inside to an airy front entry with coat closet.

• **Staircase:** This central staircase divides the layout, with a versatile den/guest room and powder room on one side and a stylish dining room on the other.

• **Kitchen:** Surrounded by counters and cabinetry, this kitchen features a centralized lunch island that is made for two but gathers more.

• **Living Room:** The fireplace is a big draw, and there's more than one way to reach the family's favorite space.

• **Bedrooms:** A bi-level staircase reaches the second-level sitting area and all three bedrooms. Two secondary bedrooms enjoy unique character as well as wall-length closets and excellent windowing.

• **Master Suite:** This area is a masterpiece, with its cathedral ceilings, L-shaped walk-in closet, corner tub, separate shower and toilet, and double sinks.

Images provided by designer/architect.

Front View

Rear View

Main Level Floor Plan

Upper Level Floor Plan

Copyright by designer/architect.

Plan #321009

Dimensions: 55'8" W x 46'4" D
Levels: 1
Square Footage: 2,295
Bedrooms: 3
Bathrooms: 2
Foundation: Basement
Materials List Available: Yes
Price Category: E

Images provided by designer/architect.

If you've got a site with great views, you'll love this home, which is designed to make the most of them.

Features:

- Porch: This wraparound porch is an ideal spot to watch the sun come up or go down. Add potted plants to create a lush atmosphere or grow some culinary herbs.

- Great Room: You couldn't ask for more luxury than this room provides, with its vaulted ceiling, large bay window, fireplace, dining balcony, and atrium window wall.

- Kitchen: No matter whether you're an avid cook or not, you'll relish the thoughtful design of this room.

- Master Suite: This suite is truly a retreat you'll treasure. It has two large walk-in closets for good storage space, and sliding doors that open to an exterior balcony where you can sit out to enjoy the stars. The amenity-filled bath adds to your enjoyment of this suite.

Rear View

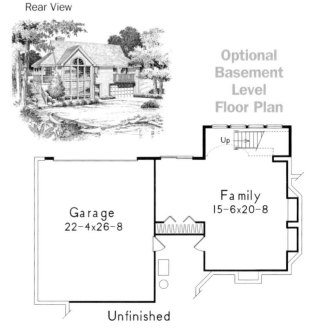

Optional Basement Level Floor Plan

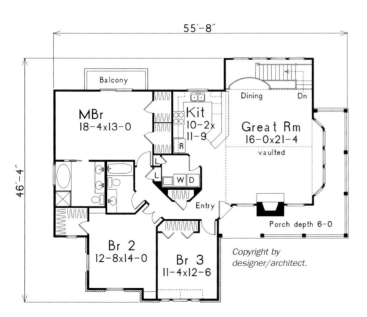

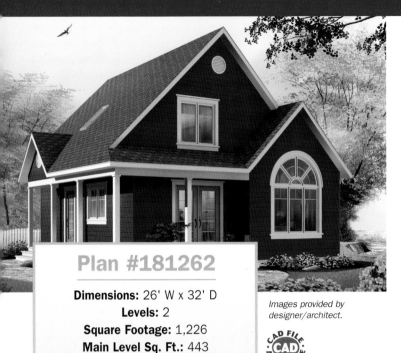

Plan #181262

Dimensions: 26' W x 32' D
Levels: 2
Square Footage: 1,226
Main Level Sq. Ft.: 443
Upper Level Sq. Ft.: 783
Bedrooms: 2
Bathrooms: 2
Foundation: Basement
Materials List Available: Yes
Price Category: B

Images provided by designer/architect.

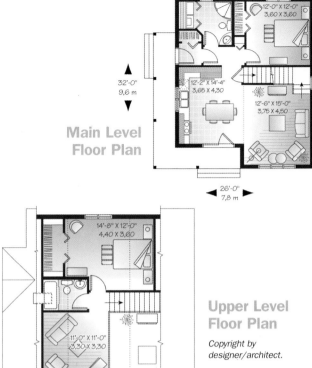

Main Level Floor Plan

Upper Level Floor Plan

Copyright by designer/architect.

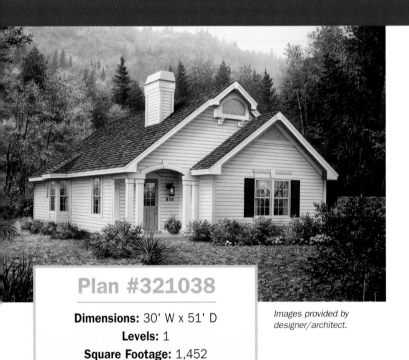

Plan #321038

Dimensions: 30' W x 51' D
Levels: 1
Square Footage: 1,452
Bedrooms: 4
Bathrooms: 2
Foundation: Basement
Materials List Available: Yes
Price Category: B

Images provided by designer/architect.

Copyright by designer/architect.

Plan #111040

Dimensions: 37' W x 52' D
Levels: 2
Square Footage: 1,650
Main Level Sq. Ft.: 1,122
Upper Level Sq. Ft.: 528
Bedrooms: 4
Bathrooms: 2
Foundation: Pier
Materials List Available: No
Price Category: C

Images provided by designer/architect.

Main Level Floor Plan

Upper Level Floor Plan

Copyright by designer/architect.

Plan #111042

Dimensions: 34' W x 30' D
Levels: 2
Square Footage: 1,779
Main Level Sq. Ft.: 907
Upper Level Sq. Ft.: 872
Bedrooms: 3
Bathrooms: 2½
Foundation: Pier
Materials List Available: No
Price Category: C

Images provided by designer/architect.

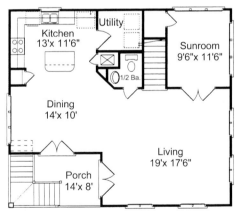

Main Level Floor Plan

Copyright by designer/architect.

Upper Level Floor Plan

Plan #401049

Dimensions: 77'10" W x 55'8" D
Levels: 2
Square Footage: 4,087
Main Level Sq. Ft.: 2,403
Upper Level Sq. Ft.: 1,684
Bedrooms: 4
Bathrooms: 4½
Foundation: Basement
Materials List Available: Yes
Price Category: I

Finished in stucco, with an elegant entry, this dramatic two-story home is the essence of luxury.

CAD FILE AVAILABLE

Features:

- **Foyer:** Double doors open to this foyer, with a sunken living room on the right and a den on the left.

- **Dining Room:** An archway leads to this formal room, mirroring its own bow window and the curved window in the living room.

- **Den:** This den and the nearby computer room have use of a full bathroom — making them handy as extra guest rooms when needed.

- **Family Room:** This room, like the living room, is sunken and warmed by a hearth, but it also has built-in bookcases.

- **Kitchen:** A snack-bar counter separates this U-shaped kitchen from the light-filled breakfast room.

Images provided by designer/architect.

- **Master Suite:** This gigantic space has his and her vanities, an oversized shower, a walk-in closet, and a sitting area.

Main Level Floor Plan

Optional Upper Level Floor Plan

Copyright by designer/architect.

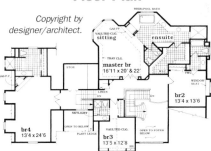

Upper Level Floor Plan

Basement Level Floor Plan

Plan #441027

Dimensions: 63' W x 90' D
Levels: 2
Square Footage: 3,638
Main Level Sq. Ft.: 2,654
Upper Level Sq. Ft.: 984
Bedrooms: 4
Bathrooms: 3½
Foundation: Crawl space; slab or basement available for fee
Materials List Available: No
Price Category: H

Cape Cod style is universally appealing as evidenced in this home. Cedar shingle siding, three dormers, and a grand bay window are cherished exterior elements, complemented by an up-to-date floor plan.

Features:

- **Great Room:** This room is the center of the design and serves well as both formal and casual living space. It features an exposed-beam ceiling, a fireplace flanked by built-ins, a columned arched entry, and double doors to a rear porch.

- **Kitchen:** Sitting between the formal dining room and the breakfast nook, this kitchen has a snack-bar counter, which is open to the great room. A handy butler's pantry makes for easy entertaining.

- **Master Suite:** Located on the main level for convenience and privacy, this retreat features a decorative ceiling and a large sleeping area. The master bath offers a large walk-in closet, dual vanities, a spa tub, and a shower.

Images provided by designer/architect.

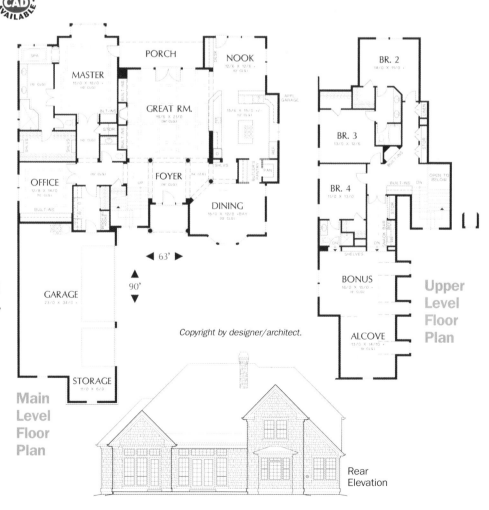

Copyright by designer/architect.

Main Level Floor Plan

Upper Level Floor Plan

Rear Elevation

Plan #111010

Dimensions: 34' W x 38' D
Levels: 3
Square Footage: 1,804
Main Level Sq. Ft.: 731
Upper Level Sq. Ft.: 935
Third Level Sq.Ft.: 138
Bedrooms: 3
Bathrooms: 3
Foundation: Piers
Materials List Available: No
Price Category: D

Copyright by designer/architect.

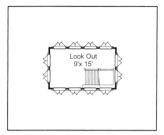

Third Level Floor Plan

Images provided by designer/architect.

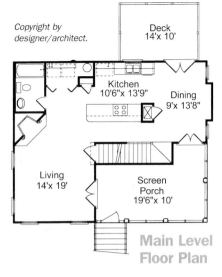

Deck 14'x 10'

Kitchen 10'6"x 13'9"
Dining 9'x 13'8"

Living 14'x 19'

Screen Porch 19'6"x 10'

Main Level Floor Plan

Bedroom 11'6"x 11'

Master Bedroom 18'6"x 15'

Bedroom 12'x 10'

Upper Level Floor Plan

Look Out 9'x 15'

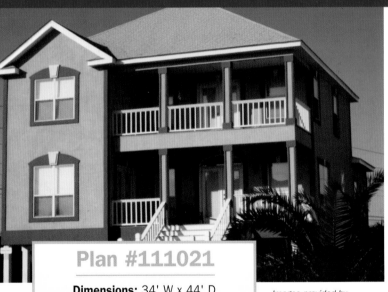

Plan #111021

Dimensions: 34' W x 44' D
Levels: 2
Square Footage: 2,221
Main Level Sq. Ft.: 1,307
Upper Level Sq. Ft.: 914
Bedrooms: 4
Bathrooms: 3
Foundation: Pier
Materials List Available: No
Price Category: E

Images provided by designer/architect.

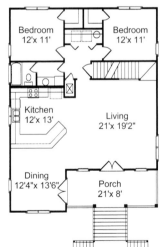

Bedroom 12'x 11'
Bedroom 12'x 11'

Kitchen 12'x 13'
Living 21'x 19'2"

Dining 12'4"x 13'6"
Porch 21'x 8'

Main Level Floor Plan

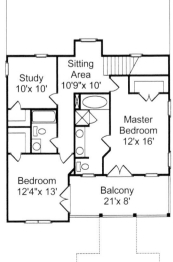

Study 10'x 10'
Sitting Area 10'9"x 10'

Master Bedroom 12'x 16'

Bedroom 12'4"x 13'
Balcony 21'x 8'

Upper Level Floor Plan

Copyright by designer/architect.

Copyright by designer/architect.

Plan #181279

Dimensions: 42' W x 46' D

Levels: 1

Square Footage: 1,452

Bedrooms: 2

Bathrooms: 1½

Foundation: Basement

Materials List Available: Yes

Price Category: B

Images provided by designer/architect.

CAD FILE **CAD** AVAILABLE

14'-0" X 15'-0"
4,20 X 4,50

11'-0" X 16'-0"
3,30 X 4,80

12'-0" X 13'-0"
3,60 X 3,90

16'-8" X 17'-9"
5,00 X 5,33

13'-0" X 20'-0"
3,90 X 6,00

10'-0" X 11'-0"
3,00 X 3,30

46'-0"
13,8 m

42'-0"
12,6 m

Plan #181271

Dimensions: 36' W x 46' D

Levels: 1

Square Footage: 1,246

Bedrooms: 2

Bathrooms: 1

Foundation: Basement

Materials List Available: Yes

Price Category: B

Images provided by designer/architect.

CAD FILE **CAD** AVAILABLE

Copyright by designer/architect.

11'-0" X 13'-4"
3,30 X 4,00

10'-0" X 10'-0"
3,00 X 3,00

11'-0" X 15'-0"
3,30 X 4,50

13'-0" X 12'-4"
3,90 X 3,70

12'-0" X 20'-0"
3,60 X 6,00

12'-0" X 16'-4"
3,60 X 4,90

46'-0"
13,8 m

36'-0"
10,8 m

Images provided by designer/architect.

Plan #151778

Dimensions: 44' W x 45' D
Levels: 1.5
Square Footage: 1,810
Main Level Sq. Ft.: 1,276
Upper Level Sq. Ft.: 534
Bedrooms: 3
Bathrooms: 2½
Foundation: Crawl space
CompleteCost List Available: Yes
Price Category: D

Just imagine watching a sunset on the charming front porch of this log home.

Features:

- **Open Plan:** This open floor plan allows viewing the great room fireplace from both the dining room and kitchen, adding to the true enjoyment of the authentic log design.

- **Dining Room:** French doors in this room lead to a grilling porch, which has a handy eating bar to use as a buffet.

- **Master Suite:** This suite is privately located on the main level and is complete with a soothing whirlpool tub.

- **Loft Area:** This upstairs area leads to two additional bedrooms with ample closet space and plenty of natural light.

Upper Level Floor Plan

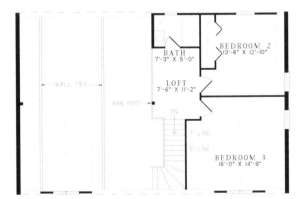

Copyright by designer/architect.

Main Level Floor Plan

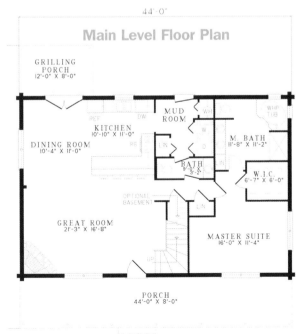

Images provided by designer/architect.

Plan #111041

Dimensions: 34' W x 32' D

Levels: 2

Square Footage: 1,743

Main Level Sq. Ft.: 912

Upper Level Sq. Ft.: 831

Bedrooms: 3

Bathrooms: 3

Foundation: Pier

Materials List Available: No

Price Category: C

You'll love the way this vacation home can accommodate a crowd or make a small family feel cozy and comfortable.

Features:

- **Living Area:** This easy-care living area is perfect for those times when you want to get away from it all—including extra housework.

- **Kitchen:** This kitchen is large enough for friends and family to chat with the cook or help with the dishes after a meal. You'll use the breakfast bar all day long for setting out drinks and snacks.

- **Master Suite:** Relax on the balcony off this master suit, and luxuriate in the bath with double vanities, a whirlpool tub, and a walk-in closet.

- **Study:** Adjacent to the master suite, this room lets you catch up on reading in a quiet spot.

- **Porch:** Let guests spill onto this convenient porch when you're hosting a party, or use it as outdoor space where the children can play.

Copyright by designer/architect.

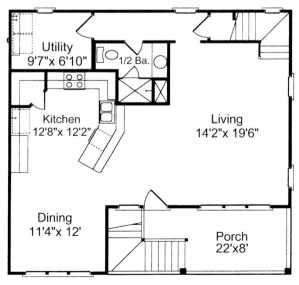

Main Level Floor Plan

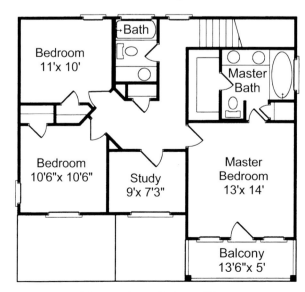

Upper Level Floor Plan

Plan #151789

Dimensions: 106'4" W x 57'8" D

Levels: 1.5

Square Footage: 2,521

Main Level Sq. Ft.: 1,645

Upper Level Sq. Ft.: 876

Bedrooms: 3

Bathrooms: 2

Foundation: Crawl space

CompleteCost List Available: Yes

Price Category: E

Images provided by designer/architect.

The full window view adds elegance to this log home, with its covered porches in the front and rear.

Features:

- **Living Room:** This room with fireplace has a soaring vaulted ceiling and is open to the kitchen and dining room.

- **Dining Room:** To the right of the living room is this formal room, which opens to the kitchen with eating bar and has access to the laundry room and breezeway to the garage.

- **Master Suite:** This suite includes a walk-in closet and private bath, as well as access to the covered porch.

- **Upper Level:** This upper floor contains a loft and full bathroom between two bedrooms with ample closet space and access to the attic.

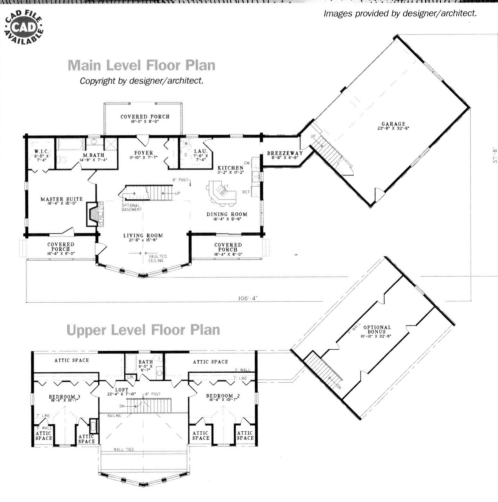

Main Level Floor Plan
Copyright by designer/architect.

Upper Level Floor Plan

Plan #151751

Dimensions: 39'10" W x 39'5" D
Levels: 1.5
Square Footage: 1,449
Main Level Sq. Ft.: 1,059
Upper Level Sq. Ft.: 390
Bedrooms: 2
Bathrooms: 2½
Foundation: Crawl space
CompleteCost List Available: Yes
Price Category: B

Images provided by designer/architect.

Comfort is the key with this magnificent log home.

Features:

- Entry: Step up to the covered porch, which has two sets of French doors that open into the great room: inside, you are greeted with a fireplace.

- Kitchen: Open to the great room, this cooking space has bar seating and view of a bay-shaped dining area.

- Master Suite: This main-level suite includes a large walk-in closet and a bath with an extra-large shower, double vanities, and a closet for a stacked washer-dryer.

- Upper Level: This space has a bedroom and bathroom with creative ceiling heights and a balcony view to the great room below.

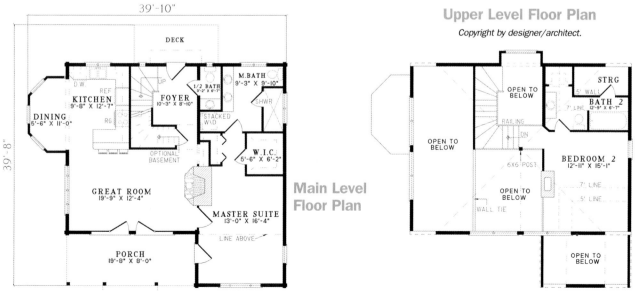

Upper Level Floor Plan

Copyright by designer/architect.

Main Level Floor Plan

Images provided by designer/architect.

Plan #441024

Dimensions: 90'6" W x 84' D
Levels: 2
Square Footage: 3,517
Main Level Sq. Ft.: 2,698
Upper Level Sq. Ft.: 819
Bedrooms: 3
Bathrooms: 3½
Foundation: Crawl space; slab or basement available for fee
Materials List Available: No
Price Category: H

You'll feel like royalty every time you pull into the driveway of this European-styled manor house.

Features:

- **Kitchen:** This gourmet chef's center hosts an island with a vegetable sink. The arched opening above the primary sink provides a view of the fireplace and entertainment center in the great room. A walk-in food pantry and a butler's pantry are situated between this space and the dining room.

- **Master Suite:** Located on the main level, this private retreat boasts a large sleeping area and a sitting area. The grand master bath features a large walk-in closet, dual vanities, a large tub, and a shower.

- **Bedrooms:** Two secondary bedrooms are located on the upper level, and each has its own bathroom.

- **Laundry Room:** This utility room houses cabinets, a folding counter, and an ironing board.

Rear View

- **Garage:** This large three-car garage has room for storage. Family members entering the home from this area will find a coat closet and a place to stash briefcases and backpacks.

Main Level
Floor Plan

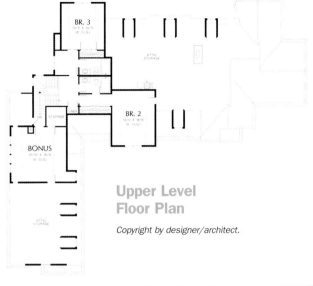

Upper Level
Floor Plan

Copyright by designer/architect.

Kitchen

Great Room

Master bath

Master Bedroom

Plan #111049

Dimensions: 60' W x 50' D
Levels: 2
Square Footage: 2,205
Main Level Sq. Ft.: 1,552
Upper Level Sq. Ft.: 653
Bedrooms: 3
Bathrooms: 2
Foundation: Pier
Materials list available: No
Price Code: E

Images provided by designer/architect.

This stately beach home offers many waterfront views.

Features:

- Ceiling Height: 8 ft.
- Entrance: This home features raised stairs, with two wings that lead to the central staircase.
- Front Porch: This area is 110 square feet.
- Living Room: This huge room features a wood-burning fireplace and large windows, and it leads to the rear covered porch and a spacious deck. It is also open to the kitchen and dining area.
- Kitchen: This room has ample counter space

and an island that is open to the dining area.

- Master Suite: This upper level room has a large balcony. This balcony is a perfect place to watch the sun set over the beach. This room also a walk-in closet.
- Master Bath: This room has all the modern amenities, with separate vanities, large corner tub and walk-in shower.
- Lower Level Bedrooms: These rooms each have a walk in closet and share a bathroom.

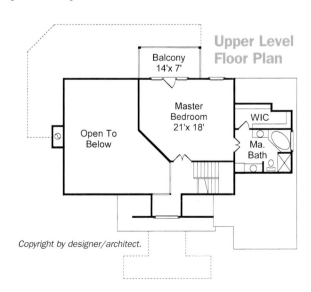

Copyright by designer/architect.

Plan #151747

Dimensions: 39' W x 36'10" D
Levels: 2
Square Footage: 1,477
Main Level Sq. Ft.: 1,131
Upper Level Sq. Ft.: 346
Bedrooms: 3
Bathrooms: 2
Foundation: Crawl space
CompleteCost List Available: Yes
Price Category: B

Images provided by designer/architect.

You'll step back into time when you come home to this simple log home with three bedrooms and a full covered porch.

Features:

- **Great Room:** This room with fireplace opens to the kitchen and dining area with a door to the rear yard.
- **Kitchen:** This U-shaped work area has an abundance of cabinets and counter space.

Enjoy the open feeling as you look into the great room.

- **Master Bedroom:** This main-level bedroom has two closets and a nearby bathroom and convenient laundry closet.
- **Upper Level:** The upper level has a bathroom with a corner shower and a large bedroom with attic-space access for seasonal storage.

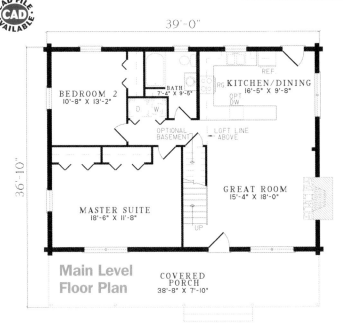

Main Level Floor Plan

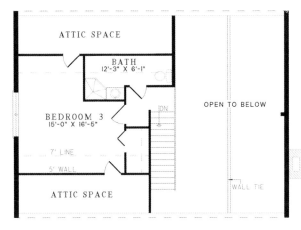

Upper Level Floor Plan

Copyright by designer/architect.

Plan #271087

Dimensions: 43'5½" W x 43'5½" D

Levels: 2

Square Footage: 2,734

Main Level Sq. Ft.: 1,564

Basement Level Sq. Ft.: 1,170

Bedrooms: 4

Bathrooms: 3

Foundation: Daylight basement or crawl space

Materials List Available: No

Price Category: F

Images provided by designer/architect.

This octagonal home offers a choice of exterior finish: wood or stucco.

Features:

• Entry: A seemingly endless deck leads to the main entry, which includes a coat closet.

• Living Room: A fireplace enhances this

spacious room, which offers great outdoor views, plus deck access via sliding glass doors.

• Master Suite: At the end of a hallway, the quiet master bedroom boasts a private bath.

• Lower Level: The basement includes a versatile general area, which could be a nice playroom. A handy den, an extra bedroom and a two-car garage round out this level.

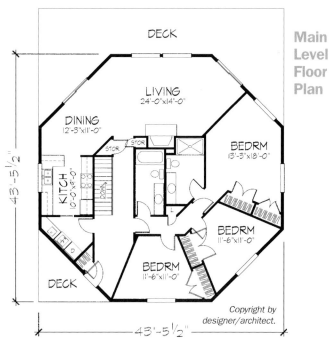

Main Level Floor Plan

Basement Level Floor Plan

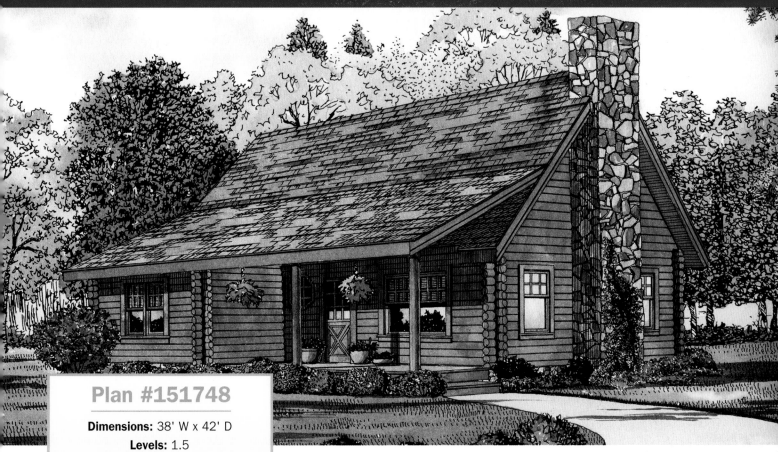

Plan #151748

Dimensions: 38' W x 42' D

Levels: 1.5

Square Footage: 1,382

Main Level Sq. Ft.: 1,040

Upper Level Sq. Ft.: 342

Bedrooms: 2

Bathrooms: 2

Foundation: Crawl space

CompleteCost List Available: Yes

Price Category: B

Images provided by designer/architect.

This log home lends itself a romantic feel with its front covered porch.

Features:

- **Great Room:** This room with cozy fireplace has access to the rear deck and is open to the loft above. The skylights flood this area with natural light.

- **Kitchen:** This kitchen with a range island and washer-dryer closet opens to the dining room.

- **Master Suite:** You ascend the stairs to this retreat, with its walk-in closet, private deck, and full bathroom with linen closet.

- **Bedroom:** Located on the main floor, this secondary bedroom has a large closet.

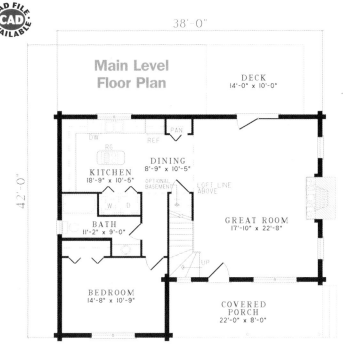

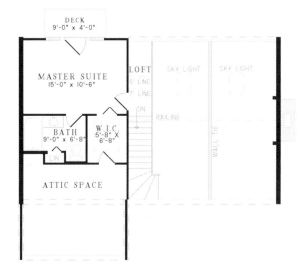

Upper Level Floor Plan

Copyright by designer/architect.

Plan #131032

Dimensions: 69'2" W x 46' D
Levels: 2
Square Footage: 2,455
Main Level Sq. Ft.: 1,499
Upper Level Sq. Ft.: 956
Bedrooms: 4
Bathrooms: 3
Foundation: Crawl space, slab, or basement
Materials List Available: Yes
Price Category: F

If you love Victorian styling, you'll be charmed by the ornate, rounded front porch and the two-story bay that distinguish this home.

Images provided by designer/architect.

Features:

- **Living Room:** You'll love the 13-ft. ceiling in this room, as well as the panoramic view it gives of the front porch and yard.

- **Kitchen:** Sunlight streams into this room, where an angled island with a cooktop eases both prepping and cooking.

- **Breakfast Room:** This room shares an eating bar with the kitchen, making it easy for the family to congregate while the family chef is cooking.

- **Guest Room:** Use this lovely room on the first level as a home office or study if you wish.

- **Master Suite:** The dramatic bayed sitting area with a high ceiling has an octagonal shape that you'll adore, and the amenities in the private bath will soothe you at the end of a busy day.

Rear View

Main Level Floor Plan

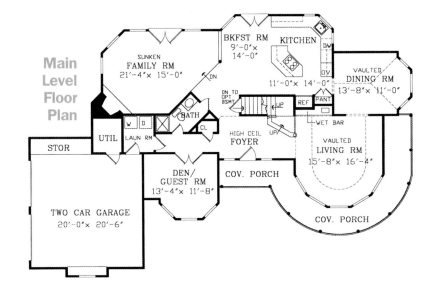

Upper Level Floor Plan

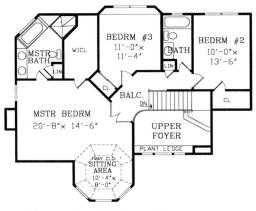

Copyright by designer/architect.

Main Level Floor Plan

Images provided by designer/architect.

Plan #151756

Dimensions: 54' W x 52' D
Levels: 1.5
Square Footage: 2,137
Main Level Sq. Ft.: 1,556
Upper Level Sq. Ft.: 581
Bedrooms: 3
Bathrooms: 2½
Foundation: Crawl space
CompleteCost List Available: Yes
Price Category: D

Upper Level Floor Plan

Copyright by designer/architect.

Plan #441030

Dimensions: 117'6" W x 63'6" D
Levels: 2
Square Footage: 5,180
Main Level Sq. Ft.: 3,030
Upper Level Sq. Ft.: 2,150
Bedrooms: 6
Bathrooms: 5
Foundation: Crawl space;
slab or basement available for fee
Materials List Available: No
Price Category:

Images provided by designer/architect.

Main Level Floor Plan

Upper Level Floor Plan

Copyright by designer/architect.

Images provided by designer/architect.

Main Level Floor Plan

Dining 12'8"x 12'

Bedroom 13'x 12'

Living 18'6"x 22'

Bedroom 13'x 11'9"

Porch

Deck

Upper Level Floor Plan

Copyright by designer/architect.

Master Bedroom 18'6"x 20'

Study 13'x 15'6"

Balcony

Plan #111027

Dimensions: 48' W x 57' D

Levels: 2

Square Footage: 2,601

Main Level Sq. Ft.: 1,623

Upper Level Sq. Ft.: 978

Bedrooms: 3

Bathrooms: 2

Foundation: Pier

Materials List Available: No

Price Category: F

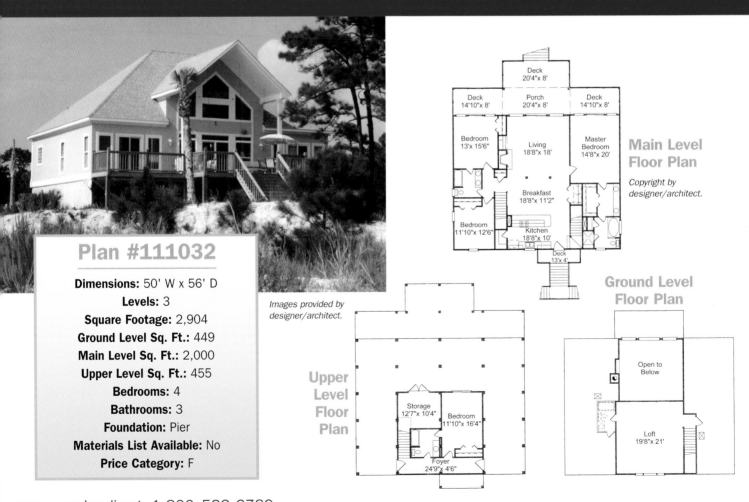

Deck 20'4"x 8'

Deck 14'10"x 8'

Porch 20'4"x 8'

Deck 14'10"x 8'

Bedroom 13'x 15'6"

Living 18'8"x 18'

Master Bedroom 14'8"x 20'

Main Level Floor Plan

Copyright by designer/architect.

Breakfast 18'8"x 11'2"

Bedroom 11'10"x 12'6"

Kitchen 18'8"x 10'

Deck 13'x 4'

Ground Level Floor Plan

Images provided by designer/architect.

Upper Level Floor Plan

Storage 12'7"x 10'4"

Bedroom 11'10"x 16'4"

Foyer 24'9"x 4'6"

Open to Below

Loft 19'8"x 21'

Plan #111032

Dimensions: 50' W x 56' D

Levels: 3

Square Footage: 2,904

Ground Level Sq. Ft.: 449

Main Level Sq. Ft.: 2,000

Upper Level Sq. Ft.: 455

Bedrooms: 4

Bathrooms: 3

Foundation: Pier

Materials List Available: No

Price Category: F

Plan #151759

Dimensions: 70'10" W x 83'8" D
Levels: 1.5
Square Footage: 3,098
Main Level Sq. Ft.: 1,870
Upper Level Sq. Ft.: 1,228
Bedrooms: 4
Bathrooms: 3
Foundation: Crawl space
CompleteCost List Available: Yes
Price Category: G

Images provided by designer/architect.

- Kitchen: This large island kitchen is open to the great room and dining area and has a large walk-in pantry.
- Master Suite: Located on the main level, this suite includes double vanities and a corner whirlpool tub in the bath.

- Bedrooms: Bedroom 2 is located on the main level. Two additional bedrooms with walk-in closets are located on the upper level and share a common bathroom.

An impressive 8-ft.-deep covered porch nearly encircles this log home.

CAD FILE AVAILABLE

Features:
- Great Room: This room with fireplace is open to the loft and has three skylights above.

Main Level Floor Plan

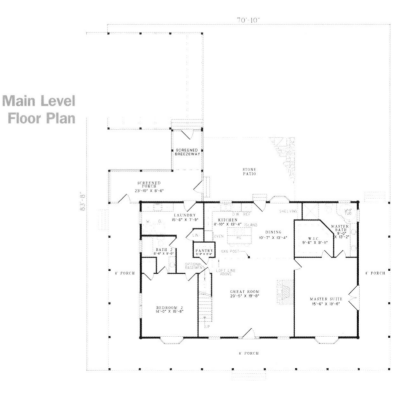

Upper Level Floor Plan

Copyright by designer/architect.

Plan #271053

Dimensions: 70' W x 34' D
Levels: 2
Square Footage: 2,458
Main Level Sq. Ft.: 1,067
Upper Level Sq. Ft.: 346
Bedrooms: 3
Bathrooms: 2½
Foundation: Daylight basement or crawl space
Materials List Available: No
Price Category: E

The octagonal shape and window-filled walls of this home create a powerful interior packed with panoramic views.

Features:

• Great Room: Straight back from the angled entry, this room is brightened by sunlight through windows and sliding glass doors. Beyond the doors, a huge wraparound deck offers plenty of space for tanning or relaxing. A spiral staircase adds visual interest.

• Kitchen: This efficient space includes a convenient pantry.

• Master Suite: On the upper level, this romantic master suite overlooks the great room below. Several windows provide scenic outdoor views. A walk-in closet and a private bath round out this secluded haven.

• Basement: The optional basement includes a recreation room, as well as an extra bedroom and bath.

Images provided by designer/architect.

Copyright by designer/architect.

Main Level Floor Plan

BEDROOM
12'-0" x 13'-8"

GREAT ROOM
16'-0" x 26'-0"
(AVERAGE)

GARAGE
21'-0" x 23'-4"

OPEN TO ABOVE

BATH

GUEST 2'-6"

ENTRY

STORAGE

KITCHEN

DECK

Upper Level Floor Plan

MASTER BEDROOM
14'-0" x 14'-0"

STORAGE

STORAGE

BATH

ACCESS DOORS

OPEN TO BELOW

WALK-IN CLOSET

Optional Basement Level Floor Plan

BEDROOM
22/0 x 10/0

RECREATION
16/0 x 21/6

CLOSET 4/0

CLOSET 4/0

BATH

LAUNDRY

STOR 3/6

LIN

CLOSET 7/6

STORAGE

WH

furnace

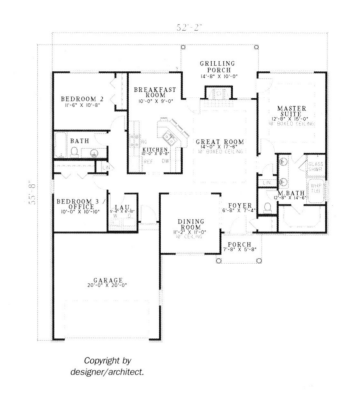

Plan #151513

Dimensions: 52'2" W x 55'8" D

Levels: 1

Square Footage: 1,560

Bedrooms: 3

Bathrooms: 2

Foundation: Crawl space or slab

CompleteCost List Available: Yes

Price Category: C

Images provided by designer/architect.

Copyright by designer/architect.

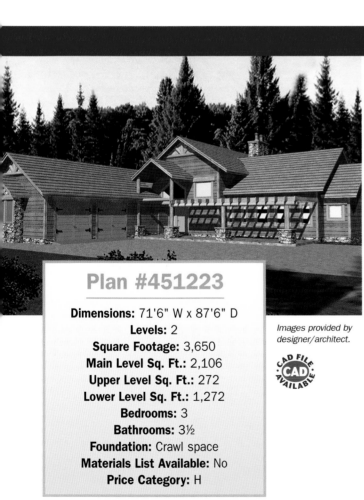

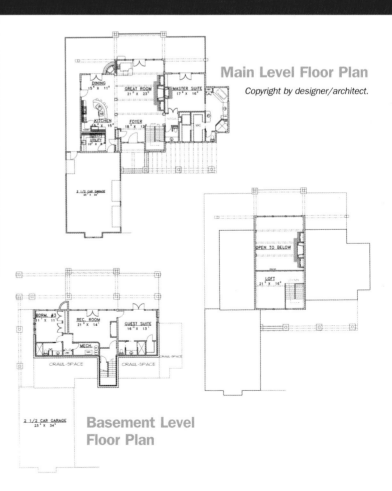

Plan #451223

Dimensions: 71'6" W x 87'6" D

Levels: 2

Square Footage: 3,650

Main Level Sq. Ft.: 2,106

Upper Level Sq. Ft.: 272

Lower Level Sq. Ft.: 1,272

Bedrooms: 3

Bathrooms: 3½

Foundation: Crawl space

Materials List Available: No

Price Category: H

Images provided by designer/architect.

Main Level Floor Plan

Copyright by designer/architect.

Basement Level Floor Plan

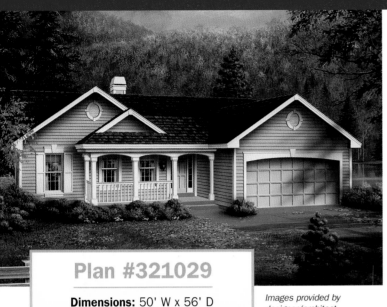

Plan #321029

Dimensions: 50' W x 56' D

Levels: 1

Square Footage: 2,334

Bedrooms: 3

Bathrooms: 2

Foundation: Daylight basement

Materials List Available: Yes

Price Category: E

Images provided by designer/architect.

Rear View

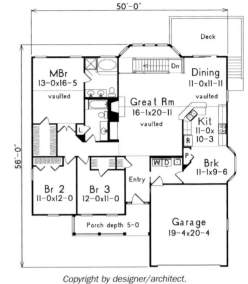

Optional Basement Level Floor Plan

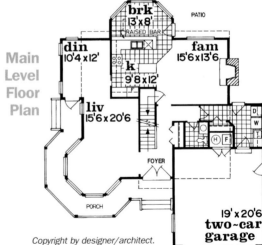

Copyright by designer/architect.

Plan #401012

Dimensions: 48' W x 52'6" D

Levels: 2

Square Footage: 2,301

Main Level Sq. Ft.: 1,180

Upper Level Sq. Ft.: 1,121

Bedrooms: 3-4

Bathrooms: 2½

Foundation: Basement

Materials List Available: Yes

Price Category: E

Images provided by designer/architect.

Main Level Floor Plan

Copyright by designer/architect.

CAD FILE AVAILABLE

Optional Upper Level

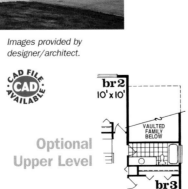

Upper Level Floor Plan

Plan #181245

Dimensions: 44' W x 44' D

Levels: 1

Square Footage: 1,707

Bedrooms: 3

Bathrooms: 1

Foundation: Basement

Materials List Available: Yes

Price Category: C

Images provided by designer/architect.

CAD FILE AVAILABLE

Copyright by designer/architect.

Plan #321031

Dimensions: 79'4" W x 59'6' D

Levels: 1

Square Footage: 3,200

Bedrooms: 3

Bathrooms: 2½

Foundation: Daylight basement

Materials List Available: Yes

Price Category: G

Images provided by designer/architect.

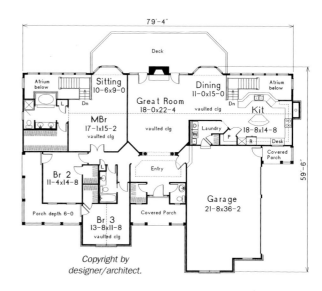

Copyright by designer/architect.

Optional Basement Level Floor Plan

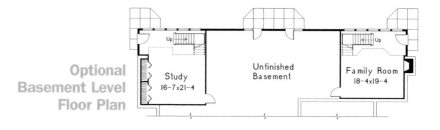

Plan #271085

Dimensions: 55' W x 66' D
Levels: 2
Square Footage: 1,541
Main Level Sq. Ft.: 1,028
Upper Level Sq. Ft.: 513
Bedrooms: 3
Bathrooms: 2
Foundation: Basement, crawl space
Materials List Available: Yes
Price Category: C

CAD FILE AVAILABLE

Images provided by designer/architect.

The soaring, wing-like roof of this plan makes a unique statement and offers fabulous scenic views.

Features:

• Conversation Pit: This central, sunken conversation pit is anchored by a massive stone fireplace and will be a popular gathering place at any time of the day.

• Living Room: This area is augmented by a high ceiling and provides outdoor views through tall windows.

• Dining Room: Enjoy all of your meals in this versatile space. Sliding glass doors allow you to step onto the wraparound deck for dessert and coffee under the stars.

• Kitchen: The U-shaped design of this efficient work space keeps everything you need at your fingertips. A nearby laundry alcove facilitates multitasking.

• Bedrooms: One bedroom has deck access, while another overlooks the living room.

Main Level Floor Plan

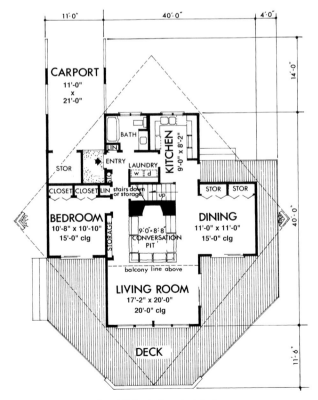

Copyright by designer/architect.

Upper Level Floor Plan

Plan #221033

Dimensions: 63' W x 61'4" D

Levels: 1

Square Footage: 1,948

Bedrooms: 3

Bathrooms: 2

Foundation: Basement

Materials List Available: No

Price Category: D

The spacious front porch on this ranch home is perfect for a relaxing evening at home.

Features:

- Kitchen: You'll love this spacious cooking center, with its breakfast bar that overlooks the dining room.

- Great Room: Columns lead you into this room from the dining-kitchen area, and you'll be impressed as you enter by the fireplace that is flanked by built-ins.

- Master Suite: This restful area features his and her walk-in closets, a corner Jacuzzi in the bath, and a stepped ceiling in the bedroom.

- Bedrooms: Two additional bedrooms face the front of the home, along with a full bathroom.

- Garage: This three-stall garage has additional space for storage; the laundry leads you from the garage into the home so that muddy shoes stay out of sight.

Images provided by designer/architect.

Copyright by designer/architect.

Rear Elevation

Plan #271070

Dimensions: 70'3" W x 60' D
Levels: 2
Square Footage: 2,144
Main Level Sq. Ft.: 1,156
Upper Level Sq. Ft.: 988
Bedrooms: 4
Bathrooms: 2½
Foundation: Basement, crawl space
Materials List Available: No
Price Category: D

Images provided by designer/architect.

Features:

- Living Room: To the left of the foyer, this secluded space offers a moment of peace and quiet after a long day at the office.

- Dining Room: An interesting ceiling treatment makes this elegant room even more sophisticated.

- Kitchen: You won't find a more well-appointed space than this! You'll love the central work island, this useful menu desk

and nearby pantry. The adjacent dinette hosts casual meals and offers outdoor access via sliding glass doors.

- Family Room: A handsome fireplace sets the mood in this expansive area.

- Master Suite: A vaulted ceiling presides over the sleeping room, while a walk-in closet organizes your entire wardrobe. The private bath boasts a refreshing shower and a linen closet.

A nice example of a country farmhouse design on the outside, this home is thoroughly modern on the inside.

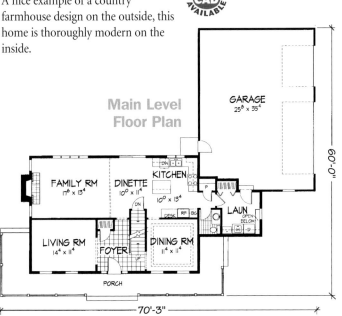

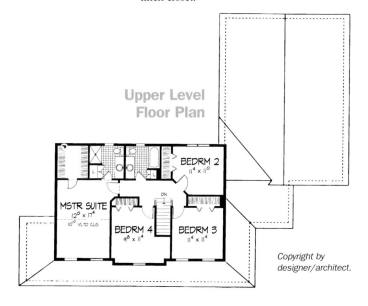

Copyright by designer/architect.

Plan #151752

Dimensions: 58' W x 40' D
Levels: 1.5
Square Footage: 2,402
Main Level Sq. Ft.: 1,584
Upper Level Sq. Ft.: 818
Bedrooms: 3
Bathrooms: 2½
Foundation: Crawl space
CompleteCost List Available: Yes
Price Category: E

Any mountain or picturesque building lot would be a terrific setting for this gorgeous log home.

Features:

- **Great Room:** Separating the master suite from the family areas that contain the kitchen and dining room, this central room provides each area with privacy.

- **Dining Room:** This room has French door access to the deck—perfect for grilling and after-dinner conversation.

- **Master Suite:** Complete with private bath and access to the deck, this suite is located on the main level of the home.

- **Kitchen:** This large eat-in kitchen is open to the dining room and has a built-in pantry.

Images provided by designer/architect.

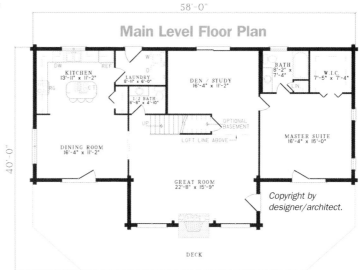

Main Level Floor Plan

Copyright by designer/architect.

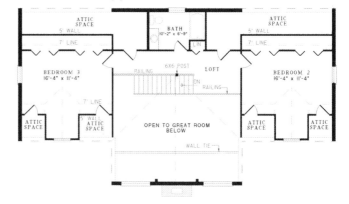

Upper Level Floor Plan

Plan #101015

Dimensions: 28' W x 46' D
Levels: 2
Square Footage: 1,647
Main Level Sq. Ft.: 1,288
Upper Level Sq. Ft.: 359
Bedrooms: 2
Bathrooms: 1
Foundation: Slab
Materials List Available: No
Price Category: C

This comfortable vacation retreat has handsome board-and-batten siding with stone accents.

Features:

• Ceiling Height: 20 ft. unless otherwise noted.

• Front Porch: This delightful front porch is perfect for spending relaxing vacation time in an old-fashioned rocker or porch swing.

• Great Room: From the porch you'll enter this enormous great room, where the whole family will enjoy spending time together under its 20-ft. vaulted ceiling.

• Kitchen: Within the great room is this open kitchen. An island provides plenty of food-preparation space, and there's a breakfast bar for casual vacation meals. The large pantry area provides space for a stacked washer and dryer.

Images provided by designer/architect.

• Bath: Also located downstairs is a compartmented bath with a 2-ft.-8-in. door that allows wheelchair access.

• Loft: Upstairs is an enormous loft with an 11-ft. ceiling. Use it to augment the two downstairs bedrooms or for recreation space.

Main Level Floor Plan

Upper Level Floor Plan

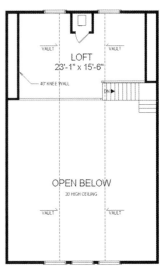

Copyright by designer/architect.

Plan #271050

Dimensions: 40' W x 40' D
Levels: 2
Square Footage: 1,188
Main Level Sq. Ft.: 936
Upper Level Sq. Ft.: 252
Bedrooms: 3
Bathrooms: 2
Foundation: Daylight basement
Materials List Available: Yes
Price Category: B

This open and attractive design features multilevel construction and efficient use of living space.

Images provided by designer/architect.

Features:

- Living Room: A fireplace and a dramatic 15-ft. vaulted ceiling make family and friends gravitate to this area.

- Kitchen/Dining: A U-shaped counter with a snack bar facilitates meals and entertaining. A stacked washer/dryer unit makes weekend chores a breeze.

- Secondary Bedrooms: Five steps up, two sizable bedrooms with vaulted ceilings share

a nice hall bath. One of the bedrooms could serve as a den and features sliding glass doors to a deck.

- Master Suite: On a level of its own, this private space includes a personal bathroom and a romantic deck for stargazing.

- Basement/Garage: The home's lower level offers plenty of space for expansion or storage, plus a tandem, tuck-under garage.

CAD FILE AVAILABLE

Basement Level Floor Plan

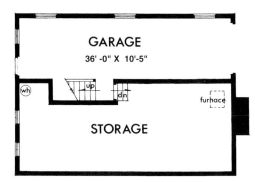

GARAGE
36'-0" X 10'-5"

STORAGE

Copyright by designer/architect.

Main Level Floor Plan

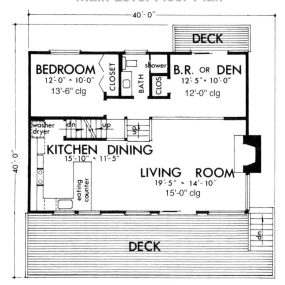

— 40'-0" —

DECK

BEDROOM
12'-0" × 10'-0"
13'-6" clg

CLOSET

BATH

CLOS

shower

B.R. OR DEN
12'-5" × 10'-0"
12'-0" clg

washer dryer

KITCHEN DINING
15'-10" × 11'-5"

eating counter

LIVING ROOM
19'-5" × 14'-10"
15'-0" clg

40'-0"

DECK

Upper Level Floor Plan

BATH

shower

CLOS

BEDROOM
11'-7" × 11'-5"
10'-0" clg

DECK

Plan #151768

Dimensions: 35' W x 39' D
Levels: 1.5
Square Footage: 1,122
Main Level Sq. Ft.: 775
Upper Level Sq. Ft.: 347
Bedrooms: 3
Bathrooms: 2
Foundation: Crawl space
CompleteCost List Available: Yes
Price Category: B

Images provided by designer/architect.

From the covered porch to the screened side porch, this log home was designed for comfort and convenience.

Features:

- Living Room: This room with corner fireplace has access to the screened porch and opens to the kitchen/dining area.

- Kitchen: This L-shaped kitchen is open to the living room and is located just off the entry.

- Master Suite: Upstairs you'll find this suite, with its large closet and private bath with double vanities.

- Bedrooms: The two secondary bedrooms, which share a common bathroom, are located on the main level and have ample closet space.

Main Level Floor Plan

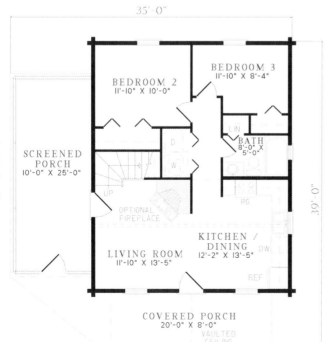

Upper Level Floor Plan

Copyright by designer/architect.

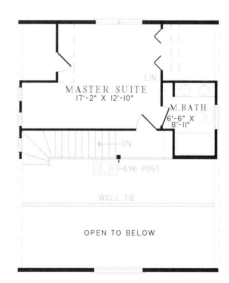

Plan #221049

Dimensions: 62'4" W x 60' D

Levels: 2

Square Footage: 2,698

Main Level Sq. Ft.: 1,852

Upper Level Sq. Ft.: 846

Bedrooms: 4

Bathrooms: 3½

Foundation: Basement

Materials List Available: No

Price Category: F

Images provided by designer/architect.

The curb appeal of this European-style two-story home is sure to please both family and friends.

CAD FILE AVAILABLE

Features:

• **Great Room:** You'll love the 12-ft.-high tray ceiling of this room, as well as the fireplace, with its impressive built-ins on either side.

• **Kitchen:** This convenient work center features a large eat-in island and corner sink, which look out to the front and side yards.

• **Master Suite:** This suite is sure to please, with its stepped ceiling, large walk-in closet, and spacious bath, complete with Jacuzzi tub.

• **Bedrooms:** Upstairs you will be amazed to find two bedrooms that share a Jack and Jill bathroom and a fourth bedroom that looks out the front of the home.

Rear Elevation

Main Level Floor Plan

Upper Level Floor Plan

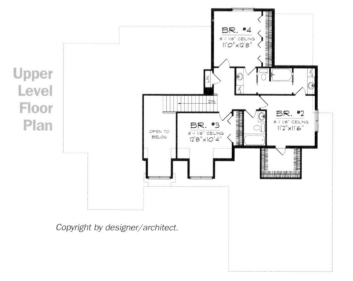

Copyright by designer/architect.

Plan #271096

Dimensions: 66' W x 98' D
Levels: 2
Square footage: 3,190
Main Level Sq. Ft.: 2,152
Upper Level Sq. Ft.: 1,038
Bedrooms: 4
Bathrooms: 3½
Foundation: Crawl space
Materials List Available: No
Price Category: G

Images provided by designer/architect.

This traditional home contains quite possibly everything you're dreaming of, and even more!

Features:

- **Formal Rooms:** These living and dining rooms flank the entry foyer, making a large space for special occasions.

- **Family Room:** A fireplace is the highlight of this spacious area, where the kids will play with their friends and watch TV.

- **Kitchen:** A central island makes cooking a breeze. The adjoining dinette is a sunny spot for casual meals.

- **Master Suite:** A large sleeping area is followed by a deluxe private bath with a whirlpool tub and a walk-in closet. Step through a French door to the backyard, which is big enough to host a deck with an inviting hot tub!

- **Guest Suite:** One bedroom upstairs has its own private bath, making it perfect for guests.

- A future room above the garage awaits your decision on how to use it.

Main Level Floor Plan

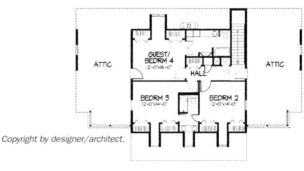

Upper Level Floor Plan

Copyright by designer/architect.

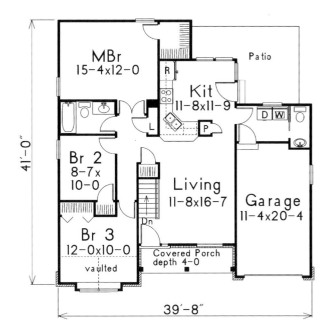

Plan #321023

Dimensions: 39'8" W x 41' D
Levels: 1
Square Footage: 1,092
Bedrooms: 3
Bathrooms: 1½
Foundation: Basement
Materials List Available: Yes
Price Category: B

Images provided by designer/architect.

Copyright by designer/architect.

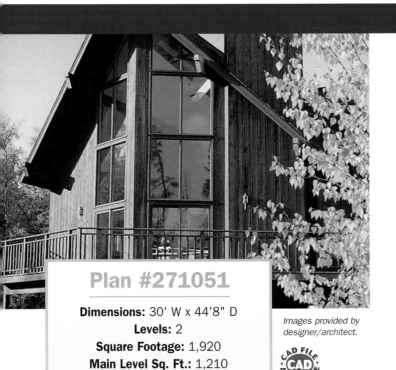

Plan #271051

Dimensions: 30' W x 44'8" D
Levels: 2
Square Footage: 1,920
Main Level Sq. Ft.: 1,210
Upper Level Sq. Ft.: 710
Bedrooms: 3
Bathrooms: 2
Foundation: Crawl space or Walk-out
Materials List Available: Yes
Price Category: D

Images provided by designer/architect.

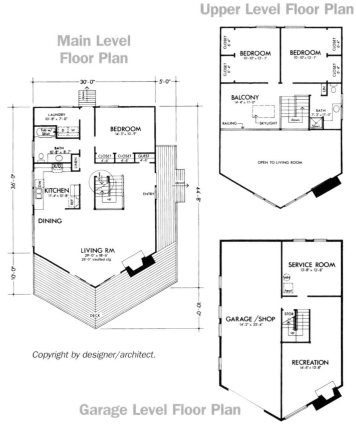

Main Level Floor Plan

Upper Level Floor Plan

Garage Level Floor Plan

Copyright by designer/architect.

Plan #181250

Dimensions: 71' W x 53' D
Levels: 2
Square Footage: 3,733
Main Level Sq. Ft.: 1,526
Upper Level Sq. Ft.: 2,207
Bedrooms: 4
Bathrooms: 3½
Foundation: Basement
Materials List Available: Yes
Price Category: H

Images provided by designer/architect.

Main Level Floor Plan

Upper Level Floor Plan

Copyright by designer/architect.

Plan #181251

Dimensions: 78' W x 64' D
Levels: 2
Square Footage: 4,075
Main Level Sq. Ft.: 2,228
Upper Level Sq. Ft.: 1,847
Bedrooms: 4
Bathrooms: 3½
Foundation: Basement
Materials List Available: Yes
Price Category: I

Images provided by designer/architect.

Main Level Floor Plan

Upper Level Floor Plan

Copyright by designer/architect.

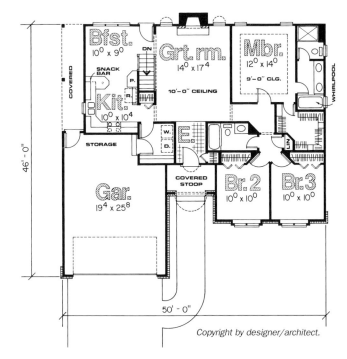

Images provided by designer/architect.

CAD FILE AVAILABLE

Copyright by designer/architect.

Plan #121060

Dimensions: 50' W x 46' D
Levels: 1
Square Footage: 1,339
Bedrooms: 3
Full Bathrooms: 2
Foundation: Basement
Materials List Available: Yes
Price Category: B

Images provided by designer/architect.

CAD FILE AVAILABLE

Copyright by designer/architect.

Rear Elevation

Plan #221031

Dimensions: 60' W x 52' D
Levels: 1
Square Footage: 1,896
Bedrooms: 3
Bathrooms: 2
Foundation: Basement
Materials List Available: No
Price Category: D

Plan #271010

Dimensions: 46'8" W x 43' D
Levels: 2
Square Footage: 1,724
Main Level Sq. Ft.: 922
Upper Level Sq. Ft.: 802
Bedrooms: 3
Bathrooms: 2½
Foundation: Basement
Materials List Available: Yes
Price Category: C

Images provided by designer/architect.

This traditional home features a wide assortment of windows that flood the interior with light and accentuate the open, airy atmosphere.

Features:

- Entry: A beautiful Palladian window enlivens this two-story-high space.

- Great Room: A second Palladian window brightens this primary gathering area, which is topped by a vaulted ceiling.

- Dining Room: Sliding glass doors connect this formal area to a large backyard deck.

- Kitchen: Centrally located, this kitchen includes a boxed-out window over the sink, providing a nice area for plants.

- Family/Breakfast Area: Smartly joined, this open space hosts a snack bar and a wet bar, in addition to a warming fireplace.

- Master Suite: Located on the upper floor, the master bedroom boasts corner windows, a large walk-in closet, and a split bath with a dual-sink vanity.

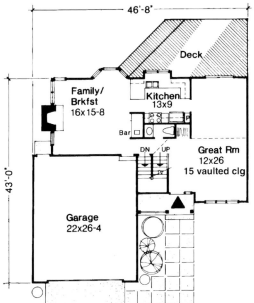

Main Level Floor Plan

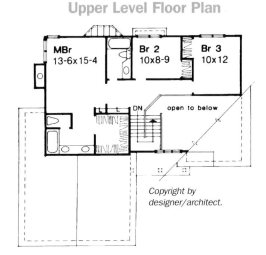

Upper Level Floor Plan

Copyright by designer/architect.

Plan #221001

Dimensions: 87' W x 60' D

Levels: 1

Square Footage: 2,600

Bedrooms: 3

Bathrooms: 2½

Foundation: Basement

Materials List Available: No

Price Category: F

Images provided by designer/architect.

Copyright by designer/architect.

You'll love this traditional ranch for its unusual spaciousness and many comfortable amenities.

Features:

- **Great Room:** As you enter the home, you'll have a clear view all the way to the backyard through the many windows in this huge room. Built-ins here provide a practical touch, and the fireplace makes this room cozy when the weather's cool.

- **Kitchen:** This large kitchen has been thoughtfully designed to make cooking a pleasure. It flows into a lovely dining nook, so it's also a great place to entertain.

- **Master Suite:** Relaxing will come naturally in this lovely suite, with its two walk-in closets, private sitting area, and large, sumptuous bathroom that features a Jacuzzi tub.

- **Additional Bedrooms:** Located on the opposite side of the house from the master suite, these bedrooms are both convenient to a full bath. You can use one room as a den if you wish.

Rear Elevation

Kitchen

Main Level Floor Plan

Upper Level Floor Plan

Optional Upper Level Floor Plan

Plan #181232

Dimensions: 33' W x 26' D
Levels: 2
Square Footage: 1,325
Main Level Sq. Ft.: 741
Upper Level Sq. Ft.: 584
Bedrooms: 2
Bathrooms: 1½
Foundation: Basement or walkout
Materials List Available: Yes
Price Category: B

Images provided by designer/architect.

Copyright by designer/architect.

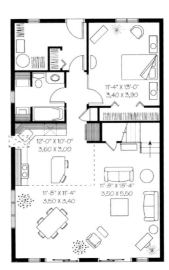

Main Level Floor Plan

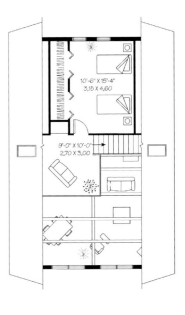

Upper Level Floor Plan

Copyright by designer/architect.

Plan #181111

Dimensions: 24'8" W x 38'4" D
Levels: 2
Square Footage: 1,304
Main Level Sq. Ft.: 945
Upper Level Sq. Ft.: 359
Bedrooms: 2
Bathrooms: 1
Foundation: Crawl space
Materials List Available: Yes
Price Category: B

Images provided by designer/architect.

Plan #401048

Dimensions: 57'8" W x 103'6" D
Levels: 2
Square Footage: 5,159
Main Level Sq. Ft.: 2,473
Upper Level Sq. Ft.: 2,686
Bedrooms: 4
Bathrooms: 4½
Foundation: Basement
Materials List Available: Yes
Price Category: I

Images provided by designer/architect.

This unusual stucco-and-siding design opens with a grand portico to a foyer that extends to the living room with fireplace.

CAD FILE AVAILABLE

Features:

• **Dining Room:** Step up a few steps to this dining room, with its coffered ceiling and butler's pantry, which connects to the gourmet kitchen.

• **Hearth Room:** Attached to the kitchen, this hearth room has the requisite fireplace and three sets of French doors that lead to the covered porch.

• **Family Room:** This room features a coffered ceiling and a fireplace flanked by French doors.

• **Master Suite:** This area includes a tray ceiling, covered deck, and lavish bath.

• **Bedrooms:** All bedrooms are located on the second floor. Two full bathrooms serve the family bedrooms and a bonus room that might be used as an additional bedroom or hobby space.

Main Level Floor Plan

Copyright by designer/architect.

Upper Level Floor Plan

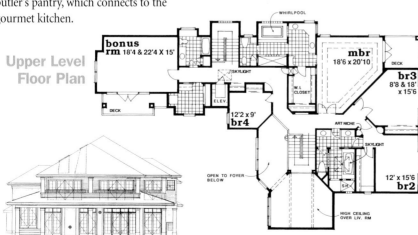

Rear Elevation

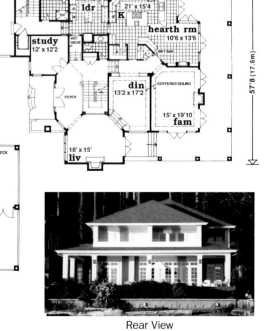

Rear View

Images provided by designer/architect.

Plan #181062

Dimensions: 58' W x 55' D
Levels: 2
Square Footage: 1,953
Main Level Sq. Ft.: 1,301
Second Level Sq. Ft.: 652
Bedrooms: 2
Bathrooms: 2½
Foundation: Half basement, half crawl space
Materials List Available: Yes
Price Category: D

Features:

- Ceiling Height: 8 ft.
- Wall of Doors: The entire back of the house is filled by five sets of multi-pane glass doors.
- Formal Dining Room: This dining room is located adjacent to the kitchen for convenient entertaining.
- Kitchen: This efficient kitchen is a pleasure in which to work, thanks to plenty of counter

space, a pantry, double sinks, and access to the laundry room.

- Great Room: This great room is open to the atrium. As a result it is filled with warmth and natural light. You'll love gathering around the handsome fireplace.
- Master Suite: This private first-floor retreat features a walk-in closet and a luxurious full bath with dual vanities.

CAD FILE AVAILABLE

A magnificent glass enclosed vertical atrium is the focal point of this beautiful country home.

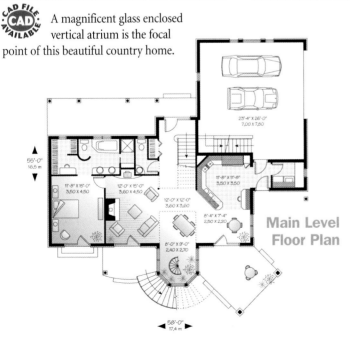

Main Level Floor Plan

Copyright by designer/architect.

Upper Level Floor Plan

Main Level
Floor Plan

Copyright by designer/architect.

Plan #181234

Dimensions: 39'8" W x 36'8" D
Levels: 3
Square Footage: 2,392
Main Level Sq. Ft.: 967
Upper Level Sq. Ft.: 1,076
Third Level Sq. Ft.: 349
Bedrooms: 5
Bathrooms: 3½
Foundation: Pier/pole
Materials List Available: Yes
Price Category: E

Images provided by designer/architect.

CAD FILE AVAILABLE

Upper Level Floor Plan

Basement
Level
Floor Plan

Plan #181235

Dimensions: 22' W x 26'4" D
Levels: 2
Square Footage: 1,077
Main Level Sq. Ft.: 550
Upper Level Sq. Ft.: 527
Bedrooms: 3
Bathrooms: 1
Foundation: Basement
Materials List Available: Yes
Price Category: B

Images provided by designer/ architect.

CAD FILE AVAILABLE

Main Level
Floor Plan

Upper Level
Floor Plan

Copyright by designer/architect.

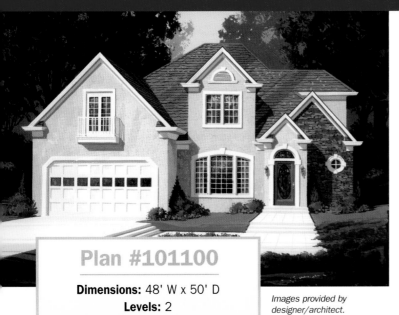

Main Level Floor Plan

Images provided by designer/architect.

CAD FILE AVAILABLE

Plan #101100

Dimensions: 48' W x 50' D
Levels: 2
Square Footage: 2,479
Main Level Sq. Ft.: 1,720
Upper Level Sq. Ft.: 759
Bedrooms: 3
Bathrooms: 2½
Foundation: Crawl space or basement
Materials List Available: Yes
Price Category: E

Upper Level Floor Plan

Copyright by designer/architect.

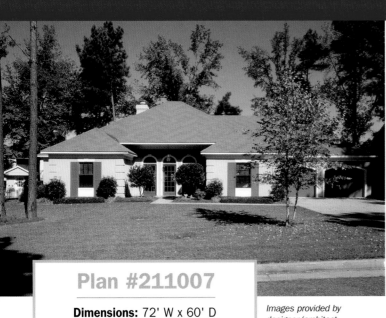

Copyright by designer/architect.

Plan #211007

Dimensions: 72' W x 60' D
Levels: 1
Square Footage: 2,252
Bedrooms: 4
Bathrooms: 2
Foundation: Slab
Materials List Available: Yes
Price Category: E

Images provided by designer/architect.

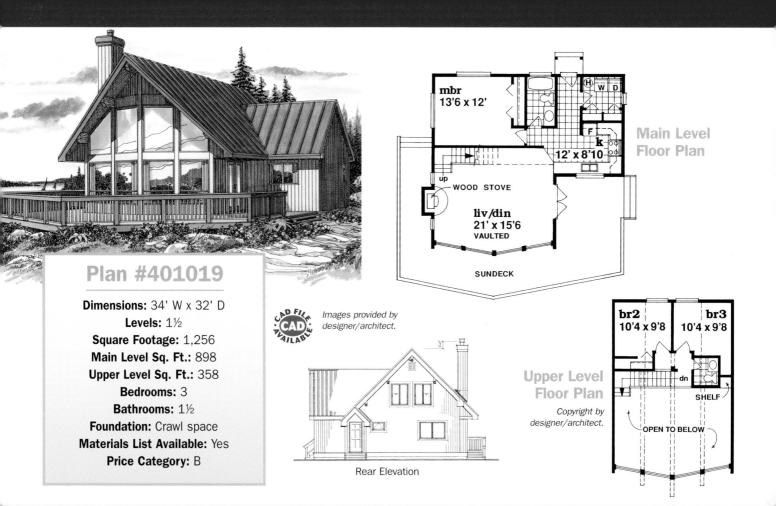

mbr
13'6 x 12'

H W D

F

k

12' x 8'10

Main Level Floor Plan

up

WOOD STOVE

liv/din
21' x 15'6
VAULTED

SUNDECK

CAD FILE AVAILABLE

Images provided by designer/architect.

Rear Elevation

br2
10'4 x 9'8

br3
10'4 x 9'8

dn

SHELF

Upper Level Floor Plan

Copyright by designer/architect.

OPEN TO BELOW

Plan #401019

Dimensions: 34' W x 32' D
Levels: 1½
Square Footage: 1,256
Main Level Sq. Ft.: 898
Upper Level Sq. Ft.: 358
Bedrooms: 3
Bathrooms: 1½
Foundation: Crawl space
Materials List Available: Yes
Price Category: B

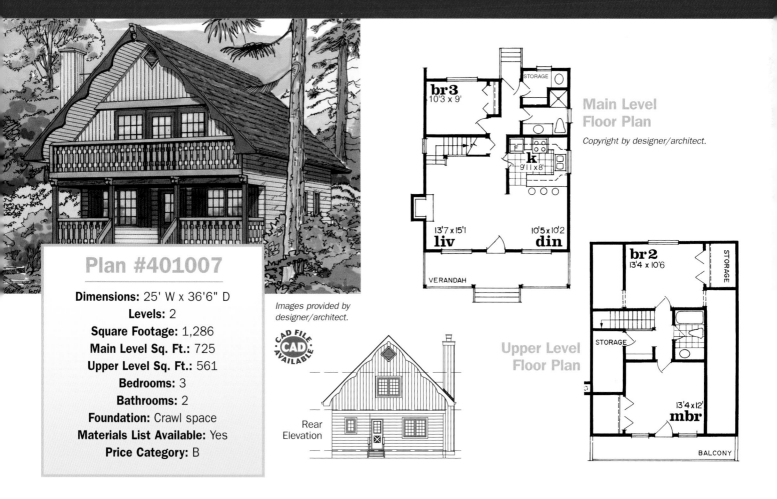

br3
10'3 x 9'

STORAGE

Main Level Floor Plan

Copyright by designer/architect.

F

k
9'11 x 8'

13'7 x 15'1
liv

10'5 x 10'2
din

VERANDAH

Plan #401007

Dimensions: 25' W x 36'6" D
Levels: 2
Square Footage: 1,286
Main Level Sq. Ft.: 725
Upper Level Sq. Ft.: 561
Bedrooms: 3
Bathrooms: 2
Foundation: Crawl space
Materials List Available: Yes
Price Category: B

Images provided by designer/architect.

CAD FILE AVAILABLE

Rear Elevation

br2
13'4 x 10'6

STORAGE

STORAGE

Upper Level Floor Plan

13'4 x 12'
mbr

BALCONY

Plan #181218

Dimensions: 38' W x 28'8" D

Levels: 1

Square Footage: 946

Bedrooms: 2

Bathrooms: 1

Foundation: Basement

Materials List Available: No

Price Category: A

Images provided by designer/architect.

With a showcase front porch trimmed by quaint railings and carved brackets, this design uses all of its space beautifully and practically.

Features:

• Living room: This company-loving room waits just inside the entrance.

• Kitchen: This creative U-shaped kitchen has a bounty of counter and cabinet space as well as a breakfast counter that stretches into the dining area and doubles as a serving board.

• Utility Areas: The full bathroom is paired with the laundry area, and a side door near the kitchen leads to a smaller covered porch.

• Bedrooms: Two spacious bedrooms sit comfortably beside each other.

Copyright by designer/architect.

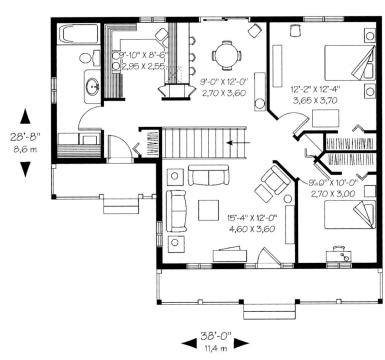

Plan #131023

Dimensions: 78'8" W x 36'2" D
Levels: 2
Square Footage: 2,460
Main Level Sq. Ft.: 1,377
Upper Level Sq. Ft.: 1,083
Bedrooms: 4
Bathrooms: 3½
Foundation: Crawl space, slab, or basement
Materials List Available: Yes
Price Category: F

You'll love the modern floor plan inside this traditional two-story home, with its attractive facade.

Features:

- Ceiling Height: 8 ft.

- Living Room: The windows on three sides of this room make it bright and sunny. Choose the optional fireplace for cozy winter days and the wet bar for elegant entertaining.

- Family Room: Overlooking the rear deck, this spacious family room features a fireplace and a skylight.

- Dining Room: The convenient placement of this large room lets guests flow into it from the living room and allows easy to access from the kitchen.

- Kitchen: The island cooktop and built-in desk make this space both modern and practical.

Images provided by designer/architect.

Rear Elevation

Main Level Floor Plan

Copyright by designer/architect.

Upper Level Floor Plan

Plan #271017

Dimensions: 50' W x 37'2" D
Levels: 2
Square Footage: 1,835
Main Level Sq. Ft.: 928
Upper Level Sq. Ft.: 907
Bedrooms: 3
Bathrooms: 2½
Foundation: Basement
Materials List Available: Yes
Price Category: D

Images provided by designer/architect.

This inviting and popular home combines interesting window arrangements and brick accents for a winning facade.

Features:

• Entry: A high ceiling expands this welcome center, for a dramatic effect.

• Living Room: A handsome fireplace is the highlight here. A dramatic vaulted ceiling is shared with the adjacent formal dining room. Imagine entertaining your extended family in this space during the holidays.

• Country Kitchen: An efficient layout keeps the family chef happy and productive in this room. The home's second fireplace warms family members while they enjoy casual meals or simply relax. A bay window is a nice touch.

• Master Suite: This suite's bedroom area is certainly generous, and the master bath features a private toilet and a walk-in closet, as well as a separate tub and shower.

Main Level Floor Plan

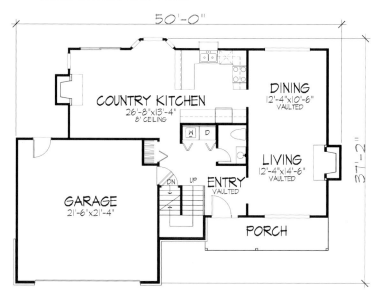

Upper Level Floor Plan

Copyright by designer/architect.

Plan #401005

Dimensions: 24' W x 28' D

Levels: 2

Square Footage: 1,073

Main Level Sq. Ft.: 672

Upper Level Sq. Ft.: 401

Bedrooms: 3

Bathrooms: 1½

Foundation: Basement

Materials List Available: Yes

Price Category: B

Scalloped fascia boards in the steep gable roof and the fieldstone chimney detail enhance this chalet.

Features:

- Outdoor Living: The front-facing deck and covered balcony are ideal outdoor living spaces.

- Living Room: The fireplace is the main focus in this living room, separating it from the dining room.

- Bedrooms: One bedroom is found on the first floor; two additional bedrooms and a full bath are upstairs.

- Storage: You'll find three large storage areas on the second floor.

Images provided by designer/architect.

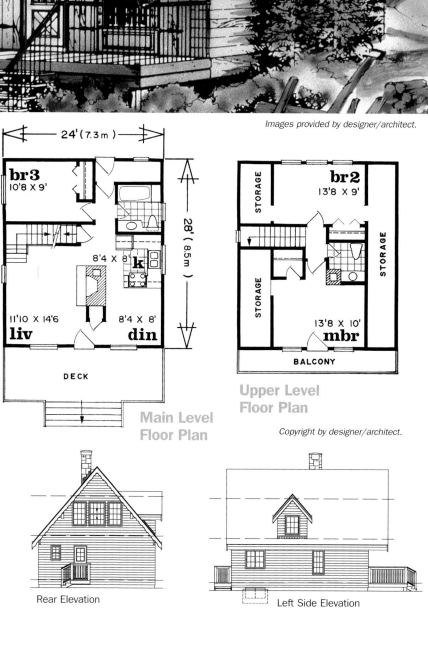

Main Level Floor Plan

Upper Level Floor Plan

Copyright by designer/architect.

Rear Elevation

Left Side Elevation

Plan #271074

Dimensions: 68' W x 86' D
Levels: 1
Square Footage: 2,400
Bedrooms: 4
Bathrooms: 3
Foundation: Crawl space or slab
Materials List Available: No
Price Category: E

Images provided by designer/architect.

Perfect for families with aging relatives or boomerang children, this home includes a completely separate suite at the rear.

Features:

- **Living Room:** A corner fireplace casts a friendly glow over this gathering space.
- **Kitchen:** This efficient space offers a serving bar that extends toward the eating nook

and the formal dining room.

- **Master Suite:** A cathedral ceiling presides over this deluxe suite, which boasts a whirlpool tub, dual-sink vanity, and walk-in closet.
- **In-law Suite:** This separate wing has its own vaulted living room, plus a kitchen, a dining room, and a bedroom suite.

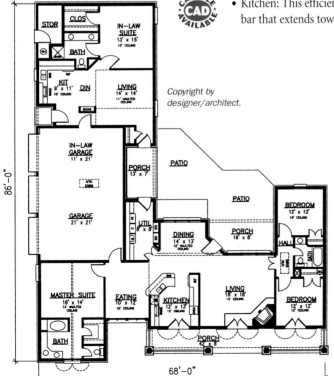

Copyright by designer/architect.

SMARTtip

Adding Professional Flair to Window Treatments

You can give your window treatment designs a professional look by using decorator tricks to customize readymades or dress your own home-sewn designs. These could include contrast linings, tassels, cording, ribbons, or couture trimmings such as buttons, coins, or bows applied to edges. Another trick is to sew a fine wire into the hem of curtains or valances to create a pliable edge that you can shape yourself. Small weights that you can sew into the hem of drapery panels or jabots will make them hang better. For more inspiration look at fashion magazines and visit showrooms.

Plan #401020

Dimensions: 55'6" W x 30' D
Levels: 1
Square Footage: 1,230
Bedrooms: 3
Bathrooms: 2
Foundation: Basement
Materials List Available: Yes
Price Category: B

This is a grand vacation or retirement home, designed for views and the outdoor lifestyle. The full-width deck complements the abundant windows in the rooms that face it.

Features:

• Living Room: This area, with a vaulted ceiling, a fireplace, and full-height windows overlooking the deck, is made for gathering.

• Dining Room: This room is open to the living room; it has sliding glass doors that lead to the outdoors.

• Kitchen: This room has a pass-through counter to the dining room and is U-shaped in design.

• Bedrooms: Two family bedrooms in the middle of the plan share a full bath.

• Master Suite: This area has a private bath and deck views.

Images provided by designer/architect.

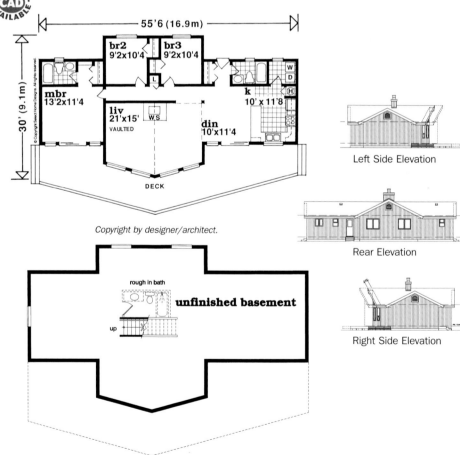

Copyright by designer/architect.

Left Side Elevation

Rear Elevation

Right Side Elevation

Optional Basement Level Floor Plan

the new Smart Approach to

home decorating

CREATIVE HOMEOWNER

The following article was reprinted from *The New Smart Approach to Home Decorating* (Creative Homeowner 2003)

Adding Color and Texture

T he colors and textures you choose will set the tone for your home decor. If you are a traditionalist decorating a formal living room, you may find yourself drawn to a dove gray and cream color scheme. A kid's play room, on the other hand, may call for bright colors and bold patterns. Of course, the size of the room and its light levels will also play a part in your choices. They not only lead to color schemes but also help in selecting patterns and textures for the room. Pattern creates rhythm, a measured flow between a number of elements throughout a room. Texture is like a visual caesura, a pause that prevents the design from becoming predictable.

The trick in decorating is to create a harmonious balance between all of the elements. By investing some time in learning those theories behind the selection of color, pattern, and texture, you can begin to develop a mix that soothes your senses the way a pastoral piece of music does. The science of color is partly concerned with its precise measurement and the intricate chemistry of dyes and pigments. It also ventures into the more subjective realm of perception and psychology: exploring how colors relate to one another, how they affect the viewer, and how quantities, textures, and patterns alter the effects. A bit of color theory can provide a further foundation for the art of interior design.

Working with Color

Color is the most versatile tool a designer can employ. It is both the easiest way to improve space and an effective way to alter it. It is the most exciting decorating element. Yet many of us find the power of color intimidating and, fearful of stepping into new territory, stick with neutrals. The palette for walls is often white or cream—colors that work fine as a backdrop for more richly hued furnishings but are less successful in rooms with neutral-colored pieces. Aside from the strength of color itself, the enormity of color choices available in paints, wallpapers, fabrics, and flooring options can also overwhelm us, making us retreat to the safety of white for the walls and neutrals throughout. So how do you break the monotony and establish an exciting color scheme? First you'll have to overcome your fear of color, then narrow your choices. An explanation of the color wheel is a good place to begin.

How Color Works

Light reflected through a prism creates a rainbow, known as the color spectrum. Each band of color blends into the next, from red to violet. The longest band is red, then orange, yellow, green, blue, and violet. Modern color theory takes those bands from the spectrum and forms them into a circle, called the color wheel, to show the relationship of one color to another.

The color wheel includes *primary colors* (red, blue, and yellow), *secondary colors* (green, orange, violet), and *tertiary colors* (red-blue, blue-red, and so on). Secondary colors are made by mixing two primaries together, such as blue and yellow to make green. A primary color and a secondary color are mixed to make tertiary colors, such as blue and green to make turquoise.

Right: Yellow w alls not only brighten this small living room, they also serve as a backdrop for the many bold patterns in the space. Many of the fabric prints pick up the yellow of the w alls.

Intensity and Value. Colors, or hues, vary in their intensity—that is, the level of the color's purity or saturation. The primaries, secondaries, and tertiaries represent colors at their full intensity. There are several ways to lessen a color's intensity. You can lighten it with white to form a tint, darken it with black to create a shade, or add gray to arrive at a tone. In addition to changing the intensity of a color, these methods affect what is known as the color's value. Value is the lightness or darkness of the color. Tinting gives a color a lighter value, and shading, of course, makes it a darker value.

Color Wheel Combinations

The color wheel is the designer's most useful tool for pairing colors. Basically, it presents the spectrum of pigment hues as a circle. The primary colors (yellow, blue, and red) are combined in the remaining hues (orange, green, and purple). The following are the most-often used configurations for creating color schemes.

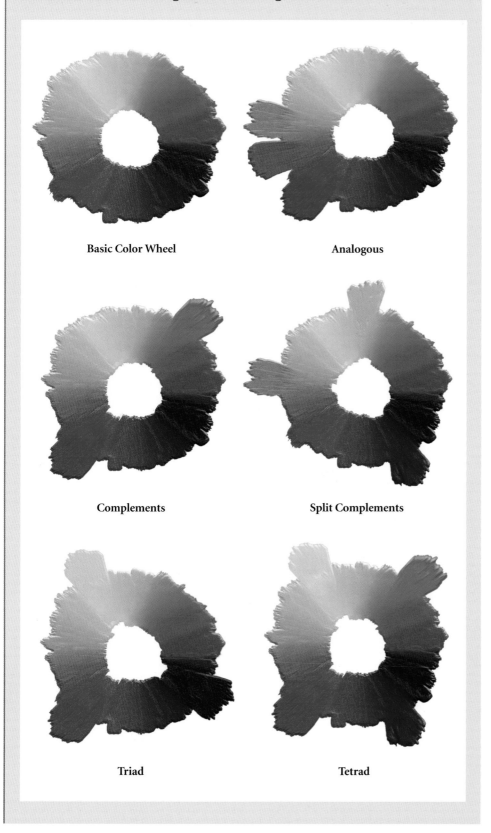

Basic Color Wheel

Analogous

Complements

Split Complements

Triad

Tetrad

Putting the Color Wheel to Work for You

Now that you've got it in front of you, use the color wheel to help you envision certain color combinations. An *analogous* scheme involves neighboring colors that share an underlying hue.

Complementary colors lie opposite each other on the color wheel and often work well together. What, you ask? A red and green living room? Well, yes, in full intensity that might be hard to stomach, but consider a rosy pink room with sage green accents. The same complements in varying intensities can make attractive, soothing combinations. A *double complementary* color scheme involves an additional set of opposites, such as green-blue and red-orange.

Alternatively, you could go with a *monochromatic* scheme, which involves using one color in a variety of intensities. That way your décor is sure to be harmonious. When developing a monochromatic scheme, lean toward several tints or several shades, but avoid too many contrasting values—that is, combinations of tints and shades. This can make your scheme look uneven.

If you want a more complex palette of three or more colors, look at the *triads* formed by three equidistant colors, such as red/yellow/blue or green/purple/orange. *A split complement* is composed of three colors—one primary or intermediate and two colors on either side of its opposite. For example, instead of teaming purple with yellow, shift the mix to purple with orange-yellow and yellow-green. Lastly, four colors equally spaced around the wheel, such as yellow/green/purple/red, form a *tetrad*. If such combinations sound a bit like Technicolor, remember that colors intended for interiors are rarely undiluted. Thus yellow might be cream, blue-purple a dark eggplant, and orange-red a muted terra-cotta or whisper-pale peach. With less jargon, the color combinations fall into these two basic camps:

- *harmonious*, or *analogous*, schemes, derived from nearby colors on the wheel—less than halfway around; and

- *contrasting*, or *complementary*, schemes, involving directly opposite slices of the pie.

The Psychology of Color

Few of us get past kindergarten without acquiring a favorite color. Over the years our tastes change and we allow ourselves to appreciate more than one hue, but most of us can still name a preference when pressed. Picking out a few colors you like best—colors that make you feel happy—is as good a place as any to begin establishing your color scheme because it is largely an emotional decision. In narrowing down your choices and combining them with the preferences of those who will share the space, try to include both warm and cool colors. The warm hues—reds, yellows, oranges, peaches, and creams—are generally most effectively used in rooms where there will be a lot of activity because they make us feel livelier. Kitchens, office spaces, even bedrooms if you're a morning person, are all natural places for brighter, warmer, more uplifting hues. Cool colors tend to be more soothing and restful. You may want to reserve your blues, greens, and lilacs for the rooms where you go to unwind.

However, color responses are subjective and changeable. The pervasive use of green in schools and hospitals in decades past, for example, has prompted a visceral dislike of the color's "institutional" shades for many people. Some studies have suggested that red rooms may heighten blood pressure and yellow rooms make the occupants more argumentative.

Sharp contrasts or schemes that feature bold colors can be fun in rooms used only occasionally, but they can become tiresome on a daily basis. Of course,

Above: Because dining rooms aren't used as often as kitchens or family rooms, many people feel comfortable experimenting with bold color schemes for these spaces.

these are general guidelines. Some people never tire of a favorite color—even if it is repeated in every room of the house.

Cultural Effects. We may be less aware of how our culture and era shape our color responses. In America and much of Europe, blue is a perennial favorite color, while red ranks first in other locales, such as Spain and Japan. Western brides dress in joyful white—a mourning color in some Far Eastern societies. Even within one culture, the accustomed palette changes. In the Victorian era, early Impressionist paintings shocked viewers, who saw them as garishly bright. Yet to our jaded eyes, the same paintings seem restfully pastel. Even closer to our own times, we might chuckle or wince at colors and combinations from a decorating guide dated 1955 or 1969—colors that struck the readers of the day as perfectly keen or groovy. And a few decades hence, our own most stylish efforts may suffer a similar fate.

The pull of comfortable, traditional colors and the push for novel, fashionable choices have shaped the American palette since the nation's early days. But the home decorator can hold to one constant: human beings seek variety in their surroundings. Light colors seem upbeat, clean, and lively but turn cold and monotonous if unrelieved. Dark colors are plush and enclosing but in excess can turn gloomy. Midtones are attractively comfortable, but a room decked completely in midtones can be dull and monotonous. Bright, saturated hues are eye-catching accents but uncomfortably demanding in quantity. In short, one could do worse than to follow the old decorating maxim, "Something dark, something light, something dull, something bright."

Altering Space with Color

As a designer, you can use warm colors and cool colors quite effectively to manipulate the way a room is perceived visually, as well as emotionally. For instance, you can cozy up a large room with warm colors. Because warm colors appear to advance, walls swathed in sunny hues seem closer together and make a room feel more intimate. Conversely, cool tones and neutrals appear to recede and can be used to open up a smaller space.

These color tricks can be employed more subtly as well. For example, suppose you've got your heart set on a cheery, predominantly yellow living room. But it's a smaller room and you'd also like to expand it visually as much as is possible. Do you have to switch your palette to blues and neutrals? Not necessarily. The less-intense version of a

Below: Blue is a cool, soothing color and a good choice for a child's bedroom. Here the designer selected different shades of blue for the walls, furniture, and window treatments.

natural light changes through the course of the day, too. Make sure you consider this when choosing a color. The best way to do that is to paint some test sample colors on the wall, and watch how the colors change depending on the position of the sun. Do they need to be adjusted? Rooms with a northern exposure will be filled with bluer, cooler light, which weakens warm colors but intensifies cool hues. Ones facing south will have a warmer, yellowish light. That light can have the opposite effect on colors. All in all, colors interact in complex ways, so these generalizations are not absolute, but they're good starting points for making initial judgements. Your best approach is to see how color behaves in the rooms you want to decorate.

Introducing Pattern

You can add pattern to a room in a variety of ways—wallpaper and fabric being the two most popular. Because pattern is largely a vehicle for color, the same rules that guide the selection of color effectively narrow the field when it comes to selecting a pattern or complement of patterns. The designer's old friend, scale, is the other important consideration when picking patterns.

Large-scale patterns are like warm colors in that they appear to come toward you. They can create a lively and stimulating atmosphere and generally make a large space seem cozier. In a small space, handle a large-scale pattern with care or it can overpower the room. That doesn't mean rule it out completely, but perhaps use it sparingly. Small-scale patterns appear to recede, making small spaces seem larger. They can also be used effectively to camouflage odd angles or corners that you find in attic ceilings. Try a subtle, non-directional pattern for this kind of application. In a large room, the effect of a small pattern can be bland. From a distance, it may read as a single color. If you're using a small-scale pattern in a large space, pick one with vibrant colors.

Above: Mix patterns the same way you mix colors—by looking for a connection. Here the designer chose small patterns for the wallcovering, curtains, and pillows.

color will generally reduce its apparent tendency to advance or recede. Investigate the other intensities, the shades and tones of yellow, to see whether there's one that does the job.

Generally speaking, sharp contrasts have the same impact as a dark color, reduc-

ing perceived space. Monochromatic schemes enlarge space. Neutrals of similar value make walls retreat and can flow unobtrusively from room to room.

Light and Color. Lighting can change color dramatically as well. The quality of

How to Mix Patterns. Mixing patterns can be intimidating, in part because it's subjective to experimentation, judgement, and "eye." Responding to this fear, manufacturers provide an abundance of coordinated wallcovering and fabric collections, available through wallpaper books and in-store design services. Such collections, selected by professionals, can save you a lot of legwork and still leave scope for your own input. If you prefer to mix your own patterns, try to match the scale of the pattern to that of the area over which it is to be used. The general rule is to use large prints on large-sized furnishings, medium prints on medium pieces, and small prints on accent pieces. A sofa, for instance, looks better than a dining room chair with a large-scale pattern. A delicate stencil makes a better border for a tabletop than on a wall. But these rules are not hard and fast.

Another trick for mixing patterns is to provide links of scale, motif, and color. The regularity of checks, stripes, textural looks, and geometrics, particularly if small-scale and low-contrast, tends to make them easy-to-mix "neutral" patterns. A small floral can play off a thin ticking stripe, while a cabbage-rose chintz may require a bolder stripe as a same-scale foil. You may choose to use the same or similar patterns in varying sizes or develop a theme by focusing on florals, geometrics, or ethnic prints.

The most effective link is shared colors or a similar level of intensity between the prints. A solid-color companion that pulls out a hue shared by two prints provides another connection. Exact matches are the backbone of manufacturers' coordinated collections. But to arrive at your own personal mix, you can interpret the principle loosely, and experiment to see which pattern combinations work for you.

Adding Texture

Texture doesn't have the obvious impact on a room that color and pattern wield. The overall effect is much more subtle. But how a material feels, as well as how it looks, does influence room design. Incorporating a variety of textures in a room adds to its richness in a way that's most comparable to the subtle inclusion of the line varieties. A mix of textures plays upon the senses and adds another layer of complexity and sophistication to a design scheme. As with every aspect of decorating, mixing textures involves a balancing act. To give a room a distinctive character, you might let one texture predominate the room, but the right contrast can make the scheme more intriguing.

Below: Texture plays a subtle, often subjective, role in a decorating scheme. This sitting area contains a small print wallcovering, a voluminous window treatment, and a rich fabric for the chair and table covering.

Types of Texture

The easiest way to incorporate texture into a design is with fabric. Brocades and damasks, moirés and chenilles, tweeds and chintzes—all conjure up different looks and sensations. Fabrics, however, are just the beginning. Tactile interest can emanate from any material or surface that is coarse or smooth, hard or soft, matte or shiny. Coarse and matte surfaces, such as stone, rough-hewn wood, stucco, corduroy, or terra cotta, absorb light and sound. Glossy and smooth surfaces, which range from metal and glass to silk and enamel, reflect light.

Spatial Effects. To start adding texture into your design, assess your room's needs. Does it lack warmth? Or does it feel too closed in? Texture affects a room spatially. Coarse or matte surfaces will make a room seem smaller and cozier. A living room of only glossy surfaces can seem cold and impersonal without a velvet slipcover on the sofa to add warmth and contrast. Smooth and shiny surfaces do the reverse—they make a room look larger and brighter. A study that feels too stuffy, for instance, may benefit from the addition of a mirror or a glass-topped table. Light reflected off of either object will brighten the space.

Above: This unusually designed room feels comfortable and intimate thanks to the selection of rich fabrics used on the comforter and furniture, and the distinctive wall treatment.

Pattern and Color. Keep in mind that texture also affects pattern and color. With fabrics, texture can either soften or enhance a pattern. For instance, patterns are crisp on glazed chintz but are blurred on terrycloth. A coarsely textured surface tones down the intensity of a paint color, and gives the color subtle variations.

Above: Think a neutral color scheme has to be boring? This room shows how adding texture—here it is the layering of different window treatments to create a certain mood—can completely change the look and feel of a space. Bright colors would be out of place here.

High-gloss surfaces increase the intensity of a color. Think of how the gray color of a tweed jacket looks "heathered" and muted. On a silk shirt, however, the same gray color would look shimmery and more intense—a completely different effect. Every room has an existing element of texture—a stone fireplace, brass hardware, a gleaming hardwood floor, a stuccoed wall, or an iridescent tile border—that you may want to take into consideration when planning your design.

Relatively featureless rooms may be improved by adding contrasting textures. Wallpaper comes in a variety of textures—foils, flocks, embossed papers, and real fabric, to list a few. Paint can be applied in matte or gloss finishes and special painted effects that can add texture. Tile and other architectural embellishments, such as cornices, moldings, and other trimwork, such as wainscoting can also imbue a room with more tactile richness.

Window treatments are another natural outlet for texture. Fabric choices for draperies and curtains, as well as the fabrics and other materials available for blinds and shades, are enormous and varied. Texture can be enhanced by the way fabric is hung. Pleating, for example, creates a play of light and shadow. You can combine layers of fabric or fabric and blinds to show off different textures.

On the floor, carpets can be smooth, knobby, sculpted, or flecked for visual texture. Rugs, rush, coir, sisal, wood, or cork are warming texture options. Quarry tiles, ceramic tiles, marble, and slate make a room cooler. Varying the materials can make the effect more interesting. An Oriental rug over a varnished wood floor is a classic example of using two different materials to create a rich texture.

Plan #341004

Dimensions: 56'10" W x 28'6" D
Levels: 1
Square Footage: 1,101
Bedrooms: 3
Bathrooms: 2
Foundation: Crawl space, slab
Materials List Available: Yes
Price Category: B

Images provided by designer/architect.

Copyright by designer/architect.

DECK

GARAGE
21'-0" X 14'-0"

W. D WH PAN

DINING/KITCH.
18'-6" X 9'-0"

BEDROOM 3
11'-4" X 9'-0"

BA. 1

COATS

LIVING ROOM
15'-6" X 12'-0"

BA. 2

LIN

BEDROOM 1
11'-4" X 12'-8"

PORCH

BEDROOM 2
11'-4" X 10'-8"

28'-6"

56'-10"

Plan #201004

Dimensions: 60'10" W x 34'10" D
Levels: 1
Square Footage: 1,121
Bedrooms: 3
Bathrooms: 2
Foundation: Crawl space, slab
(basement option for fee)
Materials List Available: Yes
Price Category: B

Images provided by designer/architect.

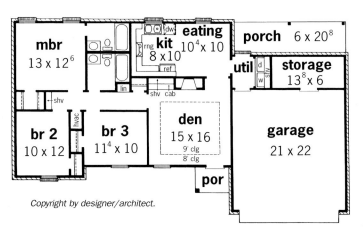

Copyright by designer/architect.

mbr
13 x 12⁶

eating
10⁴ x 10

porch 6 x 20⁸

kit
8 x 10

util

storage
13⁸ x 6

br 2
10 x 12

br 3
11⁴ x 10

den
15 x 16
9' clg
8' clg

garage
21 x 22

por

SMARTtip
Color Basics

Use color effectively to enhance the perception of the space itself. Make a large room feel cozy with warm colors, which tend to advance. Conversely, open up a small room with cool colors or neutrals, which tend to recede.

Plan #351016

Dimensions: 52' W x 38'4" D

Levels: 1

Square Footage: 1,002

Bedrooms: 2

Bathrooms: 2

Foundation: Crawl space or slab

Materials List Available: Yes

Price Category: B

Images provided by designer/architect.

Copyright by designer/architect.

This design includes many popular features, including a two-car garage.

Features:

- **Living Room:** This room welcomes you into the cozy home. It features a gas fireplace with built-in shelves on each side.

- **Kitchen:** This kitchen boasts two raised bars. One is open to the breakfast area and the other is open to the living room.

- **Bedrooms:** These two bedrooms have large closets, and bedroom 1 has direct access to the bathroom, which features a jetted tub.

- **Garage:** This two-car garage has a storage area, plus room for two nice-sized cars.

Floor plan labels:

Patio 12-8 x 10

Laun. 5-2 x 6

Breakfast Area 12 x 6 9' Ceiling

Stor. 10-0 x 4-0

Bedroom #1 11-6 x 13 9' Ceiling

Raised Bar

Jet Tub

Bath

Kitchen 12 x 10-4

Raised Bar

Garage 21-8 x 22-0

Clos.

Lin.

Tub/Shr

Bath

Br.

Clos.

Hall

Living Room 17-6 x 13 (CLEAR) 9' Ceiling

Gas Logs

Built-Ins

Bedroom #2 11-6 x 13 9' Ceiling

Front Porch 17-10 x 5

Plan #391034

Dimensions: 72'4" W x 43' D

Levels: 1

Square Footage: 1,737

Bedrooms: 3

Bathrooms: 2

Foundation: Crawl space, slab, or basement

Materials List Available: Yes

Price Category: C

Images provided by designer/architect.

This lovely home brings together traditional single-level architectural elements, current features, and just the right amount of living space.

Features:

- Entry: A demure covered porch and well-mannered foyer deliver all the important rooms.

- Dining Room: This formal room features exquisite vaulted ceilings.

- Kitchen: This close-knit kitchen with pantry embraces a cheerful breakfast nook with sliding doors to the deck.

- Master Suite: This suite is a visual treat, with its own vaulted ceiling as well as a skylight over the master bathtub and shower area.

- Bedrooms: The two secondary bedrooms are pampered with good closeting, proximity to a shared bath with double sink vanities, and wonderful windows that enhance the spacious atmosphere.

Rear Elevation

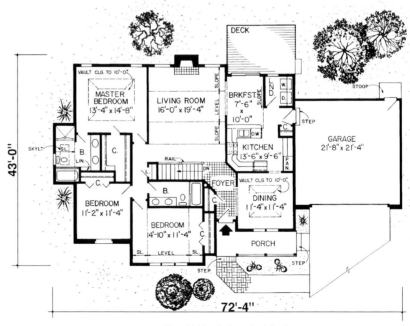

Copyright by designer/architect.

Plan #221004

Dimensions: 67'8" W x 43' D

Levels: 1

Square Footage: 1,763

Bedrooms: 3

Bathrooms: 2

Foundation: Basement

Materials List Available: No

Price Category: C

Images provided by designer/architect.

You'll love the spacious feeling provided by the open design of this traditional ranch.

Features:

- Ceiling Height: 8 ft.

- Dining Room: This formal room is perfect for entertaining groups both large and small, and the open design makes it easy to serve.

- Living Room: The vaulted ceiling here and in the dining room adds to the elegance of these rooms. Use window treatments that emphasize these ceilings for a truly sumptuous look.

- Kitchen: Designed for practicality and efficiency, this kitchen will thrill all the cooks in the family. An attached dining nook makes a natural gathering place for friends and family.

- Master Suite: The private bath in this suite features a double vanity and whirlpool tub. You'll find a walk-in closet in the bedroom.

- Garage: You'll love the extra storage space in this two-car garage.

Rear Elevation

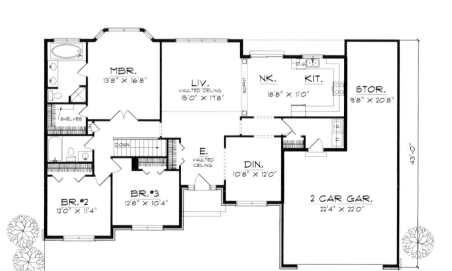

Copyright by designer/architect.

Plan #211003

Dimensions: 62' W x 64' D
Levels: 1
Square Footage: 1,865
Bedrooms: 3
Bathrooms: 2
Foundation: Slab
Materials List Available: Yes
Price Category: D

Images provided by designer/architect.

The traditional style of this home is blended with all the amenities required for today's lifestyle.

Features:

- Ceiling Height: 8 ft. unless otherwise noted.

- Front Porch: Guests will feel welcome arriving at the front door under this sheltering front porch.

- Dining Room: This large room will accommodate dinner parties of all sizes, from large formal gatherings to more intimate family get-togethers.

- Living Room: Guests and family alike will feel right at home in this inviting room. Sunlight streaming through the skylights in the 12-ft. ceiling, combined with the handsome fireplace, makes the space both airy and warm.

- Back Patio: When warm weather comes around, step out the sliding glass doors in the living room to enjoy entertaining or just relaxing on this patio.

- Kitchen: A cathedral ceiling soars over this efficient modern kitchen. It includes an eating area that is perfect for informal family meals.

SMARTtip

Fire Extinguishers

The word PASS is an easy way to remember the proper way to use a fire extinguisher.

Pull the pin at the top of the extinguisher that keeps the handle from being accidentally pressed.

Aim the nozzle of the extinguisher toward the base of the fire.

Squeeze the handle to discharge the extinguisher. Stand approximately 8 feet away from the fire.

Sweep the nozzle back and forth at the base of the fire. After the fire appears to be out, watch it carefully because it may reignite!

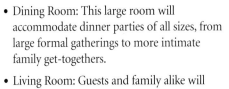

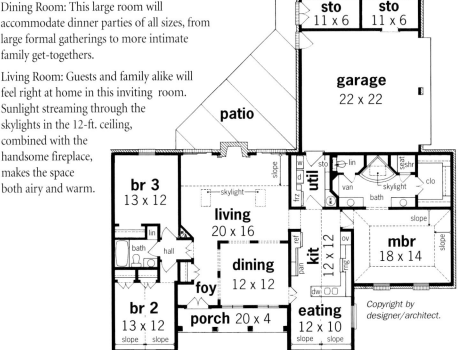

Copyright by designer/architect.

Plan #401047

Dimensions: 38' W x 34' D
Levels: 1
Square Footage: 1,064
Bedrooms: 2
Bathrooms: 1
Foundation: Basement
Materials List Available: Yes
Price Category: B

Images provided by designer/architect.

This farmhouse squeezes space-efficient features into its compact plan. Twin dormer windows flood the vaulted interior with natural light and accentuate the high ceilings.

CAD FILE AVAILABLE

Features:

- Porch: This cozy front porch opens into a vaulted great room and its adjoining dining room.

- Great Room: A warm hearth in this gathering place for the family adds to its coziness.

- Kitchen: This U-shaped kitchen has a breakfast bar open to the dining room and a sink overlooking a flower box. Nearby side-door access is found in the handy laundry room.

- Bedrooms: Vaulted bedrooms are positioned along the back of the plan. They contain wall closets and share a full bathroom with a soaking tub.

- Future Expansion: An open-rail staircase leads to the basement, which can be developed into living or sleeping space at a later time, if needed.

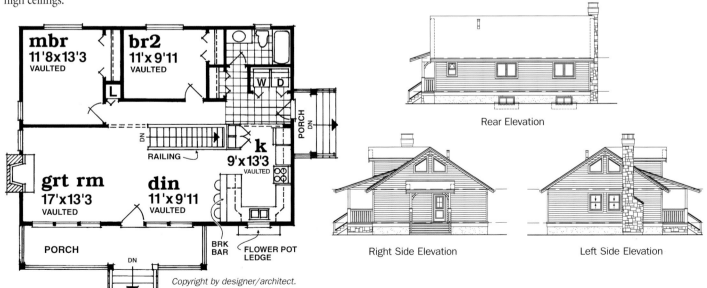

Copyright by designer/architect.

Rear Elevation

Right Side Elevation

Left Side Elevation

Plan #401050

Dimensions: 81' W x 61' D
Levels: 2
Square Footage: 6,841
Main Level Sq. Ft.: 2,596
Upper Level Sq. Ft.: 2,233
Finished Basement Sq. Ft.: 2,012
Bedrooms: 4
Bathrooms: 3 full, 2 half
Foundation: Basement
Materials List Available: Yes
Price Category: I

This grand two-story European home is adorned with a facade of stucco and brick, meticulously appointed with details for gracious living.

Features:

• Foyer: Guests enter through a portico to find this stately two-story foyer.

• Living Room: This formal area features a tray ceiling and a fireplace and is joined by a charming dining room with a large bay window.

• Kitchen: A butler's pantry joins the dining room to this gourmet kitchen, which holds a separate wok kitchen, an island work center, and a breakfast room with double doors that lead to the rear patio.

• Family Room: Located near the kitchen, this room enjoys a built-in aquarium, media center, and fireplace.

• Den: This room with a tray ceiling, window seat, and built-in computer center is tucked in a corner for privacy.

• Master Suite: The second floor features this spectacular space, which has a separate sitting room, an oversized closet, and a bath with a spa tub.

Images provided by designer/architect.

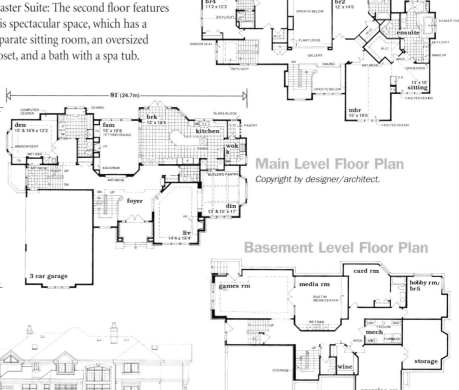

Upper Level Floor Plan

Main Level Floor Plan
Copyright by designer/architect.

Basement Level Floor Plan

Rear Elevation

Plan #401024

Dimensions: 70' W x 36' D

Levels: 1

Square Footage: 1,298

Bedrooms: 3

Bathrooms: 2

Foundation: Basement

Materials List Available: Yes

Price Category: B

A front veranda, cedar lattice, and a solid-stone chimney enhance the appeal of this one-story country-style home.

Features:

• Great Room: The open plan begins with this great room, which includes a fireplace and a plant ledge over the wall separating the living space from the country kitchen.

• Kitchen: This U-shaped kitchen provides an island work counter and sliding glass doors to the rear deck and screened porch.

• Master Suite: This area has a wall closet and a private bath with window seat.

Images provided by designer/architect.

Copyright by designer/architect.

Optional Floor Plan

Left Side Elevation

Right Side Elevation

Rear Elevation

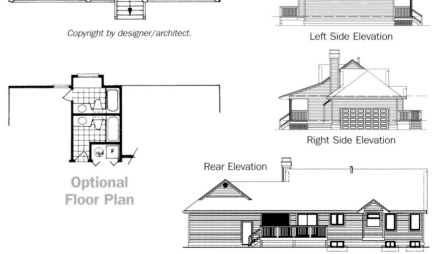

Plan #321001

Dimensions: 83' W x 42' D

Levels: 1

Square Footage: 1,721

Bedrooms: 3

Bathrooms: 2

Foundation: Crawl space, slab, or basement

Materials List Available: Yes

Price Category: C

Images provided by designer/architect.

You'll love the atrium which creates a warm, naturally lit space inside this gracious home, as well as the roof dormers that give the house wonderful curb appeal from the outside.

Features:

- **Great Room:** Bathed in light from the atrium window wall, this room, with its vaulted ceiling, will be the hub of your family life.

- **Dining Room:** This room also has a vaulted ceiling and is lit by the atrium, but you can draw drapes at night to create a cozy, warm feeling.

- **Kitchen:** Designed for functionality, this step-saving kitchen is easy to organize and makes cooking a pleasure.

- **Breakfast Room:** For convenience, this room is located between the kitchen and the rear covered porch.

- **Master Suite:** Retire with pleasure to this lovely retreat, with its luxurious bath.

Rear View

Copyright by designer/architect.

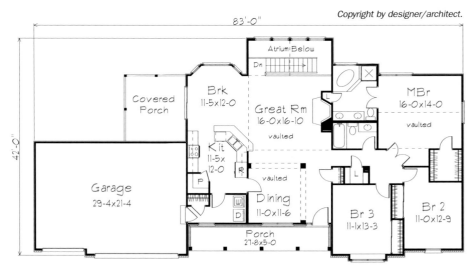

Plan #351043

Dimensions: 65' W x 50'10" D
Levels: 1
Square Footage: 1,802
Bedrooms: 3
Bathrooms: 2
Foundation: Crawl space, slab, or basement
Materials List Available: Yes
Price Category: D

This three-bedroom brick home has a wonderful split bedroom plan with open living spaces.

Features:

- Great Room: This large room with vaulted ceiling has a gas fireplace that has built-in cabinets on each side.

- Kitchen: This kitchen has an optional pocket door to the great room and a raised bar that's open to the dining room.

- Dining Room: This dining room has a view of the backyard and access to the rear covered porch.

- Master Suite: This area boasts a vaulted ceiling and his and her closets. There is also a private master bath.

- Bedrooms: The two additional bedrooms share a bathroom located in the hall.

Images provided by designer/architect.

Copyright by designer/architect.

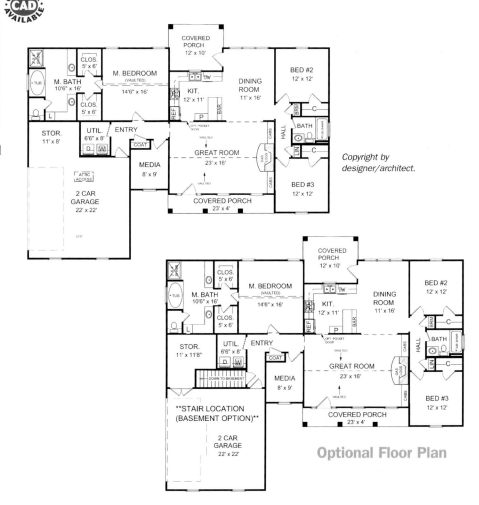

Optional Floor Plan

Plan #351020

Dimensions: 54' W x 48' D

Levels: 1

Square Footage: 1,488

Bedrooms: 3

Bathrooms: 2

Foundation: Crawl space, slab, or basement

Materials List Available: Yes

Price Category: B

Images provided by designer/architect.

This is a lot of house for its size and is an excellent example of the popular split bedroom layout.

Features:

• Great Room: This large room is open to the dining room.

• Kitchen: This fully equipped kitchen has a peninsula counter and is open into the dining room.

• Master Suite: This private area, located on the other side of the home from the secondary bedrooms, features large walk-in closets and bath areas.

• Bedrooms: The two secondary bedrooms have large closets and share a hall bathroom.

Copyright by designer/architect.

Plan #401023

Dimensions: 76' W x 63'4" D
Levels: 1
Square Footage: 2,806
Bedrooms: 3
Bathrooms: 2½
Foundation: Basement, walkout
Materials List Available: Yes
Price Category: F

Images provided by designer/architect.

The lower level of this magnificent home includes unfinished space that could have a future as a den and a family room with a fireplace. This level could also house extra bedrooms or an in-law suite.

CAD FILE AVAILABLE

Features:

- **Foyer:** On the main level, this foyer spills into a tray ceiling living room with a fireplace and an arched, floor-to-ceiling window wall.

- **Family Room:** Up from the foyer, a hall introduces this vaulted room with built-in media center and French doors that open to an expansive railed deck.

- **Kitchen:** Featured in this gourmet kitchen are a food-preparation island with a salad sink, double-door pantry, corner-window sink, and breakfast bay.

- **Master Bedroom:** The vaulted master bedroom opens to the deck, and the deluxe bath offers a raised whirlpool spa and a double-bowl vanity under a skylight.

- **Bedroom:** Two family bedrooms share a compartmented bathroom.

Rear Elevation

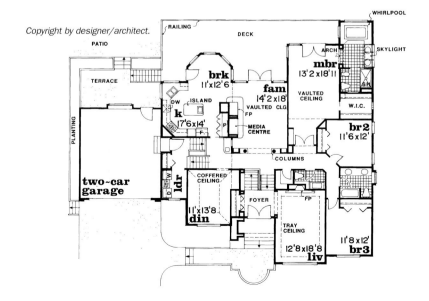

Copyright by designer/architect.

Optional Floor Plan

Plan #101005

Dimensions: 63' W x 57'2" D

Levels: 1

Square Footage: 1,992

Bedrooms: 3

Bathrooms: 2½

Foundation: Crawl space, slab, or basement

Materials List Available: Yes

Price Category: D

Images provided by designer/architect.

Rear View

This midsized ranch is accented with Palladian windows and inviting front porch.

Features:

- Ceiling Height: 9 ft. unless otherwise noted.

- Special Ceilings: Tray or vaulted ceilings adorn the living room, family room, dining room, and master suite.

- Kitchen: This bright and airy kitchen is designed to be a pleasure in which to work. It shares a big bay window with the contiguous breakfast room.

- Breakfast Room: The light streaming in from the bay window makes this the perfect place to linger with coffee and the Sunday paper.

- Master Suite: This lovely suite is exceptional, with its sitting area and direct access to the deck, as well as a full-featured bath, and spacious walk-in closet.

- Secondary Bedrooms: The other bedrooms each measure about 13 ft. x 11 ft. They have walk-in closets and share a "Jack-and-Jill" bath.

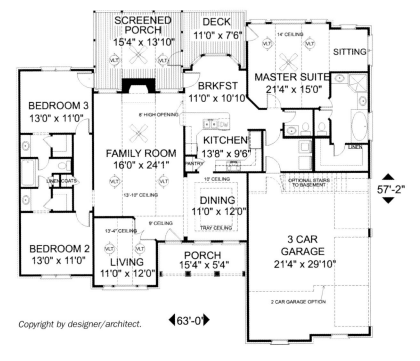

Copyright by designer/architect.

Kitchen

Living Room

Dining Room

Family Room

Master Bedroom

Master Bath

Plan #141001

Dimensions: 48' W x 29' D
Levels: 1
Square Footage: 1,208
Bedrooms: 3
Bathrooms: 2
Foundation: Basement
Materials List Available: Yes
Price Category: B

Copyright by designer/architect.

Images provided by designer/architect.

SMARTtip

Hydro-seeding

An alternative to traditional seeding is hydro-seeding. In this process, a slurry of grass seed, wood fibers, and fertilizer is spray-applied in one step. Hydro-seeding is relatively inexpensive. Compared with seeding by hand, hydro-seeding is also very fast.

Plan #341003

Dimensions: 60' W x 30' D
Levels: 1
Square Footage: 1,200
Bedrooms: 3
Bathrooms: 2
Foundation: Crawl space, slab
Materials List Available: Yes
Price Category: B

Images provided by designer/architect.

CAD FILE AVAILABLE

Copyright by designer/architect.

Plan #321030

Dimensions: 61' W x 51' D

Levels: 1

Square Footage: 2,029

Bedrooms: 4

Bathrooms: 2

Foundation: Crawl space, slab, basement, or walkout

Materials List Available: Yes

Price Category: D

Images provided by designer/architect.

Two covered porches and a rear patio make this lovely home fit right into a site with a view.

Features:

- **Great Room:** Boxed entryway columns, a vaulted ceiling, corner fireplace, widowed wall, and door to the patio are highlights in this spacious room.

- **Study:** Tucked into the back of the house for privacy, the study also opens to the rear patio.

- **Dining Area:** The windowed alcove lets natural light flow into this room, which adjoins the kitchen.

- **Kitchen:** A central island, deep pantry, and ample counter area make this room a cook's delight.

- **Master Suite:** You'll love the two walk-in closets, decorative bedroom window, and double doors opening to the private porch. The bath includes a garden tub, a separate shower, and two vanities.

- **Additional Bedrooms:** Both bedrooms have a walk-in closet.

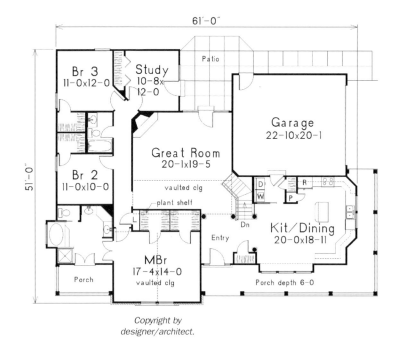

Copyright by designer/architect.

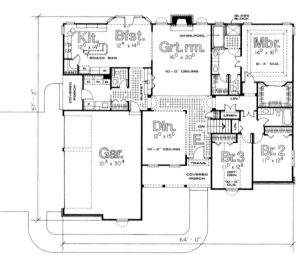

68'-0"

Patio

Garage
22-4x23-5

Kit/Din
17-6x14-6

MBr
12-9x14-6

30'-0"

Family
17-6x14-7

Br 3
12-1x11-3

Br 2
12-2x11-3

workshop
10-8x6-0

Covered Porch
23-0x8-0

Copyright by designer/architect.

Plan #321013

Dimensions: 68' W x 30' D
Levels: 1
Square Footage: 1,360
Bedrooms: 3
Bathrooms: 2
Foundation: Crawl space, slab, or basement
Materials List Available: Yes
Price Category: B

Images provided by designer/architect.

SMARTtip

Glass Doors and Fire Safety

Professionals recommend keeping glass doors open while a fire is burning. When the doors are left completely open, the burning flame has a more realistic appearance and the glass doesn't become soiled by swirling ashes. When the doors are closed, heat from a large hot fire can break the glass.

Kit.

Bfst.
12⁰ x 14⁰

Grt. rm.
16⁰ x 20⁰
10'-0" CEILING

Mbr.
14⁰ x 16⁰
9'-4" CLG.

57'-2"

Gar.
21³ x 30⁴

Din.
12⁰ x 15⁰
10'-0" CEILING

Br. 3
11⁰ x 12⁸
OPT. DEN
10'-0" CLG.

Br. 2
11⁰ x 12⁸

64'-0"

Copyright by designer/architect.

Plan #121057

Dimensions: 64' W x 57'2" D
Levels: 1
Square Footage: 2,311
Bedrooms: 3
Bathrooms: 2½
Foundation: Basement
Materials List Available: Yes
Price Category: E

Images provided by designer/architect.

CAD FILE AVAILABLE

SMARTtip

Installing Crown Molding

Test for the direction and location of ceiling joists with a stud sensor, by tapping with a hammer to hear the sound of hollow or solid areas or by tapping in test finishing nails.

Plan #131004

Dimensions: 59'4" W x 35'8" D
Levels: 1
Square Footage: 1,097
Bedrooms: 3
Bathrooms: 2
Foundation: Crawl space, slab, or basement
Materials List Available: Yes
Price Category: B

Images provided by designer/architect.

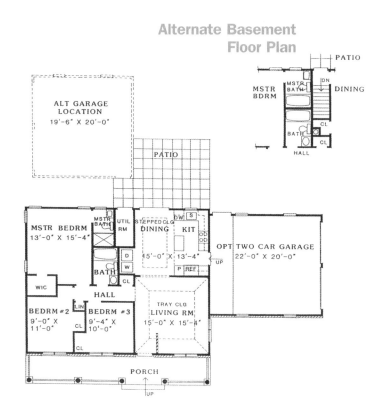

Alternate Basement Floor Plan

Plan #391006

Dimensions: 50' W x 45'4" D
Levels: 1
Square Footage: 1,456
Bedrooms: 3
Bathrooms: 2
Foundation: Crawl space, slab, or basement
Materials List Available: Yes
Price Category: B

Images provided by designer/architect.

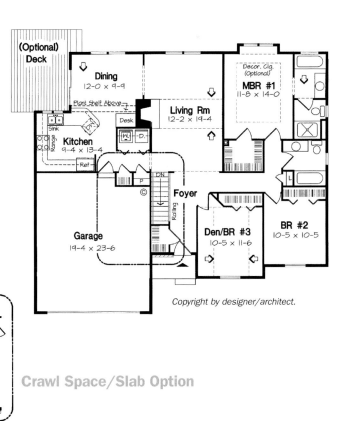

Copyright by designer/architect.

Crawl Space/Slab Option

Covered Porch 18'-5" X 4'-0"

BREAKFAST ROOM 9'-4" X 10'-11"

BEDROOM 4 13'-6" X 14'-6"

MASTER SUITE 15'-0" X 15'-0" 9' PAN CEILING

GREAT ROOM 9' BOX CEILING 15'-0" X 19'-6"

BATH

KITCHEN 9'-11" X 12'-7"

BEDROOM 3 10'-0" X 10'-4"

M.BATH 15'-0" X 11'-8"

DINING ROOM 11'-6" X 9'-8"

FOYER 7'-0" X 7'-0"

STORAGE

BEDROOM 2 12'-4" X 10'-6"

4' PORCH

GARAGE 20'-10" X 20'-0"

58'-0"

54'-10"

Copyright by designer/architect.

Plan #151005

Dimensions: 58' W x 54'10" D

Levels: 1

Square Footage: 1,940

Bedrooms: 4

Bathrooms: 2

Foundation: Crawl space, slab, or basement

CompleteCost List Available: Yes

Price Category: D

Images provided by designer/architect.

CAD FILE AVAILABLE

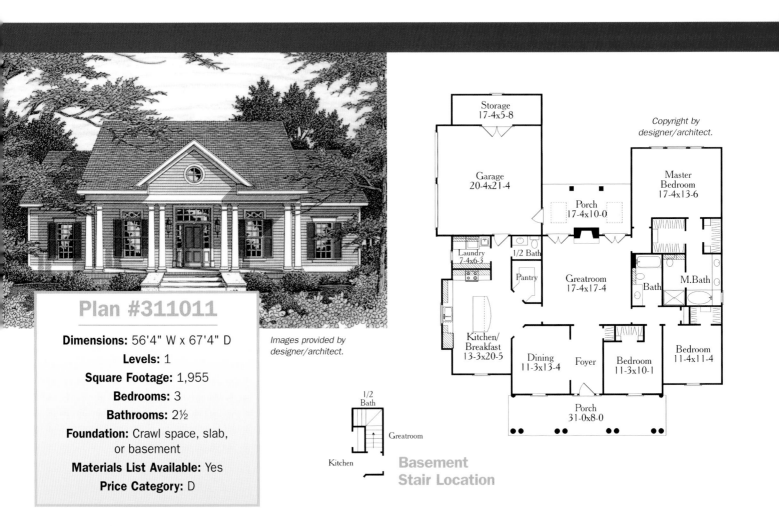

Storage 17-4x5-8

Garage 20-4x21-4

Porch 17-4x10-0

Master Bedroom 17-4x13-6

Laundry 7-4x6-3

1/2 Bath

Pantry

Greatroom 17-4x17-4

Bath

M.Bath

Kitchen/ Breakfast 13-3x20-5

Dining 11-3x13-4

Foyer

Bedroom 11-3x10-1

Bedroom 11-4x11-4

Porch 31-0x8-0

Copyright by designer/architect.

1/2 Bath

Greatroom

Kitchen

Basement Stair Location

Plan #311011

Dimensions: 56'4" W x 67'4" D

Levels: 1

Square Footage: 1,955

Bedrooms: 3

Bathrooms: 2½

Foundation: Crawl space, slab, or basement

Materials List Available: Yes

Price Category: D

Images provided by designer/architect.

Plan #401025

Dimensions: 70' W x 34' D

Levels: 1

Square Footage: 1,408

Bedrooms: 3

Bathrooms: 2

Foundation: Basement

Materials List Available: Yes

Price Category: B

An eyebrow dormer and a large veranda give guests a warm country greeting outside, while inside vaulted ceilings lend a sense of spaciousness to this three-bedroom home.

Features:

- **Front Entry:** A broad veranda shelters this area.

- **Kitchen:** This bright country kitchen boasts an abundance of counter space and cup boards, a walk-in pantry, and an island workstation.

- **Built-in Amenities:** A number of built-ins adorn the interior, including a pot shelf over the entry coat closet, an art niche, and a skylight

- **Master Suite:** A box-bay window and a spa-style tub highlight this retreat.

- **Garage:** The two-car garage provides a work shop area.

Images provided by designer/architect.

Copyright by designer/architect.

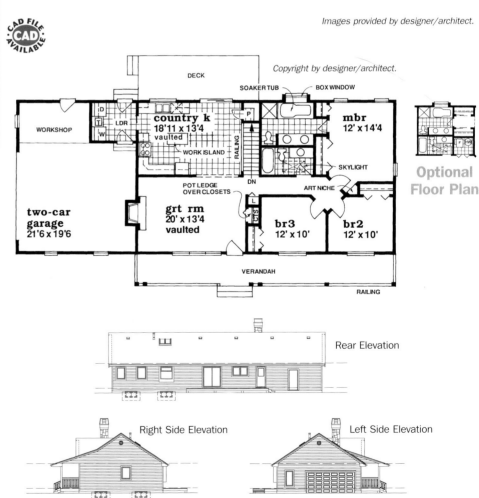

CAD FILE AVAILABLE

Optional Floor Plan

Rear Elevation

Right Side Elevation

Left Side Elevation

Plan #251001

Dimensions: 61'3" W x 40'6" D
Levels: 1
Square Footage: 1,253
Bedrooms: 3
Bathrooms: 2
Foundation: Crawl space, slab
Materials List Available: Yes
Price Category: B

Images provided by designer/architect.

- **Master Bedroom:** This master bedroom features a large walk-in closet. It has its own master bath with a single vanity, a tub, and a walk-in shower.

- **Garage:** This attached garage provides plenty of extra storage space, as well as parking for two cars.

This charming country home has a classic full front porch for enjoying summertime breezes.

Features:

- Ceiling Height: 8 ft.

- Foyer: Guests will walk through the front porch into this foyer, which opens to the family room.

- Screened Porch: A second porch is screened and is located at the rear of the home off the dining room, so your guests can step out for a bit of fresh air after dinner.

- Family Room: Family and friends will be drawn to this large open space, with its handsome fireplace and sloped ceiling.

- Kitchen: This open and airy kitchen is a pleasure in which to work. It has ample counter space and a pantry.

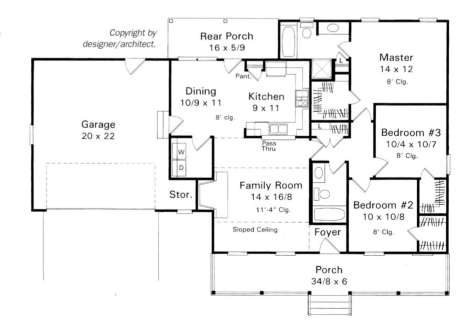

Copyright by designer/architect.

Images provided by designer/architect.

Plan #121010

Dimensions: 50' W x 62' D
Levels: 1
Square Footage: 1,902
Bedrooms: 2
Bathrooms: 2
Foundation: Basement
Materials List Available: Yes
Price Category: D

CAD FILE AVAILABLE

SMARTtip

Accentuating Your Fireplace with Faux Effects

Experiment with faux effects to add an aged look or a specific style to a fireplace mantel and surround. Craft stores sell inexpensive kits with directions for adding the appearance of antiqued or paneled wood or plaster, rusticated stone, marble, terra cotta, and other effects that make any style achievable.

Copyright by designer/architect.

Plan #321011

Dimensions: 83' W x 50'4" D
Levels: 1
Square Footage: 2,874
Bedrooms: 4
Bathrooms: 2½
Foundation: Basement
Materials List Available: Yes
Price Category: F

Images provided by designer/architect.

SMARTtip

Drilling for Kitchen Plumbing

Drill holes for plumbing and waste lines before installing the cabinets. It is easier to work when the cabinets are out in the middle of the floor, and there is no danger of knocking them out of alignment when creating the holes if they are not screwed to the wall studs or one another yet.

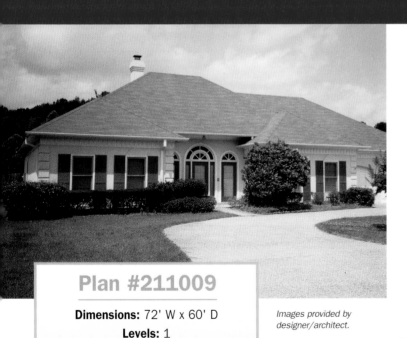

Copyright by designer/architect.

Images provided by designer/architect.

Plan #191027

Dimensions: 62' W x 42' D
Levels: 1
Square Footage: 2,354
Bedrooms: 4
Bathrooms: 2½
Foundation: Crawl space
Materials List Available: No
Price Category: E

Images provided by designer/architect.

Plan #211009

Dimensions: 72' W x 60' D
Levels: 1
Square Footage: 2,396
Bedrooms: 4
Bathrooms: 2
Foundation: Slab
Materials List Available: Yes
Price Category: E

SMARTtip

Ornaments in a Garden

Placement is everything with ornaments in a garden. Some elements are best sitting by themselves. Others are better when they are part of a cohesive whole, perhaps placed in the greenery at a corner or flanking a structure.

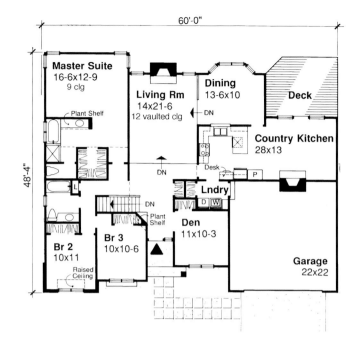

Master Suite
16-6x12-9
9 clg

Living Rm
14x21-6
12 vaulted clg

Dining
13-6x10

Deck

Country Kitchen
28x13

Plant Shelf

Desk

Lndry

Den
11x10-3

Br 2
10x11

Br 3
10x10-6

Plant Shelf

Raised Ceiling

Garage
22x22

60'-0"

48'-4"

Images provided by designer/architect.

Copyright by designer/architect.

Plan #271023

Dimensions: 60' W x 48'4" D

Levels: 1

Square Footage: 1,993

Bedrooms: 3

Bathrooms: 2

Foundation: Basement

Materials List Available: Yes

Price Category: D

Plan #101008

Dimensions: 68' W x 53' D

Levels: 1

Square Footage: 2,088

Bedrooms: 3

Bathrooms: 2½

Foundation: Basement

Materials List Available: Yes

Price Category: D

Images provided by designer/architect.

Copyright by designer/architect.

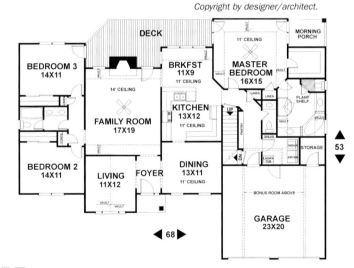

DECK

MORNING PORCH

BEDROOM 3
14X11

BRKFST
11X9
11' CEILING

MASTER BEDROOM
16X15
11' CEILING

FAMILY ROOM
17X19
14' CEILING

KITCHEN
13X12
11' CEILING

PLANT SHELF

BEDROOM 2
14X11

LIVING
11X12

FOYER

DINING
13X11
11' CEILING

STORAGE

GARAGE
23X20

BONUS ROOM ABOVE

◀ 68 ▶

53

SMARTtip

Accentuating Your Bathroom with Details

No matter how big or small the room, details will pull the style together. Some of the best details that you can include are the smallest—drawer pulls from an antique store or shells in a glass jar or just left on the countertop. Add period flavor with crown molding, or dress up contemporary fixtures with polished stone fittings.

Plan #401045

Dimensions: 78'6" W x 48' D

Levels: 1

Square Footage: 1,652

Bedrooms: 3

Bathrooms: 2

Foundation: Basement

Materials List Available: Yes

Price Category: C

This long, low ranch home has outdoor living on two porches—one to the front and one to the rear.

Features:

- High Ceilings: Vaulted ceilings in the great room, kitchen, and master bedroom add a dimension of extra space.

- Great Room: A fireplace warms this room, which opens to the country kitchen.

Images provided by designer/architect.

- Master Suite: This fine area also has doors to the rear porch and is graced by a walk-in closet, plus a full bathroom with a garden tub and dual vanity.

- Garage: This two-car garage contains space for a freezer and extra storage cabinets that are built in.

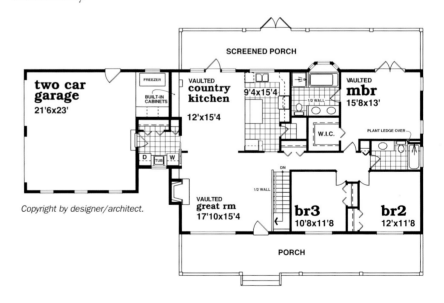

Copyright by designer/architect.

Rear Elevation

Left Side Elevation

Right Side Elevation

Plan #391004

Dimensions: 66' W x 52' D

Levels: 1

Square Footage: 1,750

Bedrooms: 2

Bathrooms: 2

Foundation: Crawl space, slab, or basement

Materials List Available: Yes

Price Category: C

This creatively compact ranch is made especially for effortless everyday living.

Features:

- Kitchen: This centralized U-shaped kitchen and look-alike breakfast nook with professional pantry have a wonderful view of the porch.

- Laundry Room: Laundry facilities are cleverly placed within reach while neatly out of the way.

- Great Room: Step into this lavish-looking sunken great room for fire-side gatherings, and move easily into the nearby formal dining area where a screened porch allows you to entertain guests after dinner.

- Master Suite: Flanking one side of the house, this master suite is serenely private and amenity-filled. Its features include full bath, a wall of walk-in closets and a dressing area.

- Bedroom: This second spacious bedroom enjoys great closeting, (with double-doors), a full bath and a close-at-hand den (or bedroom #3).

- Garage: This three-car garage goes beyond vehicle protection, providing plenty of storage and work space.

Images provided by designer/architect.

Crawl Space/Slab Option

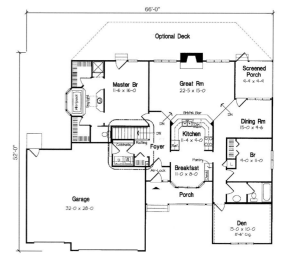

Copyright by designer/architect.

Rear View

Plan #351071

Dimensions: 51'8" W x 59' D

Levels: 1

Square Footage: 1,600

Bedrooms: 3

Bathrooms: 2½

Foundation: Basement

Materials List Available: No

Price Category: D

Images provided by designer/architect.

This charming stone-faced home will be the perfect place to come home to.

Features:

- **Great Room:** This large gathering area features a gas log fireplace and a built-in cabinet. The vaulted ceiling imparts an open and airy feeling to the space.

- **Kitchen:** This efficient U-shaped kitchen has one raised bar adjoining the dining area and another one adjoining the great room. The laundry room is located just off this space.

- **Master Suite:** This suite has a large sleeping area with a raised ceiling. The master bath boasts a jetted tub and dual vanities.

- **Bedrooms:** The secondary bedrooms are located on the opposite side of the home from the master suite for added privacy. These bedrooms have large closets and share a common bathroom.

Copyright by designer/architect.

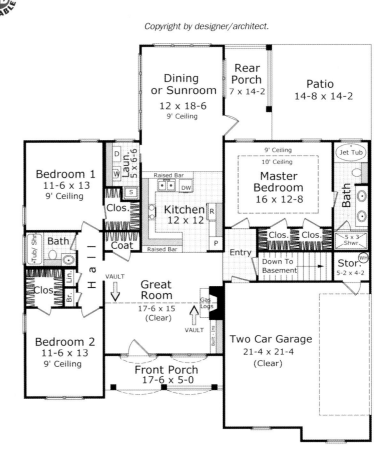

Plan #101067

Dimensions: 52'4" W x 66' D
Levels: 1
Square Footage: 1,770
Bedrooms: 3
Bathrooms: 2
Foundation: Crawl space
Materials List Available: No
Price Category: C

This nicely designed ranch is a great place to raise your family.

Features:

• Family Room: Located in the rear of the home, this room has a cozy fireplace and a tray ceiling.

• Kitchen: This well equipped kitchen boasts a raised bar open into the breakfast room. The washer and dryer are tucked away into a closet in this area.

• Master Bedroom: This private area features a tray ceiling in the sleeping area. The master bath boasts a large walk-in closet, shower, and tub.

• Bedrooms: Two secondary bedrooms share a hall bathroom and feature adequate closet space.

Images provided by designer/architect.

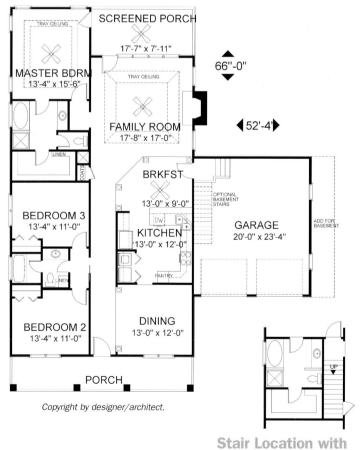

Copyright by designer/architect.

Stair Location with Bonus Room Option

Plan #391059

Dimensions: 68' W x 46' D
Levels: 1
Square Footage: 2,020
Bedrooms: 3
Bathrooms: 2½
Foundation: Basement
Materials List Available: Yes
Price Category: C

Images provided by designer/architect.

A small porch and inviting entry draw folks inside to a central dining room with elegant ceiling treatment.

Features:

• Kitchen: This clever kitchen with island boasts a corner-window breakfast area with the aura of a café.

• Great Room: This room with fireplace heads out to a large deck.

• Bedrooms: Two secondary bedrooms share a full bath.

• Master Suite: This area (with tiled tub and dual vanities) is located on the opposite side of the house from the living areas for more intimacy.

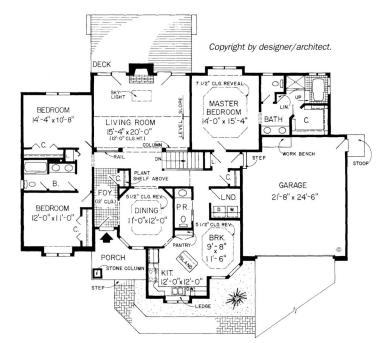

Copyright by designer/architect.

Front View/Side View

Rear View

Plan #321002

Dimensions: 72' W x 28' D

Levels: 1

Square Footage: 1,400

Bedrooms: 3

Bathrooms: 2

Foundation: Basement, crawl space

Materials List Available: Yes

Price Category: B

If you're looking for a well-designed compact home with contemporary amenities, this could be the home of your dreams.

Features:

- Porch: Just the right size for some rockers and a swing, this porch could become your outdoor living area when the weather is fine.

- Living Room: A vaulted ceiling adds to the spacious feeling in this room, where friends and family are sure to gather.

- Kitchen: This space-saving design, in combination with the ample counter and cabinet space, makes cooking a pleasure.

- Utility Room: This large room is fitted with cabinets for extra storage space. You'll find storage space in the large garage, too.

- Master Bedroom: This room is somewhat secluded for privacy, making it an ideal place for some quiet time at the end of the day.

Images provided by designer/architect.

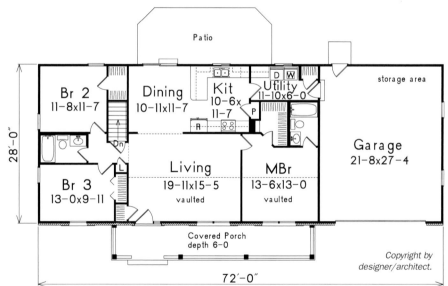

Copyright by designer/architect.

SMARTtip

Fabric Draping Ability

Test a fabric's draping ability by looking at a large piece in a fabric store. Gather at least two to three yards of material, holding one end in your hand. Check how it drapes. Does it fall into folds easily? Also look at the pattern when it is gathered. Does the design become lost in the folds? Ask a salesclerk or a friend to hold the fabric, and look at it from a few feet away.

Plan #321028

Dimensions: 79' W x 64'2" D
Levels: 1
Square Footage: 2,723
Bedrooms: 3
Bathrooms: 2½
Foundation: Basement
Materials List Available: Yes
Price Category: F

Images provided by designer/architect.

This dream brick three-bedroom home with a three-car garage has everything you are looking for in a new home.

Features:

- Great Room: This large room has a vaulted ceiling and a fireplace.

- Dining Room: Just off the entry is this formal space, with its tray ceiling.

- Kitchen: This island kitchen has a large pantry and an abundance of counter space.

- Master Suite: This retreat features a vaulted ceiling and a large walk-in closet. The master bath has a double vanity and a soaking tub.

- Bedrooms: Two additional bedrooms share a common bathroom.

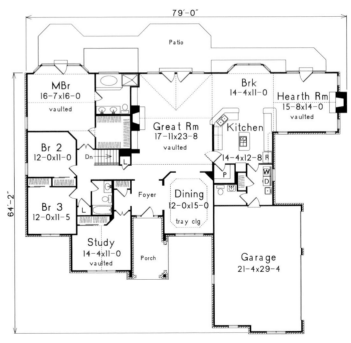

Copyright by designer/architect.

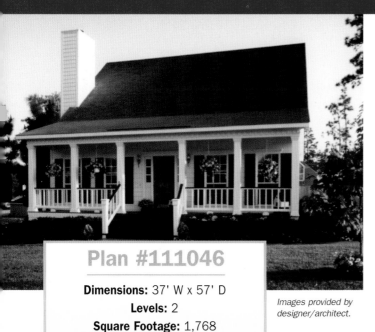

Main Level Floor Plan

Wood Deck 12'6" x 8'
Covered Porch 12'2" x 10'
Ext. Storage
Master Bath
WIC
Breakfast 11'10" x 9'6"
Utility
Master Bedroom 12'6" x 15'6"
1/2 Ba.
Kitchen 10' x 11'6"
Dining 13' x 12'
Living 14'4" x 17'6"
Porch 32' x 5'

Images provided by designer/architect.

Upper Level Floor Plan

Bedroom 10'6" x 13'2"
Balcony
Bedroom 12'6" x 14'

Copyright by designer/architect.

Plan #111046

Dimensions: 37' W x 57' D
Levels: 2
Square Footage: 1,768
Main Level Sq. Ft.: 1,247
Upper Level Sq. Ft.: 521
Bedrooms: 3
Bathrooms: 2½
Foundation: Crawl space
Materials List Available: No
Price Category: C

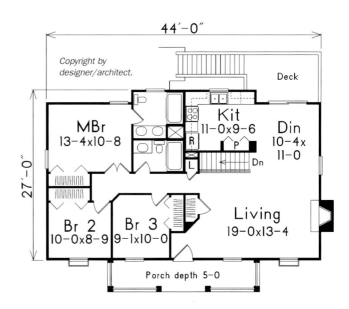

44'-0"

Copyright by designer/architect.

Deck
MBr 13-4x10-8
Kit 11-0x9-6
Din 10-4x 11-0
27'-0"
Br 2 10-0x8-9
Br 3 9-1x10-0
Living 19-0x13-4
Porch depth 5-0

Plan #321022

Dimensions: 44' W x 27' D
Levels: 1
Square Footage: 1,140
Bedrooms: 3
Bathrooms: 2
Foundation: Basement
Materials List Available: Yes
Price Category: B

Images provided by designer/architect.

SMARTtip
Basement Moldings

Keep moldings simple in a basement with lower ceilings. Elaborate moldings around the ceiling or floor can shorten the height of the room.

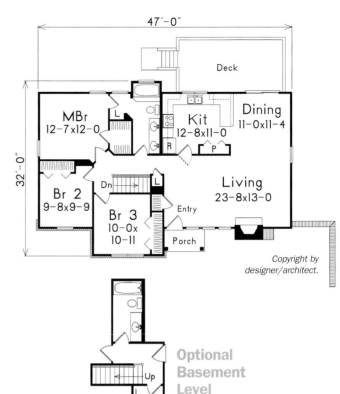

Images provided by designer/architect.

Copyright by designer/architect.

Plan #321024

Dimensions: 47' W x 32' D

Levels: 1

Square Footage: 1,403

Bedrooms: 3

Bathrooms: 1-2

Foundation: Daylight basement

Materials List Available: Yes

Price Category: B

Optional Basement Level Floor Plan

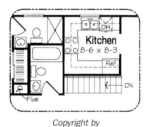

Optional Basement Level Floor Plan

Copyright by designer/architect.

Plan #391064

Dimensions: 54' W x 28' D

Levels: 1

Square Footage: 988

Bedrooms: 3

Bathrooms: 2

Foundation: Crawl space, basement

Materials List Available: Yes

Price Category: A

Images provided by designer/architect.

Images provided by designer/architect.

Copyright by designer/architect.

Plan #321014

Dimensions: 64' W x 43'8" D
Levels: 1
Square Footage: 1,676
Bedrooms: 3
Bathrooms: 2
Foundation: Basement
Materials List Available: Yes
Price Category: C

SMARTtip

Blending Architecture

An easy way to blend the new deck with the architecture of a house is with railings. Precut railings and caps come in many styles and sizes.

SMARTtip

Planning a Safe Children's Room

Keep safety in mind when planning a child's room. Make sure that there are covers on electrical outlets, guard rails on high windows, sturdy screens in front of radiators, and gates blocking any steps. Other suggestions include safety hinges for chests and nonskid backing for rugs.

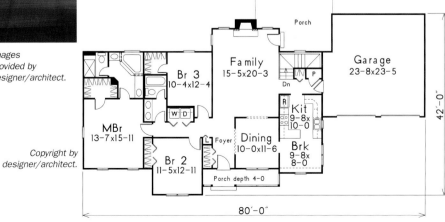

Images provided by designer/architect.

Copyright by designer/architect.

Plan #321021

Dimensions: 80' W x 42' D
Levels: 1
Square Footage: 1,708
Bedrooms: 3
Bathrooms: 2
Foundation: Crawl space or basement
Materials List Available: Yes
Price Category: C

Plan #391069

Dimensions: 56' W x 48' D

Levels: 1

Square Footage: 1,492

Bedrooms: 3

Bathrooms: 2

Foundation: Crawl space, slab, or basement

Materials List Available: Yes

Price Category: B

Images provided by designer/architect.

This design opens wide from the living room to the kitchen and dining room. All on one level, even the bedrooms are easy to reach.

Features:

- Living Room: This special room features a fireplace and entry to the deck.

- Dining Room: This formal room shows off special ceiling effects.

- Bedrooms: Bedroom 3 is inspired by a decorative ceiling, and bedroom 2 has double closet doors. There's a nearby bath for convenience.

- Master Suite: This private area features a roomy walk-in closet and private bath.

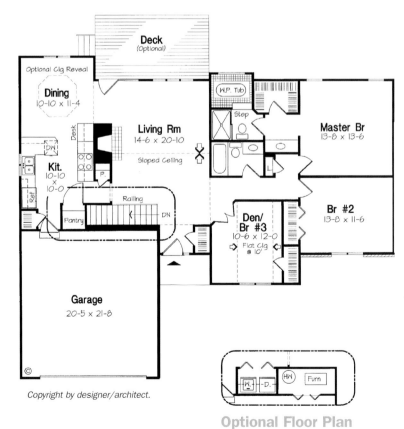

Copyright by designer/architect.

Optional Floor Plan

Plan #371072

Dimensions: 75'10" W x 38'8" D

Levels: 1

Square Footage: 1,772

Bedrooms: 3

Bathrooms: 2

Foundation: Crawl space, slab

Materials List Available: No

Price Category: C

Images provided by designer/architect.

This home, with its enclosed covered porch, defines country charm.

Features:

- **Living Room:** This large room has a 10-foot-high ceiling and large windows looking out onto a covered back porch. The cozy fireplace and built-in media center will be great for relaxing.

- **Kitchen:** This large country kitchen with breakfast nook features a raised bar.

- **Dining Room:** This beautiful room has large windows located in a boxed-out extension.

- **Master Suite:** This secluded suite has a large walk-in closet and a luxurious master bath.

Copyright by designer/architect.

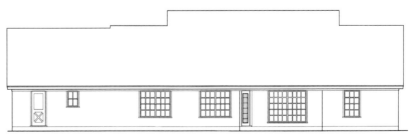

Rear Elevation

Plan #211001

Dimensions: 52' W x 66' D
Levels: 1
Square Footage: 1,655
Bedrooms: 3
Bathrooms: 2
Foundation: Slab
Materials List Available: Yes
Price Category: C

Images provided by designer/architect.

You'll love this elegant one-story home, both practical and gorgeous, with its many amenities.

Features:

• Entry: A covered porch and three glass doors with transoms announce this home.

• Living Room: At the center of the house, this living room has a 15-ft. ceiling and a fireplace. A glass door flanked by windows opens to a skylighted porch at the rear of the home.

• Dining Room: This elegant octagonal room, which is shaped by columns and cased openings, overlooks both backyard porches.

• Kitchen: A 14-ft. sloped ceiling with a skylight adds drama.

• Master Suite: Enjoy the seclusion of this area at the rear of the home, as well as its private access to a rear porch. The bath features an oval spa tub, separate shower, dual vanities, and huge walk-in closet.

Copyright by designer/architect.

SMARTtip

Plotting a Potting Space

Whether you opt for a simple corner potting bench or a multipurpose shed or greenhouse, organization is key. You'll need a work surface —a counter or table that's a convenient height for standing while at work— plus storage accommodations for hand tools, long-handled tools, watering cans, extra lengths of hose, hose nozzles, flowerpots, bags of fertilizer and potting soil, gardening books, and notebooks. Plastic garbage cans (with lids) are good for soil and seeds. Most of these spaces are small, so use hooks and stacking bins, which keep items neat and at hand's reach. High shelves free up floor space while holding least-used things.

Plan #321017

Dimensions: 77' W x 36'8" D
Levels: 1
Square Footage: 2,531
Bedrooms: 1-4
Bathrooms: 1-2½
Foundation: Daylight basement
Materials List Available: Yes
Price Category: E

Images provided by designer/architect.

Main Level Floor Plan

Copyright by designer/architect.

Optional Basement Level Floor Plan

Rear View

Plan #321012

Dimensions: 58'8" W x 51'2" D
Levels: 1
Square Footage: 1,882
Bedrooms: 3
Bathrooms: 2
Foundation: Basement
Materials List Available: Yes
Price Category: D

Images provided by designer/architect.

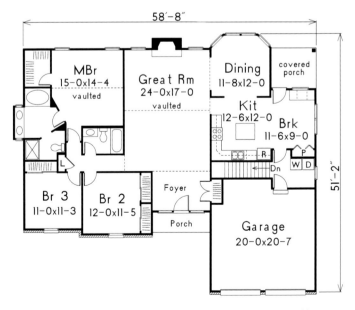

Copyright by designer/architect.

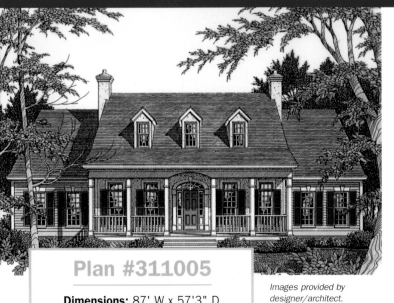

Plan #311005

Dimensions: 87' W x 57'3" D

Levels: 1

Square Footage: 2,497

Bedrooms: 3

Bathrooms: 2½

Foundation: Crawl space, slab, or basement

Materials List Available: Yes

Price Category: E

Images provided by designer/architect.

Bonus Area Floor Plan

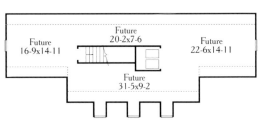

Plan #161073

Dimensions: 66' W x 69' D

Levels: 1

Square Footage: 1,895

Bedrooms: 3

Bathrooms: 2

Foundation: Basement

Materials List Available: No

Price Category: D

Images provided by designer/architect.

CAD FILE AVAILABLE

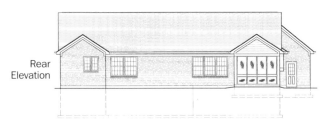

Rear Elevation

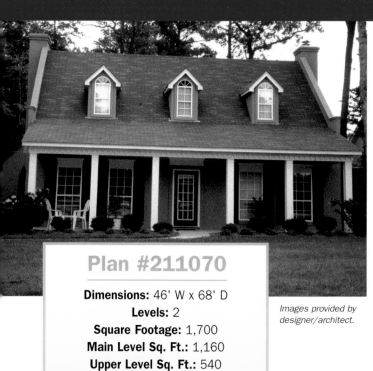

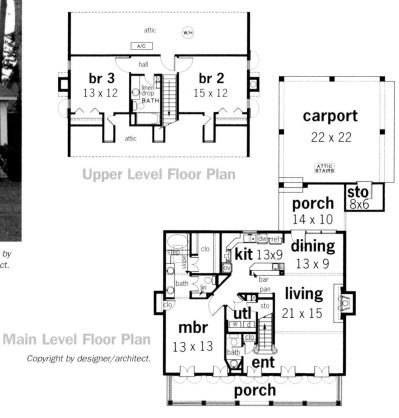

Upper Level Floor Plan

Main Level Floor Plan

Copyright by designer/architect.

Plan #211070

Dimensions: 46' W x 68' D
Levels: 2
Square Footage: 1,700
Main Level Sq. Ft.: 1,160
Upper Level Sq. Ft.: 540
Bedrooms: 3
Bathrooms: 2½
Foundation: Crawl space, optional slab, or basement
Materials List Available: Yes
Price Category: C

Images provided by designer/architect.

Plan #321033

Dimensions: 38' W x 46' D
Levels: 1
Square Footage: 1,268
Bedrooms: 3
Bathrooms: 2
Foundation: Basement
Materials List Available: Yes
Price Category: B

Images provided by designer/architect.

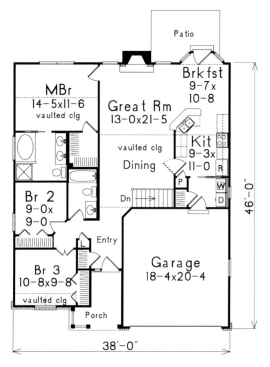

Copyright by designer/architect.

Images provided by designer/architect.

Plan #211004

Dimensions: 64' W x 62' D
Levels: 1
Square Footage: 1,828
Bedrooms: 4
Bathrooms: 2
Foundation: Crawl space, slab, or basement
Materials List Available: Yes
Price Category: D

This super-energy-efficient home has the curb appeal of a much larger house.

Features:

- Ceiling Height: 9 ft.
- Kitchen: You will love cooking in this bright, airy, and efficient kitchen. It features an angled layout that allows a great view to the outside through a window wall in the breakfast area.
- Breakfast Area: With morning sunlight streaming through the wall of windows in

this area, you won't be able to resist lingering over a cup of coffee.

- Rear Porch: This breezy rear porch is designed to accommodate the pleasure of old-fashioned rockers or swings.
- Master Bedroom: Retreat at the end of a long day to this bedroom, which is isolated for privacy yet conveniently located a few steps from the kitchen and utility area.
- Attic Storage: No need to fuss with creaky pull-down stairs. This attic has a permanent stairwell to provide easy access to its abundant storage.

Copyright by designer/architect.

SMARTtip

Resin Furniture

Resin furniture is made of molded plastic. Most resin pieces are quite affordable, but lacquered resin with brass fittings is a high-end item. Resin doesn't corrode and cleans easily, but a scratched finish cannot be repaired. However, lacquered resin can be touched up.

Plan #321006

Dimensions: 76' W x 45' D

Levels: 1, optional lower

Square Footage: 1,977

Optional Basement Level Sq. Ft.: 1,416

Bedrooms: 4

Bathrooms: 2½

Foundation: Basement

Materials List Available: Yes

Price Category: D

Images provided by designer/architect.

This design is ideal if you're looking for a home with space to finish as your family and your budget grow.

Features:

- **Great Room:** A vaulted ceiling in this room sets an elegant tone that the gorgeous atrium windows pick up and amplify.

- **Atrium:** Elegance marks the staircase here that leads to the optional lower level.

- **Kitchen:** Both experienced cooks and beginners will appreciate the care that went into the design of this step-saving kitchen, with its ample counter space and generous cabinets.

- **Master Suite:** Enjoy the luxuries you'll find in this suite, and revel in the quiet that the bedroom can provide.

- **Lower Level:** Finish the 1,416 sq. ft. here to create a family room, two bedrooms, two bathrooms, and a study.

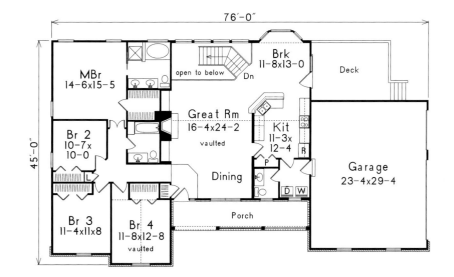

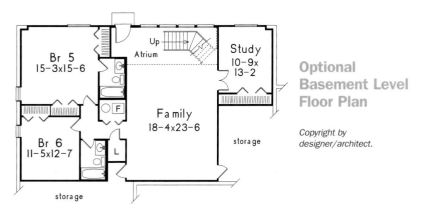

Optional Basement Level Floor Plan

Copyright by designer/architect.

Plan #101022

Dimensions: 66'2" W x 62' D

Levels: 1

Square Footage: 1,992

Bedrooms: 3

Bathrooms: 3

Foundation: Crawl space, slab, or basement

Materials List Available: Yes

Price Category: D

Images provided by designer/architect.

The exterior of this lovely home is traditional, but the unusually shaped rooms and amenities are contemporary.

Features:

- Foyer: This two-story foyer is open to the family room, but columns divide it from the dining room.

- Family Room: A gas fireplace and TV niche, flanked by doors to the covered porch, sit at the rear of this seven-sided, spacious room.

- Breakfast Room: Set off from the family room by columns, this area shares a snack bar with the kitchen and has windows looking over the porch.

- Bedroom 3: Use this room as a living room if you wish, and transform the guestroom to a media room or a family bedroom.

- Master Suite: The bedroom features a tray ceiling, has his and her dressing areas, and opens to the porch. The bath has a large corner tub, separate shower, linen closet, and two vanities.

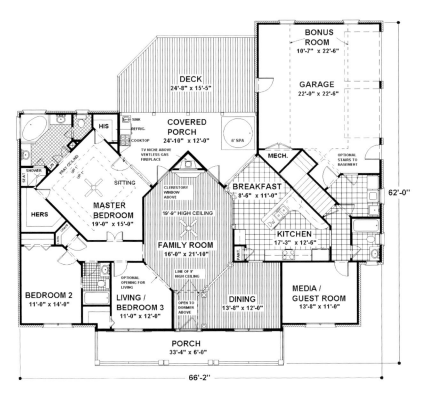

Copyright by designer/architect.

Plan #211030

Dimensions: 75' W x 37' D
Levels: 1
Square Footage: 1,600
Bedrooms: 3
Bathrooms: 2
Foundation: Slab
Materials List Available: Yes
Price Category: C

Images provided by designer/architect.

Copyright by designer/architect.

Plan #321015

Dimensions: 48' W x 64' D
Levels: 1
Square Footage: 1,501
Bedrooms: 3
Bathrooms: 2
Foundation: Crawl space, slab, or basement
Materials List Available: Yes
Price Category: C

Images provided by designer/architect.

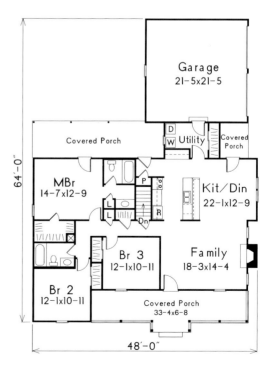

Copyright by designer/architect.

Although it is rarely noticed, a bracket plays an important role in supporting rods and poles. If a treatment rubs against a window frame, an extension bracket solves the problem. It projects from the wall at an adjustable length, providing enough clearance. A hold-down bracket anchors a cellular shade or a blind to the bottom of a door, preventing the treatment from moving when the door is opened or closed.

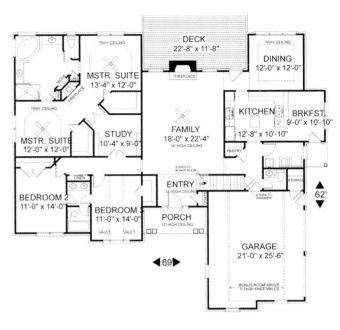

Plan #101098

Dimensions: 69' W x 62' D

Levels: 1

Square Footage: 2,398

Bedrooms: 3

Bathrooms: 2½

Foundation: Slab or basement

Materials List Available: Yes

Price Category: E

Images provided by designer/architect.

Copyright by designer/architect.

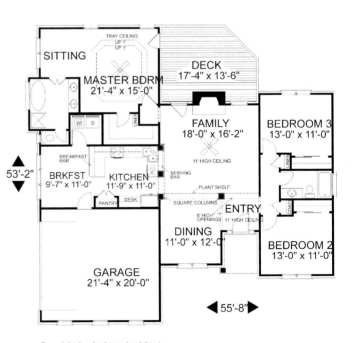

Plan #101061

Dimensions: 55'8" W x 53'2" D

Levels: 1

Square Footage: 1,681

Bedrooms: 3

Bathrooms: 2

Foundation: Crawl space or slab

Materials List Available: No

Price Category: C

Images provided by designer/architect.

Copyright by designer/architect.

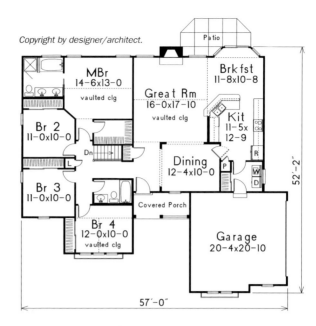

Copyright by designer/architect.

Images provided by designer/architect.

Plan #321008

Dimensions: 57' W x 52'2" D
Levels: 1
Square Footage: 1,761
Bedrooms: 4
Bathrooms: 2
Foundation: Basement
Materials List Available: Yes
Price Category: C

SMARTtip

Hanging Wallpaper

Use liner paper to smooth out a damaged wall and to provide uniform support for expensive paper.

Copyright by designer/architect.

Images provided by designer/architect.

CAD FILE AVAILABLE

Plan #221014

Dimensions: 72' W x 44'8" D
Levels: 1
Square Footage: 1,906
Bedrooms: 3
Bathrooms: 2½
Foundation: Basement
Materials List Available: No
Price Category: D

Rear Elevation

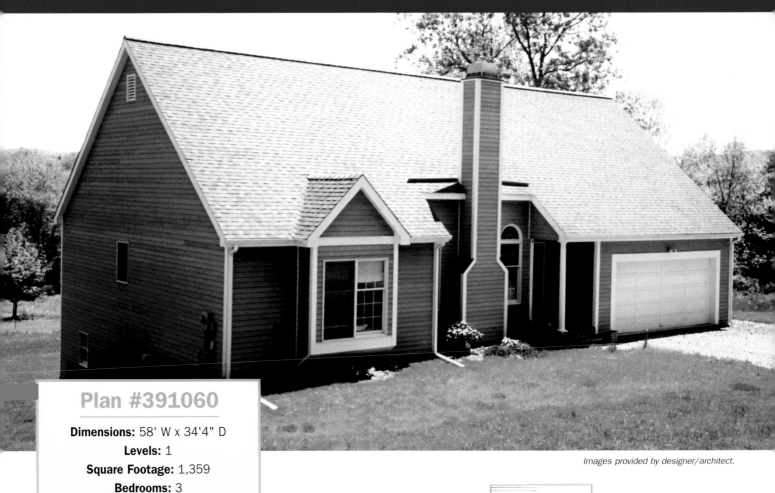

Plan #391060

Dimensions: 58' W x 34'4" D

Levels: 1

Square Footage: 1,359

Bedrooms: 3

Bathrooms: 2

Foundation: Crawl space, slab or basement

Materials List Available: Yes

Price Category: B

Big bay windows and one-story styling make this home irresistible.

Features:

- Living Room: This great-sized living room winds its way to a formal dining room and kitchen.

- Master Suite: This area (with luxury bath room) shows off a tray ceiling and a window seat with a front-yard view.

- Bedroom 2: This room has a spacious closet and a personal view of the backyard, plus a full bath.

- Den: This room with double doors can become bedroom 3 if necessary.

Images provided by designer/architect.

Copyright by designer/architect.

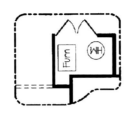

Plan #321005

Dimensions: 69' W x 53'8" D
Levels: 1
Square Footage: 2,483
Bedrooms: 3
Bathrooms: 2
Foundation: Basement
Materials List Available: Yes
Price Category: E

Images provided by designer/architect.

You'll love the grand feeling of this home, which combines with the very practical features that make living in it a pleasure.

Features:

- **Porch:** The open brick arches and Palladian door set the tone for this magnificent home.

- **Great Room:** An alcove for the entertainment center and vaulted ceiling show the care that went into designing this room.

- **Dining Room:** A tray ceiling sets off the formality of this large room.

- **Kitchen:** The layout in this room is designed to make your work patterns more efficient and to save you steps and time.

- **Study:** This quiet room can be a wonderful refuge, or you can use it for a fourth bedroom if you wish.

- **Master Suite:** Made for relaxing at the end of the day, this suite will pamper you with luxuries.

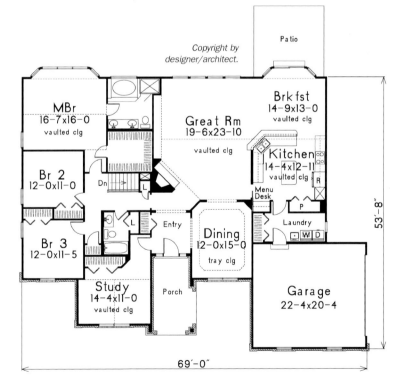

Copyright by designer/architect.

SMARTtip®
Art in Pools

The tiled walls and floor of a pool make great canvases for art, so incorporate a serious or whimsical design. Also, make the stairs wide and shallow to form a wading area for kids.

Plan #131007

Dimensions: 59'10" W x 47'8" D

Levels: 1

Square Footage: 1,595

Bedrooms: 3

Bathrooms: 2

Foundation: Crawl space, slab, basement, or walkout

Materials List Available: Yes

Price Category: D

Imagine living in this home, with its traditional country comfort and individual brand of charm.

Features:

- Exterior elements: The mixture of a front porch with a cameo front door, decorative posts, bay windows, and dormers will delight you.

- Great Room: A tray ceiling gives distinction to this large room, and a wet bar eases entertaining.

- Screened Porch: At dusk and dawn, this porch is sure to be your favorite outdoor spot.

- Kitchen: Eat any meal in this large kitchen for a touch of homey charm.

- Dining Room: Perfect for hosting a formal dinner, this bayed dining room can increase your enjoyment of simple family meals.

- Master Bedroom: For the sake of privacy, this room is somewhat secluded. Decorate to emphasize the elegant tray ceiling.

Images provided by designer/architect.

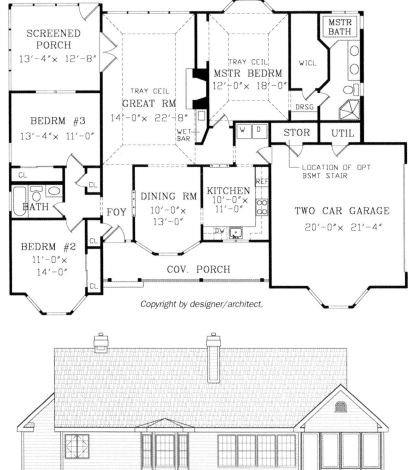

Copyright by designer/architect.

Rear Elevation

Alternate Front View

Foyer / Dining Room

Great Room

Add the Extras

Simple or plain, it's the little conveniences and miscellaneous touches that push the dining experience to perfection. Here are some extra things to think about.

- You can never have too many serving trays when you entertain outside. For carrying food or drinks from the kitchen or the grill, trays are indispensable.

- A serving cart on wheels makes a perfect movable outdoor bar and provides an additional serving surface. Look for one at yard sales or buy one new.

- Chances are you won't have a sideboard, but a few small tables to hold excess items are great substitutes for one. They're also easier to position in the different places where you need them.

- For cooler weather or even a summer's evening with a bit of nip in the air, nothing beats an outdoor fireplace for comfort. You could build one into the house, but various types of stand-alone units are sold in home centers. To add a Southwest ambiance, consider a chiminea, a clay fireplace. Try burning some piñon pine, and you'll feel as if you're in Santa Fe. Be sure to follow manufacturers' instructions when using these fireplaces. You might also have to store them during the winter.

- Pots of fragrant plants—lavender, scented geraniums, flowering tobacco, or jasmine—provide a sensual aroma. Flowers such as roses climbing up an arbor or trellis are beautiful, evoke a romantic feeling, and lend a delicate scent to the atmosphere as well.

Nothing adds romance and intrigue to an evening soiree as candlelight does. Include just a few candles for an intimate dinner. Use more for a larger gathering, placing one or more on each table. Scatter luminaries around the yard. As the beautiful evening dusk begins, light candles, a few at a time, so your eyes can adjust to the dimming light. Not only do the candles illuminate the night in a magical way but they can also keep bugs at bay.

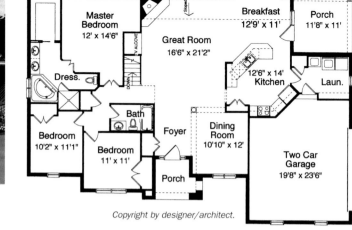

Copyright by designer/architect.

Plan #161008

Images provided by designer/architect.

Dimensions: 64'2" W x 46'6" D
Levels: 1
Square Footage: 1,860
Bedrooms: 3
Bathrooms: 2
Foundation: Slab
Materials List Available: No
Price Category: D

SMARTtip

Espaliered Fruit Trees

Try a technique used by the royal gardeners at Versailles—espalier. They trained the fruit trees to grow flat against the walls, creating patterns. It's not difficult, especially if you go to a reputable nursery and purchase an apple or pear tree that has already been espaliered. Plant it against a flat surface that's in a sunny spot.

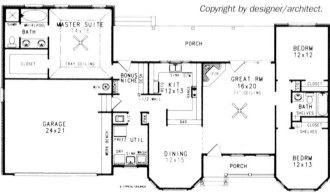

Copyright by designer/architect.

Plan #171008

Images provided by designer/architect.

Dimensions: 72' W x 40' D
Levels: 1
Square Footage: 1,652
Bedrooms: 3
Bathrooms: 2
Foundation: Slab, crawl space
Materials List Available: Yes
Price Category: C

SMARTtip

Lighting for Decorative Shadows

Use lighting to create decorative shadows. For interesting, undefined shadows, set lights at ground level aiming upward in front of a shrub or tree that is close to a wall. For silhouetting, place lights directly behind a plant or garden statue that is near a wall. In both cases, using a wide beam will increase the effect.

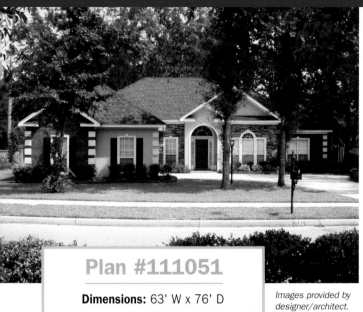

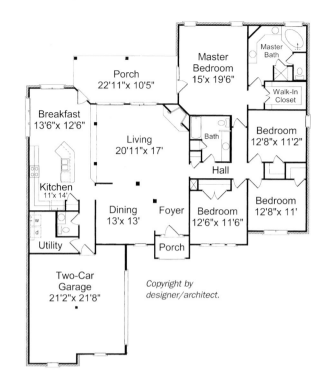

Images provided by designer/architect.

Copyright by designer/architect.

Plan #111051

Dimensions: 63' W x 76' D

Levels: 1

Square Footage: 2,471

Bedrooms: 4

Bathrooms: 2½

Foundation: Slab

Materials List Available: No

Price Category: E

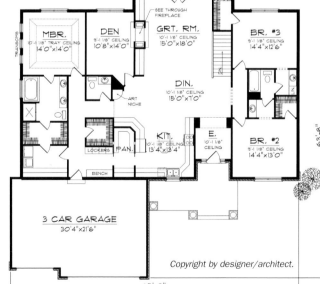

Images provided by designer/architect.

Copyright by designer/architect.

Rear Elevation

Plan #221045

Dimensions: 65' W x 63'8" D

Levels: 1

Square Footage: 2,420

Bedrooms: 3

Bathrooms: 2½

Foundation: Basement

Materials List Available: No

Price Category: E

Plan #321003

Dimensions: 67'4" W x 48' D
Levels: 1
Square Footage: 1,791
Bedrooms: 4
Bathrooms: 2
Foundation: Basement
Materials List Available: Yes
Price Category: C

Images provided by designer/architect.

The traditional good looks of the exterior of this home are complemented by the stunning contemporary design of the interior.

Features:

- Great Room: With a vaulted ceiling to highlight its spacious dimensions, this room is certain to be the central gathering spot for friends and family.

- Dining Room: Also with a vaulted ceiling, this room has an octagonal shape for added interest. Windows here and in the great room look out to the covered patio.

- Kitchen: A center island gives a convenient work space in this well-designed kitchen, which features a pass-through to the dining room for easy serving, and large, walk-in pantry for storage.

- Breakfast Room: A bay window lets sunshine pour in to start your morning with a smile.

- Master Bedroom: A vaulted ceiling and a sitting area make you feel truly pampered in this room.

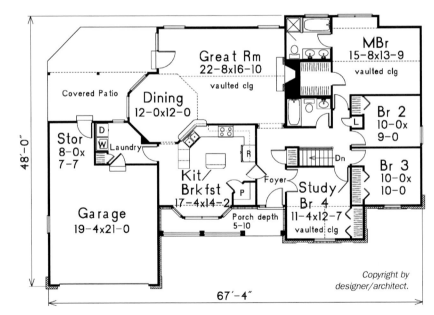

Copyright by designer/architect.

SMARTtip

Bay & Bow Windows

Occasionally too little room exists between the window frame (if there is one) and the ceiling. In this situation you might be able to use ceiling-mounted hardware. Alternatively, a cornice across the top and a rod mounted inside the cornice will give you the dual benefit of visually lowering the top of the window and concealing the hardware.

Plan #131014

Dimensions: 48' W x 43'4" D
Levels: 1
Square Footage: 1,380
Bedrooms: 3
Bathrooms: 2
Foundation: Crawl space, slab, or basement
Materials List Available: Yes
Price Category: B

The exterior of this home looks formal, thanks to its twin dormers, gables, and the bay windows that flank the columned porch, but the inside is contemporary in both design and features.

Features:

- **Great Room:** Centrally located, this great room has a 10-ft. ceiling. A fireplace, built-in cabinets, and windows that overlook the rear covered porch make it as practical as it is attractive.

- **Dining Room:** A bay window adds to the charm of this versatile room.

- **Kitchen:** This U-shaped room is designed to make cooking and cleaning jobs efficient.

- **Master Suite:** With a bay window, a walk-in closet, and a private bath with an oval tub, the master suite may be your favorite area.

- **Additional Bedrooms:** Located on the opposite side of the house from the master suite, these rooms share a full bath in the hall.

Images provided by designer/architect.

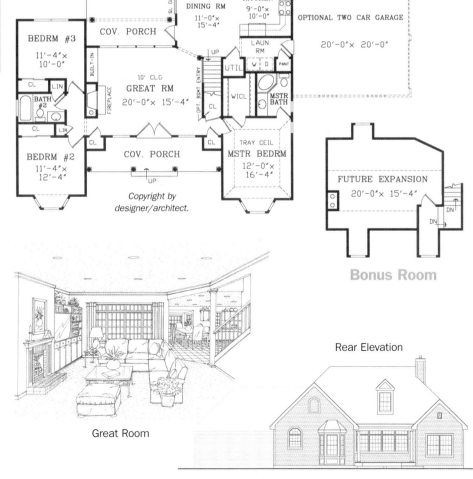

Copyright by designer/architect.

Bonus Room

Great Room

Rear Elevation

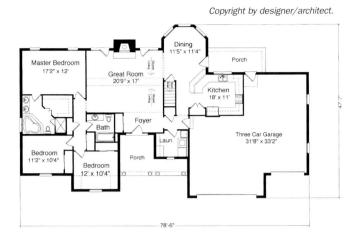

Copyright by designer/architect.

Plan #161006

Dimensions: 78'6" W x 47'7" D

Levels: 1

Square Footage: 1,755

Bedrooms: 3

Bathrooms: 2

Foundation: Basement

Materials List Available: Yes

Price Category: C

Images provided by designer/architect.

CAD FILE AVAILABLE

Rear Elevation

Copyright by designer/architect.

Plan #191003

Dimensions: 56' W x 42' D

Levels: 1

Square Footage: 1,785

Bedrooms: 3

Bathrooms: 3

Foundation: Crawl space, slab, or basement

Materials List Available: No

Price Category: C

Images provided by designer/architect.

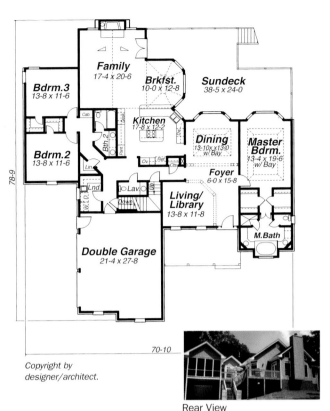

Plan #141021

Dimensions: 70'10" W x 78'9" D

Levels: 1

Square Footage: 2,614

Bedrooms: 3

Bathrooms: 2½

Foundation: Basement

Materials List Available: Yes

Price Category: F

Images provided by designer/architect.

Living Room

Dining Room

Copyright by designer/architect.

Rear View

Plan #141011

Dimensions: 54' W x 60'6" D

Levels: 1

Square Footage: 1,869

Bedrooms: 3

Bathrooms: 2

Foundation: Crawl space, slab, or basement

Materials List Available: Yes

Price Category: D

Images provided by designer/architect.

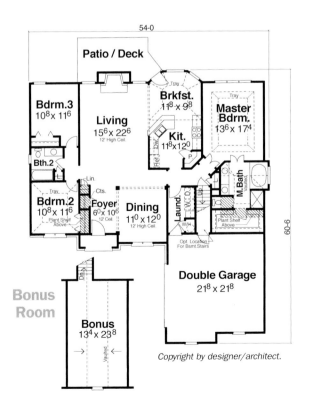

Copyright by designer/architect.

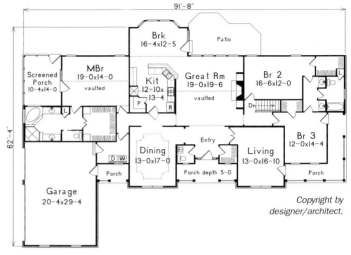

Images provided by designer/architect.

Plan #321004

Dimensions: 91'8" W x 62'4" D
Levels: 1
Square Footage: 2,808
Bedrooms: 3
Bathrooms: 2½
Foundation: Basement
Materials List Available: Yes
Price Category: F

Copyright by designer/architect.

SMARTtip

Ornaments in a Garden

Placement is everything with ornaments in a garden. Some elements are best sitting by themselves. Others are better when they are part of a cohesive whole, perhaps placed in the greenery at a corner or flanking a structure.

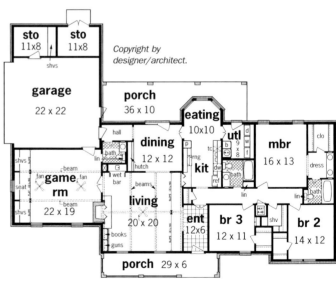

Images provided by designer/architect.

Plan #211054

Dimensions: 80' W x 62' D
Levels: 1
Square Footage: 2,358
Bedrooms: 3
Bathrooms: 2½
Foundation: Slab
Materials List Available: Yes
Price Category: E

Copyright by designer/architect.

SMARTtip

Dressing Up a Simple Fireplace

Painting a wood surround with a faux marble or faux bois (wood) is inexpensive. Adding a simple, prefabricated wooden shelf mantel can add lots of architectural character.

Plan #161072

Dimensions: 80' W x 74' D
Levels: 1
Square Footage: 2,183
Bedrooms: 3
Bathrooms: 3
Foundation: Basement
Materials List Available: Yes
Price Category: D

Features that make this house a spectacular home include a wraparound porch, a stone-and-siding exterior, and a garage that is set to the rear.

Features:

• Great Room: This large gathering area boasts a sloped ceiling, gas fireplace, and a series of windows that offer a view to the rear porch.

• Breakfast Room: This spacious breakfast room becomes a great place to start the day, with its surrounding windows and sloped ceiling.

• Kitchen: A snack bar and an abundance of counter space create this delightful kitchen. The room set in front of the kitchen can function as a formal dining room or a private study.

• Master Suite: This area is designed to pamper the homeowner with its comfortable private bath.

• Bedrooms: Two secondary bedrooms have large closets and share a hall bathroom.

Images provided by designer/architect.

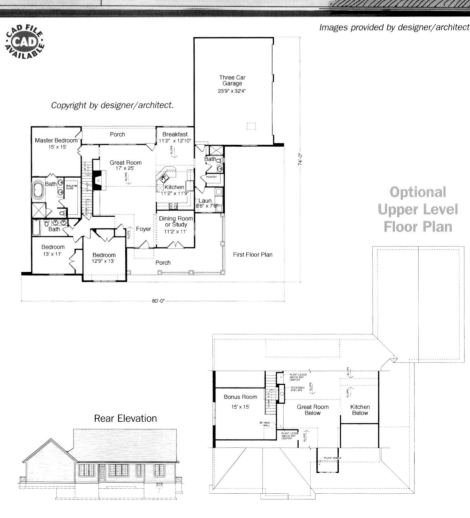

Rear Elevation

Optional Upper Level Floor Plan

Plan #401043

Dimensions: 38' W x 32' D

Levels: 1

Square Footage: 988

Bedrooms: 3

Bathrooms: 1

Foundation: Basement

Materials List Available: Yes

Price Category: A

Images provided by designer/architect.

Copyright by designer/architect.

This economical, compact home is the ultimate in efficient use of space.

Features:

- Porch: The front entry is sheltered by this casual country porch, which also protects the living room windows.

- Living Room: This central living room features a cozy fireplace and outdoor access to the front porch.

- Kitchen: This U-shaped kitchen serves both a dining area and a breakfast bar. Sliding glass doors lead from here to the rear yard.

- Master Bedroom: This room has a walk-in closet and shares a full bathroom with the secondary bedrooms.

- A single or double garage may be built to the side or to the rear of the home.

Right Side Elevation   Rear Elevation   Left Side Elevation

Plan #161098

Dimensions: 72' W x 55'10" D
Levels: 1
Square Footage: 2,283
Bedrooms: 3
Bathrooms: 2
Foundation: Basement
Material List Available: No
Price Category: E

This home, as shown in the photograph, may differ from the actual blueprints. For more detailed information, please check the floor plans carefully.

CAD FILE AVAILABLE

Images provided by designer/architect.

This spacious single-level home with 9-ft.-high ceiling heights is designed with formal and informal spaces.

Features:

• Dining Room: This open room and the great room are defined by columns and dropped ceilings.

• Great Room: This gathering area features a fireplace and a triple sliding glass door to the rear yard.

• Kitchen: This spacious kitchen with large pantry and angled counter serves the informal dining area and solarium, creating a comfortably relaxed gathering place.

• Master Suite: Designed for luxury, this suite, with its high-style tray ceiling, offers a whirlpool tub, double-bowl vanity, and large walk-in closet.

Rear Elevation

Kitchen

Copyright by designer/architect.

Breakfast 10'8" x 14'7"

Solarium 12'4" x 16'1"

Kitchen 12'6" x 15'7"

Laun.

pantry

Two-car Garage 23' x 24'

Dining Room 10'4" x 11'

Foyer

Porch

Great Room 18'3" x 18'8"

Dressing

walk-in closet

stairs dn

Hall

Bedroom /Library 12'2" x 15'8"

slope ceiling

slope ceiling

Master Bedroom 15'1" x 14'4"

Bath

Bedroom 14' x 11'4"

72'

55'10"

Plan #191028

Dimensions: 80' W x 63' D

Levels: 1

Square Footage: 2,669

Bedrooms: 4

Bathrooms: 3½

Foundation: Basement, slab

Materials List Available: No

Price Category: F

Images provided by designer/architect.

Copyright by designer/architect.

Plan #191029

Dimensions: 78' W x 67' D

Levels: 1

Square Footage: 2,726

Bedrooms: 4

Bathrooms: 3½

Foundation: Crawl space, slab, or basement

Materials List Available: No

Price Category: F

Images provided by designer/architect.

Copyright by designer/architect.

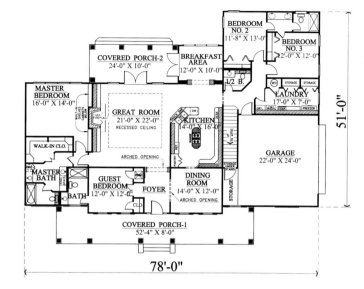

Plan #191017

Dimensions: 78' W x 51' D

Levels: 1

Square Footage: 2,605

Bedrooms: 4

Bathrooms: 2½

Foundation: Crawl space, slab, or basement

Materials List Available: No

Price Category: F

Images provided by designer/architect.

Copyright by designer/architect.

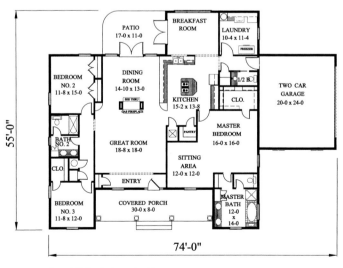

Plan #191015

Dimensions: 74' W x 55' D

Levels: 1

Square Footage: 2,340

Bedrooms: 3

Bathrooms: 2½

Foundation: Crawl space, slab

Materials List Available: No

Price Category: E

Images provided by designer/architect.

Copyright by designer/architect.

Plan #141022

Dimensions: 90' W x 93' D
Levels: 1
Square Footage: 2,911
Bedrooms: 3
Bathrooms: 2½
Foundation: Basement
Materials List Available: Yes
Price Category: F

Images provided by designer/architect.

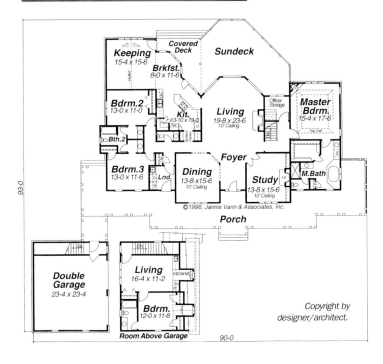

Rear View

Second-floor dormers accent this charming country ranch, which features a gracious porch that spans its entire front. A detached garage, connected by a covered extension, creates an impressive, expansive effect.

Features:

- Living Room: As you enter the foyer, you are immediately drawn to this dramatic, bayed living room.

- Study: Flanking the foyer, this cozy study features built-in shelving and a direct-vent fireplace.

- Kitchen: From a massive, partially covered deck, a wall of glass floods this spacious kitchen, breakfast bay, and keeping room with light.

- Master Suite: Enjoy the complete privacy provided by this strategically located master suite.

- Guest Quarters: You can convert the bonus room, above the garage, into a guest apartment.

Plan #131005

Dimensions: 70' W x 37'4" D
Levels: 1
Square Footage: 1,595
Bedrooms: 3
Bathrooms: 2
Foundation: Crawl space, slab, or basement
Materials List Available: Yes
Price Category: C

SMARTtip

Create a Courtyard

Create a private walled-garden retreat with fences covered by climbing vines. Add height with trellises, and divide spaces with clipped boxwood hedges. Include an (almost) instant patio by digging away an area of sod and then covering it with a layer of sand and landscaping mesh to discourage weeds. Then cover it with pea gravel, and add a garden bench, statuary, and perhaps an antique or two. The result? European ambiance for even the most nondescript suburban yard.

Images provided by designer/architect.

With the finest features of an open design in the main living areas, this home gives privacy where you need it. Best of all, it's wheelchair accessible.

Features:

- Foyer: A high ceiling gives this area real presence and serves to blend it seamlessly with the great room and the dining room.

- Great Room: The open design allows you to use this room as an extension of the dining room or, if you wish, furnish it to create a private reading nook or visually separate media center.

- Breakfast Room: Both this room and the adjacent well-appointed kitchen flow into the rest of the living area. However, access to the rear porch, where you can sit out and enjoy the weather while you eat, distinguishes this room.

- Master Suite: Located in the same wing as the other bedrooms, this suite has a separate entrance and features a vaulted ceiling, three closets, and a compartmented bath.

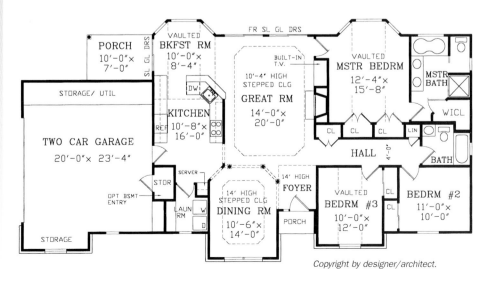

Copyright by designer/architect.

Plan #161092

Dimensions: 92'6" W x 56'8" D
Levels: 1
Square Footage: 2,110
Bedrooms: 3
Bathrooms: 2
Foundation: Walkout basement
Material List Available: Yes
Price Category: D

Brick and Stone, multiple windows, and a boxed window decorate the exterior of this one-level home.

Features:

- Great Room: This entertaining area boasts a sloped ceiling and a large fireplace. The area is open to the kitchen and breakfast area.

- Kitchen: This fully equipped island kitchen features a built-in pantry and a raised bar that looks into the breakfast area.

- Master Suite: This private area features a sloped ceiling in the sleeping area and a large window for backyard views. The master bath boasts a large bathtub, a standup shower, and dual vanities.

- Lower Level: This optional finished lower level offers a fourth bedroom, media area, wet bar, and billiards for added enjoyment.

Images provided by designer/architect.

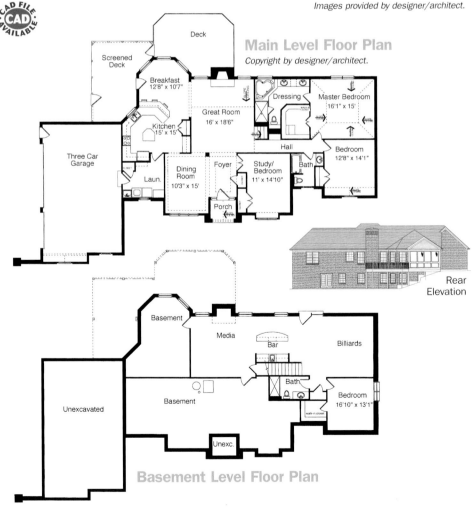

Main Level Floor Plan
Copyright by designer/architect.

Rear Elevation

Basement Level Floor Plan

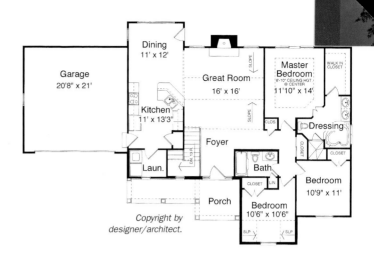

Copyright by designer/architect.

Rear Elevation

Plan #161079

Dimensions: 66'4" W x 44'10" D
Levels: 1
Square Footage: 1,498
Bedrooms: 3
Bathrooms: 2
Foundation: Basement
Materials List Available: Yes
Price Category: B

Images provided by designer/architect.

CAD FILE AVAILABLE

Rear Elevation

Plan #161088

Dimensions: 74' W x 52'10" D
Levels: 1
Square Footage: 1,824
Bedrooms: 3
Bathrooms: 2
Foundation: Basement
Materials List Available: Yes
Price Category: D

Images provided by designer/architect.

CAD FILE AVAILABLE

Copyright by designer/architect.

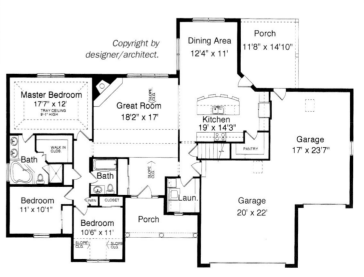

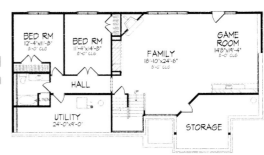

DECK

69'-0"

DINING
10'-4"x10'-0"
4'-0" CLG

HEARTH RM
13'-0"x11'-0"
4'-0" CLG

KITCHEN
13'-0"x13'-4"

GREAT RM
15'-0"x16'-0"
8'-0" VAULTED CLG

MASTER BEDROOM
12'-0"x17'-0"
4'-0" CLG

BATH

56'-0"

PANT

LAUN

ENTRY
7'-0"x9'-0"
18'-0" VAULTED CLG

WIC

PORCH

STUDY
13'-0"x13'-8"
4'-0" CLG

3 CAR GARAGE
31'-4"x23'-8"

Copyright by designer/architect.

Images provided by designer/architect.

CAD FILE AVAILABLE

Basement Level Floor Plan

BED RM
12'-4"x11'-8"
8'-0" CLG

BED RM
11'-4"x14'-8"
8'-0" CLG

FAMILY
18'-10"x24'-6"
8'-0" CLG

GAME ROOM
14'8"x19'-4"
8'-0" CLG

HALL

UTILITY
24'-0"x9'-0"

STORAGE

Plan #271073

Dimensions: 69' W x 56' D

Levels: 1

Square Footage: 1,920

Bedrooms: 3

Bathrooms: 2½

Foundation: Walk-out basement

Materials List Available: No

Price Category: D

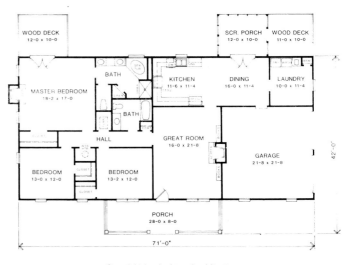

WOOD DECK
12-0 x 10-0

SCR. PORCH
12-0 x 10-0

WOOD DECK
11-0 x 10-0

MASTER BEDROOM
18-2 x 17-0

BATH

KITCHEN
11-6 x 11-4

DINING
16-0 x 11-4

LAUNDRY
10-0 x 11-4

BATH

HALL

GREAT ROOM
16-0 x 21-8

GARAGE
21-8 x 21-8

42'-0"

BEDROOM
13-0 x 12-0

BEDROOM
13-2 x 12-0

PORCH
28-0 x 8-0

71'-0"

Images provided by designer/architect.

Copyright by designer/architect.

Plan #301005

Dimensions: 71' W x 42' D

Levels: 1

Square Footage: 1,930

Bedrooms: 3

Bathrooms: 2

Foundation: Crawl space, slab

Materials List Available: Yes

Price Category: D

Plan #161091

Dimensions: 90'6" W x 42'8" D
Levels: 1
Square Footage: 3,753
Main Level Sq. Ft.: 2,198
Basement Level Sq. Ft.: 1,555
Bedrooms: 3
Bathrooms: 2
Foundation: Basement or walkout
Material List Available: No
Price Category: H

Brick and stone, multiple gables. and varied window designs decorate the exterior of this beautiful one-level home.

Features:

- **Open Plan:** The wraparound kitchen counter with seating becomes an active part of the hearth room and breakfast area.

- **Hearth Room:** This casual relaxing area boasts a corner gas log fireplace. Large windows allow the room to be flooded with natural light.

- **Master Suite:** This private area features a sloped ceiling in the sleeping area and a large window for backyard views. The master bath boasts a large bathtub, a standup shower, and dual vanities.

- **Lower Level:** This finished lower level offers two additional bedrooms, a media area, a wet bar, an exercise room, and billiards for added enjoyment.

Images provided by designer/architect.

Main Level Floor Plan

Copyright by designer/architect.

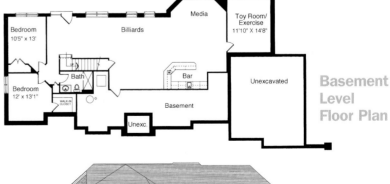

Basement Level Floor Plan

Rear Elevation

Plan #131006

Dimensions: 61' W x 53'6" D
Levels: 1
Square Footage: 2,193
Bedrooms: 3
Bathrooms: 2
Foundation: Crawl space, slab, or basement
Materials List Available: Yes
Price Category: E

This compact home is perfect for a small lot, but even so, has all the features of a much larger home, thanks to its space-saving interior design that lets one area flow into the next.

Features:

- Great Room: This wonderful room is sure to be the heart of your home. Visually, it flows from the foyer and dining room to the rear of the house, giving you enough space to create a private nook or two in it or treat it as a single, large room.

- Dining Room: Emphasize the formality of this room by decorating with subdued colors and sumptuous fabrics.

- Kitchen: Designed for efficiency, this kitchen features ample counter space and cabinets in a layout guaranteed to please you.

- Master Suite: You'll love the amenities in this private master suite, with its lovely bedroom and a bath filled with contemporary fixtures.

Images provided by designer/architect.

Kitchen

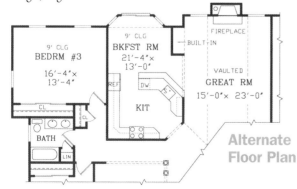

Alternate Floor Plan

Copyright by designer/architect.

Plan #321007

Dimensions: 76' W x 55'2" D
Levels: 1
Square Footage: 2,695
Bedrooms: 3
Bathrooms: 2½
Foundation: Basement
Materials List Available: Yes
Price Category: F

Images provided by designer/architect.

You'll love the way this spacious ranch reminds you of a French country home.

Features:

- **Foyer:** Come into this lovely home's foyer, and be greeted with a view of the gracious staircase and the great room just beyond.

- **Great Room:** Settle down by the cozy fireplace in cool weather, and reach for a book on the built-in shelves that surround it.

- **Kitchen:** Designed for efficient work patterns, this large kitchen is open to the great room.

- **Breakfast Room:** Just off the kitchen, this sunny room will be a family favorite all through the day.

- **Master Suite:** A bay window, walk-in closet, and shower built for two are highlights of this area.

- **Additional Bedrooms:** These large bedrooms both have walk-in closets and share a Jack-and-Jill bath for total convenience.

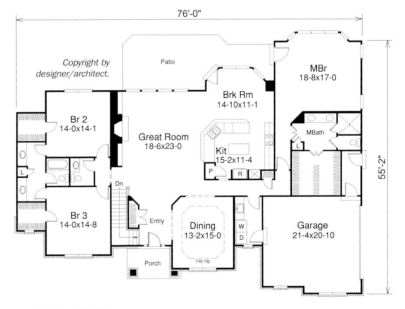

SMARTtip

Decorative Poles

Drapery poles are supported by the brackets fastened to the window frame or wall. The brackets that are provided with the poles generally coordinate and blend in with the pole finish. Brackets can be simple but also decorative. If you opt for a spectacular, attention-grabbing bracket, consider choosing less showy finials for the ends of the pole.

Plan #291016

Dimensions: 69'9" W x 58'3" D
Levels: 2
Square Footage: 2,721
Main Level Sq. Ft.: 1,447
Upper Level Sq. Ft.: 1,274
Bedrooms: 3
Bathrooms: 2½
Foundation: Basement
Materials List Available: No
Price Category: F

Images provided by designer/architect.

This fine example of Greek revival architecture begs to be visited!

Features:

- Entry: This area is the central hub of the home, with access to the kitchen, dining room, office, and upper level. There are two coat closets here.

- Living Room: This gathering area features a cozy fireplace and has access to the rear sunroom.

- Kitchen: Generous in size, this family-oriented kitchen has an informal dining area and a morning room that has access to the rear deck.

- Upper Level: Located upstairs are two secondary bedrooms that share the hall bathroom. The master suite, also on this level, features a private bath and a large walk-in closet.

Rear View

Copyright by designer/architect.

Upper Level Floor Plan

Main Level Floor Plan

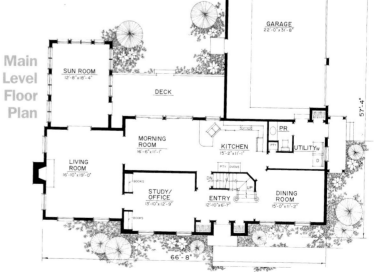

Upper Level Floor Plan

Copyright by designer/architect.

Images provided by designer/architect.

CAD FILE AVAILABLE

Main Level Floor Plan

Plan #181064

Dimensions: 91'4" W x 40'8" D
Levels: 2
Square Footage: 2,802
Main Level Sq. Ft.: 2,219
Upper Level Sq. Ft.: 583
Bedrooms: 4
Bathrooms: 2½
Foundation: Crawl space
Materials List Available: Yes
Price Category: F

Plan #201032

Dimensions: 66'10" W x 50'10" D
Levels: 1
Square Footage: 1,556
Bedrooms: 3
Bathrooms: 2
Foundation: Crawl space, slab
Materials List Available: Yes
Price Category: C

Images provided by designer/architect.

Copyright by designer/architect.

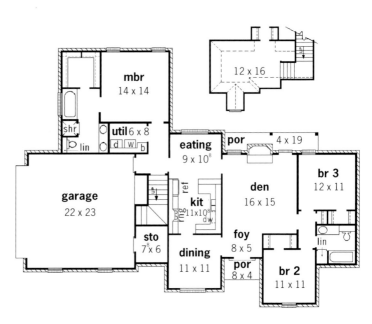

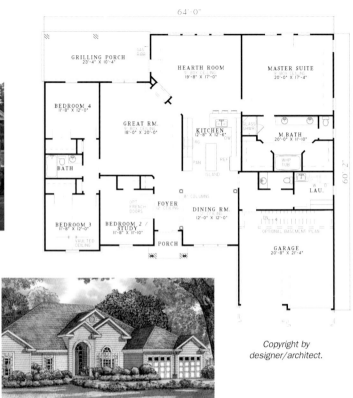

Plan #151063

Dimensions: 64' W x 60'2" D

Levels: 1

Square Footage: 2,554

Bedrooms: 4

Bathrooms: 2½

Foundation: Crawl space or slab; basement or walkout for a fee

CompleteCost List Available: Yes

Price Category: D

Images provided by designer/architect.

This home, as shown in the photograph, may differ from the actual blueprints. For more detailed information, please check the floor plans carefully.

Rear View

Copyright by designer/architect.

Plan #151486

Dimensions: 74'7" W x 70'6" D

Levels: 1

Square Footage: 2,556

Bedrooms: 4

Bathrooms: 3

Foundation: Crawl space or slab

CompleteCost List Available: Yes

Price Category: E

Images provided by designer/architect.

Copyright by designer/architect.

Plan #151008

Dimensions: 42' W x 66'10" D
Levels: 1
Square Footage: 1,892
Bedrooms: 3
Bathrooms: 2
Foundation: Crawl space, slab, basement, or daylight basement
CompleteCost List Available: Yes
Price Category: D

Images provided by designer/architect.

This home, as shown in the photograph, may differ from the actual blueprints. For more detailed information, please check the floor plans carefully.

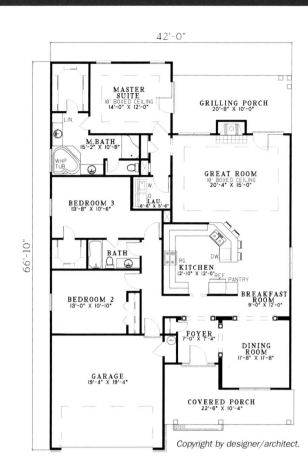

Copyright by designer/architect.

Plan #101009

Dimensions: 70'2" W x 59' D
Levels: 1
Square Footage: 2,097
Bedrooms: 3
Bathrooms: 3
Foundation: Slab
Materials List Available: Yes
Price Category: D

Images provided by designer/architect.

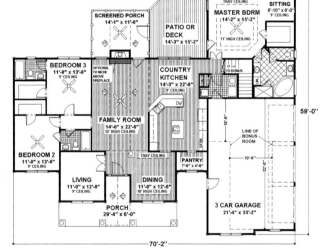

Copyright by designer/architect.

SMARTtip

Single-Level Decks

A single-level deck can use a strong vertical element, such as a pergola or a gazebo, to make it interesting. A simple and less-expensive option is a potted conical shrub or a clematis growing on a trellis.

Plan #271077

Dimensions: 69'6" W x 53' D

Levels: 1

Square Footage: 1,786

Bedrooms: 1

Bathrooms: 1½

Foundation: Basement or daylight basement

Materials List Available: No

Price Category: C

Images provided by designer/architect.

Optional Basement Level Floor Plan

Copyright by designer/architect.

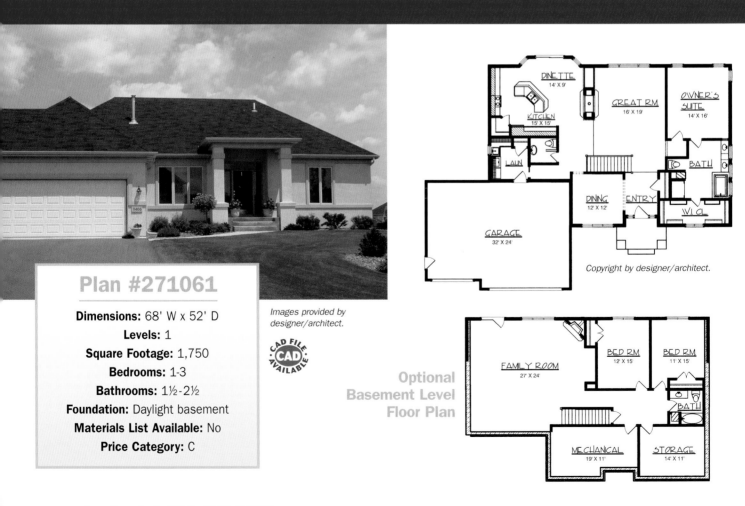

Plan #271061

Dimensions: 68' W x 52' D

Levels: 1

Square Footage: 1,750

Bedrooms: 1-3

Bathrooms: 1½-2½

Foundation: Daylight basement

Materials List Available: No

Price Category: C

Images provided by designer/architect.

Copyright by designer/architect.

Optional Basement Level Floor Plan

Plan #151351

Dimensions: 52'8" W x 60'6" D
Levels: 1
Square Footage: 1,627
Bedrooms: 3
Bathrooms: 2
Foundation: Crawl space or slab
CompleteCost List Available: Yes
Price Category: C

Images provided by designer/architect.

Entering through majestic columns into the traditional foyer, you'll instantly feel the grandeur of this home.

Features:

- **Dining Room:** Imagine an evening of exquisite cuisine as you entertain your close friends and colleagues in this elegant room, which is enhanced by 10-ft.-high ceilings and beautifully crafted columns.

- **Grilling Porch:** Located off the spacious kitchen and breakfast room, this porch makes is easy to serve your favorite barbecue recipes.

- **Master Suite:** This suite has a 10–ft.-high boxed ceiling and access to the porch. The bath has a corner whirlpool tub with glass blocks, a corner shower, and a walk-in closet.

- **Bedrooms:** The two secondary bedrooms located on the opposite side of the home from the master suite share a hall bathroom.

52' 8"

60' 6"

MASTER BATH
15'-8" X 8'-4"

MASTER SUITE
15'-8" X 12'-0"

GRILLING PORCH
11'-4" X 8'-0"

LAU.
7'-6" X 5'-6"

STORAGE
6'-9" X 5'-6"

BRKFAST RM.
11'-0" X 8'-10"

GARAGE
19'-0" X 20'-0"

BED RM. 2
10'-6" X 12'-4"

BED RM. 3
10'-6" X 13'-10"

KITCHEN
11'-0" X 13'-8"

FOYER

GREAT RM.
15'-0" X 18'-4"

ENTRY PORCH

DINING RM.
10'-8" X 11'-6"

Copyright by designer/architect.

Optional Upper Level Floor Plan

ATTIC STRG.

LIN.

BED RM. 3
14'-10" X 12'-0"

BED RM. 2
13'-0" X 12'-0"

Plan #291015

Dimensions: 88'6" W x 58'3" D
Levels: 1.5
Square Footage: 2,901
Main Level Sq. Ft.: 2,078
Upper Level Sq. Ft.: 823
Bedrooms: 3
Bathrooms: 2½
Foundation: Basement
Materials List Available: No
Price Category: F

Images provided by designer/architect.

Upon entering this home, a cathedral-like timber-framed interior fills the eye.

Features:

- **Great Room:** This large gathering area's ceiling rises up two stories and is open to the kitchen. The beautiful fireplace is the focal point of this room.

- **Kitchen:** This island kitchen is open to the great room and the breakfast nook. Warm woods of all species enhance the great room and this space.

- **Master Suite:** This suite has a sloped ceiling and adjoins a luxurious master bath with twin walk-in closets that open to a sunroom with a private balcony.

- **Upper Level:** This upper level has an open lounge that leads to two bedrooms with vaulted ceilings and a generous second bath.

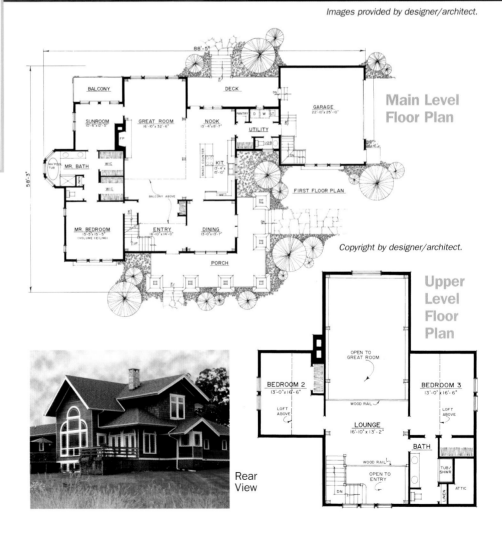

Rear View

Main Level Floor Plan

Copyright by designer/architect.

Upper Level Floor Plan

Master Bath

Kitchen

Rear Porch

Dining Room

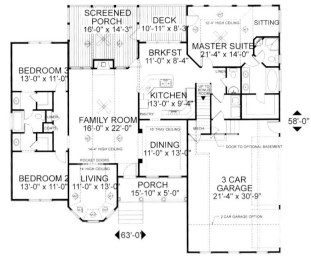

Images provided by designer/architect.

Copyright by designer/architect.

Plan #101006

Dimensions: 63' W x 58' D
Levels: 1
Square Footage: 1,982
Bedrooms: 3
Bathrooms: 2½
Foundation: Crawl space, slab basement, or walkout
Materials List Available: Yes
Price Category: D

SMARTtip

Art in Pools

The tiled walls and floor of a pool make great canvases for art, so incorporate a serious or whimsical design. Also, make the stairs wide and shallow to form a wading area for kids.

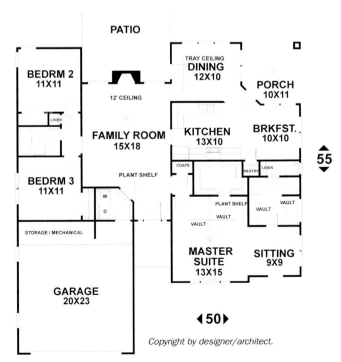

Plan #101003

Dimensions: 50' W x 55' D
Levels: 1
Square Footage: 1,593
Bedrooms: 3
Bathrooms: 2
Foundation: Slab, crawl space, or basement
Materials List Available: Yes
Price Category: C

Images provided by designer/architect.

Copyright by designer/architect.

Plan #271064

Dimensions: 76' W x 54' D
Levels: 2
Square Footage: 2,864
Main Level Sq. Ft.: 1,610
Upper Level Sq. Ft.: 1,254
Bedrooms: 4
Bathrooms: 2½
Foundation: Daylight basement
Materials List Available: No
Price Category: E

Images provided by designer/architect.

CAD FILE AVAILABLE

Main Level Floor Plan

Upper Level Floor Plan

Copyright by designer/architect.

Plan #241002

Dimensions: 65' W x 59'8" D
Levels: 1
Square Footage: 2,154
Bedrooms: 4
Bathrooms: 2½
Foundation: Slab
Materials List Available: No
Price Category: D

Images provided by designer/architect.

Copyright by designer/architect.

Plan #131028

Dimensions: 69'2" W x 50'2" D

Levels: 2

Square Footage: 2,696

Main Level Sq. Ft.: 1,960

Upper Level Sq. Ft.: 736

Bedrooms: 4

Bathrooms: 3

Foundation: Crawl space, slab, or basement

Materials List Available: Yes

Price Category: F

Images provided by designer/architect.

Imagine owning a home with Victorian styling and a dramatic, contemporary interior design.

Features:

- Foyer: Enter from the curved covered porch into this foyer with its 17-ft. ceiling.

- Great Room: A vaulted ceiling sets the tone for this large room, where friends and family are sure to congregate.

- Dining Room: A 14-ft. ceiling here accentuates the rounded shape of this room.

- Kitchen: From the angled corner sink to the angled island with a snack bar, this room has character. A pantry adds convenience.

- Master Suite: A 13-ft. tray ceiling exudes elegance, and the bath features a spa tub and designer shower.

- Upper Level: The balcony hall leads to a turreted recreation room, two bedrooms, and a full bath.

Main Level Floor Plan

Upper Level Floor Plan

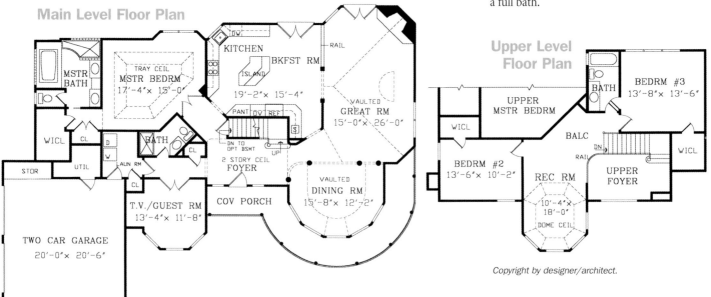

Copyright by designer/architect.

Plan #101012

Dimensions: 69'4" W x 62'9" D

Levels: 1

Square Footage: 2,288

Bedrooms: 3

Bathrooms: 2½

Foundation: Slab, crawl space, basement, or walkout

Materials List Available: No

Price Category: E

Images provided by designer/architect.

This classic brick ranch boasts traditional styling and an exciting up-to-date floor plan.

Features:

- Ceiling Height: 9 ft. unless otherwise noted.

- Front Porch: Guests will be welcome by this inviting front porch, which features a 12-ft. ceiling.

- Family Room: This warm and inviting room measures 16 ft. x 19 ft. It features a 14-ft. ceiling and a rear wall of windows. French doors lead to an enormous deck.

- Kitchen: This unique angled kitchen is open to the hearth room and eating areas, all of which enjoy vaulted ceilings and are surrounded by windows. The hearth room has a TV niche.

- Master Suite: This 16-ft. x 15-ft. master suite is truly sumptuous, with its 12-ft. ceiling, sitting area, two walk-in closets, and full-featured bath.

- Bonus Room: Here is plenty of storage or room for future expansion. Just beyond the entry are stairs leading to a bonus room measuring approximately 12 ft. x 21 ft.

Copyright by designer/architect.

Floor Plan labels:

DECK 19'-8" x 15'-0"

DINING 15'-10" x 11'-0"

HEARTH ROOM 16'-7" x 13'-0"

VAULTS TO 13'-5" PEAK

12' HIGH CEILING TV NICHE

14' HIGH CEILING

KITCHEN 16'-0" x 13'-0"

BRKFST 10'-0" x 10'-6"

13' HIGH CEILING

12' HIGH TRAY CEILING UP 1' UP 1' 14' HIGH

MASTER BDRM 16'-0" x 15'-0"

HERS HIS

FAMILY ROOM 16'-0" x 19'-0"

STAIRS TO BONUS ROOM

PANTRY

LINEN

ENTRY 12' HIGH CEILING

UP DN

STAIRS TO BASEMENT

BEDROOM 2 11'-0" x 14'-0"

13' HIGH CEILING

BEDROOM 3 11'-0" x 14'-0"

PORCH 12' HIGH CEILING

GARAGE 21'-0" x 23'-0"

BONUS ROOM ABOVE

62'-9"

69'-4'

This article was reprinted from *The New Smart Approach to Window Decor* (Creative Homeowner 2004).

Selecting Window Treatments

Selecting a window treatment provides you with a terrific opportunity for making changes that can affect how you use a room, your level of comfort or sense of well being when you are in the room, and the visual appeal or success of the overall decor. Plus a window treatment provides all of this for what is often a relatively affordable investment.

When you think of the important role a window treatment plays in your decorating plans, consider a number of factors. Do you need a way to control sunlight and glare? Can you use the window treatment to limit heat gain during the summer or heat loss during the winter? Do you want to obscure an undesirable view? Are you looking for a way to create privacy? Can you use a window treatment to modify or enhance the architectural elements of the space? Can you use it to set a mood, establish a style, or bring color, pattern, and texture into a room?

Of course, the right window treatment can do any of these things. But it can also establish or underscore a decorative style, whether it is contemporary, traditional, country, or period. On a large window or one that is situated prominently, the right dressing can also create a focal point in a space that lacks this important visual anchor.

Form Follows Function

Today, there is a wide selection of window treatments and materials to address any or all of these concerns.

Because conditions of light, heat, and lifestyle dictate changes over the course of the day or even from season to season, it's wise to select a style that is easily adjustable. For example, natural light that streams over your shoulder, while you sit in a chair with your back to the window, is lovely for reading a book. However, if you're working at a computer that is in the direct path of harsh sunlight, the glare on the monitor caused by the sun's reflection will make it difficult to read what's on the screen and may strain your eyes. A window covering that can be lowered or closed at will allows you to enjoy natural light when you want it or close it out when you don't.

Before getting started on your window-decor project, go over the following steps to make sure that you're contemplating a window treatment that does the job you need it to do.

Step One: Consider ventilation and airflow.
Sometimes you'll want to open your windows to let in fresh air and release indoor pollutants. On occasion, you may prefer a natural breeze to an air conditioner. So choose a covering that won't impede the flow of air into the room. On the other hand, if the windows are a source for draughts or heat collection, consider specially insulated curtains that can cut down on these problems and may even save you the cost of replacing old windows.

Step Two: Examine the sight lines.
What is the first thing you see when you enter a room? In most cases, it is the windows. Can you see them from outside the entry? You know what they say about first impressions, so use the window treatments to make an immediate style statement.

Left: A matchstick shade can be raised or lowered to filter light at this desk. Here, it also complements the bamboo furnishings.

Opposite: Pretty balloon shades enhance the shape and appearance of this window bay when viewed from inside and outside of the house.

Step Three: Look out, look in.
Do you want to take in the view? Then, you may want minimal window dressing. But what about privacy? You may feel as if you're living in a fishbowl, especially at night when the interior of the house is lit, unless your property is secluded. A treatment that's adjustable, such as curtains, shades, or blinds that open and close easily, is the solution. But don't ignore the way your window treatment looks from the outside. Choose a style that suits the overall style of your home.

Step Four: Observe the architecture. The window treatment you choose is the bridge from window to wall. What you select should blend harmoniously with the architecture and the home's interior design.

Above: Today's new windows can be large and window-treatment materials lightweight without compromising comfort, thanks to improved insulated glass.

Right: You can have the best of both worlds by pairing an stylish permanent treatment, such as this swag-and-jabot design, with a practical adjustable blind.

SMARTtip

Operating the Window

Consider the way a window opens and closes before choosing a window treatment. Double-hung windows pose the fewest problems. Casement windows and French doors that swing into a room require a design that will not obstruct of their paths of operation.

Right: Room-darkening shades, made from fade-resistant fabric that won't admit light, can be pulled up or down during the day, according to how you want to control the sunlight.

If there is a flaw in the design of the space, you can sometimes compensate for it with window decor. A treatment can add character that may be lacking or camouflage problems with scale and proportion.

Step Five: Look at the room's general decor.
Does it appear tired, dated, or simply unfinished? Consider how new window treatments can put a fresh face on the room.

The Practical Role of a Window Treatment

When you imagine heavy, multi-layered fabric covering a window, it's usually in a period- or historic-design context. (Although lighter-weight versions are popular in traditional homes, today.) Textiles, such as lined wool, damask, silk, brocade, velvet, and tapestries, provided much-needed insulation against extreme temperatures in an era without the luxuries of double-glazed glass, central heating, and air conditioning. Though insulation is often a factor in choosing a window treatment, ventilation and controlling natural light are more common concerns, nowadays.

Any room with an eastern orientation is subject to strong morning light, a consideration acutely important in a bedroom, for example. A room with windows facing west gets strong light in the afternoon; however, if you don't ordinarily use the room at this time of day, you may not care.

North-facing rooms, because they receive no direct sunlight, get chilly, especially during the winter. This makes a good case for insulated window treatments. Spaces with a southern exposure receive the most natural light; during the summer

months or in a warm climate, these rooms can get too hot. The right window covering can abate some of the heat buildup. Think about when and where you're most likely to be affected by natural light and whether you need a means to control it.

The rays of the sun also affect furnish-ings, so when choosing your window treatment, keep this in mind, as well. Delicate fabrics, wallcoverings, even wood finishes can be harmed by continuous direct exposure to strong natural light. Translucent fabric panels, once called "glass curtains," are often combined with draperies to filter sunlight.

Shades, Blinds, and Shutters.

All three of these treatments are usually fully adjustable and offer complete light and privacy control. Each comes in a multitude of styles, and they can be installed alone or paired with curtains or drapery.

A window treatment can pull together an entire room, often unifying a design of disparate parts. It can change the style or ambiance from casual to formal or from sterile to romantic. New curtains can punch up, tone down, or blend into a color scheme, adding pattern and texture.

Curtains and Drapery. Loosely hung fabric or panels that are attached to the window frame or sash offer some control over both light and privacy. The level depends on how many layers are installed and whether or not the fabric is lined. Sheer fabrics allow the transmission of light and don't obscure the view to the outdoors. Sometimes curtains and drapery are not adjustable; they have to be installed with a rod system or rings that allow you to open or close the panels to efficiently control light and privacy.

Opposite: Gorgeous fabric, trimming, and styling add appropriate drama to a corner of a formal room with lots of classic architectural details.

Above: A simple, understated white louvered shutter adds architectural interest to an undistinguished window in a small room. Here, it also controls light in this sunny bedroom.

Right: A lively partnership of prints, borrowed from the banquette and chair cushions, makes up a darling valance in a cheerful breakfast nook.

Main Level Floor Plan

Images provided by designer/architect.

Upper Level Floor Plan

Copyright by designer/architect.

Plan #321042

Dimensions: 71' W x 54'7" D
Levels: 2
Square Footage: 3,368
Main Level Sq. Ft.: 2,150
Upper Level Sq. Ft.: 1,218
Bedrooms: 4
Full Bathrooms: 3
Half Bathrooms: 2
Foundation: Basement
Materials List Available: Yes
Price Category: G

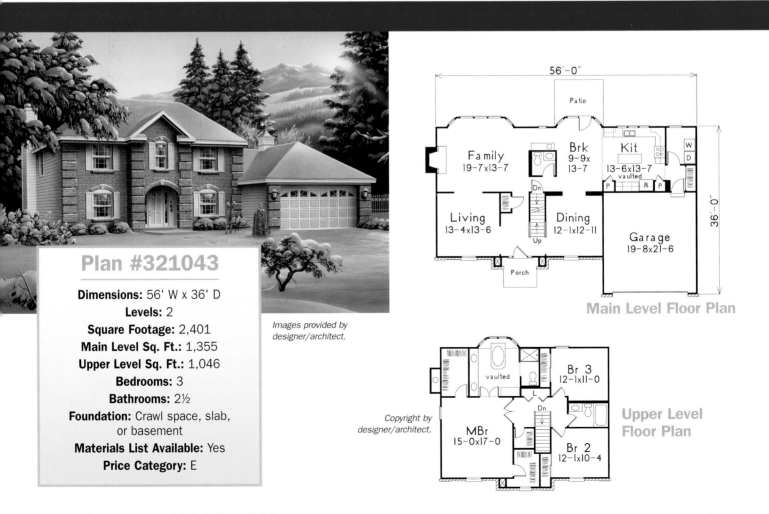

Main Level Floor Plan

Images provided by designer/architect.

Copyright by designer/architect.

Upper Level Floor Plan

Plan #321043

Dimensions: 56' W x 36' D
Levels: 2
Square Footage: 2,401
Main Level Sq. Ft.: 1,355
Upper Level Sq. Ft.: 1,046
Bedrooms: 3
Bathrooms: 2½
Foundation: Crawl space, slab, or basement
Materials List Available: Yes
Price Category: E

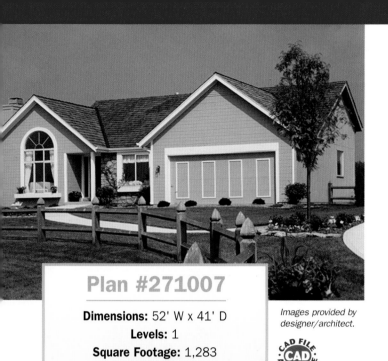

Plan #271007

Dimensions: 52' W x 41' D
Levels: 1
Square Footage: 1,283
Bedrooms: 3
Bathrooms: 2
Foundation: Basement
Materials List Available: Yes
Price Category: B

Images provided by
designer/architect.

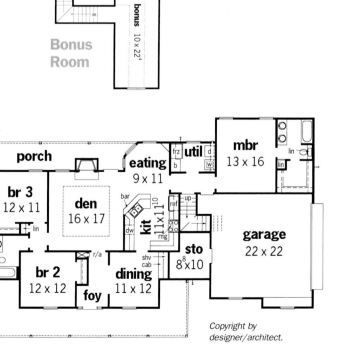

51'-5"

40'-9"

Deck

Brkfst
10-6
vaulted clg

Br 3
9x11-4

MBr
14-6x14-6

Kit
10-6x
18-8

Dining

Great Room
13-6x21
13-6 vaulted clg

Br 2
11x10-3

Garage
19-4x19-4

dn

P

Copyright by
designer/architect.

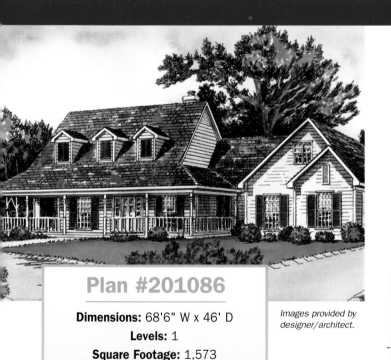

Plan #201086

Dimensions: 68'6" W x 46' D
Levels: 1
Square Footage: 1,573
Bedrooms: 3
Bathrooms: 2
Foundation: Crawl space, slab
Materials List Available: Yes
Price Category: C

Images provided by
designer/architect.

Bonus
Room

bonus
10 x 22⁴

porch

eating
9 x 11

util

mbr
13 x 16

br 3
12 x 11

den
16 x 17

kit
11x11¹⁰

bar

br 2
12 x 12

foy

dining
11 x 12

sto
8⁸x10

garage
22 x 22

Copyright by
designer/architect.

Plan #111004

Dimensions: 76' W x 85' D

Levels: 1

Square Footage: 2,968

Bedrooms: 4

Full Bathrooms: 3½

Foundation: Slab

Crawl space available for an extra fee

Materials List Available: No

Price Category: F

Images provided by designer/architect. Living Room

If you've been looking for a home that includes a special master suite, this one could be the answer to your dreams.

Features:

- Living Room: Make a sitting area around the fireplace here so that the whole family can enjoy the warmth on chilly days and winter evenings. A door from this room leads to the rear covered porch, making this room the heart of your home.

- Kitchen: An island with a cooktop makes cooking a pleasure in this well-designed kitchen, and the breakfast bar invites visitors at all times of day.

- Utility Room: A sink and a built-in ironing board make this room totally practical.

- Master Suite: A private fireplace in the corner sets a romantic tone for this bedroom, and the door to the covered porch allows you to sit outside on warm summer nights. The bath has two vanities, a divided walk-in closet, a standing shower, and a deluxe corner bathtub.

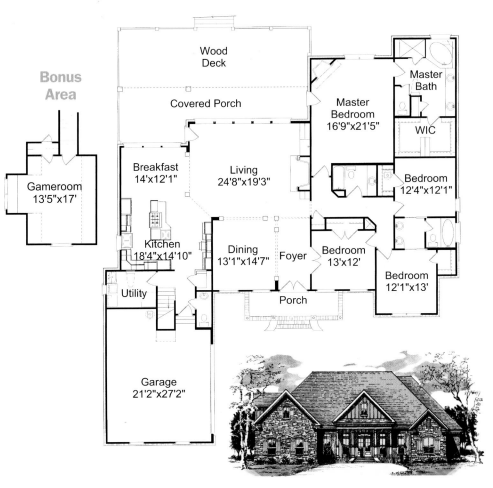

Plan #131017

Dimensions: 69'8" W x 39'4" D
Levels: 1
Square Footage: 1,480
Bedrooms: 3
Bathrooms: 2
Foundation: Crawl space, slab, or basement
Materials List Available: Yes
Price Category: C

Images provided by designer/architect.

Alternate Floor Plan

Part Plan with Optional Basement

Copyright by designer/architect.

Rear Elevation

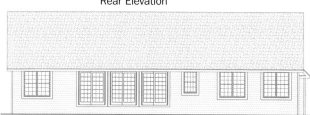

Plan #181257

Dimensions: 61'4" W x 72' D
Levels: 2
Square Footage: 2,448
Main Level Sq. Ft.: 1,448
Upper Level Sq. Ft.: 1,000
Bedrooms: 3
Bathrooms: 2½
Foundation: Basement
Materials List Available: Yes
Price Category: E

Images provided by designer/architect.

CAD FILE AVAILABLE

Main Level Floor Plan

Upper Level Floor Plan

Copyright by designer/architect.

Plan #271006

Dimensions: 50' W x 55' D

Levels: 1

Square Footage: 1,444

Bedrooms: 2

Bathrooms: 2

Foundation: Basement

Materials List Available: Yes

Price Category: B

Images provided by designer/architect.

This home, as shown in the photograph, may differ from the actual blueprints. For more detailed information, please check the floor plans carefully.

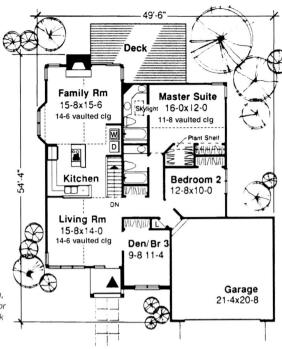

Copyright by designer/architect.

Plan #221014

Dimensions: 72' W x 44'8" D

Levels: 1

Square Footage: 1,906

Bedrooms: 3

Bathrooms: 2½

Foundation: Basement

Materials List Available: No

Price Category: D

Images provided by designer/architect.

Copyright by designer/architect.

Rear Elevation

Plan #151050

Dimensions: 69'2" W x 74'10" D

Levels: 1

Square Footage: 2,096

Bedrooms: 3

Bathrooms: 2½

Foundation: Crawl space, slab, or basement

CompleteCost List Available: Yes

Price Category: D

Images provided by designer/architect.

You'll love this spacious home for both its elegance and its convenient design.

Features:

- Ceiling Height: 8 ft.

- Great Room: A 9-ft. boxed ceiling complements this large room, which sits just beyond the front gallery. A fireplace and door to the rear porch make it a natural gathering spot.

- Kitchen: This well-designed kitchen includes a central work island and shares an angled eating bar with the adjacent breakfast room.

- Breakfast Room: This room's bay window is gorgeous, and the door to the garage is practical.

- Master Suite: You'll love the 9-ft. boxed ceiling in the bedroom and the vaulted ceiling in the bath, which also includes two walk-in closets, a corner whirlpool tub, split vanities, a shower, and a compartmentalized toilet.

- Workshop: A huge workshop with half-bath is ideal for anyone who loves to build or repair.

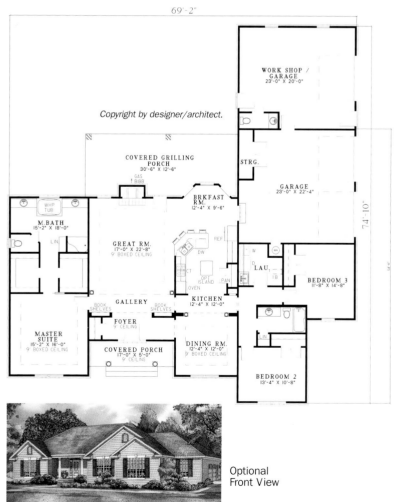

Optional
Front View

Plan #151014

Dimensions: 70'2" W x 51'4" D

Levels: 2

Square Footage: 2,698

Main Level Sq. Ft.: 1,813

Upper Level Sq. Ft.: 885

Bedrooms: 5

Bathrooms: 3

Foundation: Crawl space, slab, optional basement for fee

CompleteCost List Available: Yes

Price Category: F

Images provided by designer/architect.

A comfortable front porch welcomes you into this home that features a balcony over the great room, a study, and a kitchen designed for gourmet cooks.

Features:

- Ceiling Height: 9 ft.
- Front Porch: Stately 12-in.-wide pillars form the entryway.
- Foyer: Open to upper story.
- Great Room: A fireplace, vaulted 9-ft. ceiling, and balcony from the second floor add character to this lovely room.
- Dining Room: Open to the kitchen for convenience.
- Kitchen: A large walk-in pantry, well-designed work areas, and eat-in bar make this room a treasure.

- Breakfast Room: Enjoy this spot that opens to both the kitchen and a large covered porch at the rear of the house.
- Study: This quiet room has French doors leading to the yard.
- Master Suite: This spacious area has cozy window seats as well as his and her walk-in closets. The master bathroom is fitted with a whirlpool tub, a glass shower, and his and her sinks.

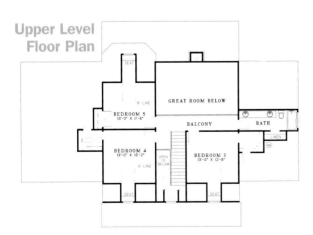

Copyright by designer/architect.

Plan #151570

Dimensions: 40' W x 43'2" D
Levels: 1
Square Footage: 1,250
Bedrooms: 3
Bathrooms: 2
Foundation: Crawl space or slab
CompleteCost List Available: Yes
Price Category: B

Images provided by designer/architect.

A starter or empty-nest home best describes this traditional style plan.

Features:

- Entry: This quaint covered space welcomes you into a foyer, which leads you past two bedrooms and a full bath to the master suite.

- Great Room: This room has a vaulted ceiling, plenty of wall space, and a sliding glass door to the backyard.

- Dining Room: Open to the kitchen, this quaint area has two large windows.

- Master Suite: Convenient to the living area, this spacious suite has a private bath with a double vanity and extra-large walk-in closet.

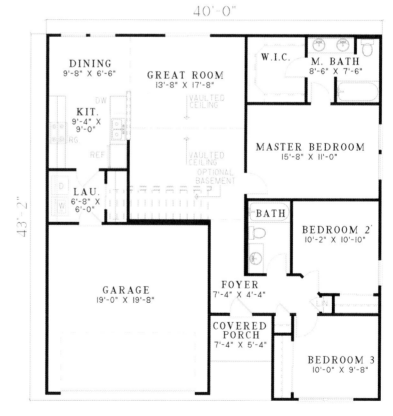

Copyright by designer/architect.

Plan #271016

Dimensions: 45'4" W x 49'6" D
Levels: 2
Square Footage: 2,170
Main Level Sq. Ft.: 1,169
Upper Level Sq. Ft.: 1,001
Bedrooms: 3
Bathrooms: 2½
Foundation: Basement
Materials List Available: Yes
Price Category: D

Images provided by designer/architect.

With plenty of living space, this attractive design is just right for a growing family.

Features:

• **Entry:** This two-story reception area welcomes guests with sincerity and style. A coat closet stands ready to take winter wraps.

• **Great Room:** This sunken and vaulted space hosts gatherings and formal meals of any

size, and a handsome fireplace adds warmth and ambiance.

• **Kitchen:** A U-shaped counter keeps the family cook organized. A bayed breakfast nook overlooks a backyard deck.

• **Family Room:** The home's second fireplace adds a cozy touch to this casual area. Relax here with the family after playing in the snow!

• **Master Suite:** A vaulted ceiling presides over the master bedroom. The private bath hosts a separate tub and shower, a dual-sink vanity, and two walk-in closets.

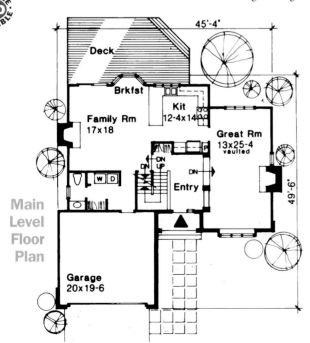

Main Level Floor Plan

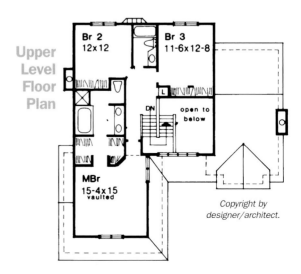

Upper Level Floor Plan

Copyright by designer/architect.

Plan #271015

Dimensions: 48' W x 28' D
Levels: 2
Square Footage: 1,359
Main Level Sq. Ft.: 668
Upper Level Sq. Ft.: 691
Bedrooms: 3
Bathrooms: 2½
Foundation: Basement
Materials List Available: Yes
Price Category: B

Images provided by designer/architect.

Strong vertical lines and pairs of narrow windows give this compact home an airy feel. Its clever floor plan makes good use of every square foot of space.

Features:

- Living Room: Beyond the sidelighted front door, the living room enjoys a vaulted ceiling and a flood of light from a striking corner window arrangement.

- Kitchen/Dining: A central fireplace separates the living room from this kitchen/dining room, where a French door opens to a rear deck.

- Master Suite: Sacrifice no luxuries in this sweet, upper-floor retreat, where a boxed-out window catches morning rays or evening stars. Next to the roomy walk-in closet, the private split bath enjoys a window of its own.

- Secondary Bedrooms: A balcony overlooks the living room and leads to one bedroom and the flexible loft.

Main Level Floor Plan

Upper Level Floor Plan

Copyright by designer/architect.

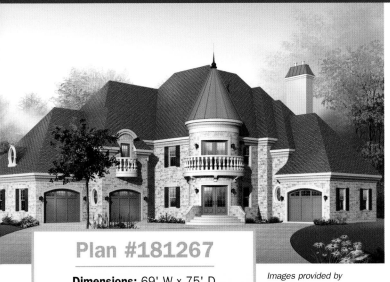

Main Level Floor Plan

Images provided by designer/architect.

Plan #181267

Dimensions: 69' W x 75' D
Levels: 2
Square Footage: 3,899
Main Level Sq. Ft.: 1,995
Upper Level Sq. Ft.: 1,904
Bedrooms: 3
Bathrooms: 2½
Foundation: Basement
Materials List Available: Yes
Price Category: H

Upper Level Floor Plan

Copyright by designer/architect.

Main Level Floor Plan

Images provided by designer/architect.

Plan #181268

Dimensions: 36' W x 43'4" D
Levels: 2
Square Footage: 2,281
Main Level Sq. Ft.: 1,019
Upper Level Sq. Ft.: 1,262
Bedrooms: 3
Bathrooms: 2½
Foundation: Basement
Materials List Available: Yes
Price Category: E

Upper Level Floor Plan

Copyright by designer/architect.

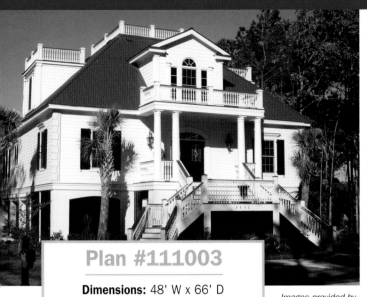

Plan #111003

Dimensions: 48' W x 66' D
Levels: 2
Square Footage: 3,319
Main Level Sq. Ft.: 2,331
Upper Level Sq. Ft.: 988
Bedrooms: 3
Bathrooms: 3½
Foundation: Pier
Materials List Available: No
Price Category: G

**Main Level
Floor Plan**

Copyright by designer/architect.

Images provided by designer/architect.

**Upper Level
Floor Plan**

Plan #111035

Dimensions: 68'6" W x 74'7" D
Levels: 2
Square Footage: 3,064
Main Level Sq. Ft.: 2,143
Upper Level Sq. Ft.: 921
Bedrooms: 4
Bathroom: 3½
Foundation: Slab
Materials List Available: No
Price Category: G

Images provided by designer/architect.

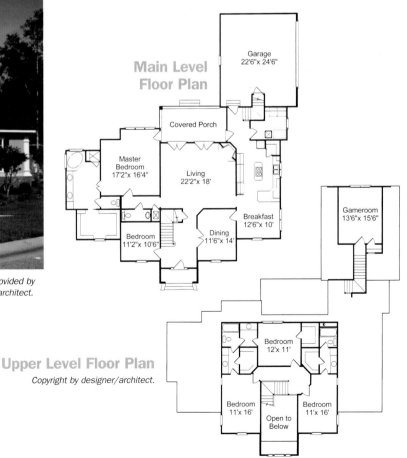

**Main Level
Floor Plan**

Upper Level Floor Plan

Copyright by designer/architect.

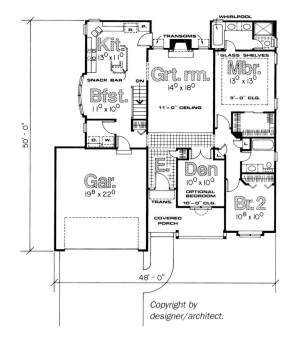

Plan #121056

Dimensions: 48' W x 50' D
Levels: 1
Square Footage: 1,479
Bedrooms: 2
Bathrooms: 2
Foundation: Basement
Materials List Available: Yes
Price Category: B

Images provided by designer/architect.

Copyright by designer/architect.

Optional Third Bedroom Floor Plan

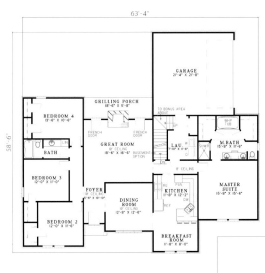

Plan #151083

Dimensions: 63'4" W x 58'6" D
Levels: 1
Square Footage: 2,034
Bedrooms: 4
Bathrooms: 2
Foundation: Crawl space, slab (basement option for fee)
CompleteCost List Available: Yes
Price Category: D

Images provided by designer/architect.

Copyright by designer/architect.

Optional Upper Level Floor Plan

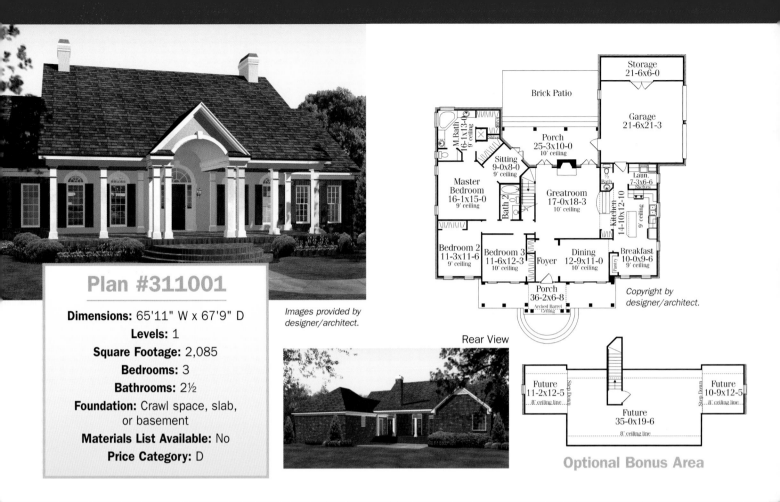

Copyright by designer/architect.

Rear View

Optional Bonus Area

Plan #311001

Dimensions: 65'11" W x 67'9" D

Levels: 1

Square Footage: 2,085

Bedrooms: 3

Bathrooms: 2½

Foundation: Crawl space, slab, or basement

Materials List Available: No

Price Category: D

Images provided by designer/architect.

Plan #351002

Dimensions: 64' W x 45'10" D

Levels: 1

Square Footage: 1,751

Bedrooms: 3

Bathrooms: 2

Foundation: Crawl space, slab, or basement

Materials List Available: Yes

Price Category: C

Images provided by designer/architect.

CAD FILE AVAILABLE

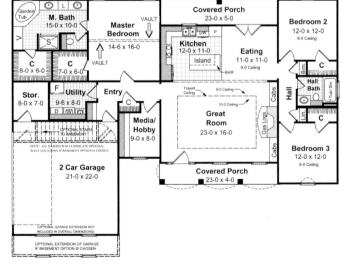

Copyright by designer/architect.

Plan #151034

Dimensions: 58'6" W x 64'6" D

Levels: 1

Square Footage: 2,133

Bedrooms: 3

Bathrooms: 2

Foundation: Crawl space, slab, or basement

CompleteCost List Available: Yes

Price Category: D

This home, as shown in the photograph, may differ from the actual blueprints. For more detailed information, please check the floor plans carefully.

Images provided by designer/architect.

You'll love the high ceilings, open floor plan, and contemporary design features in this home.

Features:

- Great Room: A pass-through tiled fireplace between this lovely large room and the adjacent hearth room allows you to notice the mirror effect created by the 10-ft. boxed ceilings in both rooms.

- Dining Room: An 11-ft. ceiling and 8-in. boxed column give formality to this lovely room, where you're certain to entertain.

- Kitchen: If you're a cook, this room may become your favorite spot in the house, thanks to its great design, which includes plenty of work and storage space, and a very practical layout.

- Master Suite: A 10-ft. boxed ceiling gives elegance to this room. A pocket door opens to the private bath, with its huge walk-in closet, glass-blocked whirlpool tub, separate glass shower, and private toilet room.

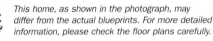

Copyright by designer/architect.

Rendering reflects floor plan

Plan #271018

Dimensions: 67' W x 37' D
Levels: 2
Square Footage: 2,445
Main Level Sq. Ft.: 1,290
Upper Level Sq. Ft.: 1,155
Bedrooms: 4
Bathrooms: 2½
Foundation: Basement
Materials List Available: Yes
Price Category: E

Images provided by designer/architect.

This traditional home re-creates the charm and character of days gone by.

Features:

- **Living Room:** A dramatic skylighted entry preludes this formal, sunken living room, which includes a stunning corner fireplace, a vaulted ceiling, and an adjoining formal dining room.

- **Dining Room:** This quiet space offers a built-in hutch beneath a vaulted ceiling.

- **Kitchen:** A built-in desk and a pantry mark this smartly designed space, which opens to a breakfast room and the family room beyond.

- **Family Room:** Sunken and filled with intrigue, this gathering room features a fireplace flanked by windows, plus French doors that open to a backyard deck.

- **Master Suite:** This luxurious upper-floor retreat boasts a vaulted ceiling, an angled walk-in closet, and a private bath.

Main Level Floor Plan

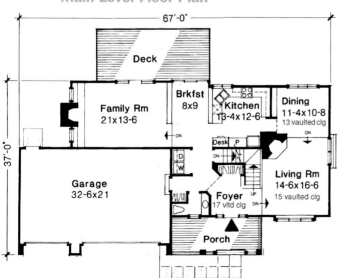

Upper Level Floor Plan

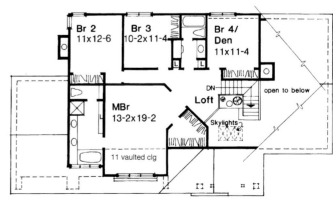

Copyright by designer/architect.

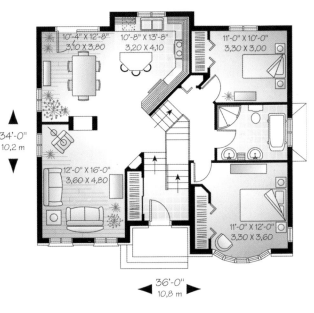

Plan #181270

Dimensions: 36' W x 34' D

Levels: 1

Square Footage: 1,127

Bedrooms: 2

Bathrooms: 1

Foundation: Basement

Materials List Available: Yes

Price Category: B

Images provided by designer/architect.

Copyright by designer/architect.

Main Level Floor Plan

Plan #181304

Dimensions: 36' W x 34' D

Levels: 2

Square Footage: 1,721

Main Level Sq. Ft.: 774

Upper Level Sq. Ft.: 947

Bedrooms: 3

Bathrooms: 1½

Foundation: Basement

Materials List Available: Yes

Price Category: C

Images provided by designer/architect.

Upper Level Floor Plan

Copyright by designer/architect.

Plan #151089

Dimensions: 84' W x 55'6" D
Levels: 1
Square Footage: 1,921
Bedrooms: 3
Bathrooms: 3
Foundation: Crawl space, slab, or basement
CompleteCost List Available: Yes
Price Category: D

Images provided by designer/architect.

If your family loves to combine indoor and outdoor living, this home's fabulous porches and deck space make it perfect.

Features:

- **Porches:** A huge wraparound front porch, sizable rear porch, and deck that joins them give you space for entertaining or simply lounging.

- **Living Room:** A fireplace and built-in media center could be the focal points in this large room.

- **Hearth Room:** Open to both the living room and kitchen, this hearth room also features a fireplace.

- **Kitchen:** This step-saving kitchen includes ample storage and work space, as well as an angled bar it shares with the hearth room. Atrium doors lead to the rear porch.

- **Bonus Upper Level:** A large game room and a full bath make this area a favorite with the children.

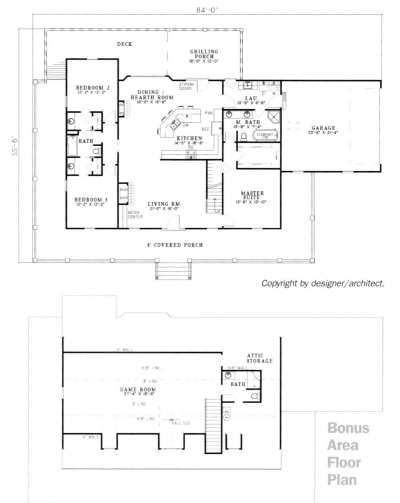

Copyright by designer/architect.

Bonus Area Floor Plan

Plan #131003

Dimensions: 60' W x 39'10" D
Levels: 1
Square Footage: 1,466
Bedrooms: 3
Bathrooms: 2
Foundation: Crawl space, slab, or basement
Materials List Available: Yes
Price Category: B

Images provided by designer/architect.

Victorian styling adds elegance to this compact and easy-to-maintain ranch design.

Features:

- Ceiling Height: 8 ft.

- Foyer: Bridging between the front door and the great room, this foyer is a surprise feature.

- Great Room: A 10-ft. ceiling adds to the spacious feeling of this room, while the corner fireplace gives it an intimate feeling. Sliding glass doors at the rear of the room open to the backyard.

- Dining Room: This formal room adjoins the great room, allowing guests and family to flow between the rooms.

- Breakfast Room: Turrets add a Victorian feeling to this room that's just off the kitchen and overlooks the front porch.

- Master Suite: Privacy is assured in this suite, which is separated from the main part of the house. A compartmented bath and large walk-in closet add convenience to its beauty.

Copyright by designer/architect.

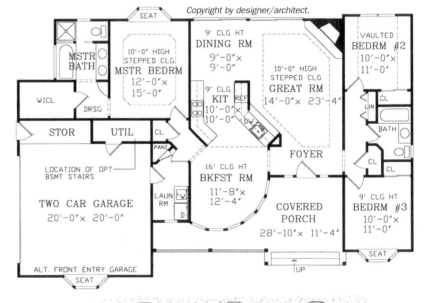

Breakfast Room

Plan #131050

Dimensions: 72'8" W x 47' D
Levels: 2
Square Footage: 2,874
Main Level Sq. Ft.: 2,146
Upper Level Sq. Ft.: 728
Bedrooms: 4
Bathrooms: 3
Foundation: Crawl space, slab, or basement
Materials List Available: Yes
Price Category: G

A gazebo and long covered porch at the entry let you know that this is a spectacular design.

Images provided by designer/architect.

Features:

• **Foyer:** This vaulted foyer divides the formal living room and dining room, setting the stage for guests to feel welcome in your home.

• **Great Room:** This large room is defined by several columns; a corner fireplace and vaulted ceiling add to its drama.

• **Kitchen:** An island work space separates this area from the bayed breakfast nook.

• **Master Suite:** You'll have privacy in this main-floor suite, which features two walk-in

closets and a compartmented bath with a dual-sink vanity.

• **Upper Level:** The two large bedrooms share a bath and a dramatic balcony.

• **Bonus Room:** Walk down a few steps into this large bonus room over the 3-car garage.

Rear Elevation

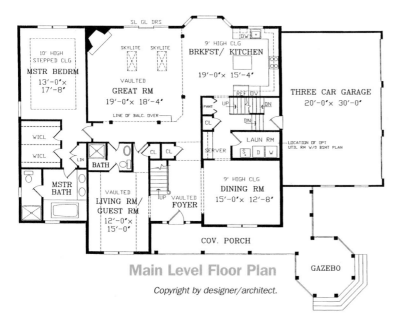

Main Level Floor Plan

Copyright by designer/architect.

Upper Level Floor Plan

Plan #161025

Dimensions: 63'4" W x 48' D
Levels: 2
Square Footage: 2,738
Main Level Sq. Ft.: 1,915
Upper Level Sq. Ft.: 823
Bedrooms: 4
Bathrooms: 3½
Foundation: Basement
Materials List Available: No
Price Category: F

This home, as shown in the photograph, may differ from the actual blueprints. For more detailed information, please check the floor plans carefully.

CAD FILE AVAILABLE

Images provided by designer/architect.

One look at the octagonal tower, boxed window, and wood-and-stone trim, and you'll know how much your family will love this home.

Features:

- Foyer: View the high windows across the rear wall, a fireplace, and open stairs as you come in.

- Great Room: Gather in this two-story-high area.

- Hearth Room: Open to the breakfast room, it's close to both the kitchen and dining room.

- Kitchen: A snack bar and an island make the kitchen ideal for family living.

- Master Suite: You'll love the 9-ft. ceiling in the bedroom and 11-ft. ceiling in the sitting area. The bath has a whirlpool tub, double-bowl vanity, and walk-in closet.

- Upper Level: A balcony leads to a bedroom with a private bath and 2 other rooms with private access to a shared bath.

Main Level Floor Plan

Upper Level Floor Plan

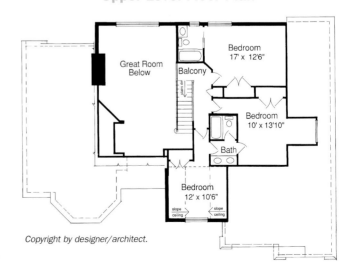

Copyright by designer/architect.

Plan #151179

Dimensions: 66'4" W x 67'2" D
Levels: 1½
Square Footage: 2,405
Opt. Bonus Level Sq. Ft.: 358
Bedrooms: 4
Bathrooms: 3
Foundation: Crawl space, slab
(basement or walk-out basement
option for fee)
CompleteCost List Available: Yes
Price Category: E

Images provided by designer/architect.

As beautiful inside as it is outside, this home will delight the most discerning family.

Features:

- **Great Room:** This room has a 10-ft. ceiling, door to the porch, fireplace, and built-ins.

- **Dining Room:** You'll love the way the columns set off this room from the great room and foyer.

- **Kitchen:** An L-shaped work area, central dining, and working island add to your efficiency.

- **Hearth Room:** A fireplace and computer center make this room a natural gathering spot.

- **Breakfast Room:** This lovely room is lit by large windows and a door that opens to the rear porch.

- **Master Suite:** You'll love the sitting room in the bayed area, walk-in closet, and luxury bath.

- **Rear Porch:** Use this porch for grilling, dining, and just relaxing—it's large enough to do it all.

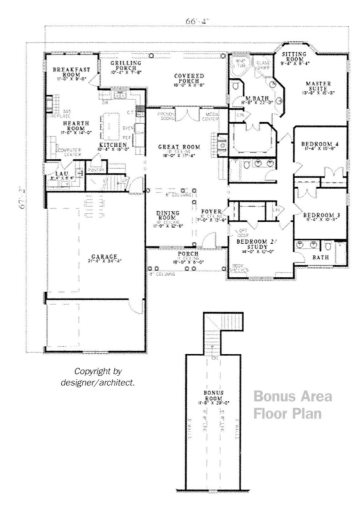

Copyright by designer/architect.

Bonus Area Floor Plan

Plan #151015

Dimensions: 72'4" W x 48'4" D
Levels: 2
Square Footage: 2,789
Main Level Sq. Ft.: 1,977
Upper Level Sq. Ft.: 812
Bedrooms: 4
Bathrooms: 3
Foundation: Crawl space, slab, or basement
CompleteCost List Available: Yes
Price Category: F

Images provided by designer/architect.

The spacious kitchen that opens to the breakfast room and the hearth room make this family home ideal for entertaining.

Features:

- Great Room: The fireplace will make a cozy winter focal point in this versatile space.

- Hearth Room: Enjoy the built-in entertainment center, built-in shelving, and fireplace here.

- Dining Room: A swing door leading to the kitchen is as attractive as it is practical.

- Study: A private bath and walk-in closet make this room an ideal spot for guests when needed.

- Kitchen: An island work area, a computer desk, and an eat-in bar add convenience and utility.

- Master Bath: Two vanities, two walk-in closets, a shower with a seat, and a whirlpool tub highlight this private space.

CAD FILE AVAILABLE

Main Level Floor Plan

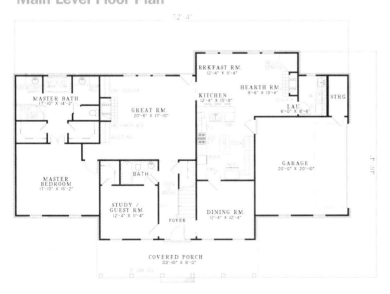

Upper Level Floor Plan

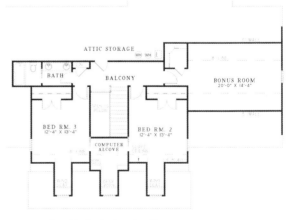

Copyright by designer/architect.

Main Level Floor Plan

Images provided by designer/architect.

CAD FILE AVAILABLE

Upper Level Floor Plan

Copyright by designer/architect.

Plan #181137

Dimensions: 68' W x 34' D

Levels: 2

Square Footage: 2,353

Main Level Sq. Ft.: 1,281

Upper Level Sq. Ft.: 1,072

Bedrooms: 3

Bathrooms: 2½

Foundation: Full basement

Materials List Available: Yes

Price Category: E

Plan #251014

Dimensions: 54' W x 61' D

Levels: 2

Square Footage: 2,210

Main Level Sq. Ft.: 1,670

Upper Level Sq. Ft.: 540

Bedrooms: 3

Bathrooms: 2½

Foundation: Crawl space, basement

Materials List Available: Yes

Price Category: E

Images provided by designer/architect.

CAD FILE AVAILABLE

Main Level Floor Plan

Upper Level Floor Plan

Copyright by designer/architect.

Plan #161035

Dimensions: 75' W x 64'11" D
Levels: 2
Square Footage: 3,688
Main Level Sq. Ft.: 2,702
Upper Level Sq. Ft.: 986
Bedrooms: 4
Bathrooms: 3½
Foundation: Basement
Materials List Available: No
Price Category: H

Images provided by designer/architect.

You'll appreciate the style of the stone, brick, and cedar shake exterior of this contemporary home.

Features:

• Hearth Room: Positioned for an easy flow for guests and family, this hearth room features a bank of windows that integrate it with the yard.

• Breakfast Room: Move through the sliding doors here to the rear porch on sunny days.

• Kitchen: Outfitted for a gourmet cook, this kitchen is also ideal for friends and family who can perch at the island or serve themselves at the bar.

• Master Suite: A stepped ceiling, crown moldings, and boxed window make the bedroom easy to decorate, while the two walk-in closets, lavish dressing area, and whirlpool tub in the bath make this area comfortable and luxurious.

Main Level Floor Plan

Upper Level Floor Plan

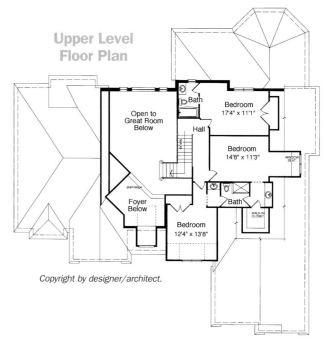

Copyright by designer/architect.

Left Elevation

Right Elevation

Kitchen

SMARTtip

How to Arrange Seating Around Your Fireplace

When the TV is near or on the same wall as the fireplace, you can arrange seating that places you at the best advantage to enjoy both. Position sofas and chairs in front of the fire, and remember that the distance between you and the TV should be at least three times the size of the screen.

Dining Room

Living Room

Master Bathroom

Main Level Floor Plan

Plan #181299

Dimensions: 41' W x 41' D

Levels: 2

Square Footage: 1,886

Main Level Sq. Ft.: 995

Upper Level Sq. Ft.: 891

Bedrooms: 3

Bathrooms: 1½

Foundation: Basement

Materials List Available: Yes

Price Category: D

Images provided by designer/architect.

Upper Level Floor Plan

Copyright by designer/architect.

Upper Level Floor Plan

Plan #181298

Dimensions: 36' W x 51' D

Levels: 2

Square Footage: 2,012

Main Level Sq. Ft.: 1,081

Upper Level Sq. Ft.: 931

Bedrooms: 3

Bathrooms: 2½

Foundation: Basement

Materials List Available: Yes

Price Category: D

Images provided by designer/architect.

Main Level Floor Plan

Copyright by designer/architect.

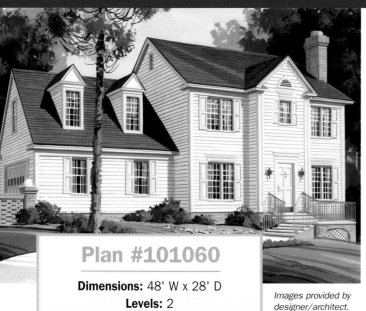

Plan #101060

Dimensions: 48' W x 28' D
Levels: 2
Square Footage: 1,653
Main Level Sq. Ft.: 816
Upper Level Sq. Ft.: 837
Bedrooms: 3
Bathrooms: 2½
Foundation: Crawl space or basement
Materials List Available: No
Price Category: C

Images provided by designer/architect.

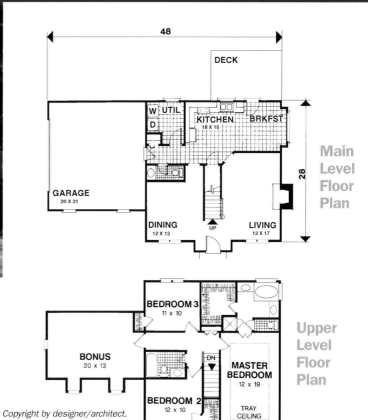

Main Level Floor Plan

Upper Level Floor Plan

Copyright by designer/architect.

Plan #321044

Dimensions: 61' W x 49'4" D
Levels: 2
Square Footage: 2,618
Main Level Sq. Ft.: 1,804
Upper Level Sq. Ft.: 814
Bedrooms: 4
Bathrooms: 2½
Foundation: Basement
Materials List Available: Yes
Price Category: F

Images provided by designer/architect.

Main Level Floor Plan

Upper Level Floor Plan

Copyright by designer/architect.

Plan #181248

Dimensions: 50' W x 54' D
Levels: 2
Square Footage: 3,321
Main Level Sq. Ft.: 1,698
Upper Level Sq. Ft.: 1,623
Bedrooms: 4
Bathrooms: 2½
Foundation: Basement
Materials List Available: Yes
Price Category: G

*Images provided by
designer/architect.*

CAD FILE AVAILABLE

**Upper Level
Floor Plan**

Copyright by designer/architect.

**Main Level
Floor Plan**

Plan #181269

Dimensions: 42' W x 46' D
Levels: 2
Square Footage: 2,628
Main Level Sq. Ft.: 1,151
Upper Level Sq. Ft.: 1,477
Bedrooms: 3
Bathrooms: 2½
Foundation: Basement
Materials List Available: Yes
Price Category: F

*Images provided by
designer/architect.*

CAD FILE AVAILABLE

**Upper Level
Floor Plan**

Copyright by designer/architect.

Plan #211077

Dimensions: 94' W x 68' D

Levels: 2

Square Footage: 5,560

Main Level Sq. Ft.: 4,208

Upper Level Sq. Ft.: 1,352

Bedrooms: 4

Bathrooms: 4 full, 2 half

Foundation: Crawl space or slab

Materials List Available: Yes

Price Category: J

This palatial home has a two-story veranda and offers room and amenities for a large family.

Features:

- Ceiling Height: 10 ft.

- Library: Teach your children the importance of quiet reflection in this library, which boasts a full wall of built-in bookshelves.

- Master Suite: Escape the pressures of a busy day in this truly royal master suite. Curl up in front of your own fireplace. Or take a long, soothing soak in the private bath, with his and her sinks and closets.

- Kitchen: This room offers many modern comforts and amenities, and free-flowing traffic patterns.

Images provided by designer/architect.

Copyright by designer/architect.

Plan #161074

Dimensions: 59'4" W x 67'10" D
Levels: 2
Square Footage: 2,427
Main Level Sq. Ft.: 1,949
Upper Level Sq. Ft.: 478
Bedrooms: 4
Bathrooms: 3½
Foundation: Basement
Materials List Available: No
Price Category: E

Images provided by designer/architect.

Brick, stone, and multiple gables decorate the exterior of this exciting home, creating curb appeal extraordinaire.

Features:

• Foyer: Along with an elegantly turned staircase, this entryway provides a view through the great room to a wall of windows on the rear wall.

• Master Suite: This suite will pamper you with a sloped ceiling, angled walls, and luxurious bathroom.

• Private Suite: A second bedroom on the first floor provides a suite for overnight guests.

• Second Floor: On the second floor a balcony overlooks the great room and foyer and leads to two additional bedrooms.

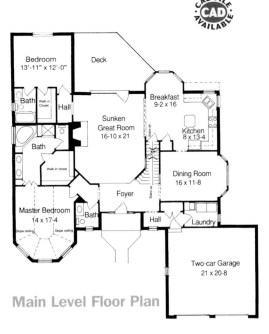

Main Level Floor Plan

Rear Elevation

Upper Level Floor Plan
Copyright by designer/architect.

Plan #161024

Dimensions: 54'4" W x 26'8" D
Levels: 2
Square Footage: 1,698
Main Level Sq. Ft.: 868
Upper Level Sq. Ft.: 830
Bonus Space Sq. Ft.: 269
Bedrooms: 3
Bathrooms: 2½
Foundation: Basement
Materials List Available: No
Price Category: C

The covered porch, dormers, and center gable that grace the exterior let you know how comfortable your family will be in this home.

Features:

- Great Room: Walk from windows overlooking the front porch to a door into the rear yard in this spacious room, which runs the width of the house.

- Dining Room: Adjacent to the great room, the dining area gives your family space to spread out and makes it easy to entertain a large group.

- Kitchen: Designed for efficiency, the kitchen area includes a large pantry.

- Master Suite: Tucked away on the second floor, the master suite features a walk-in closet in the bedroom and a luxurious attached bathroom.

- Bonus Room: Finish the 269-sq.-ft. area over the 2-bay garage as a guest room, study, or getaway for the kids.

This home, as shown in the photograph, may differ from the actual blueprints. For more detailed information, please check the floor plans carefully.   *Images provided by designer/architect.*

Main Level Floor Plan

Copyright by designer/architect.

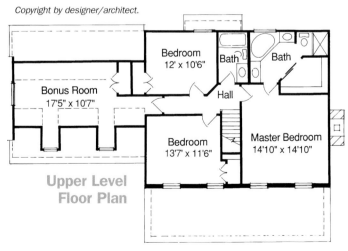

Upper Level Floor Plan

Plan #201103

Dimensions: 57'10" W x 56'10" D
Levels: 2
Square Footage: 2,490
Main Level Sq. Ft.: 1,911
Upper Level Sq. Ft.: 579
Bedrooms: 4
Bathrooms: 3
Foundation: Crawl space, slab
Materials List Available: Yes
Price Category: E

Images provided by designer/architect.

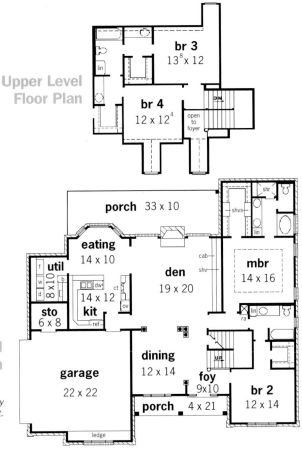

Upper Level Floor Plan

br 3
13⁸ x 12

br 4
12 x 12⁴

open to foyer

Main Level Floor Plan

porch 33 x 10

eating 14 x 10

den 19 x 20

mbr 14 x 16

util 8 x 10

kit 14 x 12

sto 6 x 8

garage 22 x 22

dining 12 x 14

foy 9x10

br 2 12 x 14

porch 4 x 21

ledge

Copyright by designer/architect.

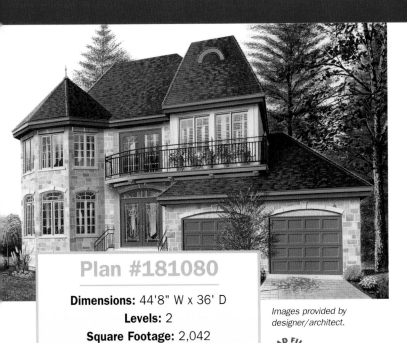

Plan #181080

Dimensions: 44'8" W x 36' D
Levels: 2
Square Footage: 2,042
Main Level Sq. Ft.: 934
Upper Level Sq. Ft.: 1,108
Bedrooms: 3
Bathrooms: 2½
Foundation: Full basement
Materials List Available: Yes
Price Category: D

Images provided by designer/architect.

CAD FILE AVAILABLE

Main Level Floor Plan

14'-0" X 9'-4"
4,20 X 2,80

18'-8" X 11'-8"
5,60 X 3,50

12'-4" X 22'-8"
3,70 X 6,80

19'-8" X 22'-0"
5,90 X 6,60

36'-0"
10,8 m

44'-8"
13,4 m

Upper Level Floor Plan

12'-0" X 10'-0"
3,60 X 3,00

11'-0" X 12'-0"
3,30 X 3,60

12'-4" X 16'-0"
3,70 X 4,80

CHAMBRE
OU BUREAU
10'-0" X 10'-0"
3,00 X 3,00

Copyright by designer/architect.

Plan #351008

Dimensions: 64'6" W x 61'4" D

Levels: 1

Square Footage: 2,002

Bedrooms: 3

Bathrooms: 2

Foundation: Basement, crawl space

Materials List Available: Yes

Price Category: D

Images provided by designer/architect.

CAD FILE AVAILABLE

Copyright by designer/architect.

Plan #271032

Dimensions: 78' W x 40' D

Levels: 2

Square Footage: 3,195

Main Level Sq. Ft.: 1,758

Upper Level Sq. Ft.: 1,437

Bedrooms: 4

Bathrooms: 2½

Foundation: Basement

Materials List Available: No

Price Category: E

Images provided by designer/architect.

CAD FILE AVAILABLE

Main Level Floor Plan

Upper Level Floor Plan

Copyright by designer/architect.

Plan #101013

Dimensions: 72' W x 66' D
Levels: 1
Square Footage: 2,564
Bedrooms: 3
Bathrooms: 2½
Foundation: Crawl space, slab, or basement
Materials List Available: Yes
Price Category: E

Images provided by designer/architect.

This exciting design combines a striking classic exterior with a highly functional floor plan.

Features:

- Ceiling Height: 9 ft. unless otherwise noted.

- Family Room: This warm and inviting room measures 18 ft. x 22 ft. It features a 14-ft. ceiling and a rear wall of windows. French doors lead to an enormous deck.

- Kitchen: This unique angled kitchen is open to the hearth room and eating areas, all of which enjoy vaulted ceilings and are surrounded by windows. The hearth room has a TV niche.

- Master Suite: This 19-ft. x 18-ft. master suite is truly sumptuous, with its 12-ft. ceiling, sitting area, two walk-in closets, and full-featured bath.

- Secondary Bedrooms: Each of the secondary bedrooms measures 11 ft. x 14 ft. and has direct access to a shared bath.

- Bonus Room: Just beyond the entry are stairs leading to this bonus room, which measures approximately 12 ft. x 21 ft.—plenty of room for storage or future expansion.

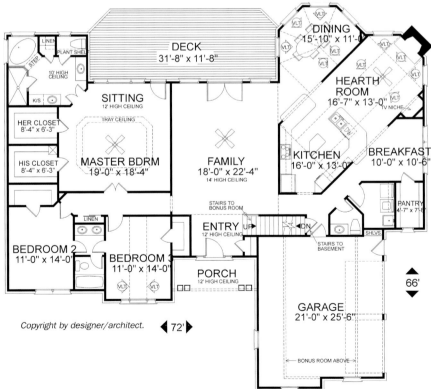

Copyright by designer/architect.

Dining Room

Hearth Room

Kitchen

Family Room

Master Bedroom

Master Bath

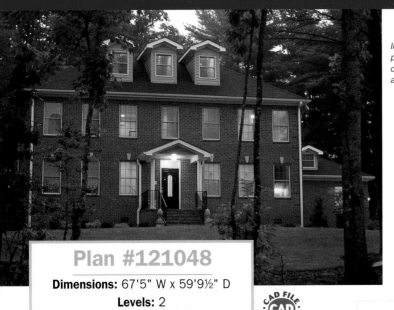

Images provided by designer/architect.

Main Level Floor Plan

Plan #121048

Dimensions: 67'5" W x 59'9½" D

Levels: 2

Square Footage: 2,975

Main Level Sq. Ft.: 1,548

Upper Level Sq. Ft.: 1,427

Bedrooms: 4

Bathrooms: 3½

Foundation: Slab

Materials List Available: Yes

Price Category: F

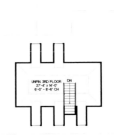

Copyright by designer/architect.

Upper Level Floor Plan

Bonus Area

Plan #121095

Dimensions: 65'4" W x 48'8" D

Levels: 2

Square Footage: 2,282

Main Level Sq. Ft.: 1,597

Upper Level Sq. Ft.: 685

Bedrooms: 4

Bathrooms: 2½

Foundation: Basement

Materials List Available: Yes

Price Category: E

Images provided by designer/architect.

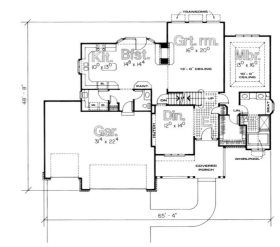

Main Level Floor Plan

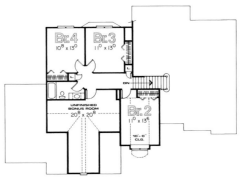

Copyright by designer/architect.

Upper Level Floor Plan

Plan #141019

Dimensions: 57' W x 41' D
Levels: 2
Square Footage: 2,826
Main Level Sq. Ft.: 1,258
Second Level Sq. Ft.: 1,568
Bedrooms: 5
Bathrooms: 3
Foundation: Basement
Materials List Available: Yes
Price Category: F

Images provided by designer/architect.

Main Level Floor Plan

Patio / Deck
Brkfst. 13⁴ x 10⁰
Office / Bdrm.5 11⁰ x 11⁴
Bth.3
Command Center
Living Area 15⁰ x 19² 11' Ceil. Boxed Tray
Kit. 13⁴ x 11⁶
Cubby Holes
Double Garage 21⁴ x 21⁸
Two Story Foyer 7⁰ x 5¹⁰
Dining 13⁴ x 11⁶

Upper Level Floor Plan

Copyright by designer/architect.

Bdrm.2 11⁰ x 13⁴
Bth.2
Children's Den / Media Room 15⁰ x 17⁴
Master Bdrm. 13⁶ x 17⁴
Bdrm.3 12⁸ x 11⁸
Opt. Tray w/ Plant Shelf
M.Bath
Balcony
Opt. Tray w/ Plant Shelf
Laund.
Linen
Two Story Foyer
Bdrm.4 11⁴ x 11²
Seat W/ Drawers

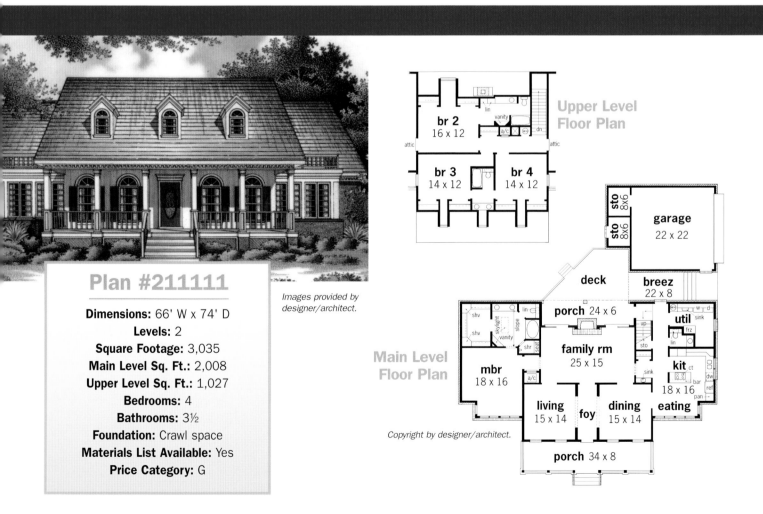

Plan #211111

Dimensions: 66' W x 74' D
Levels: 2
Square Footage: 3,035
Main Level Sq. Ft.: 2,008
Upper Level Sq. Ft.: 1,027
Bedrooms: 4
Bathrooms: 3½
Foundation: Crawl space
Materials List Available: Yes
Price Category: G

Images provided by designer/architect.

Upper Level Floor Plan

br 2 16 x 12
attic
br 3 14 x 12
br 4 14 x 12
attic

Main Level Floor Plan

Copyright by designer/architect.

sto 8x6
sto 8x6
sto 8x6
garage 22 x 22
deck
breez 22 x 8
porch 24 x 6
util
family rm 25 x 15
kit 18 x 16
mbr 18 x 16
living 15 x 14
foy
dining 15 x 14
eating
porch 34 x 8

Plan #121088

Dimensions: 56'8" W x 48' D

Levels: 2

Square Footage: 2,340

Main Level Sq. Ft.: 1,701

Upper Level Sq. Ft.: 639

Bedrooms: 4

Bathrooms: 2½

Foundation: Basement

Materials List Available: Yes

Price Category: E

Images provided by designer/architect.

You'll love this cheerful home, with its many large windows that let in natural light and cozy spaces that encourage family gatherings.

Features:

- Entry: Use the built-in curio cabinet here to display your best collector's pieces.

- Den: French doors from the entry lead to this room, with its built-in bookcase and triple-wide, transom-topped window.

- Great Room: The 14-ft. ceiling in this room accentuates the floor-to-ceiling windows that frame the raised-hearth fireplace.

- Kitchen: Both the layout and the work space make this room a delight for any cook.

- Master Suite: The bedroom has a tray ceiling for built-in elegance. A skylight helps to light the master bath, and an oval whirlpool tub, separate shower, and double vanity provide a luxurious touch.

Main Level Floor Plan

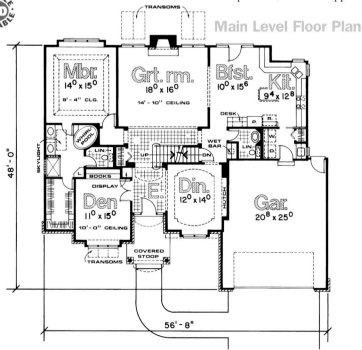

Upper Level Floor Plan

Copyright by designer/architect.

Plan #241008

Dimensions: 65' W x 56'8" D
Levels: 1
Square Footage: 2,526
Bedrooms: 4
Bathrooms: 3
Foundation: Slab
Materials List Available: No
Price Category: E

A covered back porch—with access from the master suite and the breakfast area—makes this traditional home ideal for siting near a golf course or with a backyard pool.

Features:

- **Great Room:** From the foyer, guests enter this spacious and comfortable great room, which features a handsome fireplace.

- **Kitchen:** This kitchen—the hub of this family-oriented home—is a joy in which to work, thanks to abundant counter space, a pantry, a convenient eating bar, and an adjoining breakfast area and sunroom.

- **Master Suite:** Enjoy the quiet comfort of this coffered-ceiling master suite, which features dual vanities and separate walk-in closets.

- **Additional Bedrooms:** Two secondary bedrooms, which share a full bath, are located at the opposite end of the house from the master suite. Bedroom 4—in front of the house—can be converted into a study.

Images provided by designer/architect.

Copyright by designer/architect.

Optional Bonus Area Floor Plan

SMARTtip

Traditional-Style Kitchen Cabinetry

You can modify stock kitchen cabinetry to enjoy fine furniture-quality details. Prefabricated trims may be purchased at local lumber mills and home centers. For example, crown molding, applied to the top of stock cabinetry and stained or painted to match the door style, may be all you need. Likewise, you can replace hardware with reproduction polished-brass door and drawer knobs or pulls for a finishing touch.

Plan #311002

Dimensions: 56'6" W x 82' D

Levels: 1

Square Footage: 2,402

Bedrooms: 4

Bathrooms: 2½

Foundation: Crawl space, slab

Materials List Available: Yes

Price Category: E

Images provided by designer/architect.

This lovely home has an open floor plan in the main living area but privacy in the bedrooms.

Features:

- Foyer: With an 11-ft. ceiling, this foyer opens to both the great room and the dining room.

- Great Room: A 10-ft. ceiling and handsome fireplace highlight this spacious room, which is open to both the kitchen and breakfast room.

- Dining Room: A butler's pantry and built-in china closet spell convenience in this lovely room.

- Breakfast Room: Bask in the sunshine flowing through the bay windows in this room, which opens to the rear porch.

- Kitchen: Designed for efficiency, this kitchen will charm all the cooks in the family.

- Master Suite: It's easy to feel pampered by the huge closet and bath with corner tub and two vanities.

Rear View

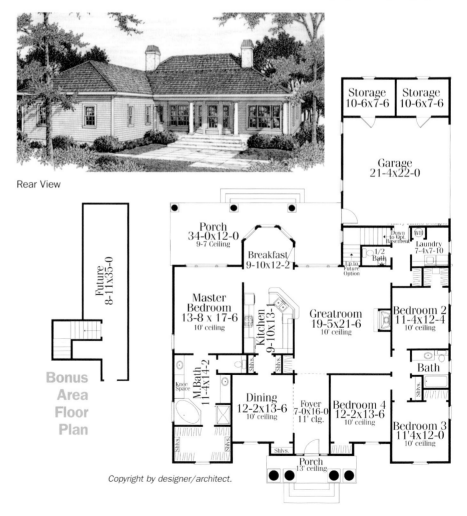

Copyright by designer/architect.

Plan #121064

Dimensions: 44' W x 40' D
Levels: 2
Square Footage: 1,846
Main Level Sq. Ft.: 919
Upper Level Sq. Ft.: 927
Bedrooms: 4
Bathrooms: 2½
Foundation: Basement
Materials List Available: Yes
Price Category: D

Images provided by designer/architect.

You'll love the features and design in this compact but amenity-filled home.

Features:

- **Entry:** A balcony overlooks this two-story entry, where a plant shelf tops the coat closet.

- **Great Room:** A trio of tall windows points up the large dimensions of this room, which is sure to be the hub of your home. Arrange the furniture to create a cozy space around the fireplace, or leave it open to the room.

- **Kitchen:** You'll love to work in this well-designed kitchen area.

- **Master Suite:** On the second floor, this master suite features a tiered ceiling and two walk-in closets. In the bath, you'll find a double vanity, whirlpool tub, and separate shower.

Main Level Floor Plan

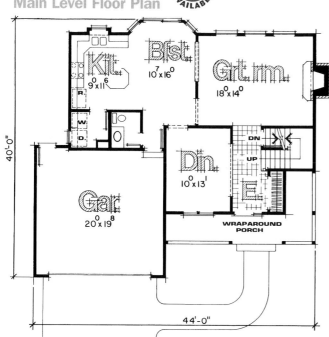

Upper Level Floor Plan

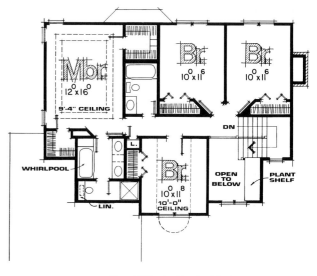

Copyright by designer/architect.

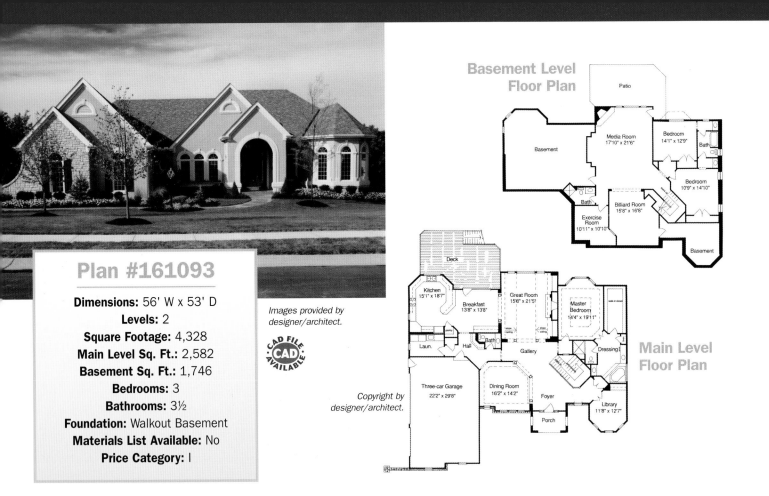

Plan #161093

Dimensions: 56' W x 53' D
Levels: 2
Square Footage: 4,328
Main Level Sq. Ft.: 2,582
Basement Sq. Ft.: 1,746
Bedrooms: 3
Bathrooms: 3½
Foundation: Walkout Basement
Materials List Available: No
Price Category: I

Images provided by designer/architect.

Basement Level Floor Plan

Main Level Floor Plan

Copyright by designer/architect.

CAD FILE AVAILABLE

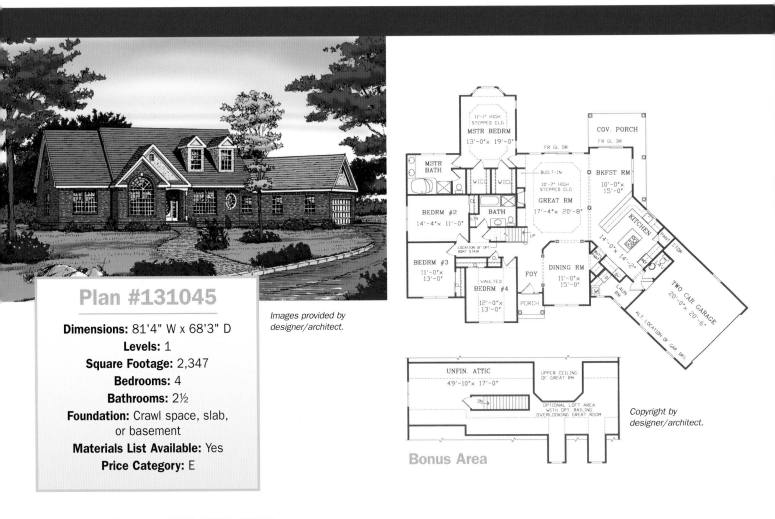

Plan #131045

Dimensions: 81'4" W x 68'3" D
Levels: 1
Square Footage: 2,347
Bedrooms: 4
Bathrooms: 2½
Foundation: Crawl space, slab, or basement
Materials List Available: Yes
Price Category: E

Images provided by designer/architect.

Copyright by designer/architect.

Bonus Area

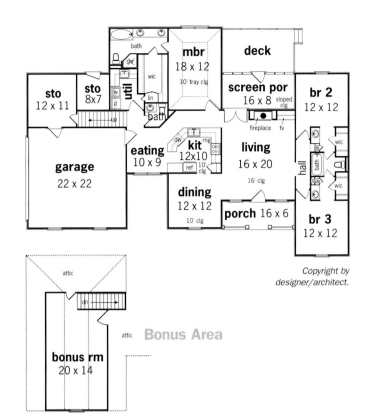

Images provided by designer/architect.

Copyright by designer/architect.

Bonus Area

Plan #211086

Dimensions: 71' W x 50' D

Levels: 1

Square Footage: 1,704

Bedrooms: 3

Bathrooms: 2½

Foundation: Crawl space

Materials List Available: Yes

Price Category: C

Main Level Floor Plan

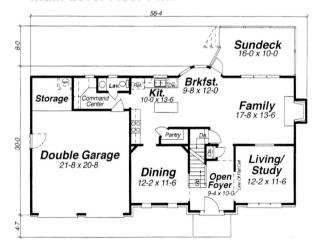

Images provided by designer/architect.

Plan #141031

Dimensions: 58'4" W x 30' D

Levels: 2

Square Footage: 2,367

Main Level Sq. Ft.: 1,025

Upper Level Sq. Ft.: 1,342

Bedrooms: 4

Bathrooms: 2½

Foundation: Basement

Materials List Available: No

Price Category: E

Upper Level Floor Plan

Copyright by designer/architect.

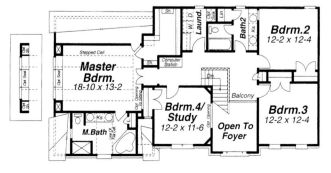

Main Level Floor Plan

Images provided by designer/architect.

Plan #251012

Dimensions: 57'9" W x 62'10" D

Levels: 2

Square Footage: 2,009

Main Level Sq. Ft.: 1,520

Upper Level Sq. Ft.: 489

Bedrooms: 3

Bathrooms: 2½

Foundation: Basement

Materials List Available: Yes

Price Category: D

Upper Level Floor Plan

Copyright by designer/architect.

Plan #251013

Dimensions: 58' W x 44' D

Levels: 2

Square Footage: 2,073

Main Level Sq. Ft.: 1,441

Upper Level Sq. Ft.: 632

Bedrooms: 4

Bathrooms: 2½

Foundation: Basement

Materials List Available: Yes

Price Category: D

Images provided by designer/architect.

Main Level Floor Plan

Upper Level Floor Plan

Copyright by designer/architect.

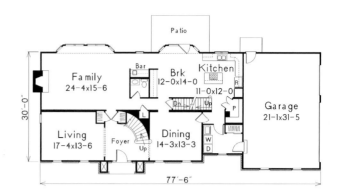

Plan #321049

Dimensions: 77'6" W x 30' D

Levels: 2

Square Footage: 3,144

Main Level Sq. Ft.: 1,724

Upper Level Sq. Ft.: 1,420

Bedrooms: 4

Bathrooms: 4½

Foundation: Basement

Materials List Available: Yes

Price Category: G

Images provided by designer/architect.

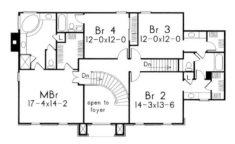

Upper Level Floor Plan

Copyright by designer/architect.

Copyright by designer/architect.

Plan #161007

Dimensions: 66'4" W x 43'10" D

Levels: 1

Square Footage: 1,611

Bedrooms: 3

Bathrooms: 2

Foundation: Basement

Materials List Available: Yes

Price Category: C

Images provided by designer/architect.

Rear Elevation

Plan #121090

Dimensions: 60' W x 58' D
Levels: 2
Square Footage: 2,645
Main Level Sq. Ft.: 1,972
Upper Level Sq. Ft.: 673
Bedrooms: 4
Bathrooms: 2½
Foundation: Basement
Materials List Available: Yes
Price Category: F

Images provided by designer/architect.

You'll be amazed at the amenities that have been designed into this lovely home.

Features:

- **Den:** French doors just off the entry lead to this lovely room, with its bowed window and spider-beamed ceiling.

- **Great Room:** A trio of graceful arched windows highlights the volume ceiling in this room. You might want to curl up to read next to the see-through fireplace into the hearth room.

- **Kitchen:** Enjoy the good design in this room.

- **Hearth Room:** The shared fireplace with the great room makes this a cozy spot in cool weather.

- **Master Suite:** French doors lead to this well-lit area, with its roomy walk-in closet, sunlit whirlpool tub, separate shower, and two vanities.

Main Level Floor Plan

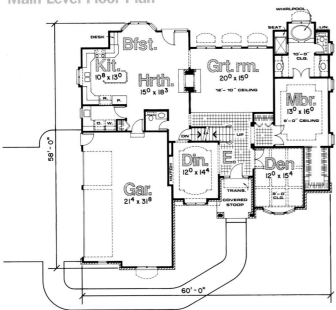

Upper Level Floor Plan

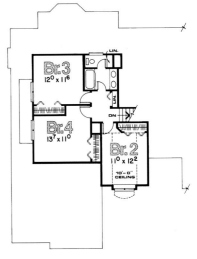

Copyright by designer/architect.

Plan #151461

Dimensions: 56'8" W x 57'4" D
Levels: 2
Square Footage: 2,360
Main Level Sq. Ft.: 1,776
Upper Level Sq. Ft.: 584
Bedrooms: 3
Bathrooms: 2½
Foundation: Crawl space or slab
CompleteCost List Available: Yes
Price Category: E

Images provided by designer/architect.

Neighbors will surely envy the elegant exterior of this charming home, with its welcoming porch and gabled roofline.

Features:

• Foyer: This two-story space blends wonderfully with the column-accented formal dining room and opens into the vast great room, which is anchored by a stately fireplace.

• Hearth Room: Enjoy casual meals by the fireplace as this room flows barrier-free into the breakfast area and kitchen.

• Master Suite: Located on the main level for convenience and privacy, this suite has a 10-ft.-tall boxed ceiling. The bath boasts a whirlpool tub, a glass shower, dual vanities, and a large walk-in closet.

• Bedrooms: Upstairs there are two bedrooms. The loft bedroom steals the show, with its extra-wide window seat, walk-in closet, and private entrance to the upstairs bathroom.

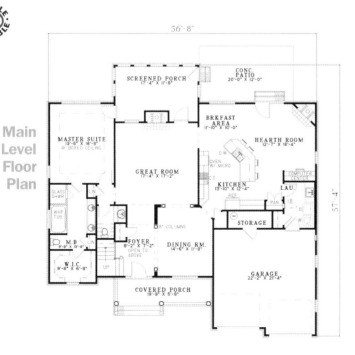

Main Level Floor Plan

Upper Level Floor Plan

Copyright by designer/architect.

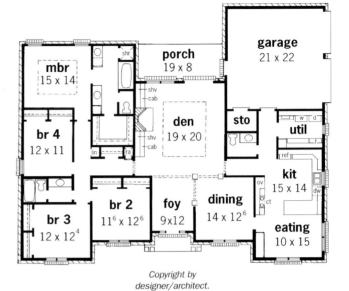

Plan #201061

Dimensions: 64'10" W x 54'10" D

Levels: 1

Square Footage: 2,387

Bedrooms: 4

Bathrooms: 2½

Foundation: Crawl space, slab

Materials List Available: Yes

Price Category: E

Images provided by designer/architect.

Copyright by designer/architect.

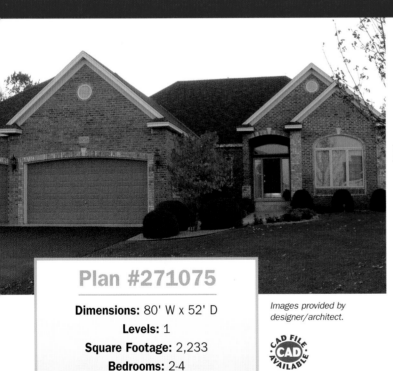

Plan #271075

Dimensions: 80' W x 52' D

Levels: 1

Square Footage: 2,233

Bedrooms: 2-4

Bathrooms: 1½-3½

Foundation: Basement

Materials List Available: No

Price Category: E

Images provided by designer/architect.

CAD FILE AVAILABLE

Optional Basement Level Floor Plan

Copyright by designer/architect.

Main Level Floor Plan

Images provided by designer/architect.

Plan #271067

Dimensions: 72'2" W x 46'5" D
Levels: 2
Square Footage: 3,015
Main Level Sq. Ft.: 1,367
Upper Level Sq. Ft.: 1,648
Bedrooms: 3
Bathrooms: 2½
Foundation: Crawl space, basement
Materials List Available: No
Price Category: G

Upper Level Floor Plan

Copyright by designer/architect.

Plan #211037

Dimensions: 66' W x 60' D
Levels: 1
Square Footage: 1,800
Bedrooms: 3
Bathrooms: 2
Foundation: Crawl space or basement; slab option for fee
Materials List Available: Yes
Price Category: D

Images provided by designer/architect.

Copyright by designer/architect.

SMARTtip

Reflected Light in the Bathroom

The addition of a large mirror can bring reflected light into a small bathroom, adding the illusion of space without the expense of renovation.

Plan #141019

Dimensions: 57' W x 41' D
Levels: 2
Square Footage: 2,826
Main Level Sq. Ft.: 1,258
Second Level Sq. Ft.: 1,568
Bedrooms: 5
Bathrooms: 3
Foundation: Basement
Materials List Available: Yes
Price Category: F

Images provided by designer/architect.

Main Level Floor Plan

Upper Level Floor Plan
Copyright by designer/architect.

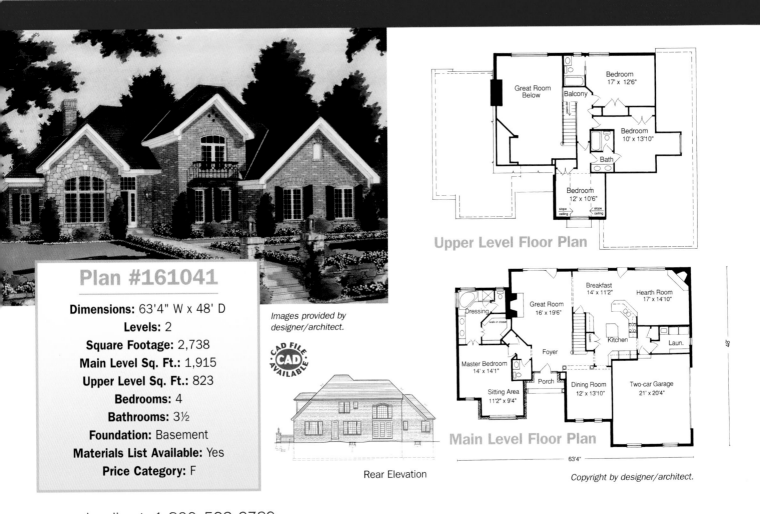

Plan #161041

Dimensions: 63'4" W x 48' D
Levels: 2
Square Footage: 2,738
Main Level Sq. Ft.: 1,915
Upper Level Sq. Ft.: 823
Bedrooms: 4
Bathrooms: 3½
Foundation: Basement
Materials List Available: Yes
Price Category: F

Images provided by designer/architect.

CAD FILE AVAILABLE

Upper Level Floor Plan

Main Level Floor Plan

Rear Elevation

Copyright by designer/architect.

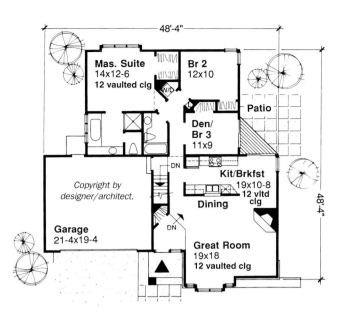

Images provided by designer/architect.

Plan #271005

Dimensions: 48'4" W x 48'4" D
Levels: 1
Square Footage: 1,368
Bedrooms: 3
Bathrooms: 2
Foundation: Basement
Materials List Available: Yes
Price Category: B

CAD FILE AVAILABLE

SMARTtip
Design with Computers

Consider using a computer-aided design (CAD) program to plan your deck. Some programs let you see three-dimensional views of your design complete with railings, stairs, planters, hot tubs, and the surrounding landscaping.

Plan #201061

Dimensions: 64'10" W x 54'10" D
Levels: 1
Square Footage: 2,387
Bedrooms: 4
Bathrooms: 2½
Foundation: Crawl space, slab
Materials List Available: Yes
Price Category: E

Images provided by designer/architect.

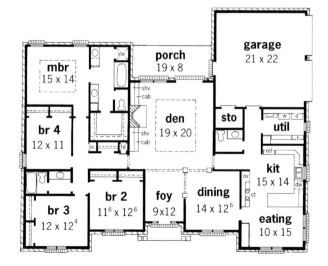

Copyright by designer/architect.

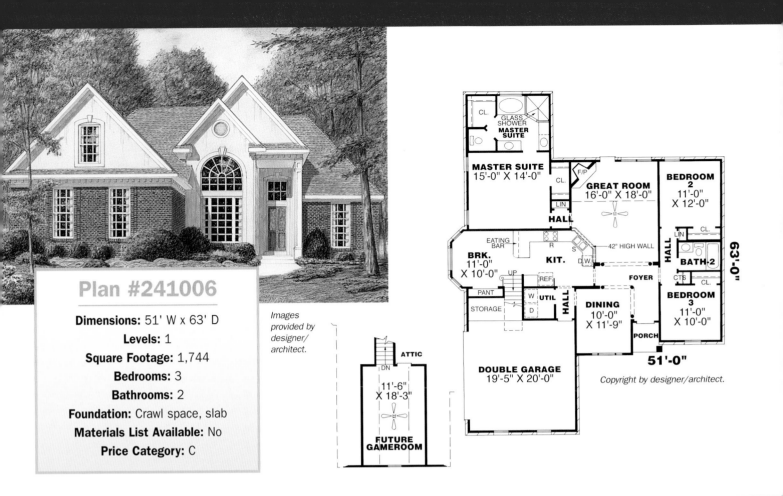

Plan #241006

Dimensions: 51' W x 63' D

Levels: 1

Square Footage: 1,744

Bedrooms: 3

Bathrooms: 2

Foundation: Crawl space, slab

Materials List Available: No

Price Category: C

Images provided by designer/architect.

Copyright by designer/architect.

Plan #271039

Dimensions: 46' W x 46' D

Levels: 2

Square Footage: 1,565

Main Level Sq. Ft.: 1,105

Upper Level Sq. Ft.: 460

Bedrooms: 3

Bathrooms: 2½

Foundation: Basement

Materials List Available: Yes

Price Category: B

Images provided by designer/architect.

Copyright by designer/architect.

Plan #151091

Dimensions: 69'2" W x 39'4" D
Levels: 1.5
Square Footage: 2,320
Main Level Sq. Ft.: 1,591
Upper Level Sq. Ft.: 729
Bedrooms: 3
Bathrooms: 2½
Foundation: Crawl space or slab
CompleteCost List Available: Yes
Price Category: C

The highlight of this glorious home plan is the morning room, with its lovely view of the backyard.

Features:

- **Great Room:** Enter this large gathering area from the entry foyer, and you'll feel the warmth from the fireplace.

- **Kitchen:** Family and weekend guests will enjoy gathering in this oversized kitchen and breakfast room with access to the side grilling porch.

- **Master Suite:** This suite features his and her walk-in closets. The master bath boasts a corner whirlpool bathtub, a corner shower, and split vanities.

- **Upper Level:** Just up the stairway you will find a loft area and two large secondary bedrooms. There is also a full bathroom on this level.

Images provided by designer/architect.

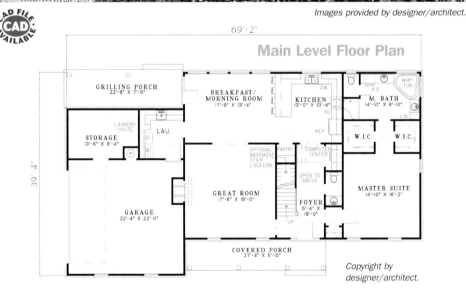

Main Level Floor Plan

Copyright by designer/architect.

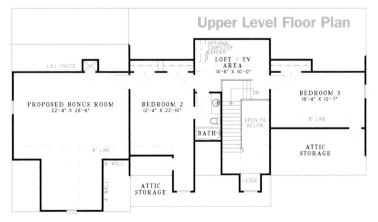

Upper Level Floor Plan

Plan #121081

Dimensions: 76'8" W x 68' D
Levels: 2
Square Footage: 3,623
Main Level Sq. Ft.: 2,603
Upper Level Sq. Ft.: 1,020
Bedrooms: 4
Bathrooms: 4½
Foundation: Basement
Materials List Available: Yes
Price Category: G

Images provided by designer/architect.

You'll love this impressive home if you're looking for perfect spot for entertaining as well as a home for comfortable family living.

Features:

• Entry: Walk into this grand two-story entryway through double doors, and be greeted by the sight of a graceful curved staircase.

• Great Room: This two-story room features stacked windows, a fireplace flanked by an

entertainment center, a bookcase, and a wet bar.

• Dining Room: A corner column adds formality to this room, which is just off the entryway for the convenience of your guests.

• Hearth Room: Connected to the great room by a lovely set of French doors, this room features another fireplace as well as a convenient pantry.

Main Level Floor Plan

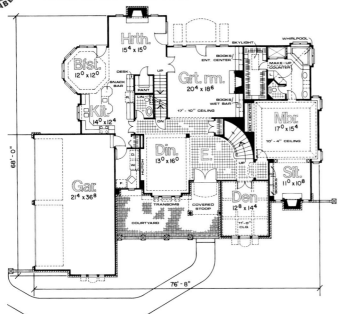

Upper Level Floor Plan

Copyright by designer/architect.

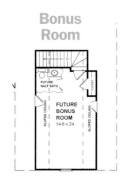

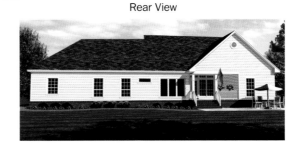

Rear View

Plan #351004

Dimensions: 78' W x 49'6" D
Levels: 1
Square Footage: 1,852
Bedrooms: 3
Bathrooms: 2½
Foundation: Crawl space, slab, or basement
Materials List Available: Yes
Price Category: D

Images provided by designer/architect.

Copyright by designer/architect.

Bonus Room

Plan #181259

Dimensions: 45' W x 54' D
Levels: 2
Square Footage: 2,279
Main Level Sq. Ft.: 1,194
Upper Level Sq. Ft.: 1,085
Bedrooms: 4
Bathrooms: 2½
Foundation: Basement
Materials List Available: Yes
Price Category: E

Images provided by designer/architect.

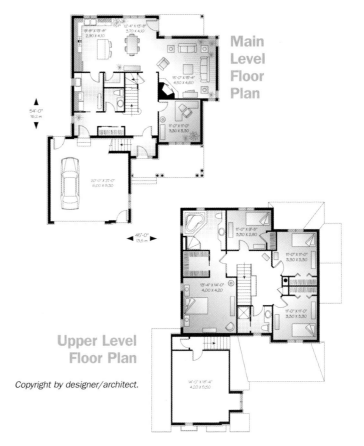

Main Level Floor Plan

Upper Level Floor Plan

Copyright by designer/architect.

As Your Landscape Grows

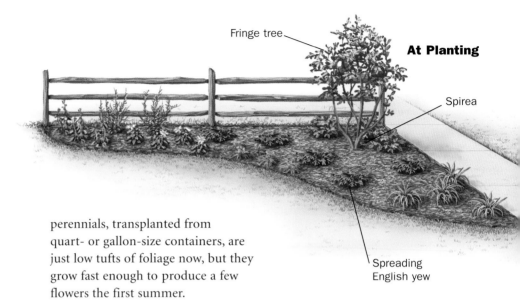

Fringe tree

At Planting

Spirea

Spreading
English yew

Landscapes change over the years. As plants grow, the overall look evolves from sparse to lush. Trees cast cool shade where the sun used to shine. Shrubs and hedges grow tall and dense enough to provide privacy. Perennials and ground covers spread to form colorful patches of foliage and flowers. Meanwhile, paths, arbors, fences, and other structures gain the patina of age.

Constant change over the years—sometimes rapid and dramatic, sometimes slow and subtle—is one of the joys of landscaping. It is also one of the challenges. Anticipating how fast plants will grow and how big they will eventually get is difficult, even for professional designers, and was a major concern in formulating the designs for this book.

To illustrate the kinds of changes to expect in a planting, these pages show one of the designs at three different "ages." Even though a new planting may look sparse at first, it will soon fill in. And because of careful spacing, the planting will look as good in ten to fifteen years as it does after three to five. It will, of course, look different, but that's part of the fun.

At Planting—Here's how the corner might appear in spring immediately after planting. The fence and mulch look conspicuously fresh, new, and unweathered. The fringe tree is only 4 to 5 ft. tall, with trunks no thicker than broomsticks. (With this or other trees, you can buy bigger specimens to start with, but they're a lot more expensive and sometimes don't perform as well in the long run.) The spireas and spreading English yews, transplanted from 2-gal. nursery containers, spread 12 to 18 in. wide. The

perennials, transplanted from quart- or gallon-size containers, are just low tufts of foliage now, but they grow fast enough to produce a few flowers the first summer.

Three to Five Years—The fringe tree has grown about 6 in. taller every year but is still quite slender. Some trees would grow faster, as much as 1 to 2 ft. a year. The spireas, like many fast-growing shrubs, have reached almost full size. From now on, they'll get thicker but not much taller. The slower-growing English yews make a series of low mounds; you still see them as individuals, not a continuous patch. Most perennials, such as the coneflowers, Shasta daisies, daylilies, and dianthus shown here, grow so crowded after a few years that they need to be divided and replanted.

Ten to Fifteen Years—The fringe tree is becoming a fine specimen, 10 to 12 ft. wide and tall. Unless you prune away enough of its lower limbs to let some sunlight in, the spireas will gradually stop blooming, get weaker, and need to be replaced with shade-tolerant shrubs such as more English yews or with shade-loving perennials and ferns. The original English yews will have formed a continuous ground cover by now and may have spread enough to limit the space available for perennials. Since the perennials get divided every few years anyway, it's no trouble to rearrange or regroup them, as shown here.

Fringe tree

Spreading
English yew

Three to Five Years

Spirea

Coneflower

Shasta daisy

Dianthus

Daylily

Fringe tree

Ten to Fifteen Years

Spreading
English yew

First Impressions

Make a Pleasant Passage to Your Front Door

First impressions are as important in the home landscape as they are on a blind date or a job interview. Why wait until a visitor reaches the front door to extend a warm greeting? Instead let your landscape offer a friendly welcome and a helpful "Please come this way." Well-chosen plants and a revamped walkway not only make a visitor's short journey a pleasant one, they can also enhance your home's most public face and help settle it comfortably in its immediate surroundings.

The ample bluestone walkway in this design invites visitors to stroll side by side through a small garden from the driveway to the entrance. The path is positioned to put the front door in full view of arriving guests. Its generous width allows for informal gatherings as guests arrive and leave, and well-chosen plants encourage lingering there to enjoy them.

Three small trees grace the entrance with spring and summer flowers, light shade, and superb fall color. Most of the perennials and shrubs are evergreen and look good year-round, providing a fine background to the flowers and an attractive foil to the fall color. In the winter, colorful tree bark and bright berries make gazing out the windows a pleasure.

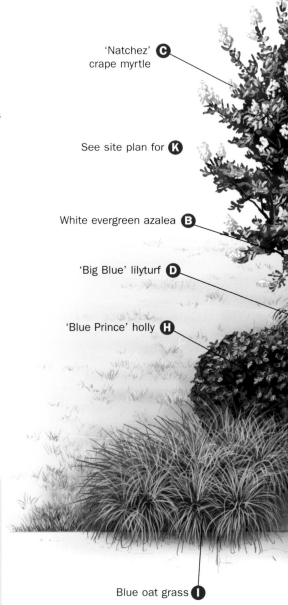

'Natchez' crape myrtle **C**

See site plan for **K**

White evergreen azalea **B**

'Big Blue' lilyturf **D**

'Blue Prince' holly **H**

Blue oat grass **I**

Note: All plants are appropriate for USDA Hardiness *Zones 5, 6, and 7.*

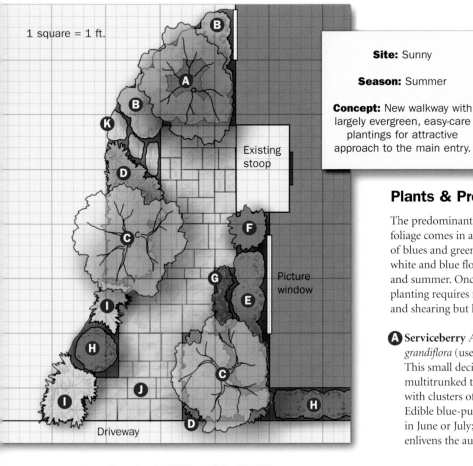

1 square = 1 ft.

Existing stoop

Picture window

Driveway

Site: Sunny

Season: Summer

Concept: New walkway with largely evergreen, easy-care plantings for attractive approach to the main entry.

Plants & Projects

The predominantly evergreen foliage comes in a surprising range of blues and greens, accented by white and blue flowers in spring and summer. Once established, the planting requires regular pruning and shearing but little else.

A **Serviceberry** *Amelanchier x grandiflora* (use 1 plant) This small deciduous, often multitrunked tree greets spring with clusters of white flowers. Edible blue-purple berries ripen in June or July; bright foliage enlivens the autumn.

B **White evergreen azalea** *Rhododendron* (use 11) Low, mounding shrubs form a soft skirt beneath the serviceberry by the door. Try the cultivar 'Helen Curtis', with white flowers in mid-to late spring.

C **'Natchez' crape myrtle** *Lagerstroemia indica* (use 2) Flanking the walk, these small multitrunked trees bear pure white crepe-papery flowers for weeks in summer. Colorful fall leaves drop to reveal attractive flaking bark in winter.

A Serviceberry

G Christmas rose

F Heavenly bamboo **J** Walkway **E** 'Otto Luyken' cherry laurel **D** 'Big Blue' lilyturf **C** 'Natchez' crape myrtle **H** 'Blue Prince' holly

D **'Big Blue' lilyturf** *Liriope muscari* (use 40)
These grassy evergreen perennials carpet the ground beneath the crape myrtles. Small spikes of blue flowers in summer produce shiny blue-black berries in fall. Brighten up spring by underplanting 75 white daffodil bulbs (*Narcissus*) in each lilyturf bed.

E **'Otto Luyken' cherry laurel** *Prunus laurocerasus* (use 4)
This evergreen shrub has thick glossy leaves and fragrant white spring flowers. Prune to form a neat block of greenery below the windows.

F **Heavenly bamboo** *Nandina domestica* (use 1)
An evergreen shrub that packs four seasons of interest into the narrow space by the door. Tiers of lacy foliage turn from copper to green to rich crimson or purple. Summer's white flowers give way to heavy sprays of shiny red berries that may last until spring.

G **Christmas rose** *Helleborus niger* (use 5)
Tucked in by the walk, this evergreen ground cover offers fine-toothed dark green leaves and white cup-size blossoms in winter and early spring. Underplant 20 white Grecian windflower bulbs (*Anemone blanda*) to add to the spring display.

H **'Blue Prince' holly** *Ilex x meserveae* (use 5)
An excellent evergreen foundation shrub between the drive and house; one is also used as a shaped specimen next to the walk. Features glossy blue-green foliage and purple twigs. Maintained by regular pruning.

I **Blue oat grass** *Helictotrichon sempervirens* (use 10)
The formality of the sheared holly is set off nicely by this small island of clump-forming grass. Blue-gray foliage looks good all year.

J **Walkway**
Rectangular flagstones in random sizes; bluestone shown here.

K **Steppingstones**
Fieldstones provide easy access to the lawn.

Create a "Living" Room

Enclose a patio with foliage and flowers

'Natchez' **A**
crape myrtle

A patio can become a true extension of your living space with the addition of plants for privacy and pleasure. The floral and foliage motifs of the "walls" in the outdoor room shown here are three-dimensional and constantly changing. The handsome brick floor accommodates a family barbecue or a large gathering. A rounded portion extends into the yard and serves, rather like a bay window, to mingle "indoors" and "outdoors."

Scale is particularly important when planting next to the house. The small, multi-trunked crape myrtles won't overwhelm the house while casting welcome shade on the patio. The room they help compose is

relatively open. Perennials and grasses fill in beneath the trees but are short enough not to obstruct views or breezes through the loose screen of trees.

We've shown the design extending in definitely into the foreground, to indicate that the patio can be made in a range of sizes. If the patio extends farther along the side of the house, you might plant additional crape myrtles along the edge that parallels the house wall. For a more open feeling, extend only the bed of grasses and perennials. The patio's other end could be similar to the end shown here, or it could have an opening to accommodate traffic to and from a garage or driveway.

'Butterfly Blue' **D**
pincushion flower

Dwarf fountain **B**
grass

Plants & Projects

This design's long-blooming, easy-care plants will make any patio, old or new, a colorful spot throughout the summer and fall.

Beneath the white flowers of the crape myrtles, shades of blue and purple cool the summer days, with yellow coreopsis as a bright accent. Purple asters, rosy sedum, and the warm golden leaves of the fountain grass extend the show into fall. When it's cold, enjoy the view from the house of the crape myrtle's striking bark. Papery dry grasses are also a pretty sight under a light snow.

A **'Natchez' crape myrtle**
Lagerstroemia indica (use 4 plants)
These small multitrunked trees provide shade and long-blooming papery white flowers in summer, good fall color, and flaky brown bark in winter. Plant bulbs around the base of the trees for a spring display.

B **Dwarf fountain grass** *Pennisetum alopecuroides* 'Hameln (use 6)
Framing the passage from patio to backyard, the arching leaves of this

perennial grass turn from summer green to autumn gold. Fluffy flower spikes wave above the foliage in late summer.

C **'Autumn Joy' sedum**
Sedum (use 6)
Large flat clusters of flower buds form atop the fleshy green foliage of this perennial in late summer. The flowers last for weeks, darkening from pale pink to rust, and the dry stalks remain standing in winter.

D **'Butterfly Blue' pincushion flower**
Scabiosa columbaria (use 14)
Tucked under the crape myrtles, these neat, compact perennials produce abundant blue flowers from May to hard frost. They make great cut flowers as well as attract butterflies.

E **'Dropmore' catmint**
Nepeta x faassenii (use 5)
This perennial's loose mounds of gray-green aromatic foliage with lavender-blue flower spikes contrast handsomely with nearby sedum. Blooms from June until frost if you shear off the spent flowers occasionally.

F **'Moonbeam' coreopsis**
Coreopsis verticillata (use 12)
A delightful perennial for the edge of the patio. Pale yellow flowers cover mounds of delicate ferny foliage from mid-summer into September.

G **'Purple Dome' aster**
Aster novae-angliae (use 3)
On dense mounds of dark green foliage this perennial bursts into bloom in early fall, drenched in small purple flowers for a month. Its round form contrasts with the spiky veronica nearby.

H **'Sunny Border Blue' veronica**
Veronica (use 5)
Beautiful spikes of tiny deep blue flowers shoot up all summer from this perennial's basal clump of shiny dark green leaves.

I **Patio**
Flagstones or pavers would look good here, too, but would make the curve more difficult to lay.

'Sunny Border **H**
Blue' veronica

F 'Moonbeam' coreopsis

C 'Autumn Joy' sedum

E 'Dropmore' catmint

G 'Purple Dome' aster

1 square = 1 ft.

Lawn

I Patio

C 'Autumn Joy' sedum

E 'Dropmore' catmint

Site: Sunny

Season: Late summer

Concept: Planting provides privacy and ambiance for entertaining guests or an early-morning cup of coffee on your own.

Note: All plants are appropriate for USDA Hardiness *Zones 5, 6, and 7.*

Make a No-Mow Slope

A terraced grove transforms a steep site

A Kousa dogwood

Site: Sunny

Season: Early summer

Concept: Retaining walls and a low-maintenance planting of trees and shrubs tame this slope.

See site plan for **G**.

F Lady's mantle

C 'Little Princess' Japanese spirea

'Boule de Neige' rhododendron **B**

E Dwarf plumbago

D 'Bronxensis' greenstem forsythia

H Retaining wall

Note: All plants are appropriate for USDA Hardiness *Zones 5, 6, and 7.*

oved by children with sleds, steep slopes can be a landscape headache for adults. They're a chore to mow, and they can present problems of erosion and maintenance if you try to establish other ground covers or plantings. One solution to this dilemma is shown here—tame the slope with low retaining walls, and plant the resulting flat (or flatter) beds with interesting low-care shrubs and perennials.

Steep slopes near the house are common on houses with walk-out basements or lower-level garages. Here, two low retaining walls create three terraces that mirror the curve of the driveway. A perennial ground cover and low-growing shrub carpet the lower and middle levels. On the top level, two small multistemmed trees and an informal underplanting of shrubs and perennials give the appearance of a small grove. Farther from the house, where the pitch of the slope lessens, the upper-level shrubs spill down the hill, marking the transition to the front lawn.

The planting is attractive whether viewed from above or below, providing good-looking flowers and foliage from spring through fall and a tracery of woody branches through the winter. When viewed from the sidewalk, it frames the house and directs attention to the front entrance. It also screens the semiprivate area of drive and garage from the more public entrance. The planting can be easily extended along the facade of the house with the addition of more rhododendrons and hostas.

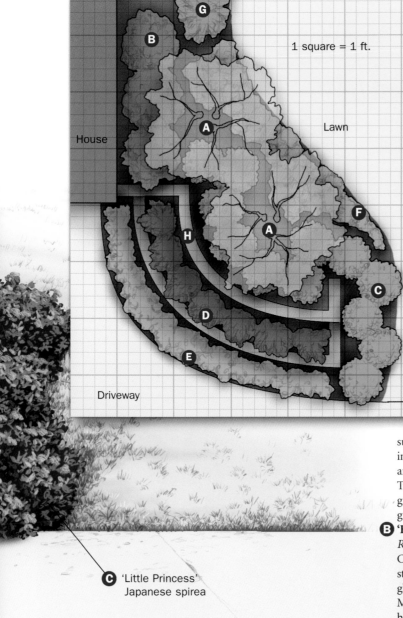

1 square = 1 ft.

House

Lawn

Driveway

C 'Little Princess' Japanese spirea

Plants & Projects

Building the retaining walls, reshaping the slope, and preparing the planting beds is a big job, so you might want to line up some energetic helpers or hire someone with a small earthmover like a Bobcat. Once that job is done and the plants are established, this design will provide years of enjoyment and needs almost no maintenance—just snap the fading flowers off the rhododendrons in June, and trim the lady's mantle and spireas in early spring. Underplanting with spring bulbs is optional, but it's an easy way to add lots more color.

A Kousa dogwood
Cornus kousa
(use 2 plants)
This small deciduous tree offers large creamy flowers for many weeks in early summer, showy edible fruits in late summer, bright fall foliage, and colorful flaky bark in winter. Two multitrunked trees will give the appearance of a small grove.

B 'Boule de Neige' rhododendron
Rhododendron (use 3)
Clusters of striking white flowers stand out against this shrub's glossy dark evergreen foliage in May or June. Its tidy rounded habit looks good against the house.

C 'Little Princess' Japanese spirea
Spiraea japonica (use 12)
A staggered row of these neat, low deciduous shrubs makes a casual edging along the upper wall. Pretty foliage topped with lots of pink flowers in June.

D 'Bronxensis' greenstem forsythia
Forsythia viridissima (use 7)
Low-growing deciduous shrub forms a tangle of attractive glossy foliage that will cascade over the lower wall with a little training. Pale yellow flowers in midspring.

E Dwarf plumbago *Ceratostigma plumbaginoides* (use 66)
Small blue flowers cover the dark green leaves of this perennial ground cover all summer. Foliage turns crimson in fall. Dies down in winter, so snow from the driveway won't hurt it. You can plant drifts of daffodils or other bulbs in the same bed; they will have plenty of time to bloom before the plumbago leafs out in May.

F Lady's mantle
Alchemilla mollis (use 30)
Broad mounds of this perennial's attractive pleated leaves make an informal edging by the lawn. Billows of chartreuse flowers in summer. Underplant with drifts of white daffodils.

G 'Royal Standard' hosta
Hosta (use 3)
The arching clusters of this perennial's green leaves stay fresh even in the sun. Fragrant trumpetlike white flowers bloom on tall stems in August and September. Underplant with pink tulips, which will bloom above emerging hosta foliage.

H Retaining wall
Curving walls built of prefabricated blocks are 18 in. tall, 4 ft. apart.

Plan #211076

Dimensions: 95' W x 90' D
Levels: 2
Square Footage: 4,242
Main Level Sq. Ft.: 3,439
Upper Level Sq. Ft.: 803
Bedrooms: 4
Bathrooms: 4 full, 3 half
Foundation: Raised slab
Materials List Available: Yes
Price Category: I

Images provided by designer/architect.

Build this country manor home on a large lot with a breathtaking view to complement its beauty.

Features:

- Foyer: You'll love the two-story ceiling here.
- Living Room: A sunken floor, two-story ceiling, large fireplace, and generous balcony above combine to create an unusually beautiful room.
- Kitchen: Use the breakfast bar at any time of the day. The layout guarantees ample working space, and the pantry gives room for extra storage.

- Master Suite: A sunken floor, wood-burning fireplace, and 200-sq.-ft. sitting area work in concert to create a restful space.
- Bedrooms: The guest room is on the main floor, and bedrooms 2 and 3, both with built-in desks in special study areas, are on the upper level.
- Outdoor Grilling Area: Fitted with a bar, this area makes it a pleasure to host a large group.

Kitchen

Kitchen

Main Level Floor Plan

garage
22 x 22

sto 15 x 6

sto

veranda

outdoor grill & bar

suggested pool & spa location

sto 12 x 7

frz

eating

porch

sunken mbr
18 x 12
fireplace

lin

shr

wic

sitting rm
17 x 12

porte cochere
12 x 20

w
d

util

ct

ref

kit
21 x 13

ov

dw

pan

sunken living room
24 x 20

a/c

wh

study
17 x 16

clo

clo

clo

shvs

clo

up

dining
17 x 13

foyer
24 x 10

guest br
17 x 13

porch 24 x 8

Copyright by designer/architect.

Master Bathroom

Upper Level Floor Plan

balcony por

balcony & Library

to attic

books

books

to attic

br 3
12 x 12

open to living room below

dn

dn

br 4
12 x 12

clo

study area

desk

open to foyer below

desk

study area

clo

Dining Room

Living Room

Plan #221015

Dimensions: 69'8" W x 46' D

Levels: 1

Square Footage: 1,926

Bedrooms: 3

Bathrooms: 2½

Foundation: Basement; optional walk-out basement available for fee

Materials List Available: No

Price Category: D

Images provided by designer/architect.

You'll love the open plan in this lovely ranch and admire its many features, which are usually reserved for much larger homes.

Features:

- Ceiling Height: 8 ft.

- Great Room: A vaulted ceiling and tall windows surrounding the centrally located fireplace give distinction to this handsome room.

- Dining Room: Positioned just off the entry, this formal room makes a lovely spot for quiet dinner parties.

- Dining Nook: This nook sits between the kitchen and the great room. Central doors in the bayed area open to the backyard.

- Kitchen: An island will invite visitors while you cook in this well-planned kitchen, with its corner pantry and ample counter space.

- Master Suite: A tray ceiling, bay window, walk-in closet, and bath with whirlpool tub, dual-sink vanity, and standing shower pamper you here.

Rear Elevation

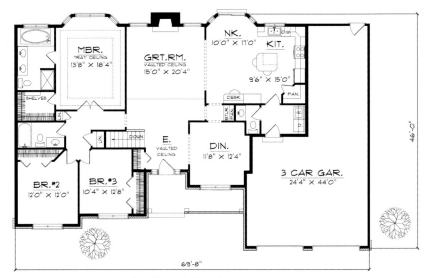

Copyright by designer/architect.

Plan #161086

Dimensions: 65'8" W x 52'8" D
Levels: 2
Square Footage: 3,610
Main Level Sq. Ft.: 1,838
Upper Level Sq. Ft.: 1,772
Bedrooms: 4
Bathrooms: 3½
Foundation: Walkout basement, optional basement available for fee
Materials List Available: Yes
Price Category: H

Images provided by designer/architect.

A brick-and-stone exterior gives a rich, solid look to this beautiful two-story home.

Features:

- **Dining Room:** Just off the foyer is this dining room, which features a dropped soffit at the ceiling to create depth.

- **Great Room:** This sunken room has a fireplace and access to the rear deck.

- **Kitchen:** This large island work space is open to the breakfast area and has a large built-in pantry.

- **Master Suite:** This private retreat features a sloped ceiling in the sleeping area. The master bath boasts a compartmentalized lavatory, large shower, soaking tub, and walk-in closet.

- **Bedrooms:** Three additional bedrooms are located on the on the second floor with the master suite. Two of the bedrooms share a Jack-and-Jill bathroom. The third bedroom has a private bathroom.

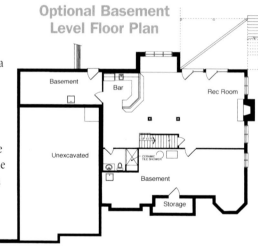

Optional Basement Level Floor Plan

Copyright by designer/architect.

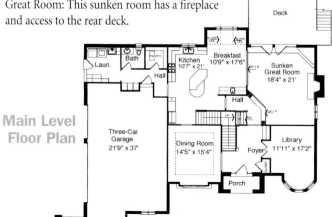

Main Level Floor Plan

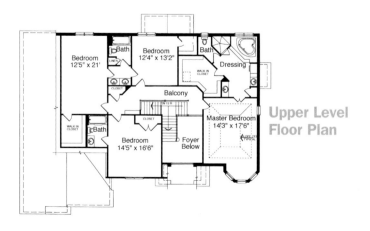

Upper Level Floor Plan

Plan #121079

Dimensions: 50' W x 60' D

Levels: 2

Square Footage: 2,688

Main Level Sq. Ft.: 1,650

Upper Level Sq. Ft.: 1,038

Bedrooms: 4

Bathrooms: 3½

Foundation: Slab

Materials List Available: Yes

Price Category: F

Images provided by designer/architect.

You'll love this open design if you're looking for a home that gives a spacious feeling while also providing private areas.

Features:

- **Entry:** The cased openings and corner columns here give an attractive view into the dining room.

- **Living Room:** Another cased opening defines the entry to this living room but lets traffic flow into it.

- **Kitchen:** This well-designed kitchen is built around a center island that gives you extra work space. A snack bar makes an easy, open transition between the sunny dining nook and the kitchen.

- **Master Suite:** An 11-ft. ceiling sets the tone for this private space. With a walk-in closet and adjoining full bath, it will delight you.

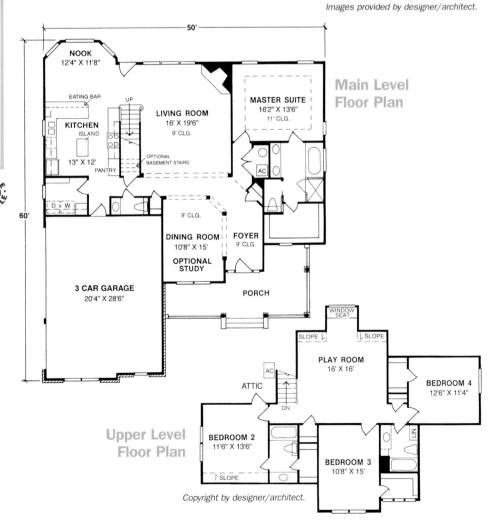

Copyright by designer/architect.

Plan #161101

Dimensions: 136'3" W x 69' D
Levels: 2
Square Footage: 8,414
Main Level Sq. Ft.: 4,011
Upper Level Sq. Ft.: 2,198
Optional Lower Level Sq. Ft.: 2,205
Bedrooms: 4
Bathrooms: 4 full, 2 half
Foundation: Walkout; basement for fee
Material List Available: Yes
Price Category: L

CAD FILE AVAILABLE · CAD ·

The grandeur of this mansion-style home boasts period stone, two-story columns, an angular turret, a second-floor balcony, and a gated courtyard.

Features:

• Formal Living: Formal areas consist of the charming living room and adjacent music room, which continues to the library, with its sloped ceilings and glass surround. Various ceiling treatments, with 10-ft. ceiling heights,

and 8-ft.-tall doors add luxury and artistry to the first floor.

• Hearth Room: This large room, with false wood-beamed ceiling, adds a casual yet rich atmosphere to the family gathering space. Dual French doors on each side of the fireplace create a pleasurable indoor-outdoor relationship.

• Kitchen: This space is an enviable work place for the gourmet cook. Multiple cabinets and expansive counter space create a room that may find you spending a surprisingly enjoyable amount of time on food preparation. The built-in grill on the porch makes

outdoor entertaining convenient and fun.

• Master Suite: This suite offers a vaulted ceiling, dual walk-in closets, and his and her vanities. The whirlpool tub is showcased on a platform and surrounded by windows for a relaxing view of the side yard. Private access to the deck is an enchanting surprise.

Images provided by designer/architect.

Rear View

Copyright by designer/architect.

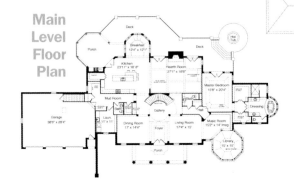

Main Level Floor Plan

Upper Level Floor Plan

Basement Level Floor Plan

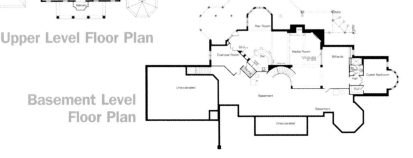

Plan #121091

Dimensions: 56' W x 50' D
Levels: 2
Square Footage: 2,689
Main Level Sq. Ft.: 1,415
Upper Level Sq. Ft.: 1,214
Bedrooms: 4
Bathrooms: 2½
Foundation: Basement
Materials List Available: Yes
Price Category: F

Images provided by designer/architect.

You'll love the unusual details that make this home as elegant as it is comfortable.

Features:

• Entry: This two-story entry is filled with natural light that streams in through the sidelights and transom window.

• Den: To the right of the entry, French doors open to this room, with its 11-ft. high, spider-beamed ceiling. A triple-wide,

transom-topped window brightens this room during the daytime.

• Family Room: A fireplace and built-in entertainment center add comfort to this room, and the cased opening to the kitchen area makes it convenient.

• Kitchen: With an adjoining breakfast area, this kitchen is another natural gathering spot.

Main Level Floor Plan

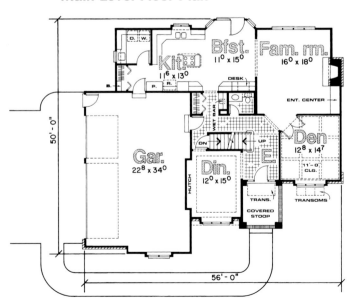

Upper Level Floor Plan

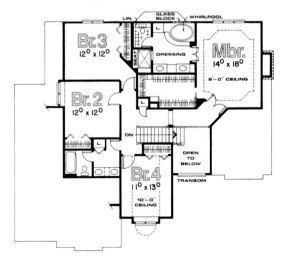

Copyright by designer/architect.

Main Level Floor Plan

Plan #341052

Dimensions: 63' W x 35' D

Levels: 1.5

Square Footage: 1,275

Main Level Sq. Ft.: 1,275

Bonus Unfinished Sq. Ft.: 473

Bedrooms: 3

Bathrooms: 2

Foundation: Crawl space

Materials List Available: No

Price Category: B

Images provided by designer/architect.

Bonus Area

Copyright by designer/architect.

Plan #211150

Dimensions: 86' W x 86' D

Levels: 2

Square Footage: 3,970

Main Level Sq. Ft.: 3,086

Upper Level Sq. Ft.: 884

Bedrooms: 4

Bathrooms: 3 full, 2 half

Foundation: Slab

Materials List Available: No

Price Category: H

Images provided by designer/architect.

Main Level Floor Plan

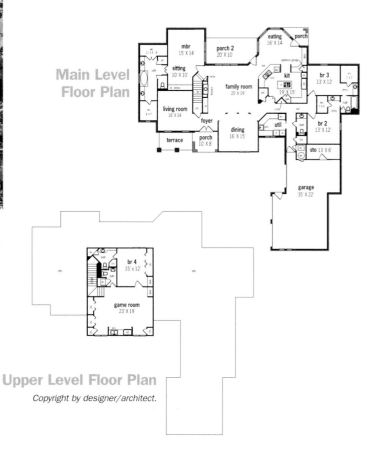

Upper Level Floor Plan

Copyright by designer/architect.

Plan #121085

Dimensions: 42' W x 54' D
Levels: 2
Square Footage: 1,948
Main Level Sq. Ft.: 1,517
Upper Level Sq. Ft.: 431
Bedrooms: 4
Bathrooms: 3
Foundation: Basement
Materials List Available: Yes
Price Category: D

You'll love the spacious feeling in this home, with its generous rooms and excellent design.

Features:

- Great Room: This room is lofty and open, thanks in part to the transom-topped windows that flank the fireplace. However, you can furnish to create a cozy nook for reading or a private spot to watch TV or enjoy some quiet music.

- Kitchen: Wrapping counters add an unusual touch to this kitchen, and a pantry gives extra storage area. A snack bar links the kitchen with a separate breakfast area.

- Master Suite: A tiered ceiling adds elegance to this area, and a walk-in closet adds practicality. The private bath features a sunlit whirlpool tub, separate shower, and double vanity.

Images provided by designer/architect.

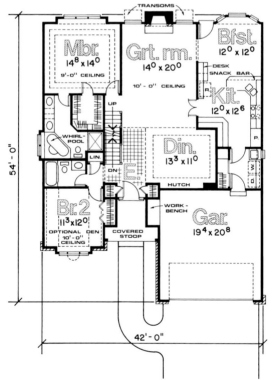

Main Level Floor Plan

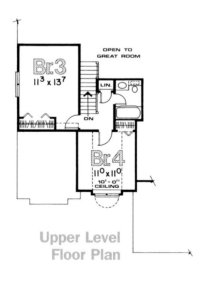

Upper Level Floor Plan

Copyright by designer/architect.

- Upper-Level Bedrooms: The upper-level placement is just right for these bedrooms, which share an amenity-filled full bathroom.

Plan #131009

Dimensions: 64'10" W x 57'8" D
Levels: 1
Square Footage: 2,018
Bedrooms: 3
Bathrooms: 2
Foundation: Crawl space, slab, or basement
Materials List Available: Yes
Price Category: D

Images provided by designer/architect.

The pavilion-styled great room at the heart of this H-shaped ranch gives it an unusual elegance that you're sure to enjoy.

Features:

- Great Room: The tray ceiling sets off this room, and a fireplace warms it on chilly nights and cool days. Two sets of sliding glass doors leading to the backyard terrace let in natural light and create an efficient traffic flow.

- Kitchen: Designed for a gourmet cook, this kitchen features a snack bar that everyone will enjoy and easy access to the breakfast room.

- Breakfast Room: Open to the columned rear porch, this breakfast room is an ideal spot for company or family brunches.

- Master Suite: A sitting area and access to the porch make the bedroom luxurious, while the private bath featuring a whirlpool tub creates a spa atmosphere.

Copyright by designer/architect.

Great Room

Plan #131044

Dimensions: 57'6" W x 42'4" D
Levels: 1
Square Footage: 1,994
Bedrooms: 3
Bathrooms: 2
Foundation: Crawl space, slab, or basement
Materials List Available: Yes
Price Category: E

Images provided by designer/architect.

Under a covered porch, Victorian-detailed bay windows grace each side of the brick-faced facade at the center of this ranch-style home, giving it a formal air.

Features:

• Ceiling Height: 10-ft. ceilings grace the central living area and the master bedroom of this home.

• Entry: Round top windows make this area and the flanking rooms bright and cheery.

• Great Room: A fireplace and built-ins that are visible from anywhere in this large room make it a natural gathering place for friends and family.

• Optional Office: Use the room just off the central hall as a home office, fourth bedroom, or study.

• Master Suite: You'll love the bay window, tray ceiling, two walk-in closets, and private bath.

• Bonus Space: Finish this large area in the attic for extra living space, or use it for storage.

Rear Elevation

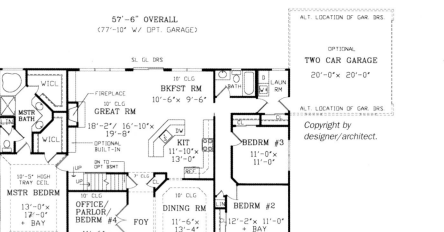

Copyright by designer/architect.

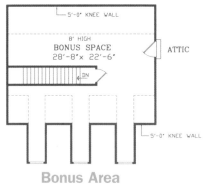

Bonus Area

Plan #121080

Dimensions: 56' W x 49' D
Levels: 2
Square Footage: 2,384
Main Level Sq. Ft.: 1,616
Upper Level Sq. Ft.: 768
Bedrooms: 4
Bathrooms: 2½
Foundation: Slab
Materials List Available: Yes
Price Category: E

This home, as shown in the photograph, may differ from the actual blueprints. For more detailed information, please check the floor plans carefully.

Images provided by designer/architect.

This design is ideal if you want a generously sized home now and room to expand later.

Features:

• Living Room: Your eyes will be drawn towards the ceiling as soon as you enter this lovely room. The ceiling is vaulted, giving a sense of grandeur, and a graceful balcony from the second floor adds extra interest to this room.

• Kitchen: Designed with lots of counter space to make your work convenient, this kitchen also shares an eating bar with the breakfast nook.

• Breakfast Nook: Eat here or go out to the adjoining private porch where you can enjoy your meal in the morning sunshine.

• Master Suite: The bayed area in the bedroom makes a picturesque sitting area. French doors in the bedroom open to a private bath that's fitted with a whirlpool tub, separate shower, two vanities, and a walk-in closet.

Main Level Floor Plan

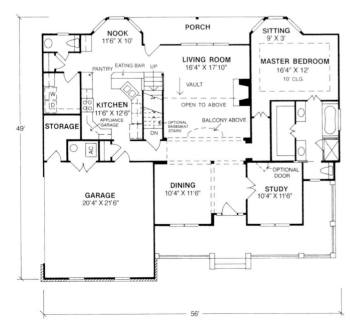

Upper Level Floor Plan

Copyright by designer/architect.

Plan #241013

Dimensions: 68' W x 46' D
Levels: 2
Square Footage: 2,779
Main Level Sq. Ft.: 1,918
Upper Level Sq. Ft.: 861
Bedrooms: 4
Bathrooms: 3½
Foundation: Crawl space, slab, basement or walkout
Materials List Available: No
Price Category: G

Images provided by designer/architect.

Main Level Floor Plan

Upper Level Floor Plan

Copyright by designer/architect.

Plan #181252

Dimensions: 92' W x 50' D
Levels: 2
Square Footage: 3,631
Main Level Sq. Ft.: 2,153
Upper Level Sq. Ft.: 1,478
Bedrooms: 3
Bathrooms: 3½
Foundation: Basement
Materials List Available: Yes
Price Category: H

Images provided by designer/architect.

Main Level Floor Plan

Upper Level Floor Plan

Copyright by designer/architect.

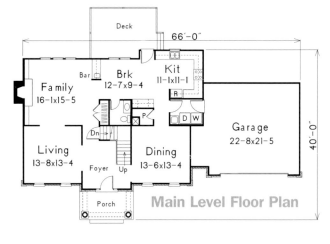

Main Level Floor Plan

Upper Level Floor Plan

Copyright by designer/architect.

Plan #321046

Dimensions: 66' W x 40' D
Levels: 2
Square Footage: 2,411
Main Level Sq. Ft.: 1,293
Upper Level Sq. Ft.: 1,118
Bedrooms: 3
Bathrooms: 2½
Foundation: Basement
Materials List Available: Yes
Price Category: E

Images provided by designer/architect.

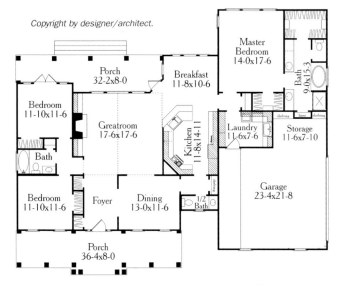

Copyright by designer/architect.

Plan #311004

Dimensions: 68'2" W x 57'4" D
Levels: 1
Square Footage: 2,046
Bedrooms: 3
Bathrooms: 2½
Foundation: Basement, crawl space, or slab
Materials List Available: Yes
Price Category: D

Images provided by designer/architect.

Rear View

Plan #221018

Dimensions: 67' W x 53' D

Levels: 1

Square Footage: 2,007

Bedrooms: 3

Bathrooms: 2

Foundation: Basement

Materials List Available: No

Price Category: D

Images provided by designer/architect.

Rear Elevation

You'll love this ranch design, with its traditional stucco facade and interesting roofline.

Features:

- Ceiling Height: 9 ft.

- Great Room: A cathedral ceiling points up the large dimensions of this room, and the handsome fireplace with tall flanking windows lets you decorate for a formal or a casual feeling.

- Dining Room: A tray ceiling imparts elegance to this room, and a butler's pantry just across from the kitchen area lets you serve in style.

- Kitchen: You'll love the extensive counter space in this well-designed kitchen. The adjoining nook is large enough for a full-size dining set and features a door to the outside deck, where you can set up a third dining area.

- Master Suite: Located away from the other bedrooms for privacy, this suite includes a huge walk-in closet, windows overlooking the backyard, and a large bath with a whirlpool tub, standing shower, and dual-sink vanity.

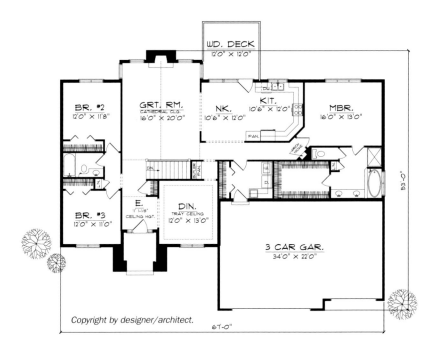

Copyright by designer/architect.

Images provided by designer/architect.

Plan #151669

Dimensions: 48' W x 48' D
Levels: 1
Square Footage: 1,381
Bedrooms: 3
Bathrooms: 2
Foundation: Crawl space, slab, basement, or walkout
CompleteCost List Available: Yes
Price Category: B

This adorable home is perfect for family gatherings and unexpected visits from friends.

Features:

- Great Room: This comfortable room accommodates everyone and features a gas fireplace and a 9-ft.-high boxed ceiling.

- Kitchen: This spacious work space will be most convenient when preparing those last minute details. The added peninsula allows you to serve breakfast for the children quickly.

- Master Suite: This suite provides distance from the children for retreat and relaxation when things get too hectic. The master bath boasts a double vanity.

- Bedrooms: One bedroom offers a spacious walk-in closet, and the other features a vaulted ceiling.

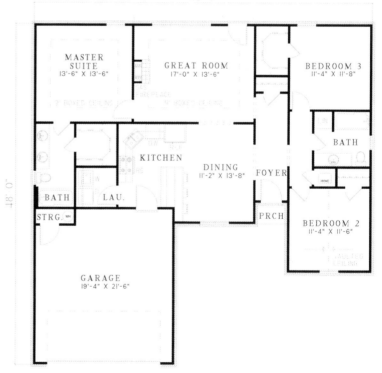

Copyright by designer/architect.

Plan #151633

Dimensions: 59'6" W x 64'2" D
Levels: 1
Square Footage: 2,486
Bedrooms: 4
Bathrooms: 3
Foundation: Crawl space or slab
CompleteCost List Available: Yes
Price Category: E

Images provided by designer/architect.

A charming exterior gives this home excellent curb appeal.

Features:

- Entry: Round columns on the front porch welcome your guests into this beautiful foyer.

- Great Room: This spacious room, with its optional built-ins and a gas fireplace, is sure to be the envy of all who see it.

- Kitchen: With this step-saving kitchen, adjoining breakfast room, and nearby grilling porch, the lack of space will never be an issue when it comes to entertaining or family gatherings.

- Master Suite: This suite is privately tucked away on the opposite side of this home and features a 10-ft.-high boxed ceiling. The bath boasts a walk-in closet, split vanities, and a corner whirlpool tub.

- Bedrooms: Two additional bedrooms with a shared bathroom and a guest room lend to plenty of sleeping accommodations.

Copyright by designer/architect.

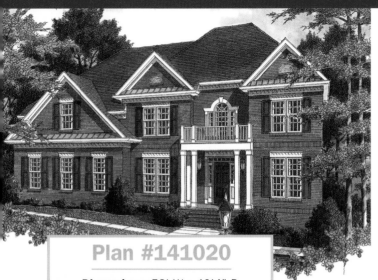

Plan #141020

Dimensions: 58' W x 40'4" D
Levels: 2
Square Footage: 3,140
Main Level Sq. Ft.: 1,553
Upper Level Sq. Ft.: 1,587
Bedrooms: 5
Bathrooms: 4
Foundation: Basement
Materials List Available: No
Price Category: G

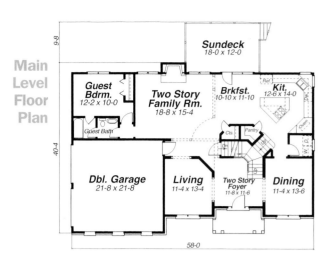

Images provided by designer/architect.

Main Level Floor Plan

Guest Bdrm. 12-2 x 10-0
Guest Bath
Two Story Family Rm. 18-8 x 15-4
Brkfst. 10-10 x 11-10
Kit. 12-6 x 14-0
Sundeck 18-0 x 12-0
Dbl. Garage 21-8 x 21-8
Living 11-4 x 13-4
Two Story Foyer 11-8 x 11-6
Dining 11-4 x 13-6

Upper Level Floor Plan

Copyright by designer/architect.

M. Bath
Two Story Family Rm.
Bdrm.4 13-2 x 11-8
Master Bdrm. 15-8 x 15-8
Bdrm.2 11-6 x 13-6
Two Story Foyer
Bdrm.3 11-6 x 13-8
Sitting 6-0 x 9-8

Plan #141028

Dimensions: 48' W x 36'4" D
Levels: 2
Square Footage: 2,215
Main Level Sq. Ft.: 1,075
Upper Level Sq. Ft.: 1,140
Bedrooms: 4
Bathrooms: 3
Foundation: Basement
Materials List Available: Yes
Price Category: E

Images provided by designer/architect.

This home, as shown in the photograph, may differ from the actual blueprints. For more detailed information, please check the floor plans carefully.

Main Level Floor Plan

Patio / Sundeck
Bdrm.4 11^0 x 12^0
Two Story Living 16^4 x 14^6
Brkfst. 10^0 x 13^4
Kitchen 9^8 x 13^4
Bath 3
Open Foyer 7^2 x 11^{10}
Dining 10^8 x 12^{10}
Pantry Ref.
Double Garage 19^4 x 21^8

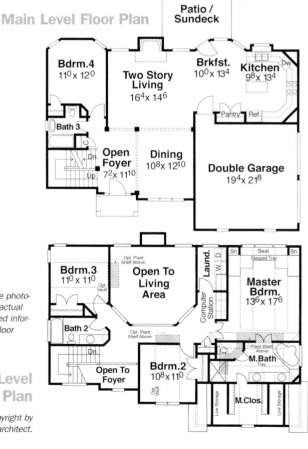

Upper Level Floor Plan

Copyright by designer/architect.

Bdrm.3 11^0 x 11^0
Open To Living Area
Laund. W. D.
Master Bdrm. 13^6 x 17^6
Bath 2
Computer Station
M.Bath
Open To Foyer
Bdrm.2 10^8 x 11^0
M.Clos.

Main Level Floor Plan

Upper Level Floor Plan

Images provided by designer/architect.

Copyright by designer/architect.

Plan #181255

Dimensions: 60' W x 46' D
Levels: 2
Square Footage: 2,577
Main Level Sq. Ft.: 1,337
Upper Level Sq. Ft.: 1,240
Bedrooms: 4
Bathrooms: 2½
Foundation: Basement
Materials List Available: Yes
Price Category: E

Main Level Floor Plan

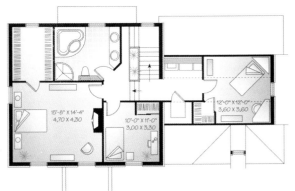

Upper Level Floor Plan

Images provided by designer/architect.

Copyright by designer/architect.

Plan #181273

Dimensions: 48' W x 28' D
Levels: 2
Square Footage: 1,889
Main Level Sq. Ft.: 908
Upper Level Sq. Ft.: 981
Bedrooms: 3
Bathrooms: 2
Foundation: Basement
Materials List Available: Yes
Price Category: D

Plan #271013

Dimensions: 43' W x 45'8" D
Levels: 2
Square Footage: 1,498
Main Level Sq. Ft.: 1,044
Upper Level Sq. Ft.: 454
Bedrooms: 2
Bathrooms: 2½
Foundation: Basement
Materials List Available: Yes
Price Category: B

Images provided by designer/architect.

CAD FILE AVAILABLE

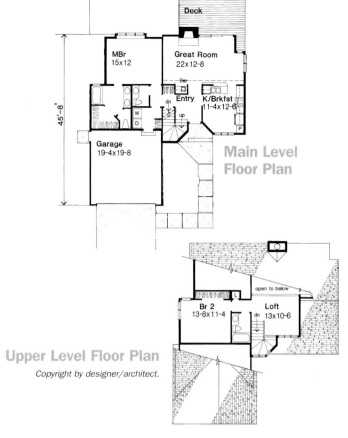

Main Level Floor Plan

Upper Level Floor Plan

Copyright by designer/architect.

Plan #261001

Dimensions: 77'8" W x 49' D
Levels: 2
Square Footage: 3,746
Main Level Sq. Ft.: 1,965
Upper Level Sq. Ft.: 1,781
Bedrooms: 4
Bathrooms: 3½
Foundation: Basement
Materials List Available: No
Price Category: H

Images provided by designer/architect.

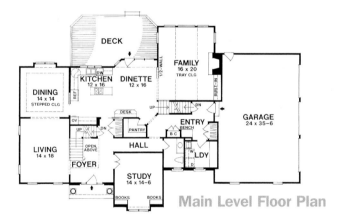

Main Level Floor Plan

Upper Level Floor Plan

Copyright by designer/architect.

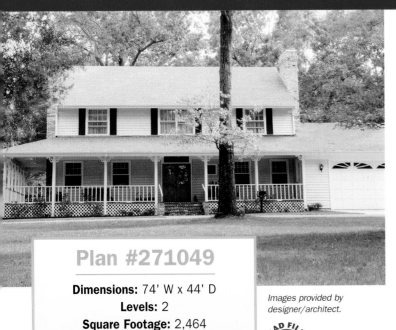

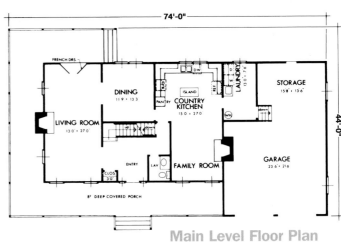

74'-0"

44'-0"

Main Level Floor Plan

Images provided by designer/architect.

Plan #271049

Dimensions: 74' W x 44' D
Levels: 2
Square Footage: 2,464
Main Level Sq. Ft.: 1,288
Upper Level Sq. Ft.: 1,176
Bedrooms: 4
Bathrooms: 2½
Foundation: Basement, crawl space
Materials List Available: Yes
Price Category: E

Upper Level Floor Plan

Copyright by designer/architect.

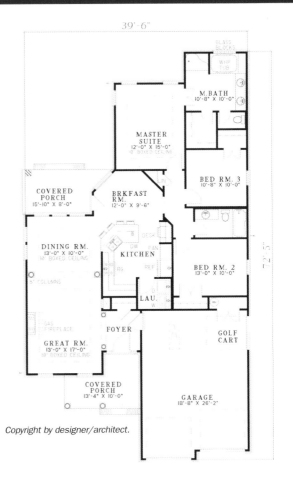

39'-6"

Images provided by designer/architect.

Plan #151337

Dimensions: 39'6" W x 72'5" D
Levels: 1
Square Footage: 1,504
Bedrooms: 3
Bathrooms: 2
Foundation: Crawl space or slab
CompleteCost List Available: Yes
Price Category: C

Copyright by designer/architect.

Plan #151037

Dimensions: 50' W x 56' D

Levels: 1

Square Footage: 1,538

Bedrooms: 3

Bathrooms: 2

Foundation: Crawl space, slab, or basement

CompleteCost List Available: Yes

Price Category: C

Images provided by designer/architect.

You'll love this traditional-looking home, with its covered porch and interesting front windows.

Features:

- Ceiling Height: 8 ft.

- Great Room: This large room has a boxed window that emphasizes its dimensions and a fireplace where everyone will gather on chilly evenings. A door opens to the backyard.

- Dining Room: A bay window overlooking the front porch makes this room easy to decorate.

- Kitchen: This well-planned kitchen features ample counter space, a full pantry, and an eating bar that it shares with the dining room.

- Master Suite: A pan ceiling in this lovely room gives an elegant touch. The huge private bath includes two walk-in closets, a whirlpool tub, a dual-sink vanity, and a skylight in the ceiling.

- Additional Bedrooms: On the opposite side of the house, these bedrooms share a large bath, and both feature excellent closet space.

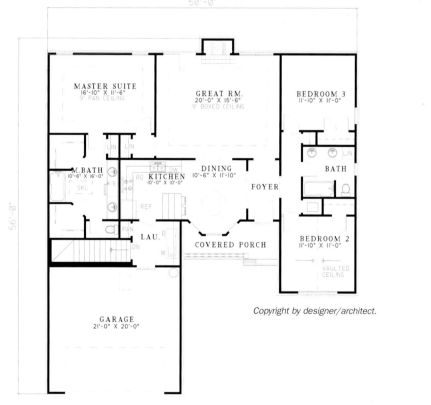

Copyright by designer/architect.

Plan #161020

Dimensions: 60' W" x 50'4" D

Levels: 2

Square Footage: 2,082; 2,349 with bonus space

Main Level Sq. Ft.: 1,524

Upper Level Sq. Ft.: 558

Bedrooms: 3

Bathrooms: 2½

Foundation: Basement

Materials List Available: Yes

Price Category: D

Images provided by designer/architect.

You'll love the textured exterior finish and interesting roofline of this charming home.

Features:

- **Great Room:** Here you can enjoy the cozy fireplace, 12-ft. ceilings, and stylish French doors.

- **Dining Room:** A grand entry prepares you for the sloped ceiling that gives charm to this room.

- **Kitchen:** Natural light floods both the well-designed kitchen and adjacent breakfast room.

- **Master Suite:** Located on the first floor, this area boasts a whirlpool tub, a double-bowl vanity, and a large walk-in closet.

- **Upper Level:** Split stairs lead to a balcony over the foyer, a computer/study area, and two additional bedrooms.

- **Bonus Room:** Use this 267-sq.-ft. area over the garage for storage or a fourth bedroom.

Main Level Floor Plan

Upper Level Floor Plan

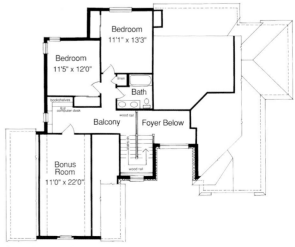

Copyright by designer/architect.

Plan #121066

Dimensions: 46' W x 41'5" D
Levels: 2
Square Footage: 2,078
Main Level Sq. Ft.: 1,113
Upper Level Sq. Ft.: 965
Bedrooms: 4
Bathrooms: 2½
Foundation: Basement
Materials List Available: Yes
Price Category: D

Images provided by designer/architect.

This lovely home has an unusual dignity, perhaps because its rooms are so well-proportioned and thoughtfully laid out.

Features:

- Family Room: This room is sunken, giving it an unusually cozy, comfortable feeling. Its abundance of windows let natural light stream in during the day, and the fireplace warms it when the weather's chilly.

- Dining Room: This dining room links to the parlor beyond through a cased opening.

- Parlor: A tall, angled ceiling highlights a large, arched window that's the focal point of this room.

- Breakfast Area: A wooden rail visually links this bayed breakfast area to the family room.

- Master Suite: A roomy walk-in closet adds a practical touch to this luxurious suite. The bath features a skylight, whirlpool tub, and separate shower.

Main Level Floor Plan

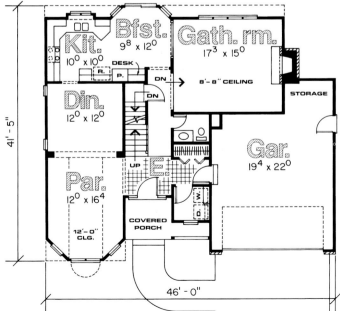

Upper Level Floor Plan

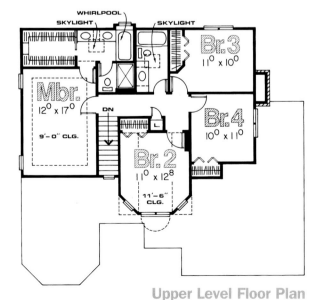

Copyright by designer/architect.

Plan #151031

Dimensions: 60'2" W x 60'2" D
Levels: 2
Square Footage: 3,130
Main Level Sq. Ft.: 1,600
Upper Level Sq. Ft.: 1,530
Bedrooms: 3
Bathrooms: 3½
Foundation: Crawl space, slab
CompleteCost List Available: Yes
Price Category: G

Images provided by designer/architect.

If you love traditional Southern plantation homes, you'll want this house with its wraparound porches that are graced with boxed columns.

Features:

- **Great Room:** Use the gas fireplace for warmth in this comfortable room, which is open to the kitchen.

- **Living Room:** 8-in. columns add formality as you enter this living and dining room.

- **Kitchen:** You'll love the island bar with a sink. An elevator here can take you to the other floors.

- **Master Suite:** A gas fireplace warms this area, and the bath is luxurious.

- **Bedrooms:** Each has a private bath and built-in bookshelves for easy organizing.

- **Optional Features:** Choose a 2,559-sq.-ft. basement and add a kitchen to it, or finish the 1,744-sq.-ft. bonus room and add a spiral staircase and a bath.

Main Level Floor Plan

Upper Level Floor Plan

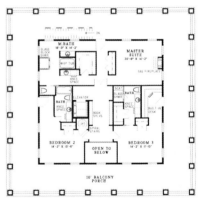

Basement Level Floor Plan

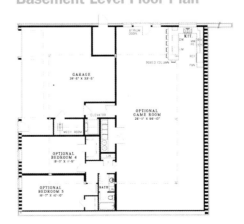

Optional Upper Level Floor Plan

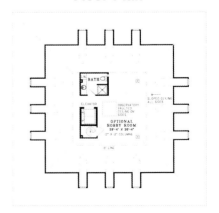

Plan #151113

Dimensions: 62'10" W x 91'4" D
Levels: 1
Square Footage: 2,186
Bedrooms: 4
Bathrooms: 3
Foundation: Crawl space, slab, or basement
CompleteCost List Available: Yes
Price Category: D

Images provided by designer/architect.

Optional Bonus Area Floor Plan

Copyright by designer/architect.

Plan #121086

Dimensions: 55'4" W x 37'8" D
Levels: 2
Square Footage: 1,998
Main Level Sq. Ft.: 1,093
Upper Level Sq. Ft.: 905
Bedrooms: 3
Bathrooms: 2½
Foundation: Basement
Materials List Available: Yes
Price Category: D

Images provided by designer/architect.

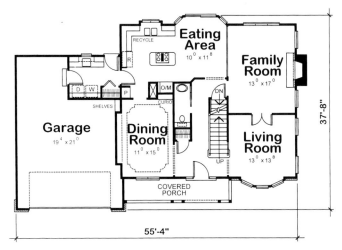

Main Level Floor Plan

Upper Level Floor Plan

Copyright by designer/architect.

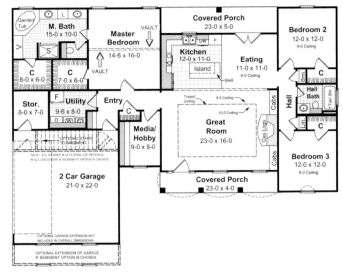

Plan #351003

Dimensions: 64' W x 45'10" D

Levels: 1

Square Footage: 1,751

Bedrooms: 3

Bathrooms: 2

Foundation: Crawl space, slab, or basement

Materials List Available: Yes

Price Category: C

Images provided by designer/architect.

CAD FILE AVAILABLE

Copyright by designer/architect.

Plan #181278

Dimensions: 54' W x 36' D

Levels: 1

Square Footage: 1,423

Bedrooms: 2

Bathrooms: 1

Foundation: Basement

Materials List Available: Yes

Price Category: B

Images provided by designer/architect.

CAD FILE AVAILABLE

Copyright by designer/architect.

Plan #111018

Dimensions: 67' W x 79' D

Levels: 1

Square Footage: 2,745

Bedrooms: 4

Bathrooms: 3½

Foundation: Basement

Materials List Available: No

Price Category: F

Images provided by designer/architect.

Rear Elevation

Copyright by designer/architect.

Plan #321010

Dimensions: 59' W x 37'8" D

Levels: 1

Square Footage: 1,787

Bedrooms: 3

Bathrooms: 2

Foundation: Basement

Materials List Available: Yes

Price Category: C

Images provided by designer/architect.

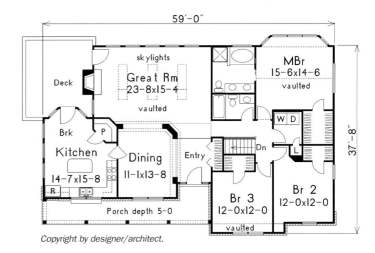

Copyright by designer/architect.

SMARTtip

Country Décor in Your Bathroom

Collections are often part of a country decor, even in the bathroom. All you need is three or more of anything that have size, shape, or color in common. You can mass them on walls, on shelves, on the windowsills, or even along the edge of the tub.

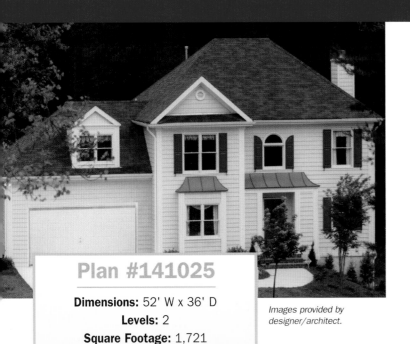

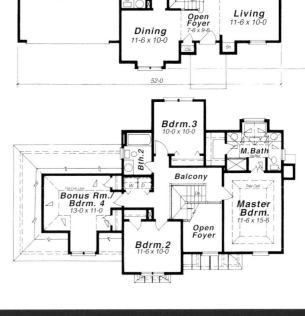

Main Level Floor Plan

Sundeck
15-6 x 12-0

Brkfst.
10-0 x 11-0

Kitchen
16-0 x 12-0

Family Rm.
16-0 x 13-6

Double Garage
19-8 x 19-4

Lav.

Living
11-6 x 10-0

Open
Foyer
7-6 x 9-6

Dining
11-6 x 10-0

36-0

52-0

Images provided by designer/architect.

Upper Level Floor Plan

Bdrm.3
10-0 x 10-0

Bth.2

M.Bath

Balcony

Bonus Rm./
Bdrm. 4
13-0 x 11-0

Master
Bdrm.
11-6 x 15-6

Open
Foyer

Bdrm.2
11-6 x 10-0

Copyright by designer/architect.

Plan #141025

Dimensions: 52' W x 36' D
Levels: 2
Square Footage: 1,721
Main Level Sq. Ft.: 902
Upper Level Sq. Ft.: 819
Bedrooms: 4
Bathrooms: 2½
Foundation: Basement
Materials List Available: Yes
Price Category: C

Main Level Floor Plan

Sundeck
21-0 x 12-0

Kitchen
12-6 x 13-4

Brkfst.
12-10 x 13-8

Living Area
20-0 x 13-4

Dining
13-0 x 14-8

Open
Foyer

Double Garage
19-8 x 21-4

38-4

Porch

46-0

Images provided by designer/architect.

Upper Level Floor Plan

M.Bath

Bdrm.3
13-0 x 10-10

Master
Bdrm.
13-0 x 18-6

W.D.

Bth.2

Open
To
Foyer

Bdrm.2
13-0 x 10-0

Copyright by designer/architect.

Plan #141027

Dimensions: 46' W x 38' D
Levels: 2
Square Footage: 2,088
Main Level Sq. Ft.: 1,048
Upper Level Sq. Ft.: 1,040
Bedrooms: 3
Bathrooms: 2½
Foundation: Basement
Materials List Available: Yes
Price Category: D

Plan #181256

Dimensions: 50'4" W x 45'4" D
Levels: 2
Square Footage: 2,245
Main Level Sq. Ft.: 1,229
Upper Level Sq. Ft.: 1,016
Bedrooms: 3
Bathrooms: 2½
Foundation: Basement
Materials List Available: Yes
Price Category: E

Images provided by designer/architect.

Main Level Floor Plan

Upper Level Floor Plan

Copyright by designer/architect.

Plan #181258

Dimensions: 45' W x 68'6" D
Levels: 2
Square Footage: 2,376
Main Level Sq. Ft.: 1,239
Upper Level Sq. Ft.: 1,137
Bedrooms: 4
Bathrooms: 2½
Foundation: Basement
Materials List Available: Yes
Price Category: E

Images provided by designer/architect.

Upper Level Floor Plan

Main Level Floor Plan

Copyright by designer/architect.

Plan #131026

Dimensions: 55'10" W x 41' D
Levels: 2
Square Footage: 2,796
Main Level Sq. Ft.: 1,481
Upper level Sq. Ft.: 1,315
Bedrooms: 4
Bathrooms: 2½
Foundation: Crawl space, slab, or basement
Materials List Available: Yes
Price Category: G

Images provided by designer/architect.

Handsome half rounds add to curb appeal.

Features:

- Ceiling Height: 8 ft.

- Library: This room features a 10-ft. ceiling with a bright bay window.

- Great Room: A 10-ft. ceiling adds to the spacious feeling of this room, while the corner fireplace gives it an intimate feeling. Sliding glass doors at the rear of the room open to the backyard.

- Dining Room: This formal room adjoins the great room, allowing guests and family to flow between the rooms, and it opens to the backyard through sliding glass doors.

- Breakfast Room: Turrets add a Victorian feeling to this room, which is just off the kitchen and overlooks the front porch.

- Master Suite: Privacy is assured in this suite, which is separated from the main part of the house. A compartmented bath and large walk-in closet add convenience to its beauty.

Master Bathroom

Family Room

Rear
Elevation

Upper Level Floor Plan

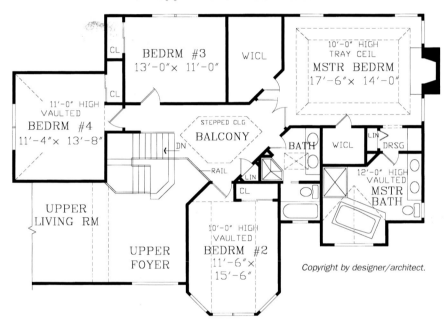

CL
BEDRM #3
13'-0" x 11'-0"

WICL

10'-0" HIGH
TRAY CEIL
MSTR BEDRM
17'-6" x 14'-0"

CL

11'-0" HIGH
VAULTED
BEDRM #4
11'-4" x 13'-8"

STEPPED CLG
BALCONY

BATH

WICL

LIN

DN

DRSG

RAIL

LIN

12'-0" HIGH
VAULTED
MSTR
BATH

CL

UPPER
LIVING RM

UPPER
FOYER

10'-0" HIGH
VAULTED
BEDRM #2
11'-6" x
15'-6"

Copyright by designer/architect.

Main Level Floor Plan

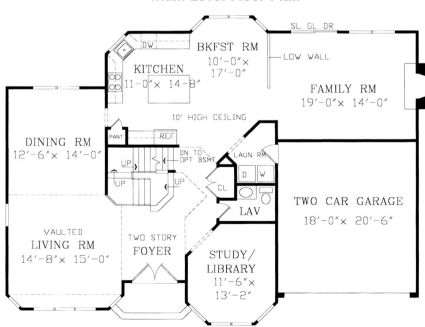

SL GL DR

DW

BKFST RM
10'-0" x
17'-0"

LOW WALL

KITCHEN
11'-0" x 14-8"

FAMILY RM
19'-0" x 14'-0"

10' HIGH CEILING

DINING RM
12'-6" x 14'-0"

PANT

REF

DN TO
OPT BSMT

LAUN RM

UP

D

W

UP

UP

CL

LAV

TWO CAR GARAGE
18'-0" x 20'-6"

VAULTED
LIVING RM
14'-8" x 15'-0"

TWO STORY
FOYER

STUDY/
LIBRARY
11'-6" x
13'-2"

SMARTtip
Paint Basics

Most interior paints are either alkyd-resin (oil-based) products or latex (water-based) varieties. Oil and water don't mix, and generally neither do the paints based on them. For multilayered effects, stick to one type or the other.

Alkyd paints are somewhat lustrous, translucent, and hard-wearing. But alkyds, and the solvents needed for cleaning up, are toxic and combustible, requiring good work-site ventilation and special disposal methods. Professional decorative painters often prefer slower-drying alkyds, which allow more time to achieve complex special effects. Alkyd paints are better suited to techniques such as combing and ragging, where glaze is brushed on in sections and then manipulated.

Latex paints, which now approach alkyd's durability and textural range, are nontoxic and quick-drying, and they clean up easily with soap and water. Most nonprofessionals find latex paint easier to deal with and capable of creating many popular decorative finishes. In general, latex paints are best suited to effects that are dabbed on over the base coat, as in sponging or stenciling. The short drying time can be an advantage, because mistakes can be painted over and redone.

Latex paint is usually the best choice for covering an entire wall, too, because the job can be completed from start to finish in just a few hours.

Plan #131031

Dimensions: 69'8" W x 48'4" D
Levels: 2
Square Footage: 4,027
Main Level Sq. Ft.: 2,198
Upper Level Sq. Ft.: 1,829
Bedrooms: 5
Bathrooms: 4½
Foundation: Crawl space, slab, or basement
Materials List Available: Yes
Price Category: I

Images provided by designer/architect.

If you love dramatic lines and contemporary design, you'll be thrilled by this lovely home.

Features:

• Foyer: A gorgeous vaulted ceiling sets the stage for a curved staircase flanked by a formal living room and dining room.

• Living Room: The foyer ceiling continues in this room, giving it an unusual presence.

• Family Room: This sunken family room features a fireplace and a wall of windows that look out to the backyard. It's open to the living room, making it an ideal spot for entertaining.

• Kitchen: With a large island, this kitchen flows into the breakfast room.

• Master Suite: The luxurious bedroom has a dramatic tray ceiling and includes two-walk-in closets. The dressing room is fitted with a sink, and the spa bath is sumptuous.

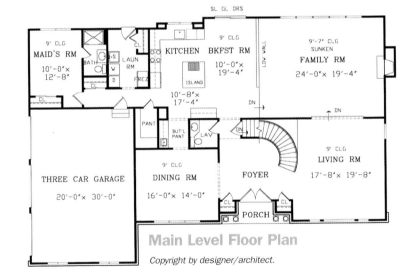

Main Level Floor Plan

Copyright by designer/architect.

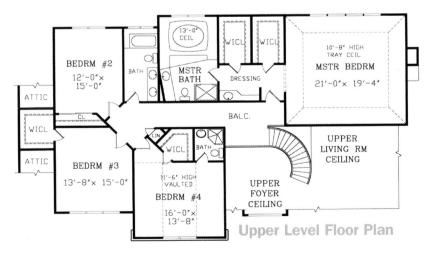

Upper Level Floor Plan

Plan #151169

Dimensions: 51'6" W x 49'10" D
Levels: 1
Square Footage: 1,525
Bedrooms: 3
Bathrooms: 2
Foundation: Crawl space, slab, basement, or daylight basement
CompleteCost List Available: Yes
Price Category: C

This comfortable home is filled with amenities that will thrill both friends and family.

Features:

• Great Room: This spacious room has a gas fireplace in the corner, 9-ft. boxed ceiling, and convenient door to the rear covered porch.

• Dining Room: Bay windows look out to the rear porch and let light flood into this room.

• Kitchen: An angled work and snack bar and large pantry are highlights in this well-planned room.

• Breakfast Room: A door to the rear porch, wide windows, and computer desk are highlights here.

• Master Suite: You'll feel pampered by the 9-ft. boxed ceiling and bath with two huge closets, whirlpool tub, separate shower, and dual vanity.

• Additional Bedrooms: Transform bedroom 3 into a study or home office if you can, and add the optional door to the foyer for total convenience.

Images provided by designer/architect.

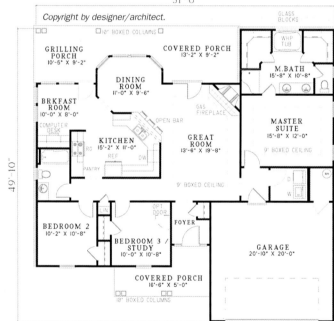

Rear View

Plan #131011

Dimensions: 75'2" W x 60'9" D
Levels: 1
Square Footage: 1,897
Bedrooms: 4
Bathrooms: 2
Foundation: Crawl space, slab, or basement
Materials List Available: Yes
Price Category: E

Images provided by designer/architect.

You'll love this home if you're looking for a plan for a sloping lot or flat one or if you want to orient the rear porch to face into or away from the sun.

Features:

• Ceiling Height: 8 ft.

• Living Area: The whole family will find it easy to congregate in this lovely room.

• Kitchen: The angle of this home makes the kitchen especially convenient while also giving it an unusual amount of character.

• Study: Located near the front door, this room can serve as a home office or fourth bedroom as easily as it does a private study.

• Master Suite: Located at the opposite end of the home from the other two bedrooms, this master suite offers privacy and quiet.

• Additional Bedrooms: These two bedrooms share a distinctive hall bathroom.

Rear View

Copyright by designer/architect.

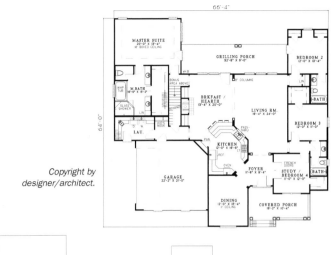

Copyright by
designer/architect.

Plan #151144

Dimensions: 66'4" W x 64' D
Levels: 1
Square Footage: 2,624
Bedrooms: 4
Bathrooms: 3
Foundation: Crawl space, slab
(basement option for fee)
CompleteCost List Available: Yes
Price Category: F

*Images provided by
designer/architect.*

CAD FILE AVAILABLE

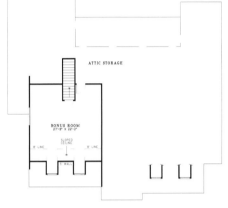

Bonus Area
Floor Plan

Main Level Floor Plan

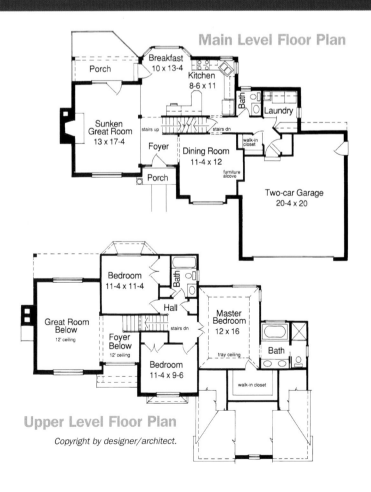

Plan #161015

Dimensions: 55'4" W x 40'4" D
Levels: 2
Square Footage: 1,768
Main Level Sq. Ft.: 960
Upper Level Sq. Ft.: 808
Bedrooms: 3
Bathrooms: 2½
Foundation: Basement
Materials List Available: Yes
Price Category: C

*Images provided by
designer/architect.*

CAD FILE AVAILABLE

Upper Level Floor Plan

Copyright by designer/architect.

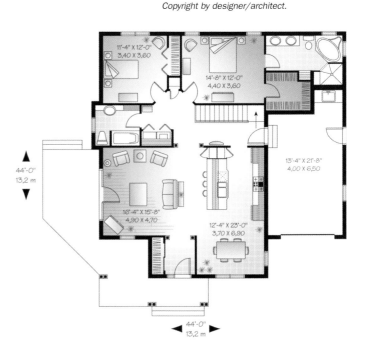

Copyright by designer/architect.

Plan #181280

Dimensions: 44' W x 44' D

Levels: 1

Square Footage: 1,452

Bedrooms: 2

Bathrooms: 2

Foundation: Basement

Materials List Available: Yes

Price Category: B

Images provided by designer/architect.

11'-4" X 12'-0"
3,40 X 3,60

14'-8" X 12'-0"
4,40 X 3,60

13'-4" X 21'-8"
4,00 X 6,50

16'-4" X 15'-8"
4,90 X 4,70

12'-4" X 23'-0"
3,70 X 6,90

44'-0"
13,2 m

44'-0"
13,2 m

Plan #161111

Dimensions: 45' W x 42'2" D

Levels: 2

Square Footage: 1,921

Main Level Sq. Ft.: 968

Upper Level Sq. Ft.: 953

Bedrooms: 4

Bathrooms: 2½

Foundation: Basement

Materials List Available: Yes

Price Category: D

Images provided by designer/architect.

WALK IN CLOSET

Master Bedroom
14'6" x 13'1"
9'-1" CEILING

Great Room Below
16'-9" CEILING

Master Bath

Bedroom
10'11" x 10'6"

Balcony

Bath

Bedroom
10'11" x 10'6"

Bedroom
11'3" x 10'6"

Upper Level Floor Plan

Copyright by designer/architect.

Main Level Floor Plan

Kitchen
12' x 13'2"

Dining Area
13'2" x 14'6"

Porch
11'-1" CEILING

Great Room
16'-9" CEILING HEIGHT
16'2" x 16'9"

Pantry

Laun.

Garage
21'9" x 21'

Bath

Foyer

Porch
11'-1" CEILING

BUILT IN ENTERTAINMENT CABINET

WALK IN CLOSET

Rear Elevation

Plan #121084

Dimensions: 40' W x 42' D
Levels: 2
Square Footage: 1,728
Main Level Sq. Ft.: 845
Upper Level Sq. Ft.: 883
Bedrooms: 4
Bathrooms: 2½
Foundation: Basement
Materials List Available: Yes
Price Category: C

Images provided by designer/architect.

Upper Level Floor Plan

Main Level Floor Plan

Copyright by designer/architect.

Plan #121034

Dimensions: 92'8" W x 59'4" D
Levels: 1
Square Footage: 2,223
Bedrooms: 1
Bathrooms: 1½
Foundation: Basement
Materials List Available: Yes
Price Category: E

Images provided by designer/architect.

Copyright by designer/architect.

Optional Basement Level Floor Plan

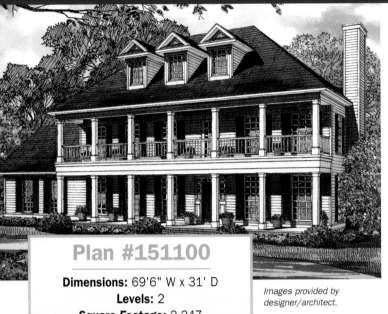

Plan #151100

Dimensions: 69'6" W x 31' D
Levels: 2
Square Footage: 2,247
Main Level Sq. Ft.: 1,154
Upper Level Sq. Ft.: 1,093
Bedrooms: 3
Bathrooms: 2½
Foundation: Crawl space, slab, or basement
CompleteCost List Available: Yes
Price Category: E

Images provided by designer/architect.

Main Level Floor Plan

Upper Level Floor Plan

Copyright by designer/architect.

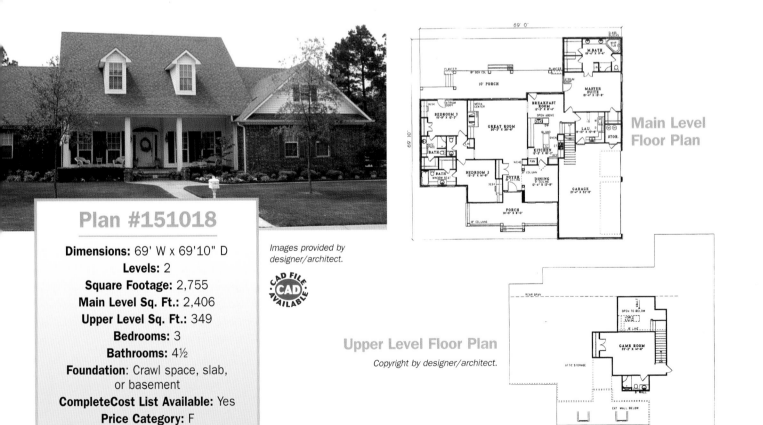

Plan #151018

Dimensions: 69' W x 69'10" D
Levels: 2
Square Footage: 2,755
Main Level Sq. Ft.: 2,406
Upper Level Sq. Ft.: 349
Bedrooms: 3
Bathrooms: 4½
Foundation: Crawl space, slab, or basement
CompleteCost List Available: Yes
Price Category: F

Images provided by designer/architect.

Main Level Floor Plan

Upper Level Floor Plan

Copyright by designer/architect.

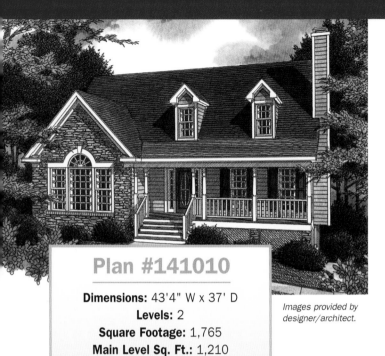

Plan #141010

Dimensions: 43'4" W x 37' D

Levels: 2

Square Footage: 1,765

Main Level Sq. Ft.: 1,210

Upper Level Sq. Ft.: 555

Bedrooms: 3

Bathrooms: 2½

Foundation: Basement

Materials List Available: Yes

Price Category: C

Main Level Floor Plan

Images provided by designer/architect.

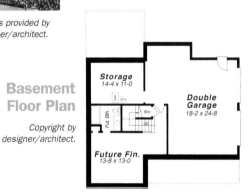

Basement Floor Plan

Copyright by designer/architect.

Upper Level Floor Plan

Plan #121094

Dimensions: 40'8" W x 46' D

Levels: 2

Square Footage: 1,768

Main Level Sq. Ft.: 905

Upper Level Sq. Ft.: 863

Bedrooms: 3

Bathrooms: 2½

Foundation: Basement

Materials List Available: Yes

Price Category: C

Images provided by designer/architect.

CAD FILE AVAILABLE

Main Level Floor Plan

Upper Level Floor Plan

Copyright by designer/architect.

Plan #221025

Dimensions: 69'8" W x 72' D

Levels: 2

Square Footage: 3,009

Main Level Sq. Ft.: 2,039

Upper Level Sq. Ft.: 970

Bedrooms: 4

Bathrooms: 2½

Foundation: Basement

Materials List Available: No

Price Category: G

Images provided by designer/architect.

Features:

- **Great Room:** You'll look into this great room as soon as you enter the two-story foyer. A fireplace flanked by built-in bookcases and large windows looking out to the deck highlight this room.

- **Dining Room:** This formal room is located just off the entry for the convenience of your guests.

- **Kitchen:** A huge central island and large pantry make this kitchen a delight for any cook. The large nook looks onto the deck and opens to the lovely three-season porch.

- **Master Suite:** You'll love this suite, with its charming bay shape, great windows, walk-in closet, luxurious bath, and door to the deck.

- **Upper Level:** Everyone will love the two bedrooms, large bath, and huge game.

Designed to resemble a country home in France, this two-story beauty will delight you with its good looks and luxurious amenities.

CAD FILE AVAILABLE

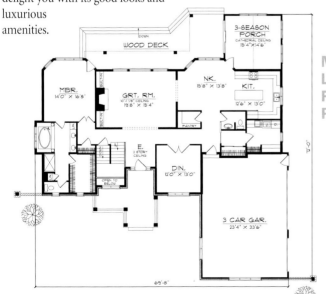

Main Level Floor Plan

Upper Level Floor Plan

Copyright by designer/architect.

Plan #121061

Dimensions: 56' W x 52' D
Levels: 2
Square Footage: 3,025
Main Level Sq. Ft.: 1,583
Upper Level Sq. Ft.: 1,442
Bedrooms: 4
Bathrooms: 3½
Foundation: Basement
Materials List Available: Yes
Price Category: G

Images provided by designer/architect.

This large home with a contemporary feeling is ideal for the family looking for comfort and amenities.

Features:

- Entry: Stacked windows bring sunlight into this two-story entry, with its stylish curved staircase.
- Library: French doors off the entry lead to this room, with its built-in bookcases flanking a large, picturesque window.
- Family Room: Located in the rear of the home, this family room is sunken to set it apart. A spider-beamed ceiling gives it a contemporary feeling, and a bay window, wet bar, and pass-through fireplace add to this impression.
- Kitchen: The island in this kitchen makes working here a pleasure. The corner pantry joins a breakfast area and hearth room to this space.

Main Level Floor Plan

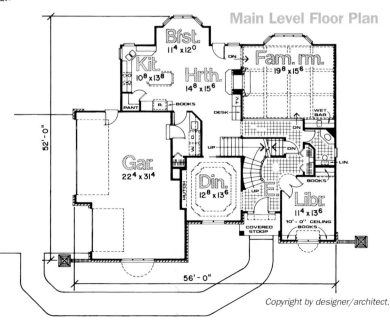

Copyright by designer/architect.

Upper Level Floor Plan

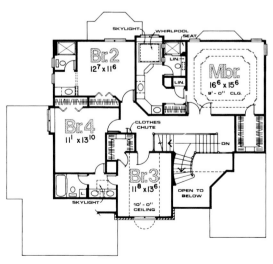

Main Level Floor Plan

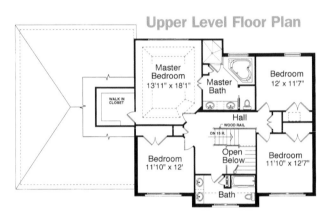

Bath
Laun.
Hall
Breakfast
11 x 14'6"
Family Room
19' x 15'3"
Garage
22' x 22'11"
Kitchen
10'4" x 11'5"
Dining Room
11'10" x 13'8"
Foyer
Study
11'10" x 11'5"
Porch

Copyright by designer/architect.

Upper Level Floor Plan

Master Bedroom
13'11" x 18'1"
Master Bath
Bedroom
12' x 11'7"
WALK IN CLOSET
Hall
Bedroom
11'10" x 12'
Open Below
Bedroom
11'10" x 12'7"
Bath

Plan #161075

Dimensions: 63' W x 38'2" D
Levels: 2
Square Footage: 2,773
Main Level Sq. Ft.: 1,498
Upper Level Sq. Ft.: 1,275
Bedrooms: 4
Bathrooms: 2½
Foundation: Basement
Materials List Available: No
Price Category: F

Images provided by designer/architect.

CAD FILE AVAILABLE

Rear Elevation

Main Level Floor Plan

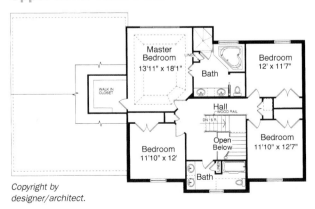

Bath
Laun.
Hall
Covered Porch
Breakfast
11' x 14'6"
Family Room
19' x 15'3"
Garage
22' x 22'11"
Kitchen
10'4" 11'5"
Dining Room
11'10" x 13'8"
Foyer
Study
11'10" x 11'5"
Porch

Upper Level Floor Plan

Master Bedroom
13'11" x 18'1"
Bath
Bedroom
12' x 11'7"
WALK IN CLOSET
Hall
Bedroom
11'10" x 12'
Open Below
Bedroom
11'10" x 12'7"
Bath

Copyright by designer/architect.

Plan #161077

Dimensions: 63' W x 41'2" D
Levels: 2
Square Footage: 2,773
Main Level Sq. Ft.: 1,498
Upper Level Sq. Ft.: 1,275
Bedrooms: 4
Bathrooms: 2½
Foundation: Basement
Materials List Available: Yes
Price Category: F

CAD FILE AVAILABLE

Images provided by designer/architect.

Rear Elevation

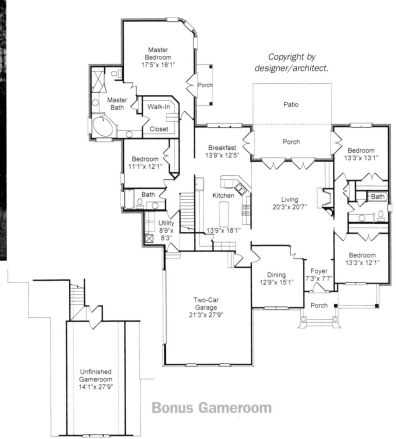

Master
Bedroom
17'5"x 18'1"

Porch

Copyright by
designer/architect.

Master
Bath

Walk-In
Closet

Patio

Porch

Bedroom
13'3" x 13'1"

Bedroom
11'1" x 12'1"

Breakfast
13'9"x 12'5"

Bath

Bath

Kitchen

Living
20'3"x 20'7"

Utility
8'9"x
8'3"

13'9"x 18'1"

Bedroom
13'3" x 12'1"

Dining
12'9" x 15'1"

Foyer
7'3"x 7'7"

Two-Car
Garage
21'3"x 27'9"

Porch

Images
provided by
designer/architect.

Unfinished
Gameroom
14'1"x 27'9"

Bonus Gameroom

Plan #111030

Dimensions: 74'10" W x 85'5" D

Levels: 1

Square Footage: 2,905

Bedrooms: 4

Bathrooms: 3

Foundation: Slab

Materials List Available: No

Price Category: F

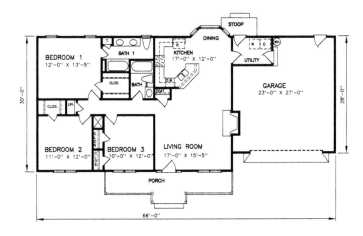

BEDROOM 1
12'-0" X 13'-5"

BATH 1

KITCHEN
17'-0" X 12'-0"

DINING

STOOP

W D

UTILITY

WH

30'-0"

CLOS.

BATH 2

GARAGE
23'-0" X 27'-0"

28'-0"

CLOS.

LIN.

BEDROOM 2
11'-0" X 12'-0"

BEDROOM 3
10'-0" X 12'-0"

LIVING ROOM
17'-0" X 15'-5"

PORCH

66'-0"

Plan #341005

Dimensions: 66' W x 30' D

Levels: 1

Square Footage: 1,334

Bedrooms: 3

Bathrooms: 2

Foundation: Crawl space, slab,
or basement

Materials List Available: Yes

Price Category: B

Images provided by
designer/architect.

CAD FILE AVAILABLE

Copyright by designer/architect.

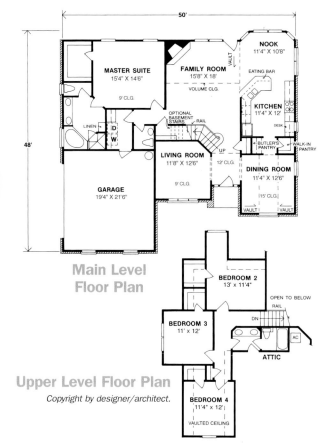

Main Level Floor Plan

Plan #121078

Dimensions: 50' W x 48' D

Levels: 2

Square Footage: 2,248

Main Level Sq. Ft.: 1,568

Upper Level Sq. Ft.: 680

Bedrooms: 4

Bathrooms: 2½

Foundation: Slab

Materials List Available: Yes

Price Category: E

Images provided by designer/architect.

This home, as shown in the photograph, may differ from the actual blueprints. For more detailed information, please check the floor plans carefully.

Upper Level Floor Plan

Copyright by designer/architect.

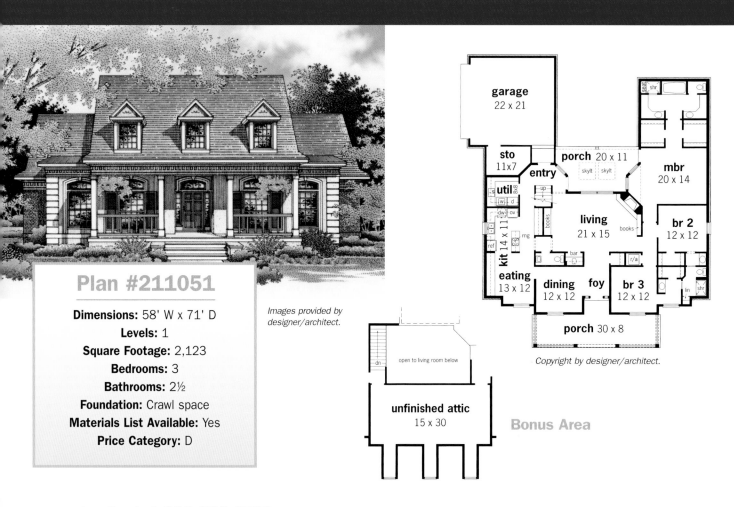

Plan #211051

Dimensions: 58' W x 71' D

Levels: 1

Square Footage: 2,123

Bedrooms: 3

Bathrooms: 2½

Foundation: Crawl space

Materials List Available: Yes

Price Category: D

Images provided by designer/architect.

Copyright by designer/architect.

Bonus Area

Plan #111006

Dimensions: 56' W x 67' D

Levels: 1

Square Footage: 2,241

Bedrooms: 4

Bathrooms: 2½

Foundation: Slab

Materials List Available: No

Price Category: E

Images provided by designer/architect.

You'll love this plan if you're looking for a home with fantastic curb appeal on the outside and comfortable amenities on the inside.

Features:

- Foyer: This lovely foyer opens to both the living and dining rooms.

- Dining Room: Three columns in this room accentuate both its large dimensions and its slightly formal air.

- Living Room: This room gives an airy feeling, and the fireplace here makes it especially inviting when the weather's cool.

- Kitchen: This G-shaped kitchen is designed to save steps while you're working, and the ample counter area adds even more to its convenience. The breakfast bar is a great gathering area.

- Master Suite: Two walk-in closets provide storage space, and the bath includes separate vanities, a standing shower, and a deluxe corner bathtub.

Front Elevation

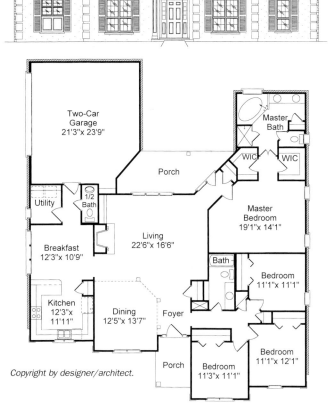

Copyright by designer/architect.

Plan #351005

Dimensions: 61' W x 47'4" D

Levels: 1

Square Footage: 1,501

Bedrooms: 3

Bathrooms: 2

Foundation: Crawl space, slab, or basement

Materials List Available: Yes

Price Category: C

Images provided by designer/architect.

This home provides a very functional split-floor-plan layout with many of the features that your family desires.

Features:

- Porches: Enjoy the beautiful weather on one of your porches, front and rear.

- Great Room: This large room, with its vaulted ceiling and gas log fireplace, is perfect for entertaining.

- Kitchen: With plenty of counter space for that growing family, this kitchen has an open layout.

- Master Suite: This expansive master bedroom and bathroom area has plenty of storage space in the separate walk-in closets.

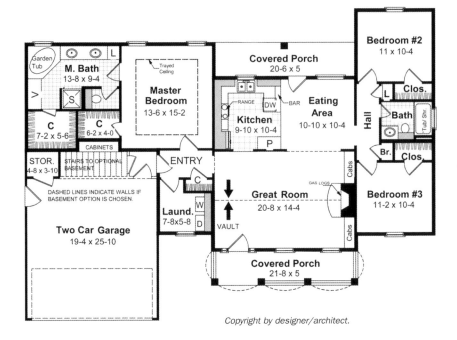

Copyright by designer/architect.

Plan #351007

Dimensions: 73'8" W x 53'2" D

Levels: 1

Square Footage: 2,251

Bedrooms: 3

Bathrooms: 2½

Foundation: Crawl space, slab, or basement

Materials List Available: Yes

Price Category: E

Images provided by designer/architect.

Bonus Room

Copyright by designer/architect.

Plan #271069

Dimensions: 63'5" W x 51'8" D

Levels: 2

Square Footage: 2,376

Main Level Sq. Ft.: 1,248

Upper Level Sq. Ft.: 1,128

Bedrooms: 4

Bathrooms: 2½

Foundation: Crawl space, basement

Materials List Available: No

Price Category: E

Images provided by designer/architect.

Main Level Floor Plan

Upper Level Floor Plan

Copyright by designer/architect.

Plan #221020

Dimensions: 69'8" W x 43' D

Levels: 1

Square Footage: 1,859

Bedrooms: 3

Bathrooms: 2½

Foundation: Basement

Materials List Available: No

Price Category: D

Images provided by designer/architect.

You'll love this design if you're looking for a compact home with amenities usually found in much larger designs.

Features:

- Ceiling Height: 8 ft.

- Living Room: A vaulted ceiling gives an elegant feeling, and a bank of windows lets natural light pour in during the daytime.

- Dining Room: Located just off the entry for the convenience of your guests, this room is ideal for intimate family meals or formal dinner parties.

- Kitchen: Just across from the dining room, this kitchen is distinguished by its ample counter space. The adjacent nook is large enough to use as a casual dining area, and it features access to the backyard.

- Master Suite: The large bay window lends interest to this room, and you'll love the walk-in closet and private bath, with its whirlpool tub, standing shower, and dual-sink vanity.

Rear Elevation

Copyright by designer/architect.

Plan #131022

Dimensions: 54'8" W x 43' D

Levels: 2

Square Footage: 2,092

Main Level Sq. Ft.: 1,152

Upper Level Sq. Ft.: 940

Bedrooms: 4

Bathrooms: 2½

Foundation: Crawl space, slab, or basement

Materials List Available: Yes

Price Category: E

Images provided by designer/architect.

You'll love the way this charming home reminds you of an old-fashioned farmhouse.

Features:

• Ceiling Height: 8 ft.

• Living Room: This large living room can be used as guest quarters when the need arises.

• Dining Room: This bayed, informal room is large enough for all your dining and entertaining needs. It could also double as an office or den.

• Garage: An expandable loft over the garage offers an ideal playroom or fourth bedroom.

Rear Elevation

Main Level Floor Plan

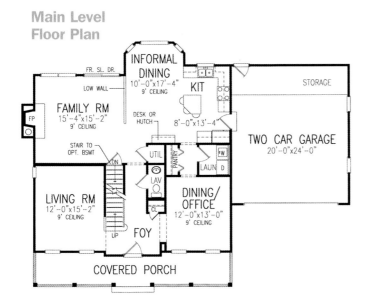

Upper Level Floor Plan

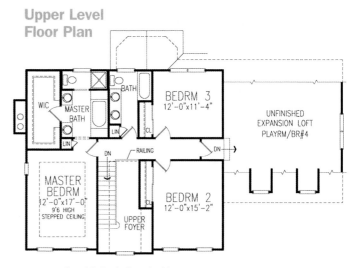

Copyright by designer/architect.

Main Level Floor Plan

Upper Level Floor Plan

Copyright by designer/architect.

Plan #181296

Dimensions: 42' W x 44' D
Levels: 2
Square Footage: 2,641
Main Level Sq. Ft.: 1,139
Upper Level Sq. Ft.: 1,502
Bedrooms: 4
Bathrooms: 3½
Foundation: Basement
Materials List Available: Yes
Price Category: F

Images provided by designer/architect.

CAD FILE AVAILABLE

Main Level Floor Plan

Plan #181292

Dimensions: 26' W x 29' D
Levels: 2
Square Footage: 1,500
Main Level Sq. Ft.: 746
Upper Level Sq. Ft.: 754
Bedrooms: 3
Bathrooms: 1½
Foundation: Basement
Materials List Available: No
Price Category: C

Images provided by designer/architect.

CAD FILE AVAILABLE

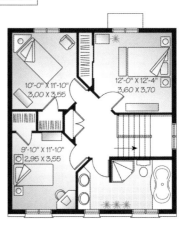

Upper Level Floor Plan

Copyright by designer/architect.

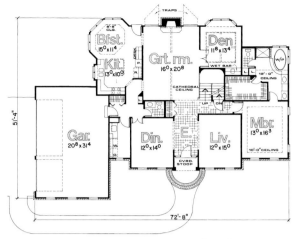

Main Level Floor Plan

Images provided by designer/architect.

Plan #121071

Dimensions: 72'8" W x 51'4" D
Levels: 2
Square Footage: 2,957
Main Level Sq. Ft.: 2,063
Upper Level Sq. Ft.: 894
Bedrooms: 4
Bathrooms: 4½
Foundation: Basement
Materials List Available: Yes
Price Category: F

Upper Level Floor Plan

Copyright by designer/architect.

Main Level Floor Plan

Images provided by designer/architect.

Plan #151237

Dimensions: 57'4" W x 55'10" D
Levels: 2
Square Footage: 2,481
Main Level Sq. Ft.: 2,084
Upper Level Sq. Ft.: 397
Bedrooms: 4
Bathrooms: 3
Foundation: Crawl space or slab
CompleteCost List Available: Yes
Price Category: E

Upper Level Floor Plan

Copyright by designer/architect.

Images provided by designer/architect.

Plan #211127

Dimensions: 94' W x 71' D
Levels: 2
Square Footage: 5,474
Main Level Sq. Ft.: 4,193
Upper Level Sq. Ft.: 1,281
Bedrooms: 4
Bathrooms: 4 full, 2 half
Foundation: Slab, crawl space
Materials List Available: No
Price Category: I

This is a truly grand southern-style home, with stately columns and eye-pleasing symmetry.

Features:

- Ceiling Height: 12 ft.

- Foyer: A grand home warrants a grand entry, and here it is. The graceful curved staircase will impress your guests as they move from this foyer to the fireplace.

- Family Room: Great for entertaining, this family room features a vaulted ceiling. A handsome fireplace adds warmth and ambiance.

- Den: Another fireplace enhances this smaller and cozier den. Here the kids can play, supervised by the family chef working in the adjacent kitchen.

- Verandas: As is fitting for a gracious southern home, you'll find verandas at front and rear.

- Master Suite: A romantic third fireplace is found in this sprawling master bedroom. The master bath provides the utmost in privacy and organization.

Main Level Floor Plan

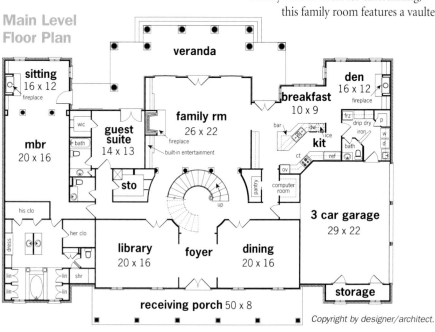

Copyright by designer/architect.

Upper Level Floor Plan

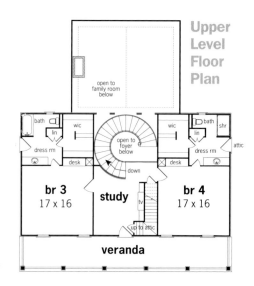

Rear View

Great Room

Kitchen

Dining Room

Master Bedroom

Master Bath

Plan #301002

Dimensions: 57'2" W x 54'10" D
Levels: 1
Square Footage: 1,845
Bedrooms: 3
Bathrooms: 2½
Foundation: Crawl space, slab
Materials List Available: Yes
Price Category: D

Images provided by designer/architect.

Although compact, this home is filled with surprisingly luxurious features.

Features:

• Ceiling Height: 8 ft. unless otherwise noted.

• Front Porch: Guests will be sheltered from the rain by this lovely little porch.

• Foyer: This elegant foyer features a 10-ft. ceiling and is open to the dining room and the rear great room.

• Dining Room: The 10-ft. ceiling from the foyer continues into this spacious dining room.

• Family Room: This family room features a vaulted ceiling and a fireplace with built-in bookcases.

• Kitchen: This kitchen boasts a pantry and plenty of storage and counter space.

• Master Bedroom: This master bedroom includes a cathedral ceiling and two walk-in closets. The master bath has two vanities, a corner spa, and a walk-in closet.

Copyright by designer/architect.

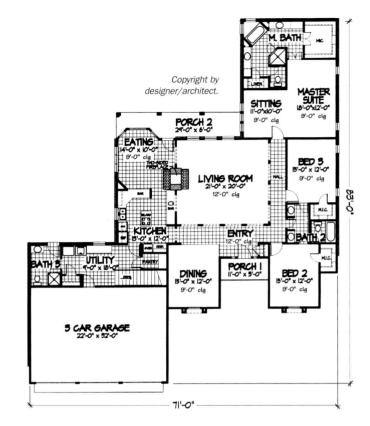

Copyright by designer/architect.

Plan #271080

Dimensions: 71' W x 83' D

Levels: 1

Square Footage: 2,581

Bedrooms: 3

Bathrooms: 3

Foundation: Basement

Materials List Available: Yes

Price Category: E

Images provided by designer/architect.

CAD FILE AVAILABLE

Main Level Floor Plan

Upper Level Floor Plan

Plan #181079

Dimensions: 60' W x 47'8" D

Levels: 2

Square Footage: 3,016

Main Level Sq. Ft.: 1,716

Upper Level Sq. Ft.: 1,300

Bedrooms: 6

Bathrooms: 4½

Foundation: Crawl space

Materials List Available: Yes

Price Category: G

Images provided by designer/architect.

CAD FILE AVAILABLE

Copyright by designer/architect.

Plan #111005

Dimensions: 61' W x 64' D
Levels: 2
Square Footage: 3,590
Main Level Sq. Ft.: 2,390
Upper Level Sq. Ft.: 1,200
Bedrooms: 4
Bathrooms: 3
Foundation: Above ground basement
Materials List Available: No
Price Category: H

Images provided by designer/architect.

Main Level Floor Plan

Copyright by designer/architect.

Upper Level Floor Plan

Living Room

Plan #341058

Dimensions: 50' W x 40'9" D
Levels: 2
Square Footage: 1,996
Main Level Sq. Ft.: 1,008
Upper Level Sq. Ft.: 988
Bedrooms: 3
Bathrooms: 2½
Foundation: Crawl space
Materials List Available: Yes
Price Category: D

Images provided by designer/architect.

CAD FILE AVAILABLE

Main Level Floor Plan

Upper Level Floor Plan

Copyright by designer/architect.

Plan #341060

Dimensions: 75'10" W x 56'2" D

Levels: 1.5

Square Footage: 2,349

Bonus unfinished Sq. Ft.: 706

Bedrooms: 3

Bathrooms: 2½

Foundation: Crawl space

Materials List Available: Yes

Price Category: E

Images provided by designer/architect.

CAD FILE AVAILABLE

Copyright by designer/architect.

Plan #161110

Dimensions: 75' W x 39'1" D

Levels: 1

Square Footage: 1,623

Bedrooms: 3

Bathrooms: 2

Foundation: Basement

Materials List Available: Yes

Price Category: C

Images provided by designer/architect.

CAD FILE AVAILABLE

Copyright by designer/architect.

Rear Elevation

Plan #321048

Dimensions: 77'6" W x 30' D
Levels: 2
Square Footage: 3,216
Main Level Sq. Ft.: 1,834
Upper Level Sq. Ft.: 1,382
Bedrooms: 4
Bathrooms: 4½
Foundation: Basement
Materials List Available: Yes
Price Category: G

Images provided by designer/architect.

You'll love the columns and well-proportioned dormers that grace the exterior of this home, which is as spacious as it is comfortable.

Features:

- **Family Room:** This large room, featuring a graceful bay window and a wet bar, is sure to be the heart of your home. On chilly evenings, the whole family will gather around the fireplace.

- **Dining Room:** Whether you're serving a family dinner or hosting a formal dinner party, everyone will feel at home in this lovely room.

- **Kitchen:** The family cooks will appreciate the thought that went into designing this kitchen, which includes ample work and storage space. A breakfast room adjoins the kitchen.

- **Hearth Room:** This room also adjoins the kitchen, creating a large area for informal entertaining.

- **Bedrooms:** Each bedroom is really a suite, because it includes a private, full bath.

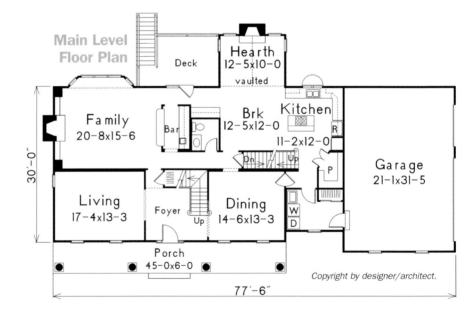

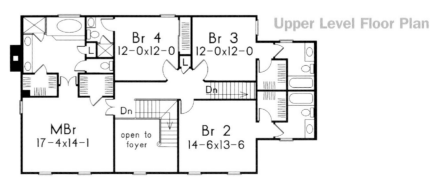

Plan #441042

Dimensions: 52' W x 45' D
Levels: 2
Square Footage: 2,538
Main Level Sq. Ft.: 1,342
Upper Level Sq. Ft.: 1,196
Bedrooms: 3
Bathrooms: 2½
Foundation: Crawl space; slab or basement available for fee
Materials List Available: No
Price Category: E

It's never too late to have a happy childhood—or the exact home you want.

Images provided by designer/architect.

Features:

- Foyer: This entry soars up two stories with a view to the open hallway above.
- Family Room: This large informal gathering area has large windows with a view to the backyard. It also has a two-sided fireplace, which it shares with the den.
- Kitchen: This fully equipped island kitchen has a built-in pantry and desk. The nook and family room are open to it.
- Master Suite: This private retreat includes a sitting area in the master bedroom that

provides ample space for a comfortable lounge in front of its fireplace. The master bath features a compartmentalized lavatory, spa tub, large shower, and his and her vanities.

- Bedrooms: The two additional bedrooms are located on the upper level with the master suite. Both rooms have large closets and share a common bathroom.

CAD FILE AVAILABLE

Rear Elevation

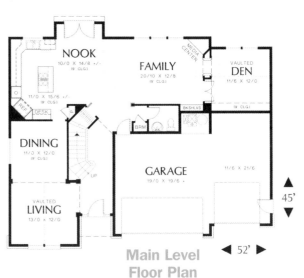

Main Level Floor Plan

◀ 52' ▶

Upper Level Floor Plan

Copyright by designer/architect.

Plan #321061

Dimensions: 55' W x 49'4" D
Levels: 2
Square Footage: 3,169
Main Level Sq. Ft.: 1,679
Upper Level Sq. Ft.: 1,490
Bedrooms: 4
Bathrooms: 2½
Foundation: Basement
Materials List Available: Yes
Price Category: G

Images provided by designer/architect.

You'll love the spacious interior of this gorgeous home, which is built for comfortable family living but includes amenities for gracious entertaining.

Features:

• Entry: This large entry gives a view of the handcrafted staircase to the upper floor.

• Living Room: Angled French doors open into this generously sized room with a vaulted ceiling.

• Family Room: You'll love to entertain in this huge room with a masonry fireplace, built-in entertainment area, gorgeous bay window, and well-fitted wet bar.

• Breakfast Room: A door in the bayed area opens to the outdoor patio for dining convenience.

• Kitchen: The center island provides work space and a snack bar, and the walk-in pantry is a delight.

• Master Suite: Enjoy the vaulted ceiling, two walk-in closets, and luxurious bath in this suite.

Main Level Floor Plan

Upper Level Floor Plan

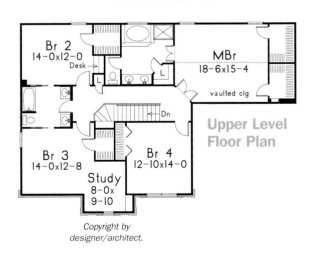

Copyright by designer/architect.

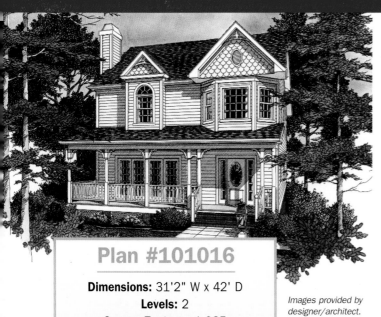

DECK
30'-6" x 11'-7"

BRKFST

KITCHEN
15'-0" x 17'-0"

DINING
14'-8" x 12'-8"

Main Level Floor Plan

FAMILY
18'-8" x 16'-0"

ENTRY
7'-11" x 15'-6"

UP

42'-0"

PORCH
30'-6" x 7'-7"

◀ 31'-2" ▶

Images provided by designer/architect.

CAD FILE AVAILABLE

Plan #101016

Dimensions: 31'2" W x 42' D

Levels: 2

Square Footage: 1,985

Main Level Sq. Ft.: 1,009

Upper Level Sq. Ft.: 976

Bedrooms: 3

Bathrooms: 2½

Foundation: Crawl space, slab, or basement

Materials List Available: No

Price Category: D

MASTER BDRM
16'-4" x 15'-0"

TRAY CEILING

DN

Upper Level Floor Plan

Copyright by designer/architect.

BEDROOM 2
12'-0" x 12'-8"

BEDROOM 3
12'-8" x 12'-0"

WINDOW SEAT AT

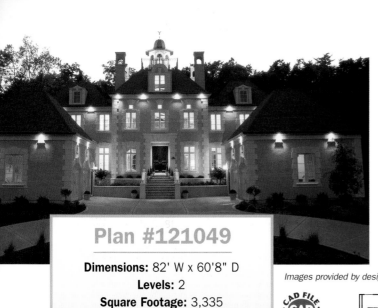

Main Level Floor Plan

82'-0"

60'-8"

Images provided by designer/architect.

CAD FILE AVAILABLE

Plan #121049

Dimensions: 82' W x 60'8" D

Levels: 2

Square Footage: 3,335

Main Level Sq. Ft.: 2,054

Upper Level Sq. Ft.: 1,281

Bedrooms: 4

Bathrooms: 3½

Foundation: Slab

Materials List Available: Yes

Price Category: G

Upper Level Floor Plan

Third Floor Bedroom Floor Plan

Copyright by designer/architect.

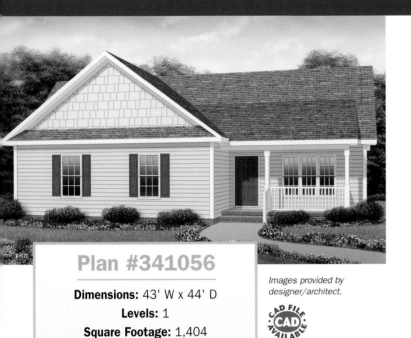

Plan #341056

Dimensions: 43' W x 44' D

Levels: 1

Square Footage: 1,404

Bedrooms: 4

Bathrooms: 2

Foundation: Crawl space

Materials List Available: Yes

Price Category: B

Images provided by designer/architect.

CAD FILE AVAILABLE

Copyright by designer/architect.

Main Level Floor Plan

Upper Level Floor Plan

Plan #341051

Dimensions: 54' W x 52' D

Levels: 2

Square Footage: 2,243

Main Level Sq. Ft.: 1,250

Upper Level Sq. Ft.: 993

Bedrooms: 4

Bathrooms: 3½

Foundation: Crawl space

Materials List Available: Yes

Price Category: E

Images provided by designer/architect.

CAD FILE AVAILABLE

Copyright by designer/architect.

Plan #271045

Dimensions: 56' W x 47' D
Levels: 2
Square Footage: 2,409
Main Level Sq. Ft.: 1,463
Upper Level Sq. Ft.: 946
Bedrooms: 4
Bathrooms: 2½
Foundation: Basement
Materials List Available: No
Price Category: E

Images provided by designer/architect.

This traditional home is so attractive, guests will walk right up to visit!

Features:

• Living Room: They'll be drawn first to this comfortable room, which boasts a vaulted ceiling and an eye-catching bump-out.

• Dining Room: From the living room, columned half walls define and introduce this formal dining room, which flaunts an elegant tray ceiling.

• Kitchen: This gourmet island-equipped kitchen offers a handy pantry. The attached breakfast bay hosts a useful menu desk and easy access to an inviting backyard deck.

• Family Room: A fireplace warms this expansive family room, which also opens onto the deck.

• Master Suite: Upstairs, the master bedroom boasts a vaulted ceiling and two walk-in closets. The private bath shows off a garden tub and a dual-sink vanity with a makeup area.

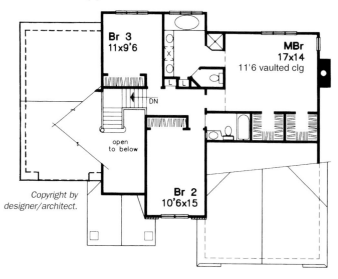

Plan #441036

Dimensions: 60' W x 50' D
Levels: 2
Square Footage: 2,902
Main Level Sq. Ft.: 1,617
Upper Level Sq. Ft.: 1,285
Bedrooms: 3
Bathrooms: 2½
Foundation: Crawl space
Materials List Available: No
Price Category: F

Images provided by designer/architect.

Features:

- Great Room: Come in and relax in this room, with its media center and fireplace. Look onto the backyard through the large windows.

- Kitchen: This kitchen is wonderfully appointed, containing an island cooktop, walk-in pantry, built-in desk, and corner sink. The laundry room is nearby.

- Master Suite: This suite is especially noteworthy, opening from double doors and boasting a walk-in closet and a bath with a spa tub, separate shower, double vanities, and compartmented toilet.

- Bedrooms: Two additional bedrooms share the upper level with the master suite. Both bedrooms have large closets and share a Jack-and-Jill bathroom.

It's a natural: a two-story traditional with board-and-batten siding, cedar shingles, stone detail at the foundation and Craftsman-inspired porch columns.

CAD FILE AVAILABLE

Main Level Floor Plan

Upper Level Floor Plan

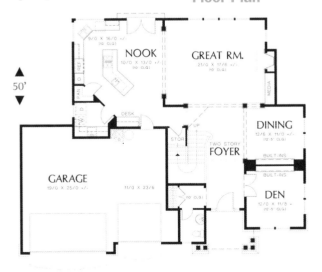

Copyright by designer/architect.

Images provided by designer/architect.

Plan #161018

Dimensions: 74'4" W x 69'11" D
Levels: 2
Square Footage: 2,816
+ 325 Sq. Ft. bonus room
Main Level Sq. Ft.: 2,231
Upper Level Sq. Ft.: 624
Bedrooms: 3
Bathrooms: 3 full, 2 half
Foundation: Basement
Materials List Available: No
Price Category: F

If you love classic European designs, look closely at this home with its multiple gables and countless conveniences and luxuries.

CAD FILE AVAILABLE

Features:

- Foyer: Open to the great room, the 2-story foyer offers a view all the way to the rear windows.

- Great Room: A fireplace makes this room cozy in any kind of weather.

- Kitchen: This large room features an island with a sink, and an angled wall with French doors to the back yard.

- Dining Room: The furniture alcove and raised ceiling make this room both formal and practical.

- Master Suite: You'll love the quiet in the bedroom and the luxuries—a whirlpool tub, separate shower, and double vanities—in the bath.

- Basement: The door from the basement to the side yard adds convenience to outdoor work.

Rear View

Main Level Floor Plan

Upper Level Floor Plan

Copyright by designer/architect.

Foyer/Dining Room

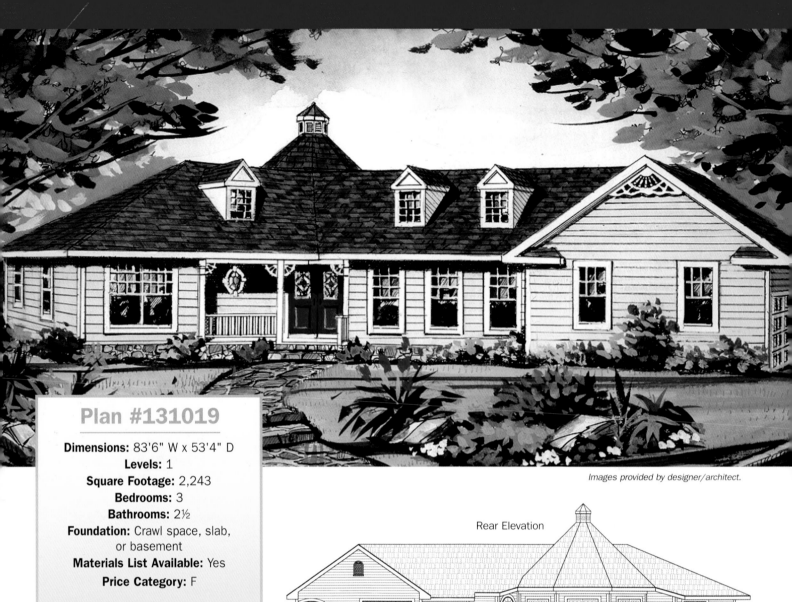

Plan #131019

Dimensions: 83'6" W x 53'4" D
Levels: 1
Square Footage: 2,243
Bedrooms: 3
Bathrooms: 2½
Foundation: Crawl space, slab, or basement
Materials List Available: Yes
Price Category: F

Images provided by designer/architect.

Drama marks this contemporary, angled ranch-style home which can be placed to suit any site, even the most difficult.

Features:

• Great Room: Imagine having an octagonal great room! The shape alone makes it spectacular, but the view to the backyard from its four exterior sides adds to the impression it creates, and you'll love its 16-ft. tray ceiling, fireplace, and wall designed to fit a large entertainment center.

• Kitchen: This room is adjacent to and visually connected to the great room but has excellent features of its own that make it an easy place to cook or clean.

• Master Suite: Separated from the other bedrooms, this suite is planned for privacy. You'll love the bath here and look forward to the quiet you can find at the end of the day.

• Additional Bedrooms: In a wing of their own, the other two bedrooms share a bath.

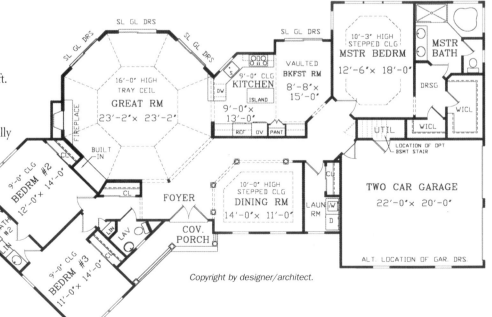

Rear Elevation

Copyright by designer/architect.

Plan #271042

Dimensions: 69'8" W x 71'4" D

Levels: 2

Square Footage: 3,469

Main Level Sq. Ft.: 2,132

Upper Level Sq. Ft.: 1,337

Bedrooms: 5

Bathrooms: 3½

Foundation: Basement

Materials List Available: No

Price Category: G

Images provided by designer/architect.

This thoroughly up-to-date home features two deluxe suites.

Features:

- Dining/Living: Flanking the soaring entry, these formal rooms are perfect for elegant parties.

- Swing Suite: At the rear of the home, this suite can house guests or an elderly parent.

- Family Room: Big and welcoming, this space includes a fireplace and a TV nook.

Kitchen

- Master Suite: The home's second suite offers all of today's best amenities, including a vaulted ceiling and private bath.

Main Level Floor Plan

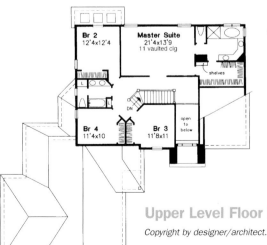

Upper Level Floor Plan

Copyright by designer/architect.

Plan #441022

Dimensions: 42' W x 53' D
Levels: 2
Square Footage: 2,820
Main Level Sq. Ft.: 1,383
Upper Level Sq. Ft.: 1,437
Bedrooms: 4
Bathrooms: 3½
Foundation: Crawl space; slab or basement available for fee
Materials List Available: No
Price Category: F

Images provided by designer/architect.

This home has all the features that are important to today's discerning homebuyer. Beautiful exterior details include multiple gables and an arched entry.

Features:

• Great Room: This spacious two-story room features a fireplace and a wall of windows to allow in an abundance of natural light.

• Kitchen: Featuring a butler's pantry and a breakfast nook, this island kitchen also has a great view of the fireplace in the great room.

• Master Suite: This suite, with its vaulted ceiling, is the perfect place for an escape after a busy day. The master bath has a walk-in closet, dual vanities, a shower, and a large tub.

• Bedrooms: A vaulted guest bedroom contains its own private bath. The two additional bedrooms and a third bath provide plenty of room for a growing family.

Rear Elevation

Main Level Floor Plan

Copyright by designer/architect.

Upper Level Floor Plan

Plan #271081

Dimensions: 86' W x 54' D

Levels: 1

Square Footage: 2,539

Bedrooms: 3

Bathrooms: 2

Foundation: Slab

Materials List Available: No

Price Category: E

Images provided by designer/architect.

This traditional home is sure to impress your guests and even your neighbors.

Features:

- **Living Room:** This quiet space off the foyer is perfect for pleasant conversation.

- **Family Room:** A perfect gathering spot, this room is nicely enhanced by a fireplace.

- **Kitchen:** This room easily serves the bayed morning room and the formal dining room.

- **Master Suite:** The master bedroom overlooks a side patio, and boasts a private bath with a skylight and a whirlpool tub.

- **Library:** This cozy room is perfect for curling up with a good novel. It would also make a great extra bedroom.

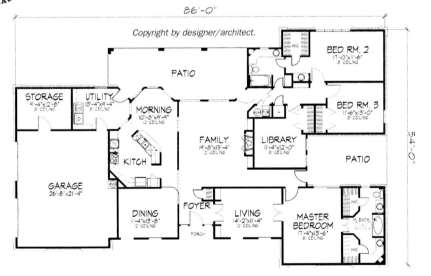

SMARTtip
Determining Curtain Length

Follow length guidelines for foolproof results, but remember that they're not rules. Go ahead and play with curtain and drapery lengths. Instead of shortening long panels at the hem, for instance, take up excess material by blousing them over tiebacks for a pleasing effect.

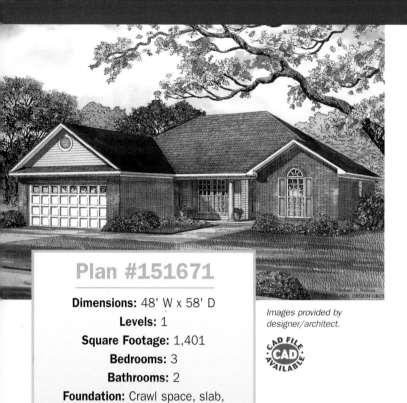

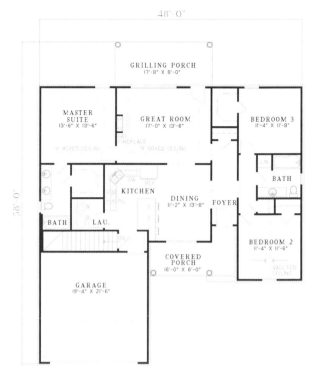

Plan #151671

Dimensions: 48' W x 58' D

Levels: 1

Square Footage: 1,401

Bedrooms: 3

Bathrooms: 2

Foundation: Crawl space, slab, basement, or walk-out

CompleteCost List Available: Yes

Price Category: B

Images provided by designer/architect.

Copyright by designer/architect.

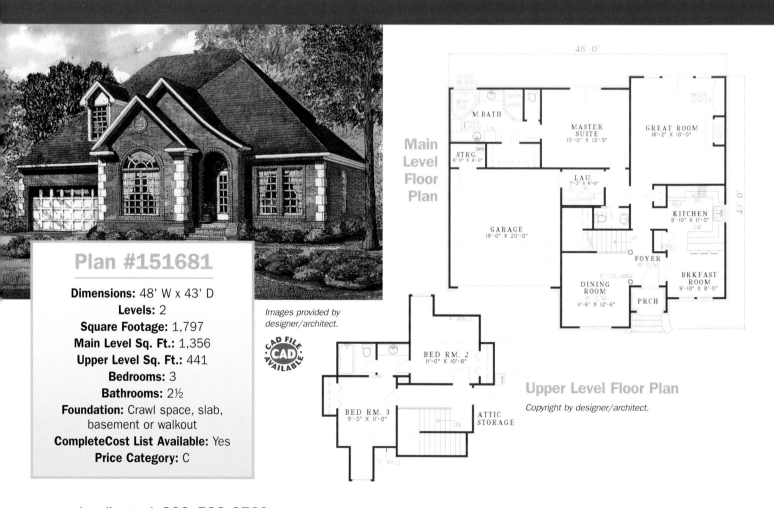

Plan #151681

Dimensions: 48' W x 43' D

Levels: 2

Square Footage: 1,797

Main Level Sq. Ft.: 1,356

Upper Level Sq. Ft.: 441

Bedrooms: 3

Bathrooms: 2½

Foundation: Crawl space, slab, basement or walkout

CompleteCost List Available: Yes

Price Category: C

Images provided by designer/architect.

Main Level Floor Plan

Upper Level Floor Plan

Copyright by designer/architect.

Plan #241005

Dimensions: 53' W x 55'9" D

Levels: 1

Square Footage: 1,670

Bedrooms: 3

Bathrooms: 2

Foundation: Crawl space or slab (basement for fee)

Materials List Available: No

Price Category: C

This charming starter home, in split-bedroom format, combines big-house features in a compact design.

Features:

- **Great Room:** With easy access to the formal dining room, kitchen, and breakfast area, this great room features a cozy fireplace.

- **Kitchen:** This big kitchen, with easy access to a walk-in pantry, features an island for added work space and a lovely plant shelf that separates it from the great room.

- **Master Suite:** Separated for privacy, this master suite offers a roomy bath with whirlpool tub, dual vanities, a separate shower, and a large walk-in closet.

- **Additional Rooms:** Additional rooms include a laundry/utility room—with space for a washer, dryer, and freezer—a large area above the garage, well-suited for a media or game room, and two secondary bedrooms.

Images provided by designer/architect.

Copyright by designer/architect.

Bonus Area Floor Plan

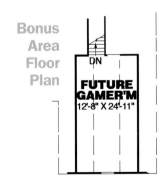

SMARTtip

Window Scarf

The best way to wrap a window scarf around a pole is as follows:

- Lay out the material on a large, clean surface. Gather the fabric at the top of each jabot, and use elastic to hold it together.

- Swing one jabot into place over the pole and, starting from there, wind the swag portion as many times as you need around the pole until you reach the elastic at the second jabot, which should have landed at the opposite pole end.

- Readjust wraps along the pole. Generally, wrapped swags just touch or slightly overlap.

- For a dramatic effect, stuff the wrapped swags with tissue paper or thin foam, depending on the translucence and weight of fabric.

- Release elastics at tops of jabots.

Plan #271002

Dimensions: 44'8" W x 50'8" D

Levels: 1

Square Footage: 1,252

Bedrooms: 3

Bathrooms: 2

Foundation: Basement

Materials List Available: Yes

Price Category: B

Images provided by designer/architect.

This traditional home combines a modest square footage with stylish extras.

Features:

- **Living Room:** Spacious and inviting, this gathering spot is brightened by a Palladian window arrangement, warmed by a fireplace, and topped by a vaulted ceiling.

- **Dining Room:** The vaulted ceiling also crowns this room, which shares the living room's fireplace. Sliding doors lead to a backyard deck.

- **Kitchen:** Smart design ensures a place for everything.

- **Master Suite:** The master bedroom boasts a vaulted ceiling, cheery windows, and a private bath.

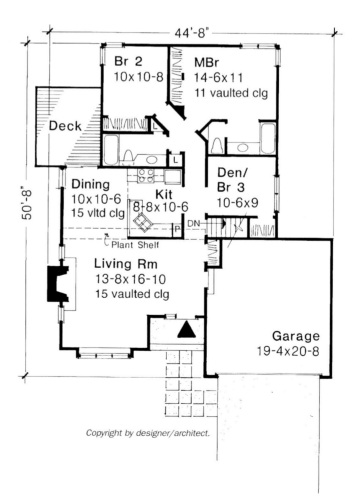

Copyright by designer/architect.

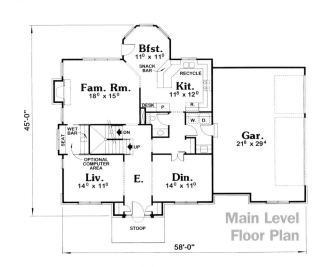

Plan #121030

Dimensions: 58' W x 45' D
Levels: 2
Square Footage: 2,613
Main Level Sq. Ft.: 1,333
Upper Level Sq. Ft.: 1,280
Bedrooms: 4
Bathrooms: 2½
Foundation: Basement
Materials List Available: Yes
Price Category: F

Images provided by designer/architect.

CAD FILE AVAILABLE

Main Level Floor Plan

Upper Level Floor Plan

Copyright by designer/architect.

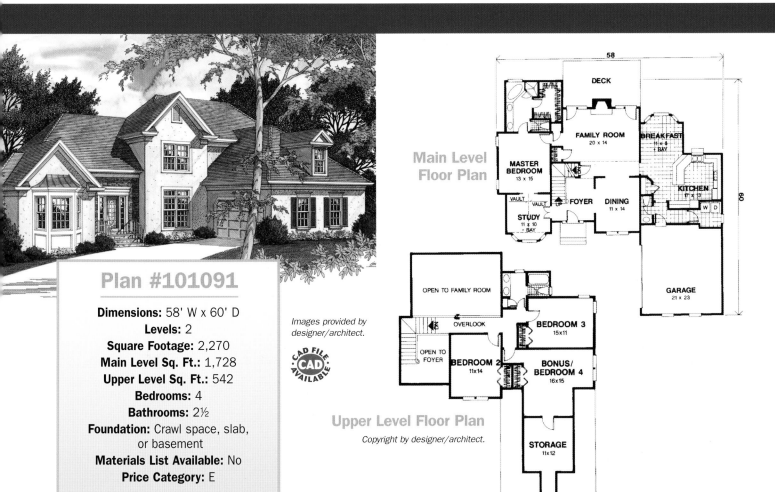

Plan #101091

Dimensions: 58' W x 60' D
Levels: 2
Square Footage: 2,270
Main Level Sq. Ft.: 1,728
Upper Level Sq. Ft.: 542
Bedrooms: 4
Bathrooms: 2½
Foundation: Crawl space, slab, or basement
Materials List Available: No
Price Category: E

Images provided by designer/architect.

CAD FILE AVAILABLE

Main Level Floor Plan

Upper Level Floor Plan

Copyright by designer/architect.

Plan #151117

Dimensions: 66' W x 55' D

Levels: 1

Square Footage: 1,957

Bedrooms: 3

Bathrooms: 3

Foundation: Crawl space, slab, or basement

CompleteCost List Available: Yes

Price Category: D

Images provided by designer/architect.

You'll love this home if you have a family-centered lifestyle and enjoy an active social life.

Features:

- **Foyer:** A 10-ft. ceiling sets the tone for this home.

- **Great Room:** A 10-ft. boxed ceiling and fireplace are the highlights of this room, which also has a door leading to the rear covered porch.

- **Dining Room:** Columns mark the entry from the foyer to this lovely formal dining room.

- **Study:** Add the French doors from the foyer to transform bedroom 3, with its vaulted ceiling, into a quiet study.

- **Kitchen:** This large kitchen includes a pantry and shares an eating bar with the adjoining, bayed breakfast room.

- **Master Suite:** You'll love the access to the rear porch, as well as the bath with every amenity, in this suite.

Copyright by designer/architect.

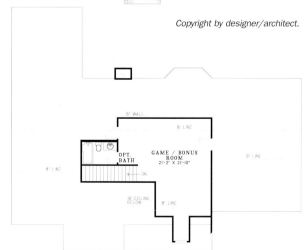

Bonus Area Floor Plan

Plan #161039

Dimensions: 61' W x 41'8" D
Levels: 2
Square Footage: 2,320
Main Level Sq. Ft.: 1,595
Upper Level Sq. Ft.: 725
Bedrooms: 4
Bathrooms: 2½
Foundation: Basement
Materials List Available: Yes
Price Category: E

A touch of old-world charm combines with the comfort and convenience of modern amenities to create a delightful home.

CAD FILE AVAILABLE

Images provided by designer/architect.

Features:

- **Great Room:** This great room is the focal point of this lovely home. The wonderful room has a two-story ceiling, fireplace, and French doors to the rear yard. Split stairs lead to a second floor balcony.

- **Dining Room:** Adjacent to the foyer, this formal dining room has a boxed window, furniture alcove, and butler's pantry.

- **Kitchen:** This kitchen is a wonderful food-preparation area, consisting of a walk-in pantry, oven cabinet, and center island.

- **Master Suite:** This master bedroom has a sloped ceiling and relaxing garden bath that showcases a whirlpool tub, shower, double-bowl vanity, and large walk-in closet.

Rear Elevation

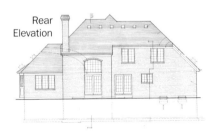

Main Level Floor Plan

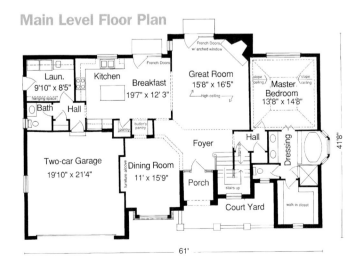

Upper Level Floor Plan

Copyright by designer/architect.

Plan #151009

Dimensions: 44' W x 86'2" D
Levels: 1
Square Footage: 1,601
Bedrooms: 3
Bathrooms: 2
Foundation: Crawl space, slab
CompleteCost List Available: Yes
Price Category: C

Images provided by designer/architect.

This can be the perfect home for a site with views you can enjoy in all seasons and at all times.

Features:

- Porches: Enjoy the front porch with its 10-ft. ceiling and the more private back porch where you can set up a grill or just get away from it all.

- Foyer: With a 10-ft. ceiling, this foyer opens to the great room for a warm welcome.

- Great Room: Your family will love the media center and the easy access to the rear porch.

- Kitchen: This well-designed kitchen is open to the dining room and the breakfast nook, which also opens to the rear porch.

- Master Suite: The bedroom has a 10-ft. boxed ceiling and a door to the rear. The bath includes a corner whirlpool tub with glass block windows.

- Bedrooms: Bedroom 2 has a vaulted ceiling, while bedroom 3 features a built-in desk.

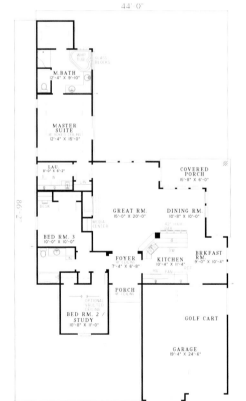

Copyright by designer/architect.

SMARTtip

Fertilizing Your Grass

Fertilizers contain nutrients balanced for different kinds of growth. The ratio of nutrients is indicated on the package by three numbers (for example, 10-10-10). The first specifies nitrogen content; the second, phosphorus; and the third, potash.

Nitrogen helps grass blades to grow and improves the quality and thickness of the turf. Fertilizers contain up to 30 percent nitrogen.

Phosphorus helps grass to develop a healthy root system. It also speeds up the maturation process of the plant.

Potash helps grass stay healthy by providing amino acids and proteins to the plants.

Plan #171013

Dimensions: 74' W x 72' D
Levels: 1
Square Footage: 3,084
Bedrooms: 4
Bathrooms: 3½
Foundation: Crawl space or slab
Materials List Available: Yes
Price Category: G

Images provided by designer/architect.

Impressive porch columns add to the country charm of this amenity-filled family home.

Features:

• Ceiling Height: 10 ft.

• Foyer: The sense of style continues from the front porch into this foyer, which opens to the formal dining room and the living room.

• Dining Room: Two handsome support columns accentuate the elegance of this dining room.

• Living Room: This living room features a cozy corner fireplace and plenty of room for the entire family to gather and relax.

• Kitchen: You'll be inspired to new culinary heights in this kitchen, which offers plenty of counter space, a snack bar, a built-in pantry, and a china closet.

• Master Suite: The bedroom of this master suite has a fireplace and overlooks a rear courtyard. The bath has two vanities a large walk-in closet, a deluxe tub, a walk-in shower, and a skylight.

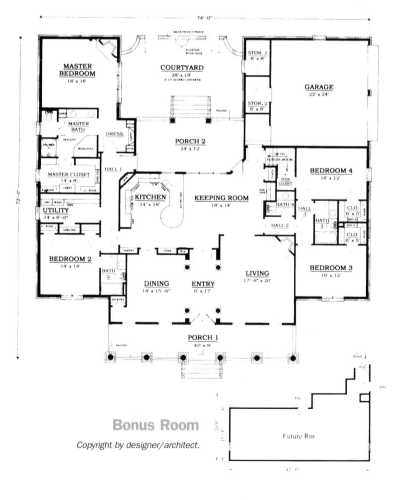

Bonus Room

Copyright by designer/architect.

Plan #161029

Dimensions: 87' W x 82' D
Levels: 2
Square Footage: 4,470
Main Level Sq. Ft.: 3,300
Upper Level Sq. Ft.: 1,170
Bedrooms: 4
Bathrooms: 3 full, 2 half
Foundation: Basement
Materials List Available: Yes
Price Category: I

Images provided by designer/architect.

This gracious home is so impressive — inside and out — that it suits the most discriminating tastes.

Features:

- **Foyer:** A balcony overlooks this gracious area decorated by tall columns.

- **Hearth Room:** Visually open to the kitchen and the breakfast area, this room is ideal for any sort of gathering.

- **Great Room:** Colonial columns also form

the entry here, and a magnificent window treatment that includes French doors leads to the terrace.

- **Library:** Built-in shelving adds practicality to this quiet retreat.

- **Kitchen:** Spread out on the oversized island with a cooktop and seating.

- **Additional Bedrooms:** Walk-in closets and private access to a bath define each bedroom.

Main Level Floor Plan

Copyright by designer/architect.

Upper Level Floor Plan

Rear View

Living Room

Living Room/Kitchen

Ideas for Entertaining

Whether an everyday family meal or a big party for 50, make it memorable and fun. With a world of options, it's easier than you think. Be imaginative with food and decoration. Although it is true that great hamburgers and hot dogs will taste good even if served on plain white paper plates, make the meal more fun by following a theme of some sort — color, occasion, or seasonal activity, for example. Be inventive with the basic elements as well as the extraneous touches, such as flowers and lighting. Here are some examples to get you started.

- For an all-American barbecue, set a picnic table with a patchwork quilt having red, white, and blue in it. Use similar colors for the napkins, and perhaps even bandannas. Include a star-studded centerpiece.

- Make a children-size dining set using an old door propped up on crates, and surround it with appropriate-size benches or chairs. Cover the table with brightly colored, easy-to-clean waxed or vinyl-covered fabric.

- If you're planning an elegant dinner party, move your dining room table outside and set it with your best linens, china, silver, and crystal. Add romantic lighting with candles in fabulous candelabras, and set a beautiful but small floral arrangement at each place setting.

- Design a centerpiece showcasing the flowers from your garden. Begin the arrangement with a base of purchased flowers, and fill in with some of your homegrown blooms. That way your flower beds will still be full of blossoms when the guests arrive.

- Base your party theme on the vegetables growing in your yard, and let them be the inspiration for the menu. When your zucchini plants are flowering, wow your family or guests by serving steamed squash blossoms. Or if the vegetables are starting to develop, lightly grill them with other young veggies — they have a much more delicate flavor than mature vegetables do.

- During berry season, host an elegant berry brunch. Serve mixed-berry crepes on your prettiest plates.

Plan #101017

Dimensions: 57' W x 51' D
Levels: 2
Square Footage: 2,253
Main Level Sq. Ft.: 1,719
Upper Level Sq. Ft.: 534
Opt. Upper Level Bonus Sq. Ft.: 247
Bedrooms: 4
Bathrooms: 3
Foundation: Basement
Materials List Available: No
Price Category: E

Images provided by designer/architect.

This alluring two-story "master-down" design blends a spectacular floor plan with a lovely facade to create a home that's simply irresistible.

Features:

- **Entry:** You're welcomed by an inviting front porch and greeted by a beautiful leaded glass door leading to this two-story entry.

- **Family Room:** A corner fireplace and a window wall with arched transoms accent this dramatic room.

- **Master Suite:** This sumptuous suite includes a double tray ceiling, sitting area, and his and her walk-in closets. The master bathroom features dual vanities, a corner tub, and a shower.

- **Bedrooms:** Located upstairs, these two additional bedrooms share a Jack-and-Jill bathroom.

Main Level Floor Plan

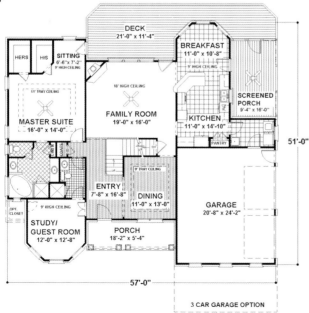

Upper Level Floor Plan

Copyright by designer/architect.

Plan #161017

Dimensions: 61' W x 37'6" D
Levels: 2
Square Footage: 2,653
Main Level Sq. Ft.: 1,365
Upper Level Sq. Ft.: 1,288
Bedrooms: 4
Bathrooms: 2½
Foundation: Basement
Materials List Available: Yes
Price Category: F

If a traditional look makes you feel comfortable, you'll love this spacious, family-friendly home.

Features:

- **Family Room:** Accessorize with cozy cushions to make the most of this sunken room. Windows flank the fireplace, adding warm, natural light. Doors leading to the rear deck make this room a family "headquarters."

- **Living and Dining Rooms:** These formal rooms open to each other, so you'll love hosting gatherings in this home.

- **Kitchen:** A handy pantry fits well with the traditional feeling of this home, and an island adds contemporary convenience.

- **Master Suite:** Relax in the whirlpool tub in your bath and enjoy the storage space in the two walk-in closets in the bedroom.

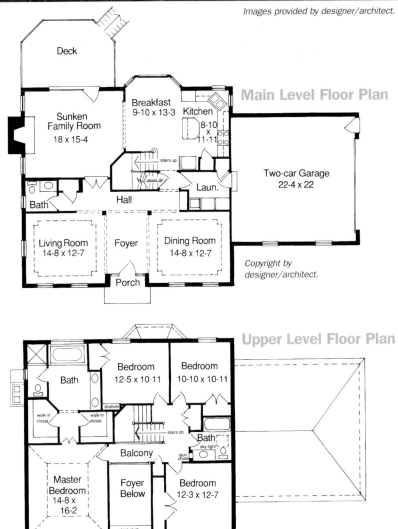

Images provided by designer/architect.

Copyright by designer/architect.

Plan #121001

Dimensions: 56' W x 58' D
Levels: 1
Square Footage: 1,911
Bedrooms: 3
Bathrooms: 2
Foundation: Basement
Materials List Available: Yes
Price Category: D

Images provided by designer/architect.

Detailed, soaring ceilings and top-notch amenities set this distinctive home apart.

Features:

- Ceiling Height: 8 ft. except as noted.

- Great Room: A soaring ceiling and six tall transom-topped windows make this a light and airy spot for entertaining.

- Formal Dining Room: The entry enjoys a pleasing view of this dining room's detailed 12-ft. ceiling and picture window.

- Great Room: At the back of the home, a see-through fireplace in this great room is joined by a built-in entertainment center.

- Hearth Room: This bayed room shares the see-through fireplace with the great room.

- Master Suite: Enjoy the stars and the sun in the private bath's whirlpool and separate shower. The bath features the same decorative ceiling as the dining room.

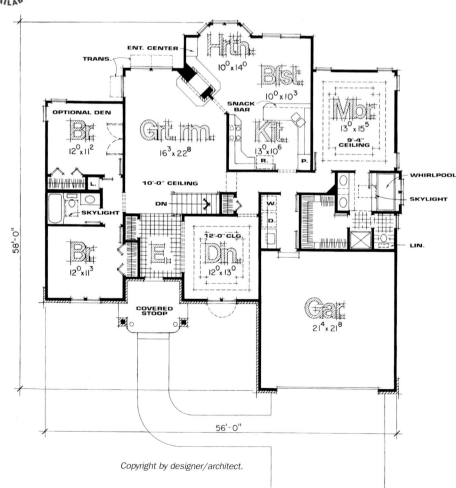

Copyright by designer/architect.

Plan #121028

Dimensions: 54'8" W x 42' D

Levels: 2

Square Footage: 2,644

Main Level Sq. Ft.: 1,366

Upper Level Sq. Ft.: 1,278

Bedrooms: 4

Bathrooms: 2½

Foundation: Basement

Materials List Available: Yes

Price Category: F

Images provided by designer/architect.

This home is filled with special touches and amenities that add up to gracious living.

Features:

- Ceiling Height: 8 ft.

- Formal Living Room: This large, inviting room is the perfect place to entertain guests.

- Family Room: This cozy, comfortable room is accessed through elegant French doors in the living room. It is sure to be the favorite family gathering place with its bay window, see-through fireplace, and bay window.

- Breakfast Area: This area is large enough for the whole family to enjoy a casual meal as they are warmed by the other side of the see-through fireplace. The area features a bay window and built-in bookcase.

- Master Bedroom: Upstairs, enjoy the gracious and practical master bedroom with its boxed ceiling and two walk-in closets.

- Master Bath: Luxuriate in the whirlpool bath as you gaze through the skylight framed by ceiling accents.

Main Level Floor Plan

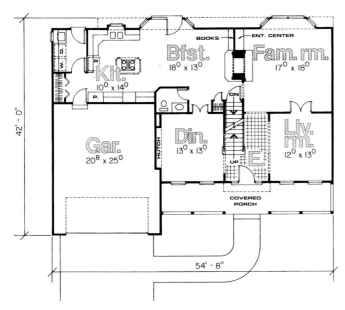

Upper Level Floor Plan

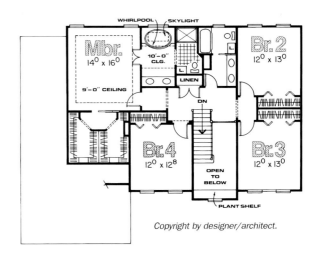

Copyright by designer/architect.

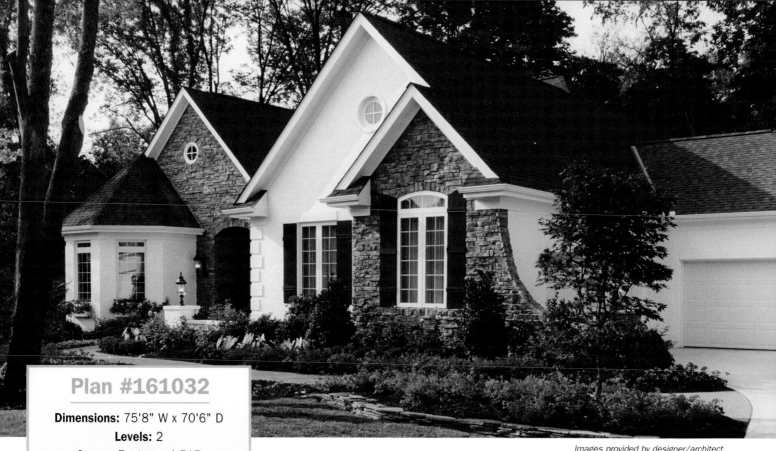

Plan #161032

Dimensions: 75'8" W x 70'6" D
Levels: 2
Square Footage: 4,517
Main Level Sq. Ft.: 2,562
Lower Level Sq. Ft.: 1,955
Bedrooms: 3
Bathrooms: 2 full, 2 half
Foundation: Basement
Materials List Available: Yes
Price Category: I

CAD FILE AVAILABLE

SMARTtip

Art Underfoot

Make a simple geometric pattern with your flooring materials. Create a focal point in a courtyard or a small area of a patio by fashioning an intricate mosaic with tile, stone, or colored concrete. By combining elements and colors, a simple garden room floor becomes a wonderful work of art. Whether you commission a craftsman or do it yourself, you'll have a permanent art installation right in your own backyard.

The brick-and-stone exterior, a recessed entry, and a tower containing a large library combine to convey the strength and character of this enchanting house.

Features:

- Hearth Room: Your family or guests will enjoy this large, comfortable hearth room, which has a gas fireplace and access to the rear deck, perfect for friendly gatherings.

- Kitchen: This spacious kitchen features a walk-in pantry and a center island.

- Master Suite: Designed for privacy, this master suite includes a sloped ceiling and opens to the rear deck. It also features a deluxe whirlpool bath, walk-in shower, separate his and her vanities, and a walk-in closet.

- Lower Level: This lower level includes a separate wine room, exercise room, sauna, two bedrooms, and enough space for a huge recreation room.

Rear Elevation

Images provided by designer/architect.

Main Level Floor Plan

Copyright by designer/architect.

Basement Level Floor Plan

Let Us Help You
Plan Your
Dream Home

Whether you've always dreamed of building your own home or you can't find the right house from among the dozens you've toured, our collection of ultimate home plans can help you achieve the home of your dreams. You could have an architect create a one-of-a-kind home for you, but the design services alone could end up costing up to 15 percent of the cost of construction—a hefty premium for any building project. Isn't it a better idea to select from among the hundreds of unique designs shown in our collection for a fraction of the cost?

What does Creative Homeowner Offer?

In this book, Creative Homeowner provides hundreds of home plans from the country's best architects and designers. Our designs are among the most popular available. Whether your taste runs from traditional to contemporary, Victorian to early American, you are sure to find the best house design for you and your family. Our plans packages include detailed drawings to help you or your builder construct your dream house. **(See page 550.)**

Can I Make Changes to the Plans?

Creative Homeowner offers three ways to help you achieve a truly unique home design. Our customizing service allows for extensive changes to our designs. **(See page 551.)** We also provide reverse images of our plans, or we can give you and your builder the tools for making minor changes on your own. **(See page 552.)**

Can You Help Me Stay on Budget?

Building a house is a large financial investment. To help you stay within your budget, Creative Homeowner can provide you with general construction costs based on your zip code. **(See page 552.)** Also, many of our plans come with the option of buying detailed materials lists to help you price out construction costs.

Is There Anything I Missed?

A typical construction crew consists of a number of skilled professionals. If you plan on doing all or part of the work yourself, or you want to keep tabs on your builder, we offer best-selling building and design books at attractive prices. (See our company Web site at www.creativehomeowner.com.) Our home-building book package covers all phases of home construction, from framing and drywalling to wiring and plumbing. **(See page 560.)**

Our Plans Packages Offer:

All of our home plans are the result of many hours of work by leading architects and professional designers. Most of our home plans include each of the following.

Frontal Sheet

This artist's rendering of the front of the house gives you an idea of how the house will look once it is completed and the property landscaped.

Detailed Floor Plans

These plans show the size and layout of the rooms. They also provide the locations of doors, windows, fireplaces, closets, stairs, and electrical outlets and switches.

Foundation Plan

A foundation plan gives the dimensions of basements, walk-out basements, crawl spaces, pier foundations, and slab construction. Each house design lists the type of foundation included. If the plan you choose does not have the foundation type you require, our customer service department can help you customize the plan to meet your needs.

Roof Plan

In addition to providing the pitch of the roof, these plans also show the locations of dormers, skylights, and other elements.

Exterior Elevations

These drawings show the front, rear, and sides of the house as if you were looking at it head on. Elevations also provide information about architectural features and finish materials.

Interior Elevations and Details

Interior elevations show specific details of such elements as fireplaces, kitchen and bathroom cabinets, built-ins, and other unique features of the design.

Cross Sections

These show the structure as if it were sliced to reveal construction requirements, such as insulation, flooring, and roofing details.

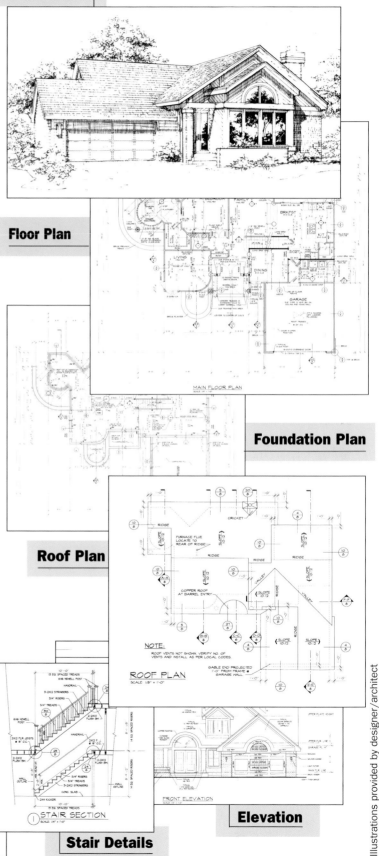

Frontal Sheet

Floor Plan

Foundation Plan

Roof Plan

Cross Sections

Stair Details

Elevation

Illustrations provided by designer/architect

Customize Your Plans in 4 Easy Steps

1 **Select the home plan** that most closely meets your needs. Purchase of a reproducible master is necessary in order to make changes to a plan.

2 **Call 1-800-523-6789 to place your order.** Tell our sales representative you are interested in customizing your plan. To receive your customization cost estimate, we will send you a checklist (via fax or email) for you to complete indicating the changes you would like to make to your plan. There is a $50 nonrefundable consultation fee for this service. If you decide to continue with the custom changes, the $50 fee is credited to the total amount charged.

3 **Fax the completed checklist** to 1-201-760-2431 or email it to us at customize@creativehomeowner.com. Within three business days of receipt of your checklist, a detailed cost estimate will be provided to you.

4 **Once you approve the estimate,** a 75% retainer fee is collected and customization work begins. Preliminary drawings typically take 10 to 15 business days. After approval, we will collect the balance of your customization order cost before shipping the completed plans. You will receive five sets of blueprints or a reproducible master, plus a customized materials list if desired.

Modification Pricing Guide

Categories	Average Cost For Modification
Add or remove living space	Quote required
Bathroom layout redesign	Starting at $120
Kitchen layout redesign	Starting at $120
Garage: add or remove	Starting at $400
Garage: front entry to side load or vice versa	Starting at $300
Foundation changes	Starting at $220
Exterior building materials change	Starting at $200
Exterior openings: add, move, or remove	$65 per opening
Roof line changes	Starting at $360
Ceiling height adjustments	Starting at $280
Fireplace: add or remove	Starting at $90
Screened porch: add	Starting at $280
Wall framing change from 2x4 to 2x6	Starting at $200
Bearing and/or exterior walls changes	Quote required
Non-bearing wall or room changes	$65 per room
Metric conversion of home plan	Starting at $400
Adjust plan for handicapped accessibility	Quote required
Adapt plans for local building code requirements	Quote required
Engineering stamping only	Quote required
Any other engineering services	Quote required
Interactive illustrations (choices of exterior materials)	Quote required

Note: *Any home plan can be customized to accommodate your desired changes. The average prices above are provided only as examples of the most commonly requested changes, and are subject to change without notice. Prices for changes will vary according to the number of modifications requested, plan size, style, and method of design used by the original designer. To obtain a detailed cost estimate, please contact us.*

Terms & Copyright
These home plans are protected under the terms of United States Copyright Law and may not be copied or reproduced in any way, by any means, unless you have purchased reproducible masters, which clearly indicate your right to copy or reproduce. We authorize the use of your chosen home plan as an aid in the construction of one single-family home only. You may not use this home plan to build a second or multiple dwellings without purchasing another blueprint or blueprints, or paying additional home plan fees.

Architectural Seals
Because of differences in building codes, some cities and states now require an architect or engineer licensed in that state to review and "seal" a blueprint, or officially approve it, prior to construction. Delaware, Nevada, New Jersey, and New York require that all plans for houses built in those states be redrawn by an architect licensed in the state in which the home will be built. We strongly advise you to consult with your local building official for information regarding architectural seals.

Before Customization

After

Decide What Type of Plan Package You Need

How many Plans Should You Order?

Standard 8-Set Package. We've found that our 8-set package is the best value for someone who is ready to start building. Once the process begins, a number of people will require their own set of blueprints. The 8-set package provides plans for you, your builder, the subcontractors, mortgage lender, and the building department.
Minimum 5-Set Package. If you are in the bidding process, you may want to order only five sets for the bidding round and reorder additional sets as needed.
1-Set Study Package. The 1-set package allows you to review your home plan in detail. The plan will be marked as a study print, and it is illegal to build a house from a study print alone. It is a violation of copyright law to reproduce a blueprint without permission.

Buying Additional Sets

If you require additional copies of blueprints for your home construction, you can order additional sets within 60 days of the original order date at a reduced price. The cost is $45.00 for each additional set. For more information, contact customer service.

Reproducible Masters

If you plan to make minor changes to one of our home plans, you can purchase reproducible masters. Printed on vellum paper, an erasable paper that you can reproduce in a copying machine, reproducible masters allow an architect, designer, or builder to alter our plans to give you a customized home design. This package also allows you to print as many copies of the modified plans as you need for construction.

CAD Files

CAD files are the complete set of home plans in an electronic file format. Choose this option if there are multiple changes you wish made to the home plans and you have a local design professional able to make the changes. Not available for all plans. Please contact our order department or visit our website to check the availability of CAD files for your plan.

Mirror-Reverse Sets/Right-Reading Reverse

Plans can be printed in mirror-reverse—we can "flip" plans to create a mirror image of the design. This is useful when the house would fit your site or personal preferences if all the rooms were on the opposite side than shown. As the image is reversed, the lettering and dimensions will also be reversed, meaning they will read backwards. Therefore, when ordering mirror-reverse drawings, you must order at least one set of right-reading plans. A $50.00 fee per plan order will be charged for mirror-reverse (regardless of the number of mirror-reverse sets ordered). Some plans are available in right-reading reverse, this feature will show the plan in reverse, but the writing on the plan will be readable. A $150.00 fee per plan order will be charged for right-reading reverse (regardless of the number of right-reading reverse sets ordered). Please contact our order department at or visit our website to check the availibility of this feature for your chosen plan.

EZ Quote: Home Cost Estimator

EZ Quote is our response to one of the most frequently asked questions we hear from customers: "How much will the house cost me to build?" EZ Quote: Home Cost Estimator will enable you to obtain a calculated building cost to construct your home, based on labor rates and building material costs within your zip code area. This summary is useful for those who want to know the total construction costs before purchasing sets of home plans. It will also provide a level of comfort when you begin soliciting bids. The cost is $29.95 for the first EZ Quote and $14.95 for each additional one. Available only in the U.S. and Canada.

CompleteCost Estimator

CompleteCost Estimator is a valuable tool for use in planning and constructing your new home. It combines the detail of a materials list with line-by-line cost estimating. The result is a complete, detailed estimate—similar to a bid. CompleteCost Estimator is only available for certain plans (please see Plan Index) and may only be ordered with the purchase of at least five sets of home plans. The cost is $125.00 for CompleteCost Estimator.

Materials List

Available for most of our plans, the Materials List provides you an invaluable resource in planning and estimating the cost of your home. Each Materials List outlines the quantity, dimensions, and type of materials needed to build your home (with the exception of mechanical systems). You will get faster, more-accurate bids from your contractors and building suppliers. A Materials List may only be ordered with the purchase of at least five sets of home plans.

Order Toll Free by Phone
1-800-523-6789
By Fax: 201-760-2431

Regular office hours are
8:30AM–7:30PM ET, Mon–Fri
Orders received 3PM ET, will be processed and
shipped within two business days.

Order Online
www.ultimateplans.com

Mail Your Order
Creative Homeowner
Attn: Home Plans
24 Park Way
Upper Saddle River, NJ 07458

Canadian Customers
Order Toll Free 1-800-393-1883

Mail Your Order (Canada)
Creative Homeowner Canada
Attn: Home Plans
113-437 Martin St., Ste. 215
Penticton, BC V2A 5L1

Before You Order

Our Exchange Policy

Blueprints are nonrefundable. However, should you find that the plan you have purchased does not fit your needs, you may exchange that plan for another plan in our collection within 60 days from the date of your original order. The entire content of your original order must be returned before an exchange will be processed. You will be charged a processing fee of 20% of the amount of the original order, the cost difference between the new plan set and the original plan set (if applicable), and all related shipping costs for the new plans. Contact our order department for more information. Please note: reproducible masters may only be exchanged if the package is unopened.

Building Codes and Requirements

At the time of creation, our plans meet the bulding code requirements published by the Building Officials and Code Administrators International, the Southern Building Code Congress International, the International Conference of Building Officials, or the Council of American Building Officials. Because building codes vary from area to area, some drawing modifications and/or the assistance of a professional designer or architect may be necessary to comply with your local codes or to accommodate specific building site conditions. We strongly advise you to consult with your local building official for information regarding codes governing your area.

Blueprint Price Schedule

Price Code	1 Set	5 Sets	8 Sets	Reproducible Masters	CAD	Materials List
A	$300	$345	$395	$530	$950	$85
B	$375	$435	$480	$600	$1,100	$85
C	$435	$500	$550	$650	$1,200	$85
D	$490	$560	$610	$710	$1,300	$95
E	$550	$620	$660	$770	$1,400	$95
F	$610	$680	$720	$830	$1,500	$95
G	$670	$740	$780	$890	$1,600	$95
H	$760	$830	$870	$980	$1,700	$95
I	$860	$930	$970	$1,080	$1,800	$105
J	$960	$1,030	$1,070	$1,190	$1,900	$105
K	$1,070	$1,150	$1,190	$1,320	$2,030	$105
L	$1,180	$1,270	$1,310	$1,460	$2,170	$105

Note: All prices subject to change

Shipping & Handling

	1-4 Sets	5-7 Sets	8+ Sets or Reproducibles	CAD
US Regular (7–10 business days)	$18	$20	$25	$25
US Priority (3–5 business days)	$25	$30	$35	$35
US Express (1–2 business days)	$40	$45	$50	$50
Canada Express (1–2 business days)	$60	$70	$80	$80
Worldwide Express (3–5 business days)	$80	$80	$80	$80

Note: All delivery times are from date the blueprint package is shipped (typically within 1-2 days of placing order).

Order Form Please send me the following:

Plan Number: _____ **Price Code:** ____ (See Plan Index.)

Indicate Foundation Type: (Select ONE. See plan page for availability.)
❏ Slab   ❏ Crawl space   ❏ Basement   ❏ Walk-out basement

❏ Optional Foundation for Fee _____ $_____
(Please enter foundation here)

Please call all our order department or visit our website for optional foundation fee

Basic Blueprint Package — Cost

❏ CAD File — $_____
❏ Reproducible Masters — $_____
❏ 8-Set Plan Package — $_____
❏ 5-Set Plan Package — $_____
❏ 1-Set Study Package — $_____
❏ Additional plan sets:
   __ sets at $45.00 per set — $_____
❏ Print in mirror-reverse: $50.00 per order — $_____
   Please call all our order department or visit our website for availibility
❏ Print in right-reading reverse: $150.00 per order — $_____
   Please call all our order department or visit our website for availibility

Important Extras

❏ Materials List — $_____
❏ CompleteCost Materials Report at $125.00 — $_____
   Zip Code of Home/Building Site _____
❏ EZ Quote for Plan #_____ at $29.95 — $_____
❏ Additional EZ Quotes for Plan #s_____
   at $14.95 each — $_____
Shipping (see chart above) — $_____
SUBTOTAL — $_____
Sales Tax (NJ residents only, add 6%) — $_____
TOTAL — $_____

Order Toll Free: 1-800-523-6789 By Fax: 201-760-2431
Creative Homeowner
24 Park Way
Upper Saddle River, NJ 07458

Name _____
(Please print or type)

Street _____
(Please do not use a P.O. Box)

City _____ State _____

Country _____ Zip _____

Daytime telephone (_____) _____

Fax (_____) _____
(Required for reproducible orders)

E-Mail _____

Payment ❏ Check/money order *Make checks payable to Creative Homeowner*

❏ VISA   ❏ MasterCard   ❏ American Express Cards   ❏ DISCOVER

Credit card number _____

Expiration date (mm/yy) _____

Signature _____

Please check the appropriate box:
❏ Licensed builder/contractor   ❏ Homeowner   ❏ Renter

SOURCE CODE CA350 www.ultimateplans.com

Copyright Notice

All home plans sold through this publication are protected by copyright. Reproduction of these home plans, either in whole or in part, including any form and/or preparation of derivative works thereof, for any reason without prior written permission is strictly prohibited. The purchase of a set of home plans in no way transfers any copyright or other ownership interest in it to the buyer except for a limited license to use that set of home plans for the construction of one, and only one, dwelling unit. The purchase of additional sets of the home plans at a reduced price from the original set or as a part of a multiple-set package does not convey to the buyer a license to construct more than one dwelling.

Similarly, the purchase of reproducible home plans (sepias, mylars) carries the same copyright protection as mentioned above. It is generally allowed to make up to a maximum of 10 copies for the construction of a single dwelling only. To use any plans more than once, and to avoid any copyright license infringement, it is necessary to contact the plan designer to receive a release and license for any extended use. Whereas a purchaser of reproducible plans is granted a license to make copies, it should be noted that because blueprints are copyrighted, making photocopies from them is illegal.

Copyright and licensing of home plans for construction exist to protect all parties. Copyright respects and supports the intellectual property of the original architect or designer. Copyright law has been reinforced over the past few years. Willful infringement could cause settlements for statutory damages to $150,000.00 plus attorney fees, damages, and loss of profits.

CRE▲TIVE HOMEOWNER®

ultimateplans.com

Order online by visiting our Web site.

Open 24 hours a day, 7 days a week.

Still haven't found your perfect home?
With thousands of plans online at ultimateplans.com, there are plenty more to choose from. Using our automated search tools, we make the process even easier. Just enter your ideal home criteria, and let our search tools find the plans for you!

Other great benefits for many plans at ultimateplans.com include:

- **More photos of both the exterior and interior of many of our most popular homes**
- **More side and rear elevations**
- **More data and information about each particular plan**

In addition, you will find more information about the building process and even free step-by-step DIY projects you can do!

Index

For pricing, see page 553.

Plan #	Price Code	Page	Total Finished Sq. Ft.	Materials List	CompleteCost
101003	C	388	1,593	Y	N
101004	C	215	1,787	Y	N
101005	D	322	1,992	Y	N
101005	D	323	1,992	Y	N
101006	D	388	1,982	Y	N
101008	D	333	2,088	Y	N
101009	D	383	2,097	Y	N
101010	D	74	2,187	Y	N
101011	D	192	2,184	Y	N
101011	D	193	2,184	Y	N
101012	E	391	2,288	N	N
101013	E	434	2,564	Y	N
101013	E	435	2,564	Y	N
101014	C	147	1,598	N	N
101015	C	278	1,647	N	N
101016	D	525	1,985	Y	N
101017	E	544	2,253	N	N
101019	F	17	2,954	N	N
101020	F	162	2,972	N	N
101022	D	352	1,992	Y	N
101060	C	427	1,653	N	N
101061	C	354	1,681	N	N
101067	C	337	1,770	N	N
101091	E	537	2,270	N	N
101098	E	354	2,398	Y	N
101100	E	292	2,479	Y	N
111003	G	411	3,319	N	N
111004	F	402	2,968	N	N
111005	H	520	3,590	N	N
111006	E	509	2,241	N	N
111010	D	254	1,804	N	N
111015	E	22	2,208	N	N
111017	E	60	2,323	N	N
111018	F	491	2,745	N	N
111021	E	254	2,221	N	N
111027	F	268	2,601	N	N
111030	F	507	2,905	N	N
111031	F	44	2,869	N	N
111031	F	45	2,869	N	N
111032	F	268	2,904	N	N
111034	G	71	3,088	N	N
111035	G	411	3,064	N	N
111039	G	188	3,335	N	N
111040	C	251	1,650	N	N
111041	C	257	1,743	N	N
111042	C	251	1,779	N	N
111046	C	341	1,768	N	N
111047	D	243	1,863	N	N
111049	E	262	2,205	N	N
111051	E	361	2,471	N	N
121001	D	546	1,911	Y	N
121003	C	55	2,498	Y	N
121004	C	99	1,666	Y	N
121006	C	139	1,762	Y	N
121007	E	76	2,512	Y	N
121008	C	67	1,651	Y	N
121009	B	11	1,422	Y	N
121010	D	331	1,902	Y	N
121011	C	12	1,724	Y	N
121014	D	145	1,869	Y	N
121015	D	15	1,999	Y	N
121017	E	31	2,353	Y	N
121018	H	88	3,950	Y	N
121019	H	65	3,775	Y	N
121020	E	35	2,480	Y	N
121021	E	159	2,270	Y	N
121023	H	56	3,904	Y	N
121024	G	39	3,057	Y	N
121025	E	24	2,562	Y	N
121027	C	187	1,660	Y	N
121028	F	547	2,644	Y	N
121029	E	14	2,576	Y	N
121030	F	537	2,613	Y	N
121031	C	21	1,772	Y	N

Plan #	Price Code	Page	Total Finished Sq. Ft.	Materials List	CompleteCost
121032	E	213	2,339	Y	N
121034	E	501	2,223	Y	N
121035	B	163	1,463	Y	N
121037	E	164	2,292	Y	N
121045	C	168	1,575	Y	N
121046	F	59	2,655	Y	N
121047	G	175	3,072	Y	N
121048	F	436	2,975	Y	N
121049	G	525	3,335	Y	N
121050	D	84	1,996	Y	N
121051	D	90	1,808	Y	N
121053	E	66	2,456	Y	N
121056	B	412	1,479	Y	N
121057	E	326	2,311	Y	N
121060	B	285	1,339	Y	N
121061	G	505	3,025	Y	N
121062	G	47	3,448	Y	N
121063	G	87	3,473	Y	N
121064	D	441	1,846	Y	N
121065	G	81	3,407	Y	N
121066	D	487	2,078	Y	N
121067	F	83	2,708	Y	N
121069	F	77	2,914	Y	N
121071	F	515	2,957	Y	N
121073	E	62	2,579	Y	N
121074	E	79	2,486	Y	N
121078	E	508	2,248	Y	N
121079	F	468	2,688	Y	N
121080	E	475	2,384	Y	N
121081	G	454	3,623	Y	N
121082	F	60	2,932	Y	N
121083	F	129	2,695	Y	N
121084	C	501	1,728	Y	N
121085	D	472	1,948	Y	N
121086	D	489	1,998	Y	N
121088	E	438	2,340	Y	N
121089	F	96	1,976	Y	N
121090	F	446	2,645	Y	N
121091	F	470	2,689	Y	N
121092	D	91	1,887	Y	N
121094	C	503	1,768	Y	N
121095	E	436	2,282	Y	N
121100	G	50	3,750	Y	N
131001	D	173	1,615	Y	N
131002	C	115	1,709	Y	N
131003	B	418	1,466	Y	N
131004	B	327	1,097	Y	N
131005	C	373	1,595	Y	N
131006	E	378	2,193	Y	N
131007	C	358	1,595	Y	N
131007	C	359	1,595	Y	N
131009	D	473	2,018	Y	N
131011	E	498	1,897	Y	N
131013	C	166	1,489	Y	N
131014	B	363	1,380	Y	N
131015	E	74	1,860	Y	N
131016	E	150	1,902	Y	N
131017	C	403	1,480	Y	N
131019	F	530	2,243	Y	N
131021	H	120	3,110	Y	N
131022	E	513	2,092	Y	N
131023	F	295	2,460	Y	N
131026	G	494	2,796	Y	N
131026	G	495	2,796	Y	N
131027	F	132	2,567	Y	N
131027	F	133	2,567	Y	N
131028	F	390	2,696	Y	N
131029	F	154	2,718	Y	N
131029	F	155	2,718	Y	N
131030	F	128	2,470	Y	N
131031	I	496	4,027	Y	N
131032	F	266	2,455	Y	N
131033	G	41	2,813	Y	N
131035	D	171	1,892	Y	N

Plan #	Price Code	Page	Total Finished Sq. Ft.	Materials List	CompleteCost
131041	D	171	1,679	Y	N
131043	D	161	1,945	Y	N
131044	D	474	1,994	Y	N
131045	E	442	2,347	Y	N
131046	F	143	2,245	Y	N
131047	C	130	1,793	Y	N
131050	G	419	2,874	Y	N
131051	F	126	2,431	Y	N
131055	E	180	2,575	Y	N
131055	E	181	2,575	Y	N
131056	B	236	1,396	Y	N
141001	B	324	1,208	Y	N
141010	C	503	1,765	Y	N
141011	D	365	1,869	Y	N
141012	D	148	1,870	Y	N
141014	D	170	2,091	Y	N
141016	E	160	2,416	Y	N
141017	E	121	2,480	N	N
141019	F	437	2,826	Y	N
141019	F	450	2,826	Y	N
141020	G	481	3,140	N	N
141021	F	365	2,614	Y	N
141022	F	372	2,911	N	N
141025	C	492	1,721	Y	N
141026	D	150	1,993	Y	N
141027	D	492	2,088	Y	N
141028	E	481	2,215	Y	N
141030	E	71	2,323	Y	N
141031	E	443	2,367	N	N
141038	C	152	1,668	Y	N
151001	G	13	3,124	N	Y
151002	E	51	2,444	N	Y
151003	C	78	1,680	N	Y
151004	D	48	2,107	N	Y
151005	D	328	1,940	N	Y
151007	C	70	1,787	N	Y
151008	D	95	1,892	N	Y
151008	D	383	1,892	N	Y
151009	C	540	1,601	N	Y
151010	B	57	1,379	N	Y
151011	G	63	3,437	N	Y
151014	F	406	2,698	N	Y
151015	F	422	2,789	N	Y
151016	C	149	1,783	N	Y
151018	F	502	2,755	N	Y
151019	F	50	2,947	N	Y
151031	G	488	3,130	N	Y
151034	D	414	2,133	N	Y
151037	C	485	1,538	N	Y
151046	E	97	2,525	N	Y
151050	D	405	2,096	N	Y
151054	C	82	1,746	N	Y
151057	F	80	2,951	N	Y
151059	B	94	1,382	N	Y
151063	D	382	2,554	N	Y
151068	D	98	1,880	N	Y
151083	D	412	2,034	N	Y
151089	D	417	1,921	N	Y
151091	C	453	2,320	N	Y
151100	E	502	2,247	N	Y
151108	F	54	2,742	N	Y
151113	D	489	2,186	N	Y
151117	D	538	1,957	N	Y
151138	C	217	2,010	N	Y
151144	F	499	2,624	N	Y
151169	C	497	1,525	N	Y
151179	E	421	2,405	N	Y
151237	E	515	2,481	N	Y
151281	B	40	1,461	N	Y
151307	B	125	1,029	N	Y
151337	C	484	1,504	N	Y
151351	C	385	1,627	N	Y
151383	E	27	2,534	N	Y
151386	D	27	1,989	N	Y

Index

For pricing, see page 553.

Plan #	Price Code	Page	Total Finished Sq. Ft.	Materials List	CompleteCost
251012	D	444	2,009	Y	N
251013	D	444	2,073	Y	N
251014	E	423	2,210	Y	N
261001	H	483	3,746	N	N
261008	E	30	2,724	N	N
271002	B	536	1,252	Y	N
271005	B	451	1,368	Y	N
271006	B	404	1,444	Y	N
271007	B	401	1,283	Y	N
271010	C	286	1,724	Y	N
271013	B	483	1,498	Y	N
271015	B	409	1,359	Y	N
271016	D	408	2,170	Y	N
271017	D	296	1,835	Y	N
271018	E	25	2,445	Y	N
271018	E	415	2,445	Y	N
271023	D	333	1,993	Y	N
271032	G	433	3,195	Y	N
271039	C	452	1,565	Y	N
271042	G	531	3,469	Y	N
271045	E	527	2,409	Y	N
271049	E	484	2,464	Y	N
271050	B	279	1,188	Y	N
271051	D	283	1,920	Y	N
271053	E	270	2,458	Y	N
271061	C	384	1,750	Y	N
271064	F	389	2,864	Y	N
271069	E	511	2,376	Y	N
271070	D	276	2,144	Y	N
271073	D	376	1,920	Y	N
271074	E	298	2,400	Y	N
271075	E	448	2,233	Y	N
271076	D	449	2,188	Y	N
271077	C	384	1,786	Y	N
271079	E	49	2,228	Y	N
271080	E	519	2,581	Y	N
271081	E	533	2,539	Y	N
271085	C	274	1,541	Y	N
271087	F	264	2,734	Y	N
271093	F	85	2,813	Y	N
271096	G	282	3,190	Y	N
281002	D	151	1,859	Y	N
281005	B	246	1,426	Y	N
281009	B	227	1,423	Y	N
281015	C	177	1,660	Y	N
281016	D	228	1,945	Y	N
281022	C	117	1,506	Y	N
291015	F	386	2,901	N	N
291015	F	387	2,901	N	N
291016	F	380	2,721	N	N
301002	D	518	1,845	Y	N
301005	D	376	1,930	Y	N
311001	D	413	2,085	N	N
311002	E	440	2,402	Y	N
311004	D	477	2,046	Y	N
311005	E	348	2,497	Y	N
311011	D	328	1,955	Y	N
321001	C	318	1,721	Y	N
321002	B	339	1,400	Y	N
321003	C	362	1,791	Y	N
321004	F	366	2,808	Y	N
321005	E	357	2,483	Y	N
321006	D	351	1,977	Y	N
321007	F	379	2,695	Y	N
321008	C	355	1,761	Y	N
321009	E	249	2,295	Y	N
321010	C	491	1,787	Y	N
321011	F	331	2,874	Y	N
321012	D	347	1,882	Y	N
321013	B	326	1,360	Y	N
321014	C	343	1,676	Y	N
321015	C	353	1,501	Y	N
321016	H	75	3,814	Y	N
321017	E	347	2,531	Y	N
321018	E	68	2,523	Y	N
321019	E	34	2,452	Y	N
321021	C	343	1,708	Y	N
321022	B	341	1,140	Y	N
321023	B	283	1,092	Y	N
321024	B	342	1,403	Y	N
321025	A	247	914	Y	N
321026	C	75	1,712	Y	N
321027	F	113	2,758	Y	N
321028	F	340	2,723	Y	N
321029	E	272	2,334	Y	N
321030	D	325	2,029	Y	N
321031	G	273	3,200	Y	N
321032	I	46	4,826	Y	N
321033	B	349	1,268	Y	N
321034	H	61	3,508	Y	N
321035	B	247	1,384	Y	N
321036	F	30	2,900	Y	N
321037	E	49	2,397	Y	N
321038	B	250	1,452	Y	N
321039	B	179	1,231	Y	N
321040	B	240	1,084	Y	N
321041	E	140	2,286	Y	N
321042	G	400	3,368	Y	N
321043	E	400	2,401	Y	N
321044	F	427	2,618	Y	N
321045	D	26	2,058	Y	N
321046	E	477	2,411	Y	N
321048	G	522	3,216	Y	N
321049	G	445	3,144	Y	N
321051	F	32	2,624	Y	N
321052	D	134	2,182	Y	N
321061	G	524	3,169	Y	N
331005	H	230	3,585	N	N
341003	B	324	1,200	Y	N
341004	B	310	1,101	Y	N
341005	B	507	1,334	Y	N
341051	E	526	2,243	Y	N
341052	B	471	1,275	N	N
341053	D	195	1,903	Y	N
341054	B	195	1,370	Y	N
341055	C	216	1,647	Y	N
341056	B	526	1,404	Y	N
341057	C	218	1,642	Y	N
341058	D	520	1,996	Y	N
341059	C	223	1,554	Y	N
341060	E	521	2,349	Y	N
351001	D	69	1,855	Y	N
351002	C	413	1,751	Y	N
351003	C	490	1,751	Y	N
351004	D	455	1,852	Y	N
351005	C	510	1,501	Y	N
351007	E	511	2,251	Y	N
351008	D	433	2,002	Y	N
351016	B	311	1,002	Y	N
351020	B	320	1,488	Y	N
351043	D	319	1,802	Y	N
351069	F	172	2,008	N	N
351070	D	138	1,818	N	N
351071	D	336	1,600	N	N
361004	D	218	2,191	N	N
371072	C	345	1,772	N	N
371092	H	18	3,836	N	N
371092	H	19	3,836	N	N
391001	D	245	2,015	Y	N
391004	C	335	1,750	Y	N
391006	B	327	1,456	Y	N
391034	C	312	1,737	Y	N
391046	D	248	1,978	Y	N
391059	C	338	2,020	Y	N
391060	B	356	1,359	Y	N
391064	A	342	988	Y	N
391069	B	344	1,492	Y	N
401005	B	297	1,073	Y	N
401007	B	293	1,286	Y	N
401012	E	272	2,301	Y	N
401019	B	293	1,256	Y	N
401020	B	299	1,230	Y	N
401023	F	321	2,806	Y	N
401024	B	317	1,298	Y	N
401025	B	329	1,408	Y	N
401029	D	89	2,163	Y	N
401043	A	368	988	Y	N
401045	C	334	1,652	Y	N
401047	B	315	1,064	Y	N
401048	J	289	5,159	Y	N
401049	I	252	4,087	Y	N
401050	K	316	6,841	Y	N
421003	C	141	1,698	Y	N
421005	C	158	1,784	Y	N
421009	F	33	2,649	Y	N
421011	E	131	2,266	Y	N
421012	F	142	2,795	Y	N
421013	E	127	2,327	Y	N
421015	D	134	2,198	Y	N
421017	E	116	2,433	Y	N
421019	F	143	2,750	Y	N
421025	E	144	2,599	Y	N
441001	D	211	1,850	N	N
441002	C	114	1,873	N	N
441003	C	126	1,580	N	N
441004	C	169	1,728	N	N
441005	D	212	1,800	N	N
441006	D	214	1,891	N	N
441007	D	28	2,197	N	N
441008	D	120	2,001	N	N
441009	F	163	2,650	N	N
441010	F	127	2,973	N	N
441011	F	131	2,898	N	N
441012	H	119	3,682	N	N
441013	G	118	3,317	N	N
441014	H	72	3,940	N	N
441014	H	73	3,940	N	N
441015	I	220	4,732	N	N
441015	I	221	4,732	N	N
441016	D	189	1,893	N	N
441017	C	169	1,707	N	N
441018	C	224	1,500	N	N
441019	D	185	2,044	N	N
441022	F	532	2,820	N	N
441024	H	260	3,517	N	N
441024	H	261	3,517	N	N
441025	G	186	3,457	N	N
441026	H	191	3,623	N	N
441027	H	253	3,638	N	N
441028	G	228	3,165	N	N
441030	J	267	5,180	N	N
441031	I	208	4,150	N	N
441031	I	209	4,150	N	N
441032	D	157	1,944	N	N
441035	D	229	2,196	N	N
441036	F	528	2,902	N	N
441038	E	231	2,518	N	N
441042	E	523	2,538	N	N
441044	E	232	2,277	N	N
441046	F	188	2,606	N	N
441048	E	233	2,453	N	N
441049	D	190	2,124	N	N
441050	E	190	2,296	N	N
451149	D	43	2,130	N	N
451165	D	216	1,933	N	N
451182	G	217	3,241	N	N
451187	I	223	4,638	N	N
451194	F	189	2,618	N	N
451200	D	22	2,142	N	N
451217	I	225	4,711	N	N
451223	H	271	3,650	N	N
451231	E	237	2,281	N	N
451249	E	225	2,281	N	N
451259	H	43	3,798	N	N

Images provided by designer/architect.

Plan #181151

Dimensions: 50' W x 46' D
Levels: 2
Square Footage: 2,283
Main Level Sq. Ft.: 1,274
Second Level Sq. Ft.: 1,009
Bedrooms: 3
Bathrooms: 2½
Foundation: Basement
Materials List Available: Yes
Price Category: E

Multiple porches, stately columns, and arched multi-paned windows adorn this country home.

Features:

- Ceiling Height: 8 ft. unless otherwise noted.

- Great Room: The second-floor mezzanine overlooks this great room. With its soaring ceiling, this dramatic room is the centerpiece of a spacious and flowing design that is just as suited to entertaining as it is to family life.

- Dining Area: Guests will naturally flow into this dining area when it is time to eat. After dinner they can step directly out onto the porch to enjoy coffee and dessert when the weather is fair.

- Kitchen: This efficient and well-designed kitchen has double sinks and offers a separate eating area for those impromptu family meals.

- Master Bedroom: This master retreat has a walk-in closet and its own sumptuous bath.

- Home Office: Whether you work at home or just need a place for the family computer and keeping track of family finances, this home office fills the bill.

Main Level Floor Plan

Upper Level Floor Plan

Copyright by designer/architect.

Featured House Plan
See page 135

Complete Your Home Plans Library with these Great Books from Creative Homeowner

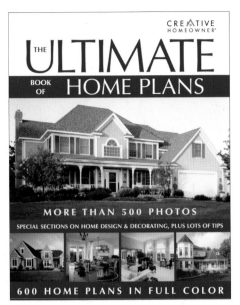

The ULTIMATE BOOK OF HOME PLANS

MORE THAN 500 PHOTOS

SPECIAL SECTIONS ON HOME DESIGN & DECORATING, PLUS LOTS OF TIPS

600 HOME PLANS IN FULL COLOR

528 pages
Book # 277039

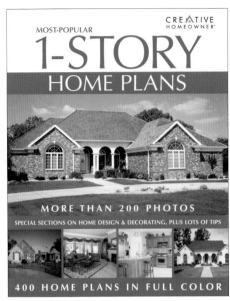

MOST-POPULAR 1-STORY HOME PLANS

MORE THAN 200 PHOTOS

SPECIAL SECTIONS ON HOME DESIGN & DECORATING, PLUS LOTS OF TIPS

400 HOME PLANS IN FULL COLOR

352 pages
Book # 277020

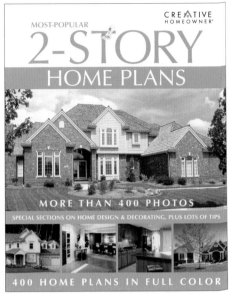

MOST-POPULAR 2-STORY HOME PLANS

MORE THAN 400 PHOTOS

SPECIAL SECTIONS ON HOME DESIGN & DECORATING, PLUS LOTS OF TIPS

400 HOME PLANS IN FULL COLOR

352 pages
Book # 277028

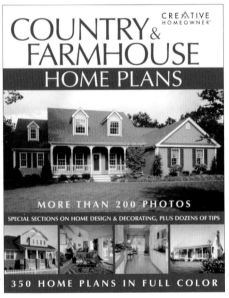

COUNTRY & FARMHOUSE HOME PLANS

MORE THAN 200 PHOTOS

SPECIAL SECTIONS ON HOME DESIGN & DECORATING, PLUS DOZENS OF TIPS

350 HOME PLANS IN FULL COLOR

320 pages
Book # 277027

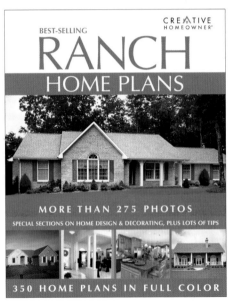

BEST-SELLING RANCH HOME PLANS

MORE THAN 275 PHOTOS

SPECIAL SECTIONS ON HOME DESIGN & DECORATING, PLUS LOTS OF TIPS

350 HOME PLANS IN FULL COLOR

320 pages
Book # 277005

The Best Home Plan Books You Can Find

- Hundreds of home designs from top residential architects and designers

- Hundreds of full-color photographs of actual home that have been built. Many of the homes also include beautiful interior photographs

- Up to 1,000 or more drawings of floor plans, side views and rear views

- Dozens of informative pages containing design and decorating ideas and tips, from working with builders to designing kitchens and installing trim work and landscaping

Books To Help You Build

Creative Homeowner offers an extensive selection of leading how-to books.

Home Building Package

Build and repair your home—inside and out—with these essential titles.

Retail Price: $74.80
Your Price: $65.95
Order #: 267095

Wiring: Complete Projects for the Home
Provides comprehensive information about the home electrical system. Over 750 color photos and 75 illustrations. 288 pages.

Plumbing: Basic, Intermediate & Advanced Projects
An overview of the plumbing system with code-compliant, step-by-step projects. Over 750 full-color photos, illustrations. 272 pages.

House Framing
Walks you through the framing basics, from assembling simple partitions to cutting compound angles for dormers. 650 full-color illustrations and photos. 240 pages.

Drywall: Pro Tips for Hanging and Finishing
Covers tools and materials, estimating, cutting, hanging, and finishing gypsum wallboard. 250 color photos and illustrations. 144 pages.

Look for these and other fine **Creative Homeowner books** wherever books are sold
For more information and to place an order, go to **www.creativehomeowner.com**